PREFACE

"The dramatist is born, not made." This common saying grants the dramatist at least one experience of other artists, namely, birth, but seeks to deny him the instruction in art granted the architect, the painter, the sculptor, and the musician. Play-readers and producers, however, seem not so sure of this distinction, for they are often heard saying: "The plays we receive divide into two classes: those competently written, but trite in subject and treatment; those in some way fresh and interesting, but so badly written that they cannot be produced." Some years ago, Mr. Savage, the manager, writing in *The Bookman* on "The United States of Playwrights," said: "In answer to the question, 'Do the great majority of these persons know anything at all of even the fundamentals of dramatic construction?' the managers and agents who read the manuscripts unanimously agree in the negative. Only in rare instances does a play arrive in the daily mails that carries within it a vestige of the knowledge of the science of drama-making. Almost all the plays, furthermore, are extremely artificial and utterly devoid of the quality known as human interest." All this testimony of managers and play-readers shows that there is something which the dramatist has not as a birthright, but must learn. Where? Usually he is told, "In the School of Hard Experience." When the young playwright whose manuscript has been returned to him but with favorable comment, asks what he is to do to get rid of the faults in his work, both evident to him and not evident, he is told to read widely in the drama; to watch plays of all kinds; to write with endless patience and the resolution never to be discouraged.

He is to keep submitting his plays till, by this somewhat indefinite method of training,he at last acquires the ability to write so well that a manuscript is accepted. This is "The School of Experience." Though a long and painful method of training, it has had, undeniably, many distinguished graduates.

Why, however, is it impossible that some time should be saved a would-be dramatist by placing before him, not mere theories of play-writing, but the practice of the dramatists of the past, so that what they have shared in common, and where their practice has differed, may be clear to him? That is all this book attempts. To create a dramatist would be a modern miracle. To develop theories of the drama apart from the practice of recent and remoter dramatists of different countries would be visionary. This book tries in the light of historical practice merely to distinguish the permanent from the impermanent in technique. It endeavors, by showing the inexperienced dramatist how experienced dramatists have solved problems similar to his own, to shorten a little his time of apprenticeship. The limitations of any such attempt I fully recognize. This book is the result of almost daily discussion for some years with classes of the ideas contained in it, but in that discussion there was a chance to treat with each individual the many exceptions, apparent or real, which he could raise to any principle enunciated. Such full discussion is impossible in a book the size of this one. Therefore I must seem to favor an instruction far more dogmatic than my pupils know from me. No textbook can do away with the value of proper classroom work. The practice of the past provides satisfactory principles for students of ordinary endowment. A person of long experience or unusually endowed, however, after grasping these principles, must at times break from them if he is to do his best work. The classroom permits a teacher such adaptations of existing usage. Such special needs no textbook can forestall. This book, then, is meant, not to replace wise classroom instruction, but to supplement it or to offer what it can when such instruction is impossible.

The contents of this book were originally brought together from notes for the classroom as eight lectures delivered before the Lowell Institute, Boston, in the winter of 1913. They were carefully reworked for later lectures before audiences in Brooklyn and Philadelphia. Indeed, both in and out of the classroom they have been slowly revised in the intervening five years. Detailed consideration of the one-act play has been reserved for later special treatment. Otherwise the book attempts to treat helpfully the many problems which the would-be dramatist must face in learning the fundamentals of a very difficult but fascinating art.

I have written for the person who cannot be content except when writing plays. I wish it distinctly understood that I have not written for the person seeking methods of conducting a course in dramatic technique. I view with some alarm the recent mushroom growth of such courses throughout the country. I gravely doubt the advisability of such courses for undergraduates. Dramatic technique is the means of expressing, for the stage, one's ideas and emotions. Except in rare instances, undergraduates are better employed in filling their minds with general knowledge than in trying to phrase for the stage thoughts or emotions not yet mature. In the main I believe instruction in the writing of plays should be for graduate students. Nor do I believe that it should be given except by persons who have had experience in acting, producing, and even writing plays, and who have read and seen the drama of different countries and times. Mere lectures, no matter how good, will not make the students productive. The teacher who is not widely eclectic in his tastes will at best produce writers with an easily recognizable stamp. In all creative courses the problem is not, "What can we make these students take from us, the teachers?" but, "Which of these students has any creative power that is individual? Just what is it? How may it be given its quickest and fullest development?" Complete freedom of choice in subject and complete freedom in treatment so that the individuality of the artist may have its best expression are indispensable in the development of great art. At first untrained and groping blindly for the means to his ends, he moves to a technique based on study of successful dramatists who have preceded him. From that he should move to a technique that is his own, a mingling of much out of the past and an adaptation of past practice to his own needs. This book will help the development from blind groping to the acquirement of a technique based on the practice of others. It can do something, but only a little, to develop the technique that is highly individual. The instruction which most helps to that must be done, not by books, not by lectures, but in frequent consultation of pupil and teacher. The man who grows from a technique which permits him to write a good play because it accords with historical practice to the technique which makes possible for him a play which no one else could have written, must work under three great Masters: Constant Practice, Exacting Scrutiny of the Work, and, above all, Time. Only when he has stood the tests of these Masters is he the matured artist.

GEO. P. BAKER

CONTENTS

DRAMATIC TECHNIQUE

CHAPTER I

TECHNIQUE IN DRAMA: WHAT IT IS. THE DRAMA AS AN INDEPENDENT ART

THIS book treats drama which has been tested before the public or which was written to be so tested. It does not concern itself with plays, past or present, intended primarily to be read — closet drama. It does not deal with theories of what the drama, present or future, might or should be. It aims to show what successful drama has been in different countries, at different periods, as written by men of highly individual gifts.

The technique of any dramatist may be defined, roughly, as his ways, methods, and devices for getting his desired ends. No dramatist has this technique as a gift at birth, nor does he acquire it merely by writing plays. He reads and sees past and present plays, probably in large numbers. If he is like most young dramatists, for example Shakespeare on the one hand and Ibsen on the other, he works imitatively at first. He, too, has his *Love's Labor's Lost*, or *Feast at Solhaug*. Even if his choice of topic be fresh, the young dramatist inevitably studies the dramatic practice just preceding his time, or that of some remoter period which attracts him, for models on which to shape the play he has in mind. Often, in whole-hearted admiration, he gives himself to close imitation of Shakespeare, one of the great Greek dramatists, Ibsen, Shaw, or Brieux. For the moment the better the imitation, the better he is satisfied; but shortly he discovers that somehow the managers or the public, if his play gets by the managers, seem to have very little taste for great dramatists at second hand. Yet the history of the drama has shown again and again that a dramatist may owe something to the plays of a preceding period and achieve success. The influence of the Greek drama on *The Servant in the House* is unmistakable. *Kismet*, Mr. Knobloch frankly states, was modeled on the loosely constructed Elizabethan plays intended primarily to tell a story of varied and exciting incident. Where lies the difficulty? Just here. Too many people do not recognize that dramatic technique — methods and devices for gaining in the theatre a dramatist's desired ends — is historically of three kinds: universal, special, and individual. First there are certain essentials which all good plays, from Æschylus to Lord Dunsany, share at least in part. They are the qualities which make a play a play. These the tyro must study and may copy. To the discussion and illustration of them the larger part of this book is devoted. Secondly, there is the special technique of a period, such as the Elizabethan, the Restoration, the period of Scribe and his influence, etc. A good illustration of this kind of technique is the difference in treatment of the Antony and Cleopatra story by Shakespeare in his play of that name, and by John Dryden in *All For Love*. Each dramatist worked sincerely, believing the technique that he used would give him best, with the public he had in mind, his desired effects. The public of Shakespeare would not have cared for Dryden's treatment: the Restoration found Shakespeare barbaric until reshaped by dramatists whose touch today often seems that of a vandal facing work the real beauty of which he does not understand. The technique of the plays of Corneille and Racine, even though they base their dramatic theory on classical practice, differs from the Greek and from Seneca. In turn the drama which aimed to copy them, the so-called Heroic Plays of England from 1660 to 1700, differed. That is, a story dramatized before when re-presented to the stage must share with the drama of the past certain characteristics if it is to be a play at all, but to some extent it must be presented differently. Why? Because, first, the dramatist is using a stage different from that of his forebears, and, secondly, because he is writing for a public of different standards in morals and art. Comparison for a moment of the stage of the Greeks with the stage of the Elizabethans, the Restoration, or of today shows the truth of the first statement. Comparison of the religious and social ideals of the Greeks with those of Shakespeare's audience, Congreve's public, Tom Robertson's, or the public of today shows the truth of the second. That is, the drama of any past time, if studied carefully, must reveal the essentials of the drama throughout time. It must reveal, too, methods and devices effective for the public of its time, but not effective at present. It is doubtless true that usually a young dramatist may gain most light as to the technique of the period on which he is entering from the practice of the playwrights just preceding him, but this does not always follow. Witness the sharp revolt, particularly in France and Germany, in the early nineteenth century, from Classicism to Romanticism. Witness, too, the change late in that century from the widespread influence of Scribe to the almost equally widespread influence of Ibsen.

The chief gift of the drama of the past to the young playwright, then, is illustration of what is essential in drama. This he safely copies. Study of the technique of a special period, if the temper of his public closely resembles the interests, prejudices, and ideals of the period he studies, may give him even larger results. Such close resemblance, however, is rare. Each period demands in part its own technique. What in that technique is added to the basal practice of the past may even be to some extent the contribution of the young dramatist in question. Resting on what he knows of the elements common to all good drama, alert to the significance of the hints which the special practice of any period may give him, he thinks his way to new methods and devices for getting with his public his desired effects. Many or most of these the other dramatists of his day discover with him. These, which make the special usage of his time, become the technique of his period.

Perhaps, however, he has added something in technique particularly his own, to be found in the plays of no other man. This, the third sort of technique, is to be seen specially in the work of the great dramatists. Usually, it is peculiarly inimitable and elusive because the result of a particular temperament working on problems of the drama peculiar to a special time. Imitation of this individual technique in most instances results, like wearing the tailor-made clothes of a friend, in a palpable misfit.

It is just because the enthusiast copies, not simply what is of universal significance in the practice of some past period, but with equal closeness what is special to the time and individual to the dramatist, that his play fails. He has produced something stamped as not of his time nor by him, but as at best a successful literary exercise in imitation. Of the three kinds of technique, then, — universal, special, and individual, — a would-be dramatist should know the first thoroughly. Recognizing the limitations of the second and third, he should study them for suggestions rather than for models. When he has mastered the first technique, and from the second has made his own what he finds useful in it, he is likely to pass to the third, his individual additions.

Why, however, should men or women who have already written stories long or short declared by competent people to be "dramatic," make any special study of the technique of plays? Like the dramatist, they must understand characterization and dialogue or they could not have written successful stories. Evidently, too, they must know something about structure. Above all, they must have shown ability so to represent people in emotion as to arouse emotional response in their readers, or their work would not be called dramatic. Why, then, should they not write at will either in the form of stories or of plays? It is certainly undeniable that many novels seem in material and at moments in treatment, as dramatic as plays on similar subjects. In each, something is said or done which moves the reader or hearer as the author wishes. These facts account for the widespread and deeply-rooted belief that any novelist or writer of short stories should write successful plays if he wishes, particularly if adapting his own work for the stage. The facts account, too, for the repeated efforts in the past to put popular novels on the stage as little changed as possible. Is it not odd that most adaptations of successful stories and most novelizations of successful plays are failures? The fact that the drama had had for centuries in England and elsewhere a fecund history before the novel as a form took shape at all would intimate that the drama is a different and independent art from that of the novel or the short story. When novelists and would-be playwrights recognize that it is, has been, and ought to be an independent art, we shall be spared many bad plays.

It is undeniable that the novelist and the dramatist start with common elements — the story, the characters, and the dialogue. If their common ability to discern in their story or characters possible emotional interests for other people, their so-called "dramatic sense," is "to achieve success on the stage it must be developed into theatrical talent by hard study and generally by long practice. For theatrical talent consists in the power of making your characters not only tell a story by means of dialogue but tell it in such skilfully devised form and order as shall, within the limits of an ordinary theatrical representation, give rise to the greatest possible amount of that peculiar kind of emotional effect, the production of which is the one great function of the theatre."[1] Certain underlying differences between the relation of the novelist to his reader and that of the dramatist to his audience reveal why the art of each must be different.

The relative space granted novelist and dramatist is the first condition which differentiates their technique. A play of three acts, say forty pages each of ordinary typewriter paper, will take in action approximately a hundred and fifty minutes, or two hours and a half. When allowance is made for waits between the acts, the manuscript should probably be somewhat shorter. A novel runs from two hundred and fifty to six hundred pages. Obviously such difference between the length of play and novel means different methods of handling material. The dramatist, if he tries for the same results as the novelist, must work more concisely. This demands very skilful selection among his materials to gain his desired effects in the quickest possible ways.

A novel we read at one or a half-dozen sittings, as we please. When we so wish, we can pause to consider what we have just read, or can re-read it. In the theatre, a play must be seen as a whole and at once. Listening to it, we cannot turn back, we cannot pause to reflect, for the play pushes steadily on to the close of each act. Evidently, then, here is another reason why a play must make its effects more swiftly than a novel. This needed swiftness requires methods of making effects more obviously and more emphatically than in the novel. In a play, then, while moving much more swiftly than in a novel, we must at any given moment be even clearer than in the novel. What the dramatist selects for presentation must be more productive of immediate effect

---

[1] *Robert Louis Stevenson: The Dramatist*, p. 7. Sir A. Pinero. Chiswick Press, London.

than is the case with the novelist, for one swingeing blow must, with him, replace repeated strokes by the novelist.

In most novels, the reader is, so to speak, personally conducted, the author is our guide. In the drama, so far as the dramatist is concerned, we must travel alone. In the novel, the author describes, narrates, analyzes, and makes his personal comment on circumstance and character. We rather expect a novelist to reveal himself in his work. On the other hand, the greatest dramatists, such as Shakespeare and Molière, in their plays reveal singularly little of themselves. It is the poorer dramatists — Dryden, Jonson, Chapman — who, using their characters as mouthpieces, reveal their own personalities. Now that soliloquy and the aside have nearly gone out of use, the dramatist, when compared with the novelist, seems, at first thought, greatly hampered in his expression. He never can use description, narration, analysis, and personal comment as his own. He may use them only in the comparatively rare instances when they befit the character speaking. His mainstay is illustrative action appropriate to his characters, real or fictitious. Surely so great a difference will affect the technique of his art. The novel, then, may be, and often is, highly personal; the best drama is impersonal.

The theatre in which the play is presented also produces differences between the practice of the dramatist and that of the novelist. No matter how small the theatre or its stage, it cannot permit the intimacy of relation which exists between reader and book. A person reads a book to himself or to a small group. In most cases, he may choose the conditions under which he will read it, indoors or out, alone or with people about him, etc. In the theatre, according to the size of the auditorium, from one hundred to two thousand people watch the play, and under given conditions of light, heat, and ventilation. They are at a distance, in most cases, from the stage. It is shut off from them more than once in the performance by the fall of the curtain. The novel appeals to the mind and the emotions through the eye. The stage appeals to both eye and ear. Scenery, lighting, and costuming render unnecessary many descriptions absolutely required in the novel. The human voice quickens the imagination as the mere printed page cannot in most cases. These unlike conditions are bound to create differences in the presentation of the same material.

It is just this greater concreteness and consequent greater vividness of the staged play which makes us object to seeing and hearing in the theatre that of which we have read with comparative calmness in the newspaper, the magazine, or the novel. Daily we read in the newspapers with unquickened pulse of horror after horror. Merely to see a fatal runaway or automobile accident sends us home sickened or unnerved. We read to the end, though horrified, the *Red Laugh* of Andreiev. Reproduce accurately on the stage the terrors of the book and some persons in the audience would probably go as mad as did people in the story. This difference applies in our attitude toward moral questions as treated in books or on the stage. "Let us instance the *Matron of Ephesus*. This acrid fable is well known; it is unquestionably the bitterest satire that was ever made on female frivolity. It has been recounted a thousand times after Petronius, and since it pleased even in the worst copy, it was thought that the subject must be an equally happy one for the stage. . . . The character of the matron in the story provokes a not unpleasant sarcastic smile at the audacity of wedded love; in the drama this becomes repulsive, horrible. In the drama, the soldier's persuasions do not seem nearly so subtle, importunate, triumphant, as in the story. In the story we picture to ourselves a sensitive little woman who is really in earnest in her grief, but succumbs to temptation and to her temperament, her weakness seems the weakness of her sex, we therefore conceive no especial hatred towards her, we deem that what she does nearly every woman would have done. Even her suggestion to save her living lover by means of her dead husband we think we can forgive her because of its ingenuity and presence of mind; or rather its very ingenuity leads us to imagine that this suggestion may have been appended by the malicious narrator who desired to end his tale with some right poisonous sting. Now in the drama we cannot harbour this suggestion; what we hear has happened in the story, we see really occur; what we would doubt of in the story, in the drama the evidence of our own eyes settles incontrovertibly. The mere possibility of such an action diverted us; its reality shows it in all its atrocity; the suggestion amused our fancy, the execution revolts our feelings, we turn our backs to the stage and say with the Lykas of Petronius, without being in Lykas's peculiar position: 'Had the emperor been just, he would have restored the body of the father to its tomb and crucified the woman.' And she seems to us the more to deserve this punishment, the less art the poet has expended on her seduction, for we do not then condemn in her weak woman in general, but an especially volatile, worthless female in particular." [1]

As Lessing points out, in the printed page we can stand a free treatment of social question after social question which on the stage we should find revolting. Imagine the horror and outcry if we were to put upon the stage a dramatized newspaper or popular magazine. Just in this intense vividness, this great reality of effect, lies a large part of the power of the stage. On the other hand, this very vividness may create difficulties. For instance, the novelist can say, "So, in a silence, almost unbroken, the long hours passed." But we watching, on the stage, the scene described in the novel, know perfectly that

---

[1] *Hamburg Dramaturgy*, pp. 329-330. Lessing. Bohn ed.

only a few minutes have elapsed. From this difficulty have arisen, to create a sense of time, the Elizabethan use of the Chorus, our *entr'acte* pauses, interpolated scenes which draw off our attention from the main story, and many other devices. But even with all the devices of the past, it is well-nigh impossible in a one-act play or in an act of one setting to create the feeling that much time has passed. Many an attempt has been made to dramatize in one act Stevenson's delightful story, *The Sire de Maletroit's Door*, but all have come to grief because the greater vividness of the stage makes the necessary lapse of considerable time too apparent. It is not difficult for the story-teller to make us believe that, between a time late one evening and early the next morning, Blanche de Maletroit lost completely her liking for one man and became more than ready to marry Denis de Beaulieu, who entered the house for the first time on this same evening. On the stage, motivation and dialogue must be such as to make so swift a change entirely convincing even though it occur merely in the time of the acting. The motivation that was easy for the novelist as he explained how profoundly Blanche was moved by winning words or persuasive action of Denis, becomes almost impossible unless the words and action when seen and heard are for us equally winning and persuasive. The time difficulty in this story has led to all sorts of amusing expedients to account for Blanche's complete change of feeling. One young author went so far as to make the first lover of Blanche flirt so desperately with a maid-servant off stage that the report of his conduct by a jealous man-servant was the last straw to bring about the change in Blanche's feelings. Though aiming at a real difficulty, this device missed because it so vulgarized the original. When all is said and done, this time difficulty caused by the greater vividness of stage presentation remains the chief obstacle in the way of the dramatist who would write of a sequence of historical events or of evolution or devolution in character. Again we foresee probable differences in technique, this time caused by the theatre, the stage, and the intense vividness of the latter.

The novel is, so to speak, the work of an individual; a play is a coöperative effort — of author, actor, producer, and even audience. Though the author writes the play, it cannot be properly judged till the producer stages it, the players act it, and the audience approves or disapproves of it. Undeniably the dialogue of a play must be very different from that of a novel because the gesture, facial expression, intonation, and general movement of the actor may in large part replace description, narration, and even parts of the dialogue of a novel. We have good dialogue for a novel when Cleopatra says, "I'll seem the thing I am not; Antony will be himself." The fact and the characterization are what count here. In the same scene, Antony, absorbed in adoration of Cleopatra, cries, when interrupted by a messenger from Rome, "Grates me; the sum." Here we need the action of the speaker, his intonation, and his facial expression, if the speech is to have its full value. In its context, however, it is as dramatic dialogue perfect. In a story or novel, mere clearness would demand more because the author could not be sure that the reader would hit the right intonation or feel the gesture which must accompany the words. It is in large part just because dramatic dialogue is a kind of shorthand written by the dramatist for the actor to fill out that most persons find plays more difficult reading than novels. Few untrained imaginations respond quickly enough to feel the full significance of the printed page of the play. On the other hand, any one accustomed to read plays often finds novels irritating because they tell so much more than is necessary for him who responds quickly to emotionalized speech properly recorded.

Just as dialogue for the stage is incomplete without the

actor, so, too, the stage direction needs filling out. Made as concise as possible by the dramatist, it is meant to be packed with meaning, not only for the actor, but for the producer. The latter is trusted to fill out, in as full detail as his means or his desires permit, the hints of stage directions as to setting and atmosphere. On the producer depends wholly the scenery, lighting, and properties used. All of this the novelist supplies in full detail for himself. An intelligent producer who reads the play with comprehension but follows only the letter of the stage directions gives a production no more than adequate at best. An uncomprehending and self-willed producer may easily so confuse the values of a well-written play as to ruin its chances. A thoroughly sympathetic and finely imaginative producer may, like an equally endowed actor, reveal genuine values in the play unsuspected even by the dramatist himself. Surely writing stage directions will differ from the narration and description of a novel.

The novelist, as has been pointed out, deals with the individual reader, or through one reader with a small group. What has just been said makes obvious that the dramatist never works directly, but through intermediaries, the actors and the producer. More than that, he seeks to stir the individual, not for his own sake as does the novelist, but because he is a unit in the large group filling the theatre. The novelist — to make a rough generalization — works through the individual, the dramatist through the group. This is not the place to discuss in detail the relation of a dramatist to his audience, but it is undeniable that the psychology of the crowd in a theatre is not exactly the same thing as the sum total of the emotional responses of each individual in it to some given dramatic incident. The psychology of the individual and the psychology of the crowd are not one and the same. The reputation of the novelist rests very largely on the verdict of his individual readers. The dramatist must move, not a considerable number of individuals, but at least the great majority of his audience. He must move his audience, too, not by emotions individual to a considerable number, but by emotions they naturally share in common or by his art can be made to share. The dramatist who understands only the psychology of the individual or the small group may write a play well characterized, but he cannot write a successful play till he has studied deeply the psychology of the crowd and has thus learned so to present his chosen subject as to gain from the group which makes the theatrical public the emotional response he desires.

Obviously, then, from many different points of view, the great art of the novelist and the equally great art of the dramatist are not the same. It is the unwise holding of an opposite opinion which has led many a successful novelist into disastrous play-writing. It is the attempt to reproduce exactly on the stage the most popular parts of successful novels which has made many an adaptation a failure surprising to author and adapter. The whole situation is admirably summed up in a letter of Edward Knobloch, author of *Kismet*. "I have found it very useful, when asked to dramatize a novel, not to read it myself, but to get some one else to read it and tell me about it. At once, all the stuffing drops away, and the vital active part, the verb of the novel comes to the fore. If the story of a novel cannot be told by some one in a hundred words or so, there is apt to be no drama in it. If I were to write a play on Hamilton, I would look up an article in an encyclopædia; then make a scenario; then read detailed biographies. Too much knowledge hampers. It is just for that reason that short stories are easier dramatized than long novels. The stories that Shakespeare chose for his plays are practically summaries. As long as they stirred his imagination, that was all he asked of them. Then he added his magic. Once the novel has been told, make the scenario. Then read the novel after. There will be very little to alter and only a certain amount of touches to add." If, in accordance with this suggestion, an adapter would plan out in scenario the mere story of the novel he wishes to adapt for the stage, would then transfer to his scenario only so much of the novel as perfectly fits the needs of the stage; and finally with the aid of the original author, would rewrite the portions which can be used only in part, and with him compose certain parts entirely anew, we should have a much larger proportion of permanently successful adaptations.

Though it is true, then, that the novelist and the dramatist work with common elements of story, characterization and dialogue, the differing conditions under which they work affect their story-telling, their characterization, and their dialogue. The differences brought about by the greater speed, greater compactness, and greater vividness of the drama, with its impersonality, its coöperative nature, its appeal to the group rather than to the individual, create the fundamental technique which distinguishes the drama from the novel. This is the technique possessed in common by the dramatists of all periods. The art of the playwright is not, then, the art of the novelist. Throughout the centuries a very different technique has distinguished them.

"But," it may be urged, "all that has been said of the differences between the play and the novel shows that the play cramps truthful presentation of life. Is not play-writing an art of falsification rather than truth?" A living French novelist once exclaimed, "I have written novels for many years, with some returns in reputation but little return in money. Now, when a young actor helps me, I adapt one of my novels to the stage and this bastard art immediately makes it possible for me to buy automobiles." Robert Louis Stevenson wrote, toward the end of his life, to Mr. Sidney

Colvin, "No, I will not write a play for Irving nor for the devil. Can you not see that the work of *falsification*, which a play demands is, of all tasks, the most ungrateful? And I have done it a long while, — and nothing ever came of it." [1] The trouble with both these critics of the drama was that they held a view of the stage which makes it necessary to shape, to twist, and to contort life when represented on it. While it is true that selection and compression underlie all dramatic art, as they underlie all of the pictorial arts, it is no longer true, as it was in the mid-nineteenth century, that dramatists believe that we should shape life to fit hampering conditions of the stage, accepted as inevitably rigid. Today we regard the stage, as we should, as plastic. If the stage of the moment forbids in any way the just representation of life, so much the worse for that stage; it must yield. The ingenuity of author, producer, scenic artist, and stage mechanician must labor until the stage is fitted to represent life as the author sees it. For many years now, the cry of the dramatist has been, not "Let us adapt life to the stage," but rather: "Let us adapt the stage, at any cost for it, at any cost of imaginative effort or mechanical labor, to adequate and truthful representation of life." The art of the playwright may be the art of fantasy or of realism, but for him who understands it rightly, not mistaking it for another art, and laboring till he grasps and understands its seeming mysteries, it can never be an art of falsification. Instead, it is the art that, drawing to its aid all its sister fine arts, in splendid coöperation, moves the masses of men as does no other art. As Sir Arthur Pinero has said, "The art — the great and fascinating and most difficult art — of the modern dramatist is nothing else than to achieve that compression of life which the stage undoubtedly demands, without falsification." [2]

[1] *Robert Louis Stevenson: the Dramatist*, p. 30. Sir A. Pinero. Chiswick Press, London.
[2] *Idem.*

CHAPTER II

THE ESSENTIALS OF DRAMA: ACTION AND EMOTION

WHAT is the common aim of all dramatists? Twofold: first, as promptly as possible to win the attention of the audience; secondly, to hold that interest steady or, better, to increase it till the final curtain falls. It is the time limit to which all dramatists are subject which makes the immediate winning of attention necessary. The dramatist has no time to waste. How is he to win this attention? By what is done in the play; by characterization; by the language the people of his play speak; or by a combination of two or more of these. Today we hear much discussion whether it is what is done, *i.e.* action, or characterization, or dialogue which most interests a public. Which is the chief essential in good drama? History shows indisputably that the drama in its beginnings, no matter where we look, depended most on action. The earliest extant specimen of drama in England, *circa* 967, shows clearly the essential relations of action, characterization, and dialogue in drama at its outset. The italics in the following show the action; the roman type the dialogue.

While the third lesson is being chanted, let four brothers vest themselves, one of whom, vested in an alb, enters as if to do something, and, in an inconspicuous way, approaches the place where the sepulchre is, and there holding a palm in his hand, sits quiet. While the third respond is chanted, let the three others approach, all alike vested in copes, bearing thuribles (censers) with incense in their hands, and, with hesitating steps, in the semblance of persons seeking something, let them come before the place of the sepulchre. These things are done, indeed, in representation of the angel sitting within the tomb and of the women who came with spices to anoint the body of Jesus. When, therefore, he who is seated sees the three approaching as if wandering *about and seeking something, let him begin to sing melodiously and in a voice moderately loud*

Whom seek you at the sepulchre, O Christians?

When this has been sung to the end, let the three respond in unison,

Jesus of Nazareth, the crucified, O heavenly one.

Then he,

He is not here; he has risen, as was foretold.
Go ye, announcing that he has risen from the dead.

Upon the utterance of this command, let the three turn to the choir and say,

Alleluia! the Lord is risen.

This said, let him, still remaining seated, say, as if calling them back, the antiphon,

Come, and see the place where the Lord lay.
Alleluia, Alleluia!

Having said this, however, let him rise and lift the veil, and show them the place empty of the cross, but the clothes, only, laid there with which the cross was wrapped. When they see this, let them set down the thuribles that they have carried within that same sepulchre, and take up the cloth and hold it up before the clergy, and, as if in testimony that the Lord has risen and is not now wrapped therein, let them sing this antiphon:

The Lord has risen from the tomb,
Who for us was crucified,

and let them lay the cloth upon the altar. The antiphon finished, let the prior, rejoicing with them in the triumph of our King, in that, death vanquished, he has risen, begin the hymn,

We praise thee, O Lord.

This begun, all the bells are rung together, at the end of which let the priest say the verse,

In thy resurrection, O Christ,

as far as this word, and let him begin Matins, saying,

O Lord, hasten to my aid! [1]

---

[1] *Early Plays*, pp. 5–6. Riverside Literature Series. C. G. Child. Houghton Mifflin Co., Boston.

Obviously in this little play the directions for imitative movement fill three quarters of the space; dialogue fills one quarter; characterization, except as the accompanying music may very faintly have suggested it, there is none. Historically studied, the English drama shows that characterization appeared as an added interest when the interest of action was already well established. The value of dialogue for its own sake was recognized even later.

What is true of the English drama is of course equally true of all Continental drama which, like the English drama, had its origin in the Trope and the Miracle Play. Even, however, if we go farther back, to the origin of Greek Drama in the Ballad Dance we shall find the same results. The Ballad Dance consisted "in the combination of speech, music, and that imitative gesture which, for lack of a better word, we are obliged to call dancing. It is very important, however, to guard against modern associations with this term. Dances in which men and women joined are almost unknown to Greek antiquity, and to say of a guest at a banquet that he danced would suggest intoxication. The real dancing of the Greeks is a lost art, of which the modern ballet is a corruption, and the orator's action a faint survival. It was an art which used bodily motion to convey thought: as in speech the tongue articulated words, so in dancing the body swayed and gesticulated into meaning. . . . In epic poetry, where thought takes the form of simple narrative, the speech (Greek *epos*) of the Ballad Dance triumphs over the other two elements. Lyric poetry consists in meditation or highly wrought description taking such forms as odes, sonnets, hymns, — poetry that lends itself to elaborate rhythms and other devices of musical art: here the music is the element of the Ballad Dance which has come to the front. And the imitative gesture has triumphed over the speech and the music in the case of the third branch of poetry; drama is thought expressed in action." [1]

Imitative movement is the drama of the savage.

"An Aleut, who was armed with a bow, represented a hunter, another a bird. The former expressed by gestures how very glad he was he had found so fine a bird; nevertheless he would not kill it. The other imitated the motions of a bird seeking to escape the hunter. He at last, after a long delay, pulled his bow and shot: the bird reeled, fell, and died. The hunter danced for joy; but finally he became troubled, repented having killed so fine a bird, and lamented it. Suddenly the dead bird rose, turned into a beautiful woman, and fell into the hunter's arms." [2]

Look where we will, then, — at the beginnings of drama in Greece, in England centuries later, or among savage peoples today — the chief essential in winning and holding the attention of the spectator was imitative movement by the actors, that is, physical action. Nor, as the drama develops, does physical action cease to be central. The most elaborate of the Miracle Plays, the Towneley *Second Shepherds' Play* and the Brome *Abraham and Isaac* [3] prove this. In the former we are of course interested in the characterization of the Shepherds and Mak, but would this hold us without the stealing of the sheep and the varied action attending its concealment and discovery in the house of Mak? Undoubtedly in the *Abraham and Isaac* characterization counts for more, but we have the journey to the Mount, the preparations for the sacrifice, the binding of the boy's eyes, the repeatedly upraised sword, the farewell embracings, the very dramatic coming of the Angel, and the joyful sacrifice of the sheep when the child is released. Without

---

[1] *The Ancient Classical Drama*, pp. 3-4. R. G. Moulton. Clarendon Press, Oxford.

[2] Quoted in *The Development of the Drama*, pp. 10-11. Copyright, 1903, by Brander Matthews. Chas. Scribner's Sons, New York.

[3] For these two plays see *Early Plays*. Riverside Literature Series. C. G. Child. Houghton Mifflin Co., Boston.

all this central action, the fine characterization of the play would lose its significance. In Shakespeare's day, audiences again and again, as they watched plays of Dekker, Heywood, and many another dramatist, willingly accepted inadequate characterization and weak dialogue so long as the action was absorbing. Just this interest in, for instance, *The Four Prentices,* or the various *Ages* [1] of Thomas Heywood, was burlesqued by Francis Beaumont in *The Knight of the Burning Pestle.* It may be urged that the plays of Racine and Corneille, as well as the Restoration Comedy in England, show characterization and dialogue predominant. It should be remembered, however, that Corneille and Racine, as well as the Restoration writers of comedy wrote primarily for the Court group and not for the public at large. Theirs was the cultivated audience of the time, proud of its special literary and dramatic standards. Around and about these dramatists were the writers of popular entertainment, which depended on action. In England, we must remember that Wycherley and Vanbrugh, who are by no means without action in their plays, belong to Restoration Comedy as much as Etherege or Congreve, and that the Heroic Drama, in which action was absolutely central, divided the favor of even the Court public with the Comedy of Manners. The fact is, the history of the Drama shows that only rarely does even a group of people for a brief time care more for plays of characterization and dialogue than for plays of action. Throughout the ages, the great public, cultivated as well as uncultivated, have cared for action first, then, as aids to a better understanding of the action of the story, for characterization and dialogue. Now, for more than a century, the play of mere action has been so popular that it has been recognized as a special form, namely, melodrama. This type of play, in which characterization and dialogue have usually

---

[1] *Works.* 6 vols. Pearson, London.

been entirely subordinated to action, has been the most
widely attended. Today the motion picture show has driven
mere melodrama from our theatres, yet who will deny that
the "movie" in its present form subordinates everything
to action? Even the most ambitious specimens, such as
Cabiria and *The Birth of a Nation*, finding their audiences
restless under frequent use of the explanatory "titles"
which make clear what cannot be clearly shown in action,
hasten to depict some man hunt, some daring leap from a
high cliff into the sea, or a wild onrush of galloping white-
clad figures of the Ku Klux Klan. From the practice of centuries the feeling that action is really central in drama has
become instinctive with most persons who write plays without preconceived theories. Watch a child making his first
attempt at play-writing. In ninety-nine cases out of a hundred, the play will contain little except action. There will
be slight characterization, if any, and the dialogue will be
mediocre at best. The young writer has depended almost
entirely upon action because instinctively, when he thinks of
drama, he thinks of action.

Nor, if we paused to consider, is this dependence of drama
upon action surprising. "From emotions to emotions" is the
formula for any good play. To paraphrase a principle of
geometry, "A play is the shortest distance from emotions to
emotions." The emotions to be reached are those of the audience. The emotions conveyed are those of the people on
the stage or of the dramatist as he has watched the people
represented. Just herein lies the importance of action for the
dramatist: it is his quickest means of arousing emotion in an
audience. Which is more popular with the masses, the man
of action or the thinker? The world at large believes, and
rightly that, as a rule, "Actions speak louder than words."
The dramatist knows that not what a man thinks he thinks,
but what at a crisis he does, instinctively, spontaneously,

best shows his character. The dramatist knows, too, that though we may think, when discussing patriotism in the abstract, that we have firm ideas about it, what reveals our real beliefs is our action at a crisis in the history of our country. Many believed from the talk of German Socialists that they would not support their Government in the case of war. Their actions have shown far more clearly than their words their real beliefs. Ulster sounded as hostile as possible to England not long ago, but when the call upon her loyalty came she did not prove false. Is it any wonder, then, that popular vote has declared action the best revealer of feeling and, therefore, that the dramatist, in writing his plays, depends first of all upon action? If any one is disposed to cavil at action as popular merely with the masses and the less cultivated, let him ask himself, "What, primarily in other people interests me — what these people do or why they do it?" Even if he belong to the group, relatively very small in the mass of humanity, most interested by "Why did these people do this?" he must admit that till he knows clearly what the people did, he cannot take up the question which more interests him. For the majority of auditors, action is of first importance in drama: even for the group which cares far more for characterization and dialogue it is necessary as preparing the way for that characterization and dialogue on which they insist.

Consider for a moment the nature of the attention which a dramatist may arouse. Of course it may be only of the same sort which an audience gives a lecturer on a historical or scientific subject, — a readiness to hear and to try to understand what he has to present, — close but unemotional attention. Comparatively few people, however, are capable of sustained attention when their emotions are not called upon. How many lectures last over an hour? Is not the "popular lecturer" popular largely because he works into

his lecture many anecdotes and dramatic illustrations in
order to avoid or to lighten the strain of close, sustained
attention? There is, undoubtedly, a public which can listen
to ideas with the same keen enjoyment which most auditors feel when listening to something which stirs them emotionally, but as compared with the general public it is
infinitesimal. Understanding this, the dramatist stirs the
emotions of his hearers by the most concrete means at his
command, his quickest communication from brain to brain,
— action just for itself or illustrating character. The infe-
riority to action of mere exposition as a creator of interest
the two following extracts show.

ACT I. SCENE 1. *Britain. The garden of Cymbeline's palace*

Enter two gentlemen

1. Gent. You do not meet a man but frowns. Our bloods
No more obey the heavens than our courtiers
Still seem as does the King.
　2. Gent.　　　　　　　　But what's the matter?
1. Gent. His daughter, and the heir of's kingdom, whom
He purpos'd to his wife's sole son — a widow
That late he married — hath referred herself
Unto a poor but worthy gentleman. She's wedded,
Her husband banish'd, she imprison'd; all
Is outward sorrow; though I think the King
Be touched at very heart.
　2. Gent.　　　　　　　None but the King?
1. Gent. He that hath lost her too; so is the Queen,
That most desir'd the match: but not a courtier,
Although they wear their faces to the bent
Of the King's look, hath a heart that is not
Glad at the thing they scowl at.
　2. Gent.　　　　　　　And why so?
1. Gent. He that hath miss'd the Princess is a thing
Too bad for bad report; and he that hath her —
I mean, that married her, alack, good man!
And therefore banish'd — is a creature such

As, to seek through the regions of the earth
For one his like, there would be something failing
In him that should compare. I do not think
So fair an outward, and such stuff within
Endows a man but he.

    2. Gent.   You speak him far.

    1. Gent. I do extend him, sir, within himself,
Crush him together rather than unfold
His measure duly.

    2. Gent.   What's his name and birth?

    1. Gent. I cannot delve him to the root. His father
Was call'd Sicilius, who did gain his honour
Against the Romans with Cassibelan,
But had his titles by Tenantius whom
He serv'd with glory and admir'd success,
So gain'd the sur-addition Leonatus;
And hath, besides this gentleman in question,
'Two other sons, who in the wars o' the time
Died with their swords in hand; for which their father
Then old and fond of issue, took such sorrow
That he quit being, and his gentle lady,
Big of this gentleman our theme, deceas'd
As he was born. The King he takes the babe
To his protection, calls him Posthumus Leonatus,
Breeds him and makes him of his bed chamber,
Puts to him all the learnings that his time
Could make him the receiver of; which he took,
As we do air, fast as 'twas minist'red,
And in's spring became a harvest; liv'd in court —
Which rare it is to do — most prais'd, most lov'd,
A sample to the youngest, to the more mature
A glass that feated them, and to the graver
A child that guided dotards; to his mistress,
For whom he is now banish'd, — her own price
Proclaims how she esteem'd him and his virtue;
By her election may be truly read
What kind of man he is.

    2. Gent.   I honour him
Even out of your report. But, pray you, tell me
Is she sole child to the King?

    1. Gent.   His only child.

He had two sons, — if this be worth your hearing,
Mark it — the eldest of them at three years old,
I' the swathing-clothes the other, from their nursery
Were stolen, and to this hour no guess in knowledge
Which way they went.
   2. Gent.   How long is this ago?
   1. Gent. Some twenty years.
   2. Gent. That a King's children should be so convey'd,
So slackly guarded and the search so slow,
That could not trace them!
   1. Gent.   Howso'er 'tis strange,
Or that the negligence may well be laughed at,
Yet it is true, sir.
   2. Gent.   I do well believe you.
   1. Gent. We must forbear; here comes the gentleman,
The Queen and Princess.   (*Exeunt.*)[1]

Here Shakespeare trusts mere exposition to rouse interest. His speakers merely question and answer, showing little characterization and practically no emotion. Is this extract as interesting as the following?

   Fitz Urse. (*Catches hold of the last flying monk.*) Where is the
      traitor Becket?
   Becket.   Here.
No traitor to the King, but Priest of God,
Primate of England.   (*Descending into the transept.*)
         I am he ye seek.
What would ye have of me?
   Fitz Urse.   Your life.
   De Tracy.   Your life.
   De Morville. Save that you will absolve the bishops.
   Becket.   Never, —
Except they make submission to the Church.
You had my answer to that cry before.
   De Morville. Why, then you are a dead man; flee!
   Becket.   I will not.
I am readier to be slain than thou to slay.
Hugh, I know well that thou hast but half a heart

    [1] *Cymbeline,* Act i, Scene 1.

To bathe this sacred pavement with my blood.
God pardon thee and these, but God's full curse
Shatter you all to pieces if ye harm
One of my flock!

Fitz Urse. Seize him and carry him!
Come with us — nay — thou art our prisoner — come!
(Fitz Urse lays hold of Archbishop's pall.)

Becket. Down!
(Throws him headlong.)

De Morville. Ay, make him prisoner, do not harm the man.

Fitz Urse. (Advances with drawn sword.) I told thee that I should remember thee!

Becket. Profligate pander!

Fitz Urse. Do you hear that? Strike, strike.
(Strikes the Archbishop and wounds him in the forehead.)

Becket. (Covers his eyes with his hand.) I do commend my cause to God.

Fitz Urse. Strike him, Tracy!

Rosamund. (Rushing down the steps from the choir.) No, no, no, no. Mercy, Mercy,
As you would hope for mercy.

Fitz Urse. Strike, I say.

Grim. O, God, O, noble knight, O, sacrilege!

Fitz Urse. Strike! I say.

De Tracy. There is my answer then.
(Sword falls on Grim's arm, and glances from it, wounding Becket.)
This last to rid thee of a world of brawls!

Becket. (Falling on his knees.) Into thy hands, O Lord — into thy hands —! *(Sinks prone.)*

De Brito. The traitor's dead, and will arise no more.
(De Brito, De Tracy, Fitz Urse rush out, crying " King's men !" De Morville follows slowly Flashes of lightning through the Cathedral. Rosamund seen kneeling at the body of Becket.)[1]

The physical action of this extract instantly grips attention. Interested at once by this action, shortly we rush on un-

---

[1] *Becket: A Tragedy.* Lord Tennyson. Arranged for the stage by Henry Irving. Macmillan & Co., London and New York.

thinking, but feeling more and more intensely. In this extract action is everywhere. The actionless *Cymbeline* is undramatic. This extract is intensely dramatic.

Just what, however, is this action which in drama is so essential? To most people it means physical or bodily action which rouses sympathy or dislike in an audience. The action of melodrama certainly exists largely for itself. We expect and get little but physical action for its own sake when a play is announced as was the well-known melodrama, *A Race for Life*.

As Melodramatically and Masterfully Stirring, Striking and Sensational as Phil Sheridan's Famous Ride.
Superb, Stupendous Scenes in Sunset Regions.
Wilderness Wooings Where Wild Roses Grow.
The Lights and Shades of Rugged Border Life.
Chinese Comedy to Make Confucius Chuckle.
The Realism of the Ranch and Race Track.
The Hero Horse That Won a Human Life.
An Equine Beauty Foils a Murderous Beast.
Commingled Gleams of Gladness, Grief, and Guilt.
Dope, Dynamite and Devilish Treachery Distanced.
Continuous Climaxes That Come Like Cloudbursts.

Some plays depend almost wholly upon mere bustle and rapidly shifting movement, much of it wholly unnecessary to the plot. Large portions of many recent musical comedies illustrate this. Such unnecessary but crudely effective movement Stevenson burlesqued more than once in the stage directions of his *Macaire*.

ACT I. SCENE 1

Aline and maids; to whom Fiddlers; afterwards Dumont and Charles. As the curtain rises, the sound of the violin is heard approaching. Aline and the inn servants. who are discovered laying the table, dance up to door L.C., to meet the Fiddlers, who enter likewise dancing to their own music. Air: "Haste to the Wedding." The Fiddlers exeunt playing into house, R.U.E. Aline and Maids dance back to table, which they proceed to arrange.

Aline. Well, give me fiddles: fiddles and a wedding feast. It tickles your heart till your heels make a runaway match of it. I don't mind extra work, I don't, so long as there's fun about it. Hand me up that pile of plates. The quinces there, before the bride. Stick a pink in the Notary's glass: that's the girl he's courting.

Dumont. (Entering with Charles.) Good girls, good girls! Charles, in ten minutes from now what happy faces will smile around that board!

ACT II. SCENE 2

To these all the former characters, less the Notary. The fiddlers are heard without, playing dolefully. Air: "O, dear, what can the matter be?" in time to which the procession enters.

Macaire. Well, friends, what cheer?
Aline. No wedding, no wedding! } *Together*
Goriot. I told 'ee he can't, and he can't!
Dumont. Dear, dear me.
Ernestine. They won't let us marry. } *Together*
Charles. No wife, no father, no nothing.
Curate. The facts have justified the worst anticipations of our absent friend, the Notary.
Macaire. I perceive I must reveal myself.[1]

If physical action in and of itself is so often dramatic, is all physical action dramatic? That is, does it always create emotion in an onlooker? No. It goes for naught unless it rouses his interest. Of itself, or because of the presentation given it by the dramatist, it must rouse in the onlooker an emotional response. A boy seeing "Crazy Mary" stalking the street in bedizened finery and bowing right and left, may see nothing interesting in her. More probably her actions will move him to jeer and jibe at her. Let some spectator, however, tell the boy of the tragedy in Crazy Mary's

[1] *Macaire.* By R. L. Stevenson and W. E. Henley. Chas. Scribner's Sons, New York. Copyright, 1895, by Stone & Kimball, Chicago.

younger life which left her unbalanced, and, if he has any right feeling, the boy's attitude will begin to change. He may even give over the jeering he has begun. Reveal to him exactly what is passing in the crazed mind of the woman, and his mere interest will probably turn to sympathy. Characterization, preceding and accompanying action, creates sympathy or repulsion for the figure or figures involved. This sympathy or repulsion in turn converts mere interest into emotional response of the keenest kind. Though physical action is undoubtedly fundamental in drama, no higher form than crude melodrama or crude farce can develop till characterization appears to explain and interpret action.

The following extracts from Robertson's *Home* show physical action, silly it is true, yet developing characterization by illustrative action. The first, even as it amuses, characterizes the timid Bertie, and the second shows the mild mentality and extreme confusion of the two central figures.

Mr. Dorrison. Will you give Mrs. Pinchbeck your arm, Colonel? Dora, my dear. (*Taking Dora's.*) Lucy, Captain Mountraffe will — (*Sees him asleep.*) Ah, Lucy, you must follow by yourself.
> (*Colonel takes off Mrs. Pinchbeck; Dorrison, Dora. At that moment, Bertie enters window, R., and runs to Lucy, kneels at her feet, and is about to kiss her hand. Mountraffe yawns, which frightens Bertie. He is running off as the drop falls quickly.*)

End of Act I

Colonel. I'd always give my eyes to be alone with this girl for five minutes, and whenever I am alone with her, I haven't a word to say for myself. (*Aloud.*) That music, Miss Thornhaugh?

Dora. (*At piano.*) Yes.

Col. (*Aside.*) As if it could be anything else. How stupid of me. (*Aloud.*) New music?

Dora. Yes.

Col. New laid — I mean, fresh from the country — fresh from London, or — yes — I — (*Dora sits on music stool at piano. This scene is played with great constraint on both sides. Colonel bends over Dora at piano.*) Going to play any of it now?

Dora. No. I must practise it first. I can't play at sight.

Col. Can't you really? Don't you believe in — music — at first sight?

(*Dora drops a music book. Colonel picks it up. Dora tries to pick it up. They knock their heads together; mutual confusion. As they rise, each has hold of the book.*)

Dora. }
Col. } I beg your pardon. (*Both trembling.*)

Dora. It's nothing.

Col. Nothing, quite so.

(*Dora sits on music stool. As she does so, both leave hold of the book and it falls again.*)

Dora. I thought you had the book.

Col. (*Picking it up.*) And I thought you had it, and it appears that neither of us had it. Ha! ha! (*Aside.*) Fool that I am! (*Dora sits thoughtfully, Colonel bending over her; a pause.*) Won't you play something?

Dora. I don't know how to play.

Col. Oh, well, play the other one. (*They resume their attitudes; a pause.*) The weather has been very warm today, has it not?

Dora. Very.

Col. Looks like thunder to me.

Dora. Does it?

Col. Are you fond of thunder — I mean fond of music? I should say are you fond of lightning? (*Dora touches keys of piano mechanically.*) Do play something.

Dora. No, I — I didn't think of what I was doing. What were you talking about?

Col. About? You — me — no! About thunder — music — I mean lightning.

Dora. I'm afraid of lightning. (Act II.) [1]

The first scene of Act I of *Romeo and Juliet* is full of interesting physical action — quarrels, fighting, and the halting of the fight by the angry Prince. The physical action, however, characterizes in every instance, from the servants of the two factions to Tybalt, Benvolio, the Capulets, the Mon-

[1] R. M. DeWitt, New York City.

tagues, and the Prince. Moreover, this interesting physical action, which is all the more interesting because it characterizes, is interesting in the third place because in every instance it helps to an understanding of the story. It shows so intense an enmity between the two houses that even the servants cannot meet in the streets without quarreling. By its characterization it prepares for the parts Benvolio and Tybalt are to play in later scenes. It motivates the edict of banishment which is essential if the tragedy of the play is to occur.

SCENE 1. *Verona. A public place*

Enter Sampson and Gregory, of the house of Capulet, with swords and bucklers

Sampson. Gregory, on my word, we'll not carry coals.
Gregory. No, for then we should be colliers.
Sam. I mean, an we be in choler, we'll draw.
Gre. Ay, while you live, draw your neck out o' the collar.
Sam. I strike quickly, being mov'd.
Gre. But thou art not quickly mov'd to strike.
Sam. A dog of the house of Montague moves me.

.   .   .   .

Draw thy tool; here comes two of the house of Montague.

Enter two other serving-men. (Abraham and Balthasar.)

Sam. My naked weapon is out. Quarrel, I will back thee.
Gre. How! turn thy back and run?
Sam. Fear me not.
Gre. No, marry; I fear thee!
Sam. Let us take the law of our sides; let them begin.
Gre. I will frown as I pass by, and let them take it as they list.
Sam. Nay, as they dare. I will bite my thumb at them; which is disgrace to them if they bare it.
Abraham. Do you bite your thumb at us, sir?
Sam. I do bite my thumb, sir.
Abr. Do you bite your thumb at us, sir?
Sam. (Aside to Gre.) Is the law of our side, if I say ay?

Gre. No.

Sam. No, sir, I do not bite my thumb at you, sir; but I bite my thumb, sir.

Gre. Do you quarrel, sir?

Abr. Quarrel, sir? No, sir.

Sam. But if you do, sir, I am for you. I serve as good a man as you.

Abr. No better.

Sam. Well, sir.

Enter Benvolio.

Ger. Say "better"; here comes one of my master's kinsmen.

Sam. Yes, better, sir.

Abr. You lie.

Sam. Draw, if you be men. Gregory, remember thy swashing blow. (*They fight.*)

Benvolio. Part, fools!
Put up your swords; you know not what you do.

(*Beats down their swords.*)

Enter Tybal

Tybalt. What, art thou drawn among these heartless hinds?
Turn thee, Benvolio, look upon thy death.

Ben. I do but keep the peace. Put up thy sword,
Or manage it to part these men with me.

Tyb. What, drawn, and talk of peace! I hate the word
As I hate hell, all Montagues, and thee.
Have at thee, coward! (*They fight.*)

Enter three or four citizens, and officers, with clubs or partisans

Officer. Clubs, bills, and partisans! Strike! Beat them down!
Down with the Capulets! down with the Montagues!

Enter Capulet in his gown and Lady Capulet

Capulet. What noise is this? Give me my long sword, ho!

Lady Capulet. A crutch, a crutch! Why call you for a sword?

Cap. My sword, I say! Old Montague is come,
And flourishes his blade in spite of me.

Enter Montague and Lady Montague

Montague. Thou villain, Capulet, — Hold me not, let me go.

Lady Montague. Thou shalt not stir one foot to seek a foe.

Enter Prince, with his train

Prince. Rebellious subjects, enemies to peace,
Profaners of this neighbour-stained steel, —
Will they not hear? — What, ho! you men, you beasts,
That quench the fire of your pernicious rage
With purple fountains issuing from your veins,
On pain of torture, from those bloody hands
Throw your mistemper'd weapons to the ground,
And hear the sentence of your moved prince.
Three civil brawls, bred of an airy word,
By thee, old Capulet, and Montague,
Have thrice disturb'd the quiet of our streets,
And made Verona's ancient citizens
Cast by their grave beseeming ornaments,
To wield old partisans, in hands as old,
Cank'red with peace, to part your cank'red hate;
If ever you disturb our streets again
Your lives shall pay the forfeit of the peace.
For this time, all the rest depart away.
You, Capulet, shall go along with me;
And Montague, come you this afternoon,
To know our farther pleasure in this case,
To old Free-town, our common judgement place,
Once more, on pain of death, all men depart.
    (*Exeunt all but Montague, Lady Montague, and Benvolio.*)

Even physical action, then, may interest for itself, or because it characterizes, or because it helps on the story, or for two or more of these reasons.

If we examine other extracts from famous plays we shall, however, find ourselves wondering whether action in drama must not mean something besides mere physical action. In the opening scene of *La Princesse Georges*, by Dumas fils, the physical action is neither large in amount nor varied, but the scene is undeniably dramatic, for emotions represented create prompt emotional response in us.

ACT I. SCENE 1

A Drawing Room

Severine, watching near the window, with the curtain drawn a
little aside, then Rosalie

Severine. Rosalie! At last! What a night I have gone through!
Sixteen hours of waiting! (*To Rosalie, who enters.*) Well?
Rosalie. Madame, the Princess must be calm.
Severine. Don't call me Princess. That's wasting time.
Rosalie. Madame has not slept?
Severine. No.
Rosalie. I suspected as much.
Severine. Tell me, is it true?
Rosalie. Yes.
Severine. The details, then.
Rosalie. Well, then, last evening I followed the Prince, who
went to the Western Railway, as he had told Madame that he would
do, to take the train at half past nine; only, instead of buying a
ticket for Versailles, he took one for Rouen.
Severine. But he was alone?
Rosalie. Yes. But five minutes after he arrived, she came.
Severine. Who was the woman?
Rosalie. Alas, Madame knows her better than I!
Severine. It is some one whom I know?
Rosalie. Yes.
Severine. Not one of those women? —
Rosalie. It is one of your intimate friends, of the best social
position.
Severine. Valentine? Bertha? No. — The Baroness?
Rosalie. The Countess Sylvanie.
Severine. She? Impossible! She stayed here, with me, until at
least nine o'clock. We dined alone together.
Rosalie. She was making sure that you didn't suspect anything.
Severine. Indeed, nothing. And she came to the train at what
hour?
Rosalie. At twenty-five minutes past nine.
Severine. So, in twenty-five minutes —
Rosalie. She went home; she changed her dress (she arrived all
in black); she went to the St. Lazare Station. It is true that only
your garden and hers separate her house from yours; that she has

the best horses in Paris; and that she is accustomed to doing this
sort of thing, if I may believe what I have heard.

Severine. To what a pass we have come! My most intimate
friend! Did they speak to each other? [1]

This scene wins our attention because it reveals in Severine a mental state which in itself interests and moves us far
more than the mere physical action.

What has been said of *La Princesse Georges* is even more
true of the ending of Marlowe's *Faustus.*

Faustus. Ah, Faustus:
Now hast thou but one bare hour to live,
And then thou must be damn'd perpetually!
Stand still, you ever-moving spheres of heaven,
That time may cease, and midnight never come;
Fair Nature's eye, rise, rise again and make
Perpetual day; or let this hour be but
A year, a month, a week, a natural day,
That Faustus may repent and save his soul!
O lente, lente currite, noctis equi!
The stars move still, time runs, the clock will strike,
The devil will come, and Faustus will be damn'd.
. . . . All beasts are happy,
For when they die,
Their souls are soon dissolv'd in elements;
But mine must live still to be plagu'd in hell.
Curs'd be the parents that engender'd me!
No, Faustus, curse thyself, curse Lucifer
That hath deprived thee of the joys of heaven.
                              (*The clock strikes twelve.*)
O, it strikes, it strikes! Now body, turn to air,
Or Lucifer will bear thee quick to hell!
                              (*Thunder and lightning.*)
O, soul, be chang'd into little water-drops,
And fall into the ocean, ne'er be found!

Enter Devils

My God, my God, look not so fierce on me!
Adders and serpents, let me breathe a while!

---

[1] *Théâtre Complet,* vol. v. Dumas fils. Calmann Lévy, Paris.

Ugly hell, gape not! come not, Lucifer!
I'll burn my books! — Ah, Mephistophilis!

(Exeunt Devils with Faustus.)[1]

Though this scene doubtless requires physical action as
the tortured Faustus flings himself about the stage, would
that action be clear enough to move us greatly were it not
for the characterization of the preceding scenes and the masterly phrasing which exactly reveals the tortured soul? Is it
not a mental state rather than physical action which moves
us here? Surely.

The fact is, the greatest drama of all time, and the larger
part of the drama of the past twenty years, uses action much
less for its own sake than to reveal mental states which are
to rouse sympathy or repulsion in an audience. In brief,
marked mental activity may be quite as dramatic as mere
physical action. Hamlet may sit quietly by his fire as he
speaks the soliloquy "To be, or not to be," yet by what we
already know of him and what the lines reveal we are moved
to the deepest sympathy for his tortured state. There is almost no physical movement as Percinet reads to Sylvette
from *Romeo and Juliet* in the opening pages of Rostand's
Romancers, yet we are amused and pleased by their excited
delight.

ACT I

*The stage is cut in two by an old wall, mossy and garlanded by luxu-
rious vines. To the right, a corner of Bergamin's park; to the left a
corner of Pasquinot's. On each side, against the wall, a bench.*

SCENE 1. *Sylvette. Percinet. When the curtain rises, Percinet
is seated on the wall, with a book on his knees, from which he is reading to Sylvette. She stands on the bench in her father's park, her chin
in her hands, her elbows against the wall, listening attentively.*

Sylvette. O Monsieur Percinet, how beautiful it is!
Percinet. Isn't it? Hear Romeo's reply! (*He reads.*)

---

[1] Marlowe's *Faustus*, Act v. Mermaid Series or Everyman's Library.

"It was the lark, the herald of the morn,
No nightingale; look, love, what envious streaks
Do lace the severing clouds in yonder east:
Night's candles are burnt out and jocund day
Stands tiptoe on the misty mountain tops:
I must be gone. . . ."

Sylvette. (*Alert, with animation.*) Sh!

Percinet. (*Listens a moment, then*) No one! So, mademoiselle,
don't have the air of an affrighted birdling on a branch, ready
to spread wing at the slightest sound. Hear the immortal lovers
talking:

She. "Yon light is not day-light, I know it, I:
It is some meteor that the sun exhales,
To be to thee this night a torch bearer."

He. "Let me be ta'en, let me be put to death;
I am content, so thou wilt have it so.
I'll say yon gray is not the morning's eye;
'Tis but the pale reflex of Cynthia's brow;
Nor that is not the lark, whose notes do beat
The vaulty heaven so high above our heads;
I have more care to stay than will to go:
Come, death, and welcome! Juliet wills it so."

Sylvette. Oh, no! I won't have him talk of that; if he does, I shall
cry.

Percinet. Then we'll shut our book till tomorrow, and, since you
wish it, let sweet Romeo live.

(*He closes the book and looks about him.*)

What an adorable spot! It seems made for lulling one's self with
the lines of the great William.[1]

Here is great activity, but it is mental rather than physical action. To make it rouse us to the desired emotional response, good characterization and wisely chosen words are
necessary.

Examine also the opening scene of Maeterlinck's *The Blind*.
A group of sightless people have been deserted in a wood by
their guide, and consequently are so bewildered and timor-
ous that they hardly dare move. Yet all their trepidation,

---

[1] *The Romancers.* Translated by Mary Hendee. Doubleday & McClure Co., New York.

doubt, and awe are clearly conveyed to us, with a very small amount of physical action, through skilful characterization, and words specially chosen and ordered to create and intensify emotion in us.

An ancient Norland forest, with an eternal look, under a sky of deep stars.

In the centre and in the deep of the night, a very old priest is sitting, wrapped in a great black cloak. The chest and the head, gently upturned and deathly motionless, rest against the trunk of a giant hollow oak. The face is fearsome pale and of an immovable waxen lividness, in which the purple lips fall slightly apart. The dumb, fixed eyes no longer look out from the visible side of Eternity and seem to bleed with immemorial sorrows and with tears. The hair, of a solemn whiteness, falls in stringy locks, stiff and few, over a face more illuminated and more weary than all that surrounds it in the watchful stillness of that melancholy wood. The hands, pitifully thin, are clasped rigidly over the thighs.

On the right, six old men, all blind, are sitting on stones, stumps, and dead leaves.

On the left, separated from them by an uprooted tree and fragments of rock, six women, also blind, are sitting opposite the old men. Three among them pray and mourn without ceasing, in a muffled voice. Another is old in the extreme. The fifth, in an attitude of mute insanity, holds on her knees a little sleeping child. The sixth is strangely young and her whole body is drenched with her beautiful hair. They, as well as the old men, are all clad in the same ample and sombre garments. Most of them are waiting, with their elbows on their knees and their faces in their hands; and all seem to have lost the habit of ineffectual gesture and no longer turn their heads at the stifled and uneasy noises of the Island. Tall funereal trees, — yews, weeping-willows, cypresses, — cover them with their faithful shadows. A cluster of long, sickly asphodels is in bloom, not far from the priest, in the night. It is unusually oppressive, despite the moonlight that here and there struggles to pierce for an instant the glooms of the foliage.

First Blind Man. (*Who was born blind.*) He hasn't come back yet?
Second Blind Man. (*Who also was born blind.*) You have awakened me.
First Blind Man. I was sleeping, too.
Third Blind Man. (*Also born blind.*) I was sleeping, too.

First Blind Man. He hasn't come yet?

Second Blind Man. I hear something coming.

Third Blind Man. It is time to go back to the Asylum.

First Blind Man. We ought to find out where we are.

Second Blind Man. It has grown cold since he left.

First Blind Man. We ought to find out where we are!

The Very Old Blind Man. Does any one know where we are?

The Very Old Blind Woman. We were walking a very long while; we must be a long way from the Asylum.

First Blind Man. Oh! the women are opposite us?

The Very Old Blind Woman. We are sitting opposite you.

First Blind Man. Wait, I am coming over where you are. (*He rises and gropes in the dark.*) Where are you? — Speak! let me hear where you are!

The Very Old Blind Woman. Here; we are sitting on stones.

First Blind Man. (*Advances and stumbles against the fallen tree and the rocks.*) There is something between us.

Second Blind Man. We had better keep our places.

Third Blind Man. Where are you sitting? — Will you come over by us?

The Very Old Blind Woman. We dare not rise!

Third Blind Man. Why did he separate us?

First Blind Man. I hear praying on the women's side.

Second Blind Man. Yes; the three old women are praying.

First Blind Man. This is no time for prayer!

Second Blind Man. You will pray soon enough, in the dormitory!

(*The three old women continue their prayers.*)

Third Blind Man. I should like to know who it is I am sitting by.

Second Blind Man. I think I am next to you.

(*They feel about them.*)

Third Blind Man. We can't reach each other.

First Blind Man. Nevertheless, we are not far apart. (*He feels about him and strikes with his staff the fifth blind man, who utters a muffled groan.*) The one who cannot hear is beside us.

Second Blind Man. I don't hear anybody; we were six just now.

First Blind Man. I am going to count. Let us question the women, too; we must know what to depend upon. I hear the three old women praying all the time; are they together?

The Very Old Blind Woman. They are sitting beside me, on a rock.

First Blind Man. I am sitting on dead leaves.
Third Blind Man. And the beautiful blind girl, where is she?
The Very Old Blind Woman. She is near them that pray.
Second Blind Man. Where is the mad woman, and her child?
The Young Blind Girl. He sleeps; do not awaken him!
First Blind Man. Oh! How far away you are from us! I thought
you were opposite me!
Third Blind Man. We know — nearly — all we need to know.
Let us chat a little, while we wait for the priest to come back.[1]

Many an inexperienced dramatist fails to see the force of
these words of Maeterlinck: "An old man, seated in his arm-
chair, waiting patiently, with his lamp beside him — submitting with bent head to the presence of his soul and his
destiny — motionless as he is does yet live in reality a deeper,
more human, and more universal life than the lover who
strangles his mistress, the captain who conquers in battle, or
the husband who 'avenges his honor.'" If an audience can
be made to feel and understand the strong but contained
emotion of this motionless figure, he is rich dramatic material.

In the extracts from *La Princesse Georges, Faustus, The
Romancers, The Blind,* in the soliloquy of Hamlet referred to,
and the illustration quoted from Maeterlinck, it is not physical outward expression but the vivid picture we get of a
state of mind which stirs us. Surely all these cases prove that
we must include mental as well as physical activity in any
definition of the word *dramatic.* Provided a writer can convey to his audience the excited mental state of one or more
of his characters, then this mental activity is thoroughly
dramatic. That is, neither physical nor mental activity is
in itself dramatic; all depends on whether it naturally arouses,
or can be made by the author to arouse, emotion in an audience. Just as we had to add to physical action which arouses
emotional response of itself, physical action which is made

[1] *The Blind.* Translated by Richard Hovey. Copyright, 1894 and 1896, by Stone &
Kimball, Chicago.

to arouse response because it develops the story or illustrates character, we must now add action which is not physical, but mental.

There is even another chance for confusion. A figure sitting motionless not because he is thinking hard but because blank in mind may yet be dramatic. Utter inaction, both physical and mental, of a figure represented on the stage does not mean that it is necessarily undramatic. If the dramatist can make an audience feel the terrible tragedy of the contrast between what might have been and what is for this perfectly quiet unthinking figure, he rouses emotion in his hearers, and in so doing makes his material dramatic. Suppose, too, that the expressionless figure is an aged father or mother very dear to some one in the play who has strongly won the sympathy of the audience. The house takes fire. The flames draw nearer and nearer the unconscious figure. We are made to look at the situation through the eyes of the character — some child or relative — to whom the scene, were he present, would mean torture. Instantly the figure, because of the way in which it is represented, becomes dramatic. Here again, however, the emotion of the audience could hardly be aroused except through characterization of the figure as it was or might have been, or of the child or relative who has won our sympathy. Again, too, characterization so successful must depend a good deal on well-chosen words.

This somewhat elaborate analysis should have made three points clear. First, we may arouse emotion in an audience by mere physical action; by physical action which also develops the story, or illustrates character, or does both; by mental rather than physical action, if clearly and accurately conveyed to the audience; and even by inaction, if characterization and dialogue by means of other figures are of high order. Secondly, as the various illustrations have been examined, it must have become steadily more clear that while action is popularly held to be central in drama, emotion is really the essential. Because it is the easiest expression of emotion to understand, physical action, which without illuminating characterization and dialogue can express only a part of the world of emotion, has been too often accepted as expressing all the emotion the stage can present. Thirdly, it should be clear that a statement one meets too frequently in books on the drama, that certain stories or characters, above all certain well-known books, are essentially undramatic material is at least dubious. The belief arises from the fact that the story, character, or idea, as usually presented, seems to demand much analysis and description, and almost to preclude illustrative action. In the past few years, however, the drama of mental states and the drama which has revealed emotional significance in seeming or real inaction, has been proving that "nothing human is foreign" to the drama. A dramatist may see in the so-called undramatic material emotional values. If so, he will develop a technique which will create in his public a satisfaction equal to that which the so-called undramatic story, character, or idea could give in story form. Of course he will treat it differently in many respects because he is writing not to be read but to be heard, and to affect the emotions, not of the individual, but of a large group taken as a group. He will prove that till careful analysis has shown in a given story, character, or idea, no possibility of arousing the same or dissimilar emotions in an audience, we cannot say that this or that is dramatic or undramatic, but only: "This material will require totally different presentation if it is to be dramatic on the stage, and only a person of acumen, experience with audiences, and inventive technique can present it effectively."

The misapprehension just analyzed rests not only on the

misconception that action rather than emotion is the essential in drama, but also largely on a careless use of the word *dramatic*. In popular use this word means *material for drama*, or *creative of emotional response*, or *perfectly fitted for production under the conditions of the theatre*. If we examine a little, in the light of this chapter, the nature and purpose of a play, we shall see that *dramatic* should stand only for the first two definitions, and that *theatric* must be used for the third. Avoiding the vague definition *material for drama*, use *dramatic* only as *creative of emotional response* and the confusion will disappear.

A play exists to create emotional response in an audience. The response may be to the emotions of the people in the play or the emotions of the author as he watches these people. Where would satirical comedy be if, instead of sharing the amusement, disdain, contempt or moral anger of the dramatist caused by his figures, we responded exactly to their follies or evil moods? All ethical drama gets its force by creating in an audience the feelings toward the people in the play held by the author. Dumas fils, Ibsen, Brieux prove the truth of this statement. The writer of the satirical or the ethical play, obtruding his own personality as in the case of Ben Jonson, or with fine impersonality as in the case of Congreve or Molière, makes his feelings ours. It is an obvious corollary of this statement that the emotions aroused in an audience need not be the same as those felt by the people on the stage. They may be in the sharpest contrast. Any one experienced in drama knows that the most intensely comic effects often come from people acting very seriously. In *Le Bourgeois Gentilhomme* (Act I, Scene 2), the morning reception of M. Jourdain affords an instance of this in his trying on of costumes, fencing, and lessons in dancing and language. Serious entirely for M. Jourdain they are as presented by Molière, exquisitely comic for us. In brief, the dramatic may rouse the same, allied, or even contrasting emotions in an onlooker.

Nor need the emotion roused in an audience by actor or author be exactly the same in amount. The actress who abandons herself to the emotions of the part she is playing soon exhausts her nervous vitality. It would be the same if audiences listening to the tragic were permitted to feel the scenes as keenly as the figures of the story. On the other hand, in some cases, if the comic figure on the stage felt his comicality as strongly as the audience which is speechless with laughter, he could not go on, and the scene would fail. Evidently, an audience may be made, as the dramatist wills, to feel more or less emotion than the characters of the play.

That it is duplication of emotion to the same, a less, or a greater extent or the creation of contrasting emotion which underlies all drama, from melodrama, riotous farce and even burlesque to high-comedy and tragedy, must be firmly grasped if a would-be dramatist is to steer his way clearly through the many existing and confusing definitions of *dramatic*. For instance, Brunetière said, "Drama is the representation of the will of man in contrast to the mysterious powers of natural forces which limit and belittle us; it is one of us thrown living upon the stage, there to struggle against fatality, against social law, against one of his fellow mortals, against himself, if need be, against the emotions, the interests, the prejudices, the folly, the malevolence of those around him." [1] That is, by this definition, conflict is central in drama. But we know that in recent drama particularly, the moral drifter has many a time aroused our sympathy. Surely inertness, supineness, stupidity, and even torpor may be made to excite emotion in an audience. Conflict covers a large part of drama but not all of it.

Mr. William Archer, in his *Play-Making*, declares that

[1] *Études Critiques*, vol. VII, p. 207.

"a crisis" is the central matter in drama, but one immediately wishes to know what constitutes a crisis, and we have defined without defining. When he says elsewhere that that is dramatic which "by representation of imaginary personages is capable of interesting an average audience assembled in a theatre," [1] he almost hits the truth. If we rephrase this definition: "That is dramatic which by representation of imaginary personages interests, through its emotions, an average audience assembled in a theatre," we have a definition which will better stand testing.

Is all dramatic material, *theatric?* No, for *theatric* does not necessarily mean *sensational, melodramatic, artificial*. It should mean, and it will be so used in this book, *adapted for the purpose of the theatre*. Certainly all dramatic material, that is, material which arouses or may be made to arouse emotion, is not fitted for use in the theatre when first it comes to the hand of the dramatist. Undeniably, the famous revivalists, Moody, J. B. Gough, Billy Sunday, have worked from emotions to emotions; that is, they have been dramatic. Intentionally, feeling themselves justified by the ends obtained, they have, too, been *theatric* in the poor and popular sense of the word, namely, *exaggerated, melodramatic, sensational*. Yet *theatric* in the best sense of the word these highly emotional speakers, who have swept audiences out of all self-control, have not been. They worked as speakers, not as playwrights. Though they sometimes acted admirably, what they presented was in no sense a play. To accomplish in play form what they accomplished as speakers, that is, to make the material properly theatric, would have required an entire reworking. From all this it follows that even material so emotional in its nature as to be genuinely dramatic may need careful reworking if it is to succeed as a play, that is, if it is to become properly *theatric*. Drama, then, is pres-

---

[1] *Play-Making*, p. 48. William Archer. Small, Maynard & Co., ...on.

er. ation of an individual or group of individuals so as to move an audience to responsive emotion of the kind desired by the dramatist and to the amount required. This response must be gained under the conditions which a dramatist finds or develops in a theatre; that is, dramatic material must be made theatric in the right sense of the word before it can become drama.

To summarize: accurately conveyed emotion is the great fundamental in all good drama. It is conveyed by action, characterization, and dialogue. It must be conveyed in a space of time, usually not exceeding two hours and a half, and under the existing physical conditions of the stage, or with such changes as the dramatist may bring about in them. It must be conveyed, not directly through the author, but indirectly through the actors. In order that the dramatic may become theatric in the right sense of the word, the dramatic must be made to meet all these conditions successfully. These conditions affect action, characterization, and dialogue. A dramatist must study the ways in which the dramatic has been and may be made theatric: that is what technique means.

CHAPTER III

FROM SUBJECT TO PLOT. CLEARING THE WAY

A PLAY may start from almost anything: a detached thought
that flashes through the mind; a theory of conduct or of art
which one firmly believes or wishes only to examine; a bit
of dialogue overheard or imagined; a setting, real or imagined, which creates emotion in the observer; a perfectly
detached scene, the antecedents and consequences of which
are as yet unknown; a figure glimpsed in a crowd which for
some reason arrests the attention of the dramatist, or a figure
closely studied; a contrast or similarity between two people
or conditions of life; a mere incident — noted in a newspaper
or book, heard in idle talk, or observed; or a story, told only
in the barest outlines or with the utmost detail. "How do
the ideas underlying plays come into being? Under the most
varying conditions. Most often you cannot tell exactly how.
At the outset you waste much time hunting for a subject,
then suddenly one day, when you are in your study or even
in the street, you bring up with a start, for you have found
something. The piece is in sight. At first there is only an
impression, an image of the brain that wholly defies words.
If you were to write out exactly what you feel at the moment
— provided that were at all possible — it would be exceedingly difficult to indicate its attractiveness. The situation is
similar to that when you dream that you have discovered
an idea of profound significance; on awaking you write
it down; and on rereading perceive that it is commonplace or
stale. Then you follow up the idea; it tries to escape, and
when captured at last, still resists, ceaselessly changing form.
You wish to write a comedy; the idea cries, 'Make a tragedy

of me, or a story-play.' At last, after a struggle you master the idea." [1]

Back of *La Haine* of Sardou was the detached thought or query: "Under what circumstances will the profound charity of woman show itself in the most striking manner? In the preface to *La Haine*, Sardou has told how his plays revealed themselves to him. 'The problem is invariable. It appears as a kind of equation from which the unknown quantity must be found. The problem gives me no peace till I have found the answer.'" [2] Maeterlinck wrote several of his earlier plays, *The Intruder, Princess Maleine, The Blind*, to demonstrate the truth of two artistic theories of his: that what would seem to most theatre-goers of the time inaction might be made highly dramatic, and that partial or complete repetition of a phrase may have great emotional effect. *Magda (Heimat)* of Sudermann was written to illustrate the possible inherent tragedy of Magda's words: "Show them [people thoroughly sincere and honest but limited in experience and outlook] that beyond their narrow virtues there may be something true and good." In *Le Fils Naturel* of Dumas the younger, the illegitimate son, till late in the play, believes his father to be his uncle. "The logical development would seem to be obvious: father and son falling into each other's arms. Dumas, on the contrary, arranged that the son should not take the family name, and that the play should end with the following dialogue:

The Father. You will surely permit me, when we are alone together, to call you my son.
The Son. Yes, uncle.

It seems that Montigny, Director of the Gymnase Theatre, was shocked by the frigidity of this dénouement. He said to

[1] *Auteurs Dramatiques, Pailleron.* A. Binet and J. Passey. *L'Année Psychologique,* 1894, pp. 98–99.
[2] *Sardou and the Sardou Plays,* p. 127. Jerome A. Hart. J. B. Lippincott Co., Philadelphia.

Dumas, 'Make them embrace each other; the play, in that case, will have at least thirty additional performances.' Dumas answered, 'I can't suppress the last word. It is for that I wrote the piece.'"[1] One suspects that Lord Dunsany feels the same about the last words of his *King Argimenes*. The whole play apparently illustrates the almost irresistible effect of habit and environment. At the opening of the play, King Argimenes is the hungry, overworked slave of the captors who deprived him of his kingship. He talks eagerly with his fellow slaves of the King's sick dog, who will make a rich feast for them if he dies. At the end, Argimenes, completely successful in his revolt, is lord of all he surveys. Surprised by the news of the incoming messenger, he suddenly reverts to a powerful desire of his slavehood, speaking instinctively as did *Le fils* of Dumas.

Enter running, a Man of the household of King Darniak. He starts and stares aghast on seeing King Argimenes

King Argimenes. Who are you?
Man. I am the servant of the King's dog.
King Argimenes. Why do you come here?
Man. The King's dog is dead.
King Argimenes and His Men. (*Savagely and hungrily.*) Bones!
King Argimenes. (*Remembering suddenly what has happened and where he is.*) Let him be buried with the late King.
Zarb. (*In a voice of protest.*) Majesty!

Curtain.[2]

John G. Whittier's poem, *Barbara Frietchie*, provided the picture or incident which started Clyde Fitch on his play of the same name. In *Cyrano de Bergerac;* in the numerous adaptations of *Vanity Fair* usually known as *Becky Sharp;* in *Peg O' My Heart, Rip Van Winkle*, and *Louis XI*, it is characterization of a central figure which was probably the

[1] *Auteurs Dramatiques, Dumas fils*, p. 77.
[2] *Five Plays*, p. 86. Lord Dunsany. Mitchell Kennerley, New York.

point of departure for the play. Whether the source was an observed or an imagined figure, a character from history or fiction, the problem of the dramatist was like that of Sardou in *Rabagas*, — to find the story which will best illustrate the facets of character of the leading figure. Sometimes, as in *Nos Bons Villageois*, by the same author, the point of departure is a group of country people whose manners and customs must be portrayed, — in this case to illustrate the reception these rapacious peasants give pleasure-seeking Parisians, whom they detest and seek to turn to monetary advantage.[1] Mr. William Archer points out that *Strife* "arose in Mr. Galsworthy's mind from his actually having seen in conflict the two men who were the prototypes of Anthony and Roberts, and thus noted the waste and inefficacy arising from the clash of strong characters unaccompanied by balance. It was accident that led him to place the two men in an environment of capital and labour. In reality, both of them were, if not capitalists, at any rate, on the side of capital." [2] In *Theodora*, Sardou tried to reconstitute an historical epoch which interested him.[3] Still another source is this: "The point of departure of the plays of M. de Curel is psychological. What allures him is a curious situation which raises some problem. He asks himself, 'What, under such circumstances, can have been going on in our minds?' This was the case with *L'Envers d'une Sainte*. M. de Curel was thinking of this: A woman was arrested for murder; thanks to protection in high places, the action of the courts was held up. The woman was represented to be insane and shut up in an asylum. Years pass by; the woman succeeds in escaping, and returning home secretly, suddenly opens the door of the room where her children are playing. It is in this picture-like form that the idea of the piece came to him, a picture so detailed

---

[1] *Auteurs Dramatiques, Sardou. L'Année Psychologique*, 1894, p. 66.
[2] *Play-Making*, pp. 18–19, note. William Archer. Small, Maynard & Co., Boston.
[3] *Auteurs Dramatiques, Sardou*, p. 66.

and concrete that in imagination he saw the astonishment
of the children, the terror of the nurse calling for aid, and
the husband hurrying to prevent his wife from stepping into
the room."[1] The origin of *A Doll's House*, of Ibsen, we have
in these, his first, "Notes for the Modern Tragedy":

Rome, 19.10, 78.

There are two kinds of spiritual law, two kinds of conscience,
one in man, and another, altogether different, in woman. They do
not understand each other; but in practical life the woman is judged
by man's law, as though she were not a woman but a man.

The wife in the play ends by having no idea of what is right or
wrong; natural feeling on the one hand and belief in authority
on the other have altogether bewildered her.

A woman cannot be herself in the society of the present day,
which is an exclusively masculine society, with laws framed by
men and with a judicial system that judges feminine conduct from
a masculine point of view.

She has committed forgery and she is proud of it; for she did
it out of love for her husband, to save his life. But this husband
with his commonplace principles of honour is on the side of the law
and regards the question with masculine eyes.

Spiritual conflicts. Oppressed and bewildered by the belief in
authority, she loses faith in her moral right and ability to bring
up her children. Bitterness. A mother in modern society, like certain insects who go away and die when she has done her duty in the
propagation of the race. Love of life, of husband and children and
family. Here and there a womanly shaking off of her thoughts.
Sudden return of anxiety and terror. She must bear it all alone.
The catastrophe approaches, inexorably, inevitably. Despair, conflict, and destruction

(Krogstad has acted dishonourably and thereby become well-to-
do; now his prosperity does not help him, he cannot recover his
honour.)[2]

It is a truism, first, that Shakespeare wrote story plays,
and secondly that he did not endeavor to imagine a new
story. Instead, he made over plays grown out of date in his

---

[1] *Auteurs Dramatiques, M. de Curel*, p. 121.
[2] *From Ibsen's Workshop. Works*, vol. x, pp. 91–92. Chas. Scribner's Sons, New York.

time, or adapted to the stage what today we should call novelettes which came to him in the original or translation from Italy, Spain, or France. Never did he find a story which seemed to him fully shaped and ready for the stage.[1] The tales may be verbose and redundant; they may be mere bare outlines of the action, little if at all characterized, with unreal dialogue; or they may provide Shakespeare with only a part of the story he uses, the rest coming from other tales or from his own imagination. Widely different as they are, however, one and all they were points of departure for Shakespeare's plays.

No matter which one of the numerous starting points noted may be that of the dramatist, he must end in story even if he does not begin with it. Suppose that he starts with a character. He cannot merely talk about the figure. This might produce a kind of history; it cannot produce drama. Inevitably, he will try to illustrate, by means of action, some one dominant characteristic, or group of characteristics, or to the full, the many-sided nature of the man. Very nearly the same thing may be said of any attempt to dramatize an historical epoch. Its chief characteristic or characteristics must be illustrated in action. Some story is inevitable. Suppose, for the moment, that as in Morose of Ben Jonson's *Silent Woman*,[2] the dramatist is stressing one characteristic, in this instance morbid sensitiveness to noise of any kind. It is well known that Jonson cared more for character and less for story than most dramatists of his day. Yet even in this play we find the story of the tricking of Morose by his nephew, Dauphine, resulting in the marriage of Morose to Dauphine's page. The reason why the three parts of *Henry VI* of Shakespeare are little read and very rarely acted is not merely that they are somewhat crude early work, but that

---

[1] Consult the pages of W. C. Hazlitt's *Shakespeare Library*, a source book of his plays for proof of this.

[2] Belles-Lettres Series. F. E. Schelling, ed. D. C. Heath & Co., Boston and New York.

crowding incident of all kinds lacks the massing needed to give it clearness of total effect to round it out into a well-told story. Illustrative incidents, unrelated except that historically they happen to the same person, and that historically they are given in proper sequence, are likely to be confusing. We need the Baedeker of a biographer or an historian to emphasize the incidents so that the meaning they have for him may be clear to us. The first part of Marlowe's *Tamburlaine*,[1] when quickly read, seems but a succession of conquests, not greatly unlike, leading to his control of the world of his day. He who sees no deeper into the play than this praises certain scenes or passages, but finds the whole repetitious and confusing. Closer examination shows, however, that behind these many incidents of war and slaughter is an interest of Marlowe's own creation which keeps us waiting for, anticipating the final scene — the desire of Zenocrate, at first captive of Tamburlaine, and later his devoted wife, to reconcile her father, the Soldan, and her husband. The satisfaction of her desire makes the spectacular ending of Part I. This thread of interest gives a certain unity to the material presented, creates a slight story in the mass of incident, — that is, something with a beginning, a middle, and an end. What gives unity to the Second Part of *Tamburlaine* is the idea that, even as Tamburlaine declares himself all-conquering, he faces unseen forces against which he cannot stand — the physical cowardice of his son, so incomprehensible to him that he kills the boy; the illness and death of his beloved Zenocrate, though he spares nothing to save her; his own growing physical weakness, his breakdown and death even as the generals he has never called on in vain before prove unable to aid him. Again we find an element of story to unify the material.

A moment's thought will show that if, beginning with

---

[1] Mermaid Series or Everyman's Library.

character we must ultimately reach some story, however slight, this is just as true of a play which begins with an idea, a bit of dialogue, a detached scene, or a mere setting. The setting must be the background of some incident. This, in turn, must be part of a story or we shall have the episodic form already found undesirable. Similarly, a detached scene must become part of a series of scenes. Get rid of the effect of episodic scenes, that is, give them unity, and lo, we have story of some sort. The bit of dialogue must become part of a larger dialogue belonging to characters of the play; and characterization, as we have seen, results in some story. The artistic or moral idea of the dramatist can be made clear only by human figures, the pawns with which he makes his emotional moves. At once we are on the way to story. *The Red Robe* [1] of Brieux aims to illustrate the idea that in France the administration of justice has been confused by personal ambition and personal intrigue. Is it without story? Surely we have the story of Mouzon, — his hopes, his consequent intrigues for advancement, and his resulting death. Here is a group of incidents developing something from a beginning to an end, that is, providing story. The play contains, too, the story of Yanetta and Etchepare. May we not say that the Vagret family provides a third story?

A play, then, may begin in almost anything seen or thought. Speaking broadly, there is no reason why one source is better than another. The important point is that something seen or thought should so stir the emotions of the dramatist that the desire to convey his own emotion or the emotions of characters who become connected with what he has seen or thought, forces him to write till he has worked out his purpose. Undoubtedly, however, he who begins with a story is nearer his goal than he who begins with an idea or

[1] Published in translation by Brentano; also in *Chief Contemporary Dramatists*. Thomas H. Dickinson. Houghton Mifflin Co., Boston.

a character. Disconnected episodes, then, may possibly make
a vaudeville sketch or the libretto of a lower order of musical
comedy. Unless unified in story, even though it be very slight,
they cannot make a play.

This point needs emphasis for two reasons: because lately
there has been some attempt to maintain that a newer type
of play has no story, and because many a beginnner in
dramatic writing seems to agree with Bayes in *The Rehearsal*.
"What the devil's a plot except to stuff in fine things?" In
good play-writing it is not a question of bringing together as
many incidents or as many illustrations of character as you
can crowd together in a given number of acts, but of selecting the illustrative incidents, which, when properly developed will produce in an audience the largest amount of the
emotional response desired. Later this error will be considered in detail.

Nor will the recent attempt to maintain that there is a
new type of play with "absolutely no story in it" stand close
analysis. The story may be very slight, but story is present
in all such plays. Take two cases. Mr. William Archer, in
his excellent book on *Play-Making*,[1] sums up Miss Elizabeth
Baker's *Chains* [2] as follows: "A city clerk, oppressed by the
deadly monotony of his life, thinks of going to Australia —
and doesn't go: that is the sum and substance of the action.
Also, by way of underplot, a shopgirl, oppressed by the
deadly monotony and narrowness of her life, thinks of escaping from it by marrying a middle-aged widower — and
doesn't do it." He then declares that the play has "absolutely no story." Does any reader believe that this play
could have succeeded, as it has, if the audience had been
left in any doubt as to *why* the city clerk and the shopgirl
did not do what they had planned? Yet surely, if this play
makes clear, as it does, *why* these two people changed their

[1] *Note*, p. 49.   [2] J. W. Luce & Co., Boston; Sidgwick & Jackson, Ltd., London.

minds, it must have story, for it shows us people thinking
of escaping from conditions they find irksome, and explains
why they give up the idea. If that isn't story, what is it?

The Weavers of Hauptmann,[1] giving us somewhat loosely
connected pictures of social conditions among the weavers
of Germany in the forties of the nineteenth century, is said
to be another specimen of these plays without story. Now
such plays as *The Weavers* have one of two results: they rouse
us to thought on the social conditions represented, or they
do not. To succeed they must rouse us; but if our stirred
feelings are to lead anywhere, we must be not only stirred
but clear as to the meaning of the play. There have been
many who have thought that *The Weavers*, though it stirs
us to sympathy, leaves us nowhere because not clear. Be
this as it may, even *The Weavers* has some story, for it tells
us of the rise and development of a revolt of the weavers
against their employers.

Confusion as to "story" results from two causes. First,
story in drama is often taken to imply only complicated
story. To say that every play must have complicated story
is absurd. To say that every play must have some story,
though it may be very slight, is undeniable. Secondly, story
is frequently used to mean plot, and plot of the older type,
namely a play of skilfully arranged suspense and climax in
a story of complicated and extreme emotion. It is the second
cause which underlies Mr. Archer's curious statement about
Chains. He says that the play has no "emotional tension
worth speaking of," and assumes that where there is no
emotional tension there cannot be story. Tension in the sense
of suspense the play has little, but Mr. Archer states that it
held "an audience absorbed through four acts" and stirred
"them to real enthusiasm." In these words he grants the
emotional response of the audience. Miss Baker substitutes

[1] *Dramatic Works*, vol. i. Ed. Ludwig Lewisohn. B. Huebsch., New York.

sympathy for the characters and deft dealing with ironic
values (see the ends of Act II and Act III) for complicated
plot and dependence on suspense. One kind of play, however, no more precludes story than another.

What, then, is the difference between story and plot? In
treating drama, what should be meant by story is what a
play boils down to when you try to tell a friend as briefly
as possible what it is about — what Mr. Knobloch calls the
vital active part, the "verb" of the play. Here is the story
of the play, *Barbara Frietchie*, as it re-shaped itself in Clyde
Fitch's mind from Whittier's poem:[1] "A Northern man

[1] For purposes of useful comparison the lines of Whittier which suggested the subject to
Mr. Fitch are appended.

On that pleasant morn of the early fall
When Lee marched over the mountain wall;

Over the mountains winding down,
Horse and foot, into Frederick town.

Forty flags with their silver stars,
Forty flags with their crimson bars,

Flapped in the morning wind: the sun
Of noon looked down and saw not one.

Up rose old Barbara Frietchie then,
Bowed with her fourscore years and ten;

Bravest of all in Frederick town,
She took up the flag the men hauled down

In her attic window the staff she set,
To show that one heart was loyal yet.

Up the street came the rebel tread,
Stonewall Jackson riding ahead.

Under his slouched hat left and right
He glanced; the old flag met his sight.

"Halt!" — the dust-brown ranks stood fast
"Fire!" — out blazed the rifle-blast.

It shivered the window, pane and sash;
It rent the banner with seam and gash.

Quick, as it fell from the broken staff
Dame Barbara snatched the silken scarf.

loves a Southern girl. She defies her father and runs away to marry him. By a sudden battle the ceremony is prevented. The minister's house is seized by the rebels, and soldiers stationed there. Barbara, who has remained, seeing a Confederate sharpshooter about to fire on her lover passing with his regiment, drops on her knees, slowly levels a gun she has seized, and shoots the Southerner. Her lover is wounded and she struggles to protect him from her father, brother, and rebel suitor, and from every little noise which might cost his life. He dies, and she, now wholly wedded to the Northern cause, waves the flag, as does the old woman in Whittier's poem, in defiance of the Southern army, and is shot by her crazy rebel lover." [1] Note that this summary, though it makes the story clear, in no way presents the scenes of the play as to order, suspense, or climax. This is the story, not the plot of *Barbara Frietchie*. Plot, dramatically speaking, is the story so moulded by the dramatist as to gain for him in the theatre the emotional response he desires. In order to create and maintain interest, he gives his story, as seems to him wise, simple or complex structure; and discerning elements in it of suspense, surprise, and climax, he reveals

She leaned far out on the window-sill,
And shook it forth with a royal will.

"Shoot, if you must, this old gray head,
But spare your country's flag," she said.

A shade of sadness, a blush of shame,
Over the face of the leader came;

The nobler nature within him stirred
To life at that woman's deed and word:

"Who touches a hair of yon gray head
Dies like a dog! March on!" he said.

All day long through Frederick street
Sounded the tread of marching feet:

All day long that free flag tost
Over the heads of the rebel host.

[1] *The Stage in America*, p. 90. Norman Hapgood. The Macmillan Co., New York.

them to just the extent necessary for his purposes. Plot is story proportioned and emphasized so as to accomplish, under the conditions of the theatre, the purposes of the dramatist. Compare the plot of *Barbara Frietchie* with its story.

Act I. The Frietchies' front stoop facing on a street in the town of Frederick, which is in the hands of the hated Yankees. By the sentimental talk of the Southern girls sitting on the steps we learn that Barbara Frietchie is carrying on a flirtation with Captain Trumbull, a Union officer, under the noses of her outraged family, friends, and lover, Jack Negly. After a short scene, Barbara sends him off rebuffed and incensed. She is then left alone in the dusk. Her brother, Arthur Frietchie, steals round the corner of the house, wounded. Barbara takes him in and they are not yet out of earshot when Captain Trumbull appears to call on Barbara much to the wrath of the Frietchies' next-door neighbor, Colonel Negly. The Yankee lover summons Barbara, and dismisses a Union searching party, swearing on his honor that there are no rebels in the Frietchie home. Her gratitude for this leads them into a love scene, turbulent from the clash of sectional sympathies, terminating in her promise to become his wife. No sooner has the betrothal been spoken than Barbara's father, incensed to it by old Colonel Negly, forbids the Union man his house and his daughter. To complete their separation, an Orderly rushes on, announcing the departure of Captain Trumbull's Company for Hagerstown in the early morning. Leaning over the second-floor balcony, Barbara tells her lover that she will be at the minister's house at Hagerstown the next day at noon.

Act II. The Lutheran minister's house at Hagerstown. Barbara and her friend, Sue Royce, appear all aflutter and, with the minister's wife, Mrs. Hunter, await the arrival of the bridegroom and the divine. News comes that the Con-

federates are swooping into the town, and Captain Trumbull bursts into the room. An impassioned love scene follows
in which we learn that Barbara's sympathies are changing,
so much so that she presents her lover with an old Union flag
to wear next his heart. Orders for the soldier to join his
Company part Barbara and Trumbull. The Confederates
are heard coming down the street as he leaves the house.
Barbara's brother Arthur breaks into the house and sta-
tions two sharpshooters, angered deserters from Captain
Trumbull's Company, at the windows, Barbara protesting.
Arthur goes about his business and she learns that Gelwex,
the deserter with the greatest grudge against her lover, is
to have the honor of picking him off as he comes down the
street. She gets a gun for herself. Captain Trumbull's excited voice is heard outside the window. The deserter takes
careful aim, puts his finger to the trigger, and is shot from
behind by Barbara.

Act III. Two days later. The front hallway of the
Frietchie house. The Confederates have re-taken the town.
Barbara is in despair, her father exultant, not speaking to
her until she tells him that she is not married to the Union
officer. She pleads for news of her beloved, but her father
gives her little satisfaction. He has just gone upstairs when
Arthur comes in, supporting a wounded and fever-stricken
man whom he has shot. It is Captain Trumbull. Barbara
takes him to her room, and when her father, hearing who
the wounded man is, orders him thrown into the street, she
pleads with all her strength to be allowed to keep him with
her. The old man yields, and when the Confederate searching party invades the house, gives his word for its loyalty.
Barbara has placed herself at the foot of the stairs, determined to hold the fort against the enemies of her lover. The
doctor has insisted on absolute quiet for him; noise may kill
him. When the searching party has been turned back, she

summons new strength to quiet crazy Jack Negly, who has entered howling his victory. He insists that she shall marry him, and tries, pistol in hand, to force his way past Barbara to the bedside of his enemy in love and war. By sheer force of will she conquers Negly and rushes past him to the door of the room where her lover lies.

Act IV. Scene 1. The next morning. Barbara's room. Captain Trumbull lies peacefully on the bed. Mammy Lu, the colored nurse, is dozing as Barbara enters. They listen for the invalid's breathing, hear none, and find that he is dead. Half crazed, Barbara snatches the bloody flag from his bosom. The scene changes.

Scene 2. The balconied stoop in front of the house. The Confederate soldiers, headed by Stonewall Jackson, are heralded by a large crowd! Barbara, hanging the Union flag out on the balcony, is discovered by the mob, who begin to stone her, urging somebody to shoot. The lines of Whittier's poem, to fit the circumstances which Clyde Fitch has made, now become:

Shoot! You've taken a life already dearer to me than my own. Shoot, and I'll *thank* you! but *spare* your flag! [1]

General Jackson orders that no shot be fired on penalty of death. Her crazed lover, Negly, shoots her down from the street, and his own father orders the execution of the penalty.

"In many cases, no doubt, it is the plain and literal fact that the impulse to write some play — any play — exists, so to speak, in the abstract, unassociated with any particular subject, and that the would-be playwright proceeds, as he thinks, to set his imagination to work and invent a story. But this frame of mind is to be regarded with suspicion. Few plays of much value, one may guess, have resulted from such an abstract impulse. Invention in these cases is apt to

[1] *Barbara Frietchie*, p. 126. Clyde Fitch. Life Publishing Co., New York.

be nothing but recollection in disguise, the shaking of a kaleidoscope formed of fragmentary reminiscences. I remember once in some momentary access of ambition, trying to invent a play. I occupied several hours of a long country walk, in, as I believed, creating out of nothing at all a dramatic story. When at last I had modelled it into some sort of coherency, I stepped back from it in my mind as it were, and contemplated it as a whole. No sooner had I done so than it began to seem vaguely familiar. 'Where have I seen this story before?' I asked myself; and it was only after cudgelling my brains for several minutes that I found I had re-invented Ibsen's *Hedda Gabler*. Thus, when we think we are choosing a plot out of the void, we are very apt to be, in fact, ransacking the storehouse of memory."[1]

There is, of course, another group of would-be playwrights who care nothing for freshness of subject but are perfectly content to imitate the latest success, hoping thereby to win immediate notoriety, or what interests them even more, immediate money return. Undoubtedly a man may take a subject just presented in a successful play and so re-shape it by the force of his own personality as to make it an original work of power. Ordinarily, however, these imitators should remember the old adage about the crock which goes so often to the well that at last it comes back broken. He who merely imitates may have some temporary vogue, and dramatic technique may help him to win it, but whatever is very popular soon gives way to something else, for the fundamental law of art, as of life, is change. He who is content merely to imitate must be content with impermanency. It is the creator *and* perfecter whom we most remember. Even the creator *or* the perfecter we remember. The mere imitators have their brief day and pass. Today we still read the work of the initiators, Lyly, Greene, Kyd. With pleasure we turn

---

[1] *Play-Making*, pp. 24–25. William Archer. Small, Maynard & Co., Boston.

the pages of Marlowe, Jonson, and Fletcher, not to mention
Shakespeare. The dozens of mere imitators who had their
little day are known only as names.

The ambitious but inexperienced writer of plays worries
himself much in hunting a novel subject, — and in vain. Far
afield he goes, seeking the sensational, the bizarre, the occult,
for new emotions and situations, failing to recognize that
the emotional life of yesterday, today, and tomorrow can differ little fundamentally. Civilization refines or deteriorates,
kingdoms rise and fall, languages develop and pass, but love
of man and woman, of friend for friend, ambition, jealousy,
envy, selfishness, — these emotions abide. A book has been
published to show that there are but thirty-six possible dramatic situations. It is based on the dictum of the Italian
dramatist, Gozzi, that "there could be only thirty-six tragic
situations. Schiller gave himself much trouble to find more,
but was unable to find as many." [1] The very chapter headings of the book mentioned prove that the number of possible dramatic situations is a mere matter of subdivision:
"Vengeance Pursuing Crime"; "Madness"; "Fatal Impru-
dence"; "Loss of Property"; "Ambition." Obviously, there
are many different kinds of vengeance, as the person pursuing the crime is a hired detective, a wronged person, an
officer of state, etc. Moreover, differing conditions surround-
ing the crime, as well as the character of the avenger, would
make the vengeance sought different. The same may be
said of the other chapter-headings. It may be possible to
agree on the smallest number of dramatic situations possible, but disagreement surely lies beyond that, for, according to our natures, we shall wish to subdivide and increase
the number. Just what that smallest number is, here is unimportant. The important fact is: keen thinkers about the
drama agree that the stuff from which it is made may be put

---

[1] *Les 36 Situations Dramatiques.* Georges Polti. Edition du *Mercure de France*, 1895, p. 1.

into a small number of categories. This rests on the belief
that the emotions we feel today are the same old emotions,
though we may feel them in greater or less degree because
of differences in climate, civilization or ideals. Modern invention, of course, affects our emotional life. It is now a
commonplace that invention has quite changed the heroism
of warfare from what it was even a generation ago. It is still
heroism, but under conditions so different that it needs
wholly different treatment dramatically. In Restoration
Comedy the rake was the hero. The audience, viewing life
through his eyes saw the victims of his selfishness as fools
or as people who, in any combat of wits with the hero, de-
servedly came off defeated. Interest in one's fellow man, a
more just sense of life had developed in the early years of
the eighteenth century. This wholly changed the emphasis,
and gave birth to the Sentimental Comedy. The characters,
even the story, of this newer comedy are almost identical
with the Restoration Comedy, but the material is so treated
that our sympathies go to the unfortunate wife of *The Careless Husband*, not to the man himself, as they would have
a generation before. In *The Provoked Husband* [1] it is the
point of view of that husband as to Lady Townley, though
she is presented in all her charm and gaiety, with which
we are left.

The sentimentality of the present day is not the sentimentality of 1850 to 1870. The higher education of women, the
growth of suffrage, the prevailing wide discussion of scientific matters have not taken sentimentality from us, but have
changed its look. Because of changes in costume and custom
it even appears more different than it really is. A perfect
illustration of the point is *Milestones*,[2] of Mr. Edward Knobloch. Three generations live before our eyes the same story,

---

[1] For texts of *The Careless Husband* and *The Provoked Husband*, both plays by Colley
Cibber, see *Works*, vols. II and IV, 1777.
[2] Methuen & Co., Ltd., London.

but how differently because of changed costumes, ideas, and immediate surroundings. In French drama, the wet-nurse is no new figure as one employee in a household where we are watching the comedy or the tragedy of the employers. Brieux was the first, however, to study the emotions of such a household through the nurse, making her feelings of prime consequence. Hence, *Les Remplaçantes*.[1] The whole situation is summed up by William Sharp (Fiona Macleod) in his Introduction to *The House of Usna*:

The tradition of accursed families is not the fantasy of one dramatist, or of one country or of one time. . . .

Whether the poet turn to the tragedy of the Theban dynasty, or to the tragedy of the Achaian dynasty, or to the tragedy of Lear, or to the Celtic tragedy of the House of Fionn, or to the other and less familiar Gaelic tragedy of the House of Usna — whether one turn to these or to the doom of the House of Malatesta, or to the doom of the House of Macbeth, or to the doom of the House of Ravenswood, one turns in vain if he be blind and deaf to the same elemental forces as they move in their eternal ichor through the blood that has today's warmth in it, that are the same powers though they be known of the obscure and the silent, and are committed like wandering flame to the torch of a ballad as well as to the starry march of the compelling words of genius; are of the same dominion, though that be in the shaken hearts of islesfolk and mountaineers, and not with kings in Mykênai, or by the thrones of Tamburlaine and Aurungzebe, or with great lords and broken nobles and thanes. . . .

. . . I know one who can evoke modern dramatic scenes by the mere iterance of the great musical names of the imagination. Menelaos, Helen, Klytemaistra, Andromachê, Kassandra, Orestes, Blind Oidipus, Elektra, Kreusa, and the like. This is not because these names are in themselves esoteric symbols. My friend has not seen any representation of the *Agamemnon* or the *Choephoroi*, of *Aias* or *Oidipus at Kolonos*, of *Elektra* or *Ion*, or indeed of any Greek play. But he knows the story of every name mentioned in each of the dramas of the three kings of Greek Tragedy. . . . And here, he says, is his delight. "For I do not live only in the past

---

[1] Not translated. Edition in French, P. V. Stock, Paris.

but in the present, in these dramas of the mind. The names stand for the elemental passions, and I can come to them through my own gates of today as well as through the ancient portals of Aischylos or Sophocles or Euripides." . . .

It is no doubt in this attitude that Racine, so French in the accent of his classical genius, looked at the old drama which was his inspiration: that Mr. Swinburne and Mr. Bridges, so English in the accent of their genius, have looked at it; that Echegaray in Spain, looked at it before he produced his troubled modern *Elektra* which is so remote in shapen thought and coloured semblance from the colour and idea of its prototype; that Gabriele D'Annunzio looked at it before he became obsessed with the old terrible idea of the tangled feet of Destiny, so that a tuft of grass might withhold or a breath from stirred dust empoison, and wrote that most perturbing of all modern dramas, *La Città Morta*.[1]

The drama must, then, go on treating over and over emotions the same in kind. Real novelty comes in presenting them as they affect men and women who are in ideas, habits, costume, speech, and environment distinctly of their time. Their expression of the old elemental emotions brings genuine novelty. Usually it is not through an incident or an episode obviously dramatic, but through the characters involved that one understands and presents what is novel in the dramatic. Feeling this strongly, Mr. Galsworthy asserts "Character is plot." [2]

So long as characters, ideas, and treatment seem to the public fresh, they even have a weakness for a story they have heard before. Recall the drama of Æschylus, Sophocles, and Euripides in which the dramatists shared with their audiences a knowledge of the stories of the gods which was theirs by education and from repeated treatment by the dramatists of the day. That public asked, not new stories, but newness of effect because old stories which were almost fixed subjects

[1] Foreword to *The House of Usna*. Fiona Macleod. Published by Thomas B. Mosher, Portland, Maine, 1903.
[2] *Some Platitudes Concerning Drama*. John Galsworthy. *Atlantic Monthly*, December, 1909.

for their dramatists were given individuality of treatment. In a modified sense this was true of the Elizabethan public. *Romeo and Juliet*, *Lear*, probably *Titus Andronicus*, and possibly *Julius Cæsar* Londoners had known as plays just passing from popularity when Shakespeare made them over. Here again, it was freshness of treatment through better characterization, richer poetry, and finer technique, not creative story, which won the public to Shakespeare. Nor is this attitude a thing of the past. Think of the delight with which the public today watches the rejuggling of old elements of plot in the rapid succession of popular musical comedies, grateful for whatever element of freshness they may find in the total product. Was it the story, or the characterization and setting, indeed all that went with the treatment of the story, which in *Peg o' My Heart* and *Bunty Pulls the Strings* won these plays popularity? Seek for novelty, then, not by trying to invent some new story, but in an idea, the setting of the play, the technical treatment given it, above all the characters. The last, when studied, are likely so to reshape the story which first presents itself to the imagination as to make it really novel. Does the freshness of the story of the Duke, Olivia, and Viola in *Twelfth Night* rest on the story as Shakespeare found it in Barnabe Riche's book,[1] or on the characterization Shakespeare gave these suggested figures and the effect of their developed characters on the story as he found it? Surely the latter.

Another common fallacy of young dramatists is that what has happened is better dramatic material than what is imagined. Among the trite maxims a dramatist should remember, however, is: "Truth is often stranger than fiction." The test for a would-be writer of plays, choosing among several starting points, should be, not, "Is this true?"

---

[1] *Shakespeare Library*, vol. I, pp. 387–412. Ed. W. C. Hazlitt.

but "Will my audience believe it true on sight or because of the treatment I can give it?" "Aristotle long ago decided how far the tragic poet need regard historical accuracy. He does not make use of an event because it really happened, but because it happened so convincingly that for his present purpose he cannot invent conditions more convincing." [1] Any reader of manuscript plays knows that again and again, when he has objected to something as entirely improbable, he has been told indignantly: "Why, you must accept that, for it happened exactly like that to my friend, Smith." On the other hand, who refuses to see *The Merchant of Venice* because of the inherent improbability of the exaction of the pound of flesh by Shylock? Highly improbable it is, but Shakespeare makes this demand come from a figure so human in all other respects that we accept it. A subject is not to be rejected because true or false. Every dramatic subject must be presented with the probable human experience, the ethical ideas, and the imaginativeness of the public in mind. To a dramatist all subjects are possible till, after long wrestling with the subject chosen, he is forced to admit that, whether originally true or false, he cannot make it seem probable to an audience. Facts are, of course, of very great value in drama, but if they are to convince a theatrical public, the dramatist must so present them that they shall not run completely counter to what an audience thinks it knows about life.

Nor should a person who knows absolutely nothing of the theatre attempt to write plays. He should go to see plays enough to know how long a performance usually lasts, waits between the acts included, say two hours and a half to two hours and three quarters; to know about how long an act usually takes in playing; to gain some idea of the relation in time between the written or printed page and the time in

---

[1] *Hamburg Dramaturgy*, p. 279. Lessing. Bohn ed.

acting; to understand that, in general, a small cast is preferable to a large one; to know that the limited space of the stage makes some effects so difficult as to be undesirable. This is to have ordinary common sense about the theatre. Otherwise, what he puts on paper will be practically sure of immediate rejection because the manuscript proves that the writer has either not been in the theatre, or being there, has been wholly unobservant. The following quotation seems almost fantastic, but the experience of the writer in reading dramatic manuscripts fully bears it out:

Many of the manuscripts that are sent to the New York managers are such impossible oddities that few readers would regard a description of them as really accurate. It was the privilege of the writer to look over a collection of "plays" that have been mailed recently to several of the theatrical offices, and, among the number, he came across a dozen that were each about fifteen to twenty pages in length. This included the scenic descriptions and stage directions. Such "plays," if enacted, would be of about ten to eleven minutes' duration instead of two and a quarter hours. Three manuscripts called for from ninety to one hundred characters, and from nine to fourteen different scenes. Eight manuscripts were divided into nine acts each and, judging from their thickness, would have run on for days, after the fashion of a Chinese drama. One "play" was laid in the year 2200 A.D., and called for twelve actors to portray " the new race of men " — each man to be at least seven feet tall. These characters were to make all their entrances and exits in airships. Several manuscripts that the writer examined would have required professional strong men in their enactment, so difficult were the physical feats outlined for some of the actors. A great number of "modern dramas" included a ream of colloquialisms and anachronisms intermixed with Louis XV situations. And one manuscript, entitled "Love in All Ages" called for twelve different acts with a new group of nine differently built actors in each.[1]

A stage direction which ran something like this is the most naïve in the experience of the writer. "Germs of a locomo-

[1] *The United States of Playwrights*, Henry Savage. *The Bookman*, September, 1909.

tive, a cathedral, etc., detach themselves in an unknown
manner from the walls and float airily, merrily about the
room." Impossible? Possibly not for a genius of a stage
manager. Likely to recommend the play to a manager trying to judge from a manuscript the dramatic sense of its
unknown author? Hardly.

Granted then that a would-be playwright has acquired
ordinary common sense about the theatre and has some point
of departure, how does he move from it to plot? First, by
taking time enough, by avoiding hurry. Let any would-be
dramatist get rid promptly of the idea that good plays are
written in a rush. It is perfectly true that the mere writing
out of a play has often been done in what seems an amazingly
short time, — a few weeks, days, or even hours. However, in
every case of rapid composition, as for instance Sheridan's
Rivals, which was put on paper in very brief time, the
author has either mulled his material for a long time or was
so thoroughly conversant with it that it required no careful
thinking out at the moment of composition. In *The Rivals*
Sheridan drew upon his intimate knowledge for many years
of the people and the gossip of the Pump Room at Bath.
Mr. H. A. Jones has more than once testified, "I mull long
on my plot, sometimes a year, but when I have it, the rest
(the mere writing out) is easy." Sardou turned out a very
large number of plays. Nor are his plays, seemingly, such as
to demand the careful preparation required for the drama
of ideas or the drama more dependent on characterization
than incident. Yet he worked very carefully at all stages,
from point of departure to final draft. "Whenever an idea
occurred to Sardou, he immediately made a memorandum
of it. These notes he classified and filed. For example, years
before the production of *Thermidor* he had the thought of
one day writing such a play. Gradually the character of
Fabienne shaped itself; Labussière was devised later to fit

Coquelin. Everything that he read about that epoch of the French Revolution, and the ideas which his reading inspired, he wrote down in the form of rough notes. Engravings, maps, prints, and other documents of the time he carefully collected. Memoirs and histories he annotated and indexed, filing away the index references in his file cases, or dossiers. At the time of his death, Sardou had many hundreds of these dossiers, old and new. Some of the older ones had been worked up into plays, while the newer ones were merely raw material for future dramas. When the idea of a play had measurably shaped itself in his mind he wrote out a skeleton plot which he placed in its dossier. There it might lie indefinitely. In this shape *Thermidor* remained for nearly twenty years, and *Theodora* for ten. When he considered that the time was ripe for one of his embryonic plays, Sardou would take out that particular dossier, read over the material, and lay it aside again. After it had fermented in his brain for a time, he would, if the inspiration seized him, write out a scenario. After this, he began the actual writing of the play." [1]

Late in the seventeenth century, one of the most prolific of English playwrights, John Dryden, contracted to turn out four plays a year. He failed completely to carry out his promise. Some dramatists of a much more recent day should attribute to the speed with which they have turned out plays their repeated failures, or, after early successes, their waning hold on the public. Every dramatist should keep steadily in mind the words of the old French adage: "Time spares not that on which time hath been spared." Time, again time, and yet again time is the chief element in successful writing of plays.

A wandering, erratic career is forbidden the dramatist. Back in the eighteenth century Diderot stated admirably the qualities a dramatist must have if he is to plot well.

<hr>

[1] *Sardou and the Sardou Plays*, p. 125. J. A. Hart. J. B. Lippincott & Co., Philadelphia.

"He must get at the heart of his material. He must consider order and unity. He must discern clearly the moment at which the action should begin. He must recognize the situations which will help his audience, and know what it is expedient to leave unsaid. He must not be rebuffed by difficult scenes or long labor. Throughout he must have the aid of a rich imagination." [1] Selection, Proportion, Emphasis, Movement, — all making for clearness, — these as the words of Diderot suggest, are what the dramatist studies in developing his play from Subject, through Story, to Plot.

[1] *De la Poésie Dramatique.* Diderot. *Œuvres,* vol. VII, p. 321. Garnier Frères, Paris.

CHAPTER IV

FROM SUBJECT THROUGH STORY TO PLOT. CLEARNESS THROUGH WISE SELECTION

DUMAS the younger, at twenty, wishing to write his first play, asked his father for the secret of a successful play. That man of many successful novels and plays replied: "It's very simple: First Act, clear; Third Act, short; and everywhere, interest." Though play-writing is not always so easy a matter as when a man of genius like Dumas the elder wrote the relatively simple romantic dramas of his day, he emphasized one of the fundamentals of drama when he called for clearness in the first act. He might well have called for it everywhere. First of all, a dramatist who has found his point of departure must know just what it means to him, what he wants to do with it. Is he merely telling a story for its own sake, satisfied if the incidents be increasingly interesting till the final curtain falls? Is he writing his play, above all, for one special scene in it, as was Mr. H. A. Jones, in *Mrs. Dane's Defence*,[1] in its third act? Does he merely wish to set people thinking about conditions of to-day, to write a drama of ideas, like Mr. Galsworthy in *The Pigeon*,[2] or M. Paul Loyson, in *The Apostle?* [3] Has he, like Brieux in *Damaged Goods* [4] or *The Cradle*,[5] an idea he wishes to convey, and so must write a problem play? Is his setting significant for one scene only or has it symbolic values for the whole play? As Dumas the younger well

---

[1] Samuel French, New York.
[2] Chas. Scribner's Sons, New York.
[3] Drama League Series, Doubleday, Page & Co., New York.
[4] Brentano, New York.
[5] *Le Berceau.* P. V. Stock, Paris.

said, "How can you tell what road to take unless you know where you are going?"[1]

The trouble with most would-be dramatists is that they make too much of the mere act of writing, too little of the thinking preliminary to composition and accompanying it. With the point of departure clearly in mind, seeing some characters who immediately connect themselves with the subject, forecasting some scenes and a few bits of dialogue, they rush to their desks before they see with equal clearness, we will not say the plot but even the story necessary for the proposed play. What is the result? "They have a general view of their subject, they know approximately the situations, they have sketched out the characters, and when they have said to themselves, 'This mother will be a coquette, this father will be stern, this lover a libertine, this young girl impressionable and tender,' the fury of making their scenes seizes them. They write, they write, they come upon ideas, fine, delicate, and even strong; they have charming details ready to hand: but when they have worked much and come to plotting, for always one must come to that, they try to find a place for this charming bit; they can never make up their minds to put aside this delicate or strong idea, and they will do exactly the opposite of what they should, — make the plot for the sake of the scenes when the scenes should grow out of the plot. Consequently the dialogue will be constrained in movement and much trouble and time will be lost." [2]

A modern play recently submitted to the writer in manuscript showed just this trouble. Act I was in itself good. Act II was good in one scene, bad in the other. Act III was in itself right. Yet at the end of the play one queried: "What is the meaning of it all?" Nothing bound the parts

[1] Preface, *Au Public*, to *La Princesse Georges*. A. Dumas fils. *Œuvres*, vol. v, p. 79. Calmann Levy, Paris.

[2] *De la Poésie Dramatique*. Diderot. *Œuvres*, vol. vii, pp. 321–322. Garnier Frères, Paris.

together. There was no clear emphasis on some central purpose. The author, when questioned, admitted that with certain characters in mind, he had written the scenes as they came to him. When pressed to state his exact subject, he advanced first one, then another, at last admitting candidly: "I guess I never have been able to get far enough away from the play to see quite what all of it does mean." Asked whether there was not underlying all his scenes irony of fate, in that a man trying his best to do what the world holds commendable is bound in such relationship to two or three people that always they give his career a tragic turn, he said, after consideration, "Yes. What if I call my play *The Irony of Life?*" With the purpose of making that his meaning he reworked his material. Quickly the parts fell into line, with a clear and interesting play as the result. Many and many a play containing good characterization, good dialogue and some real individuality of treatment has gone to pieces in this way. A recent play opened with a well-written picture of the life of a group of architects' draughtsmen. Apparently we were started on a story of their common or conflicting interests. After that first act, however, the play turned into a story of the way in which one of these young draughtsmen, a kind of mixture of Get-Rich-Quick Wallingford and D'Artagnan, forced his way to professional and social success. Once or twice, scenes seemed intentional satire on our social classes. The fact is, the author had in the back of his mind social satire, characterization of the central figure, and a picture of the life of young draughtsmen. As material for any one of these came to him when he was writing, he gave his attention wholly to it. Though this might do for a rough draft, it must be rewritten to make the chief interest stand out as most important, and to give the other interests clearly their exact part in a perfectly clear whole. Left as written, the play seemed to have a first act somewhat off the question, and a later development going off now and then at a tangent. Its total effect, in spite of some admirable characterization, considerable truth to life, and real cleverness, was confusion for the audience and consequent dissatisfaction.

Another play, often extremely well characterized, had, as an apparent central purpose, study of a mother who has been trying to give her son such surroundings that he cannot go the way of his father who, many years since, had embezzled. Yet almost as frequently the purpose seemed to be a very close study of the son, who, although the mother, blinded by her affection, does not see it, is mentally and morally almost the duplicate of his father. Moved with sympathy, now for one and now for the other, just as the interest of the writer led him, the audience came away confused and dissatisfied. How can an audience be expected to know what a dramatist has not settled for himself, the chief of his interests among several?

When M. de Curel, with his original idea or picture for *L'Envers d'une Sainte* sat down to reflect, "he noticed that the interest in the subject lies in the feelings a woman must experience when she returns after a long absence to a place full of memories, and finds herself face to face with her past life. There was the psychological idea which seemed to him alluring, — to paint a special phase of emotion." [1] There, for him, lay the heart of his subject. Bulwer-Lytton, writing to Macready in September, 1838, of a proposed play on the life of the Chevalier de Marillac, in which Cardinal Richelieu must also be an important figure, said: "Now look well at this story, you will see that incident and position are good. But then there is one great objection. Who is to do Richelieu? Marillac has the principal part and requires you; but a bad Richelieu would spoil all. On the other hand, if you took Richelieu, there would be two great acts without you,

<hr>

[1] *Auteurs Dramatiques. F. de Curel. L'Année Psychologique*, 1874, p. 121.

which will never do; and the main interest of the plot would not fall on you. Tell me what you propose. Must we give up this idea?" [1] Bulwer-Lytton had not yet found the dramatic centre in his material. At first the story and character of Marillac blinded him to the fact that the material was best fitted for a dramatic study of the great Cardinal. When, shortly after his letter, he came to see that the dramatic centre lay in Richelieu, his famous play began developing. With that magnet in hand, he quickly drew to him the right filaments of incident to make a unified and interesting story.

Any dramatist has the right to decide first, what is the real importance of his subject to him, but before he finishes he may find that he will discard what originally seemed to him important, either because something interests him more as he reflects or because he comes to see in his subject an interest other than his own which will be stronger for the audience. M. de Curel, thinking over his proposed play, abandoned his first idea because "in ten minutes space it transformed itself. He abandoned his first idea in order to try to paint the slightly analogous feelings of a nun. He imagined a young girl who, at a former time, in a moment of madness, had wished to kill the wife of the man with whom she was infatuated. To expiate her crime, she entered a convent, took the vows, and lived in retirement for twenty years. Then she learned that the man whom she loved had just died. Whereupon, perhaps from desire for freedom, perhaps from curiosity, she comes out of her exile, returns to her family and finds herself in the presence of the widow and her child." Here was the beginning, not of *L'Envers d'une Sainte*,[2] but of another play, *L'Invitée*. "It may happen — something certainly surprising — that the idea which al-

---

[1] *Letters of Bulwer-Lytton to Macready*, p. 35. Introduction by Brander Matthews. Privately printed. The Carteret Book Club, Newark, N.J., 1911.

[2] *A False Saint*. F. de Curel. Translated by B. H. Clark. Drama League Series. Doubleday, Page & Co., New York.

lured the author into writing the piece makes no part of the piece itself. It is excluded from it; no trace of it remains. Note that the point of departure of *L'Invitée* is an idea of a woman capable of murder who is passed off as insane. Of the murder nothing remains, and as to the mother's madness it is reduced to almost nothing: it is no more than a rumor that has been going about, and the mother has not been really insane."[1]   Not to yield to such a compelling new aspect of the subject is to find one's way blocked. The resulting tragedy, or comedy, for the unyielding playwright, Mr. Archer states amusingly. "'Here,' says a well-known playwright, 'is a common experience. You are struck with an idea with which you fall in love. "Ha!" you say. "What a superb scene where the man shall find the will under the sofa! If that doesn't make them sit up, what will?" You begin the play. The first act goes all right, and the second act goes all right. You come to the third act and somehow it won't go at all. You battle with it for weeks in vain; and then it suddenly occurs to you, "Why, I see what's wrong! It's that confounded scene where the man finds the will under the sofa. Out it must come!" You cut it out and at once all goes smooth again. But you have thrown overboard the great effect that first tempted you.'"[2]

The point is not that when a dramatist first begins to think over his subject, he must decide exactly what is for him the heart of it. He may shift, reject, and change his own interest again and again, as attractive aspects of his subject suggest themselves. The point is that this shifting of interest should take place before he begins to put his play on paper. Not to be perfectly clear with one's self which of three or four possible interests offered by a subject is the one really interesting is to waste time. As the play develops, a writer

[1] *Auteurs Dramatiques. F. de Curel. L'Année Psychologique,* 1894, pp. 121–123.
[2] *Play-Making*, pp. 58–59, note. William Archer. Small, Maynard & Co., Boston.

wobbles from one subject to another and so leaves no clear final impression. Or he is obliged to rewrite the play, placing the emphasis properly for clearness. In one case he fails. In the other he does his work twice. The present writer has seen many a manuscript, after a year or more of juggling with shifting interests, given up in despair and thrown into the waste basket.

Probably it is best to leave till revision the question whether the interest presented will appeal to the general audience just as it does to the writer. It certainly can do no harm, however, and may save labor, when an author knows just what he wants to treat and how he wishes to treat it, for him to consider whether this interest is likely to be as important for his public as for him. Many years ago, Mr. A. M. Palmer produced *The Parisian Romance*, a play so trite in subject and treatment that, as written, it might easily have failed. A young actor, seeing in a minor rôle the opportunities for a popular success built up a fine piece of characterization in the part of Baron Chevrial. That gave Richard Mansfield his first real start. The play was remodeled so that this element of novelty, this fresh piece of characterization, became central. Thus re-emphasized the play became known all over the country.[1] Not long since a play written by its author to be wholly amusing, proved so hilarious in the second act that the actors rehearsed it with difficulty. When produced, however, the audience was so won by the hero in Act I that they took his mishaps in the second act with sympathetic seriousness. The play had to be rewritten.

It is at careful planning or plotting that the inexperienced dramatist balks. Scenarios, the outlines which will show any intelligent reader what plot the dramatist has in mind and its exact development, are none too popular. They are, how-

---

[1] See chapter x, "The Dramatist and His Public."

ever, the very best means by which a dramatist may force
himself to find what for him is the heart of his subject.[1] The
moment that is clear to him, it is the open sesame to whatever story his play will demand. It is, too, the magnet which
draws to him the bits of thought, character, action and dialogue which he shapes into plot.

With his purpose clearly in mind, the dramatist, as he
passes from point of departure through story to plot, selects,
and selects, and selects. Among all the possible people who
might be the main figure in accomplishing his purpose, he
picks the one most interesting him, or which he believes
will most interest his public. From all the people who might
surround his central figure he chooses the few who will best
accomplish his purpose. If his people first appear to him as
types, as in the case of *The Country Boy* to be cited in a moment, selectively he moves from type to individuals. Sooner
or later he must determine how many of the possible characteristics of his figures he cares to present. As he writes,
he selects from all that his people might say, and from all
they might do in the way of illustrative action, only what
seems to him necessary for his purpose. No dramatist uses
all that occurs to him in the way of dramatic incident, characters, or dialogue. As he shapes his story; as he reshapes
his story into plot; in many cases before he touches pen to
paper, he has rejected much, always selecting what he uses
by the touchstone of the definite purpose which knowing the
heart of his subject has given him.

Doubtless some writers see situation first, and others character, but sooner or later all must come to some story. Now
as story is only incident so unified that it has interesting
movement from a beginning to an end, ultimately the task
of all dramatists is to find illustrative action which as clearly
and quickly as possible will present the characters of the

[1] See chapter IX.

story or make clear the purpose of the dramatist. Here is
the selective process by which Mr. Selwyn got at the story
of his *Country Boy* :

It happened to be just before Christmas of last year. The season
some way impressed itself on me, and I began to think what a desolate place New York must be for a lot of fellows who had come
here from small towns and who were thinking of the homes they had
left there, and longing to go back to them for the Christmas season.
Doubtless there are hundreds of them here who came here years
ago vowing that they would never go back till they had "made
good," with the result that they have never since spent Christmas
in the old home. [*The initial idea.*] There is always somebody to
whom we are always successful, and some one to whom we are
never successful, and many times, if these fellows would go back
to their old homes, among the people who really care for them, they
would be regarded as successes, whereas in the great city they are
looked upon as failures. [*Type character.*]

It seemed to me that a character of that kind would make a good
subject for a play, and then I began to look around for some one
tangible to work from. Suddenly I thought of a newspaper man I
used to know when I lived at a boarding house on 51st Street,
here in New York. He was a free lance, and a grouchy, rheumatic,
envious, bitter fellow, who had all the "dope" on life — was a
philosopher and could tell every one else how to live, but didn't
seem to be able to apply any of his knowledge to himself. He
wouldn't even speak to any one in the boarding house but me, and
why he singled me out for the honor I don't know. But anyway
he did, and he used to tell me all of his troubles — how he had come
from a little town with great ambitions, and had vowed never to
go back till he had attained all that he had set out to get. And yet
he had never been back. He was a failure; dressed shabbily and had
given up hope for himself — and still, as I say, he could tell everybody else just what to do to succeed. When I lived there in the
boarding house and used to see him, I thought he was the only one
of his kind in town, but since then I have found that there are
many others just like him. [*Individual character.*]

So it occurred to me that he would be a good subject for *The
Country Boy*, and I worked out his life as it had actually been lived
here in New York. Though the character was good I presently
discovered that it would not do for my central figure, for the rea-

son that he had been here too long. He had gone through the mill
and knew all about it, and what I really needed was a boy who could
be shown to come from the country, and who could be taken
through the temptations and discouragements that a boy of that
sort would have to endure. So I just drew this younger character
from my imagination. [*Selection of special figure.*]

I had to have this chap a bumptious, conceited sort of youth so
as to have the contrast stronger when he met the hard knocks that
were to come to him in the city. There are many boys of that sort
in small towns. They do not see the opportunities around them
but imagine nothing short of a big city has space enough for
them to develop in. [*Purpose determining characterization.*] [1]

From idea through type-character to the individual Mr.
Selwyn worked to the life in New York of the older man,
and the story of the temptations and discouragements of the
boy. When he had reached these, Mr. Selwyn saw that the
best story for his purpose would be a mingling of the two.
The boy "worked, in very well with the character of the old
newspaper man, because it allowed him to give the youngster
the benefit of his experience, and to succeed eventually by
taking advantage of it. That brought a happy ending for
both of them." [2]

Any one of these stories as it lay in the mind of Mr. Selwyn
before he turned it into plot, was a sequence of incidents,
actions illustrative of one or both of the two characters, and,
through them, of the original idea. Just what is meant by
this "illustrative action" so often mentioned? In *Les Oberlé*,
by René Bazin, is a charming chapter describing the Alsa-
tian vintage festival. At their work the women sing the song
of the Black Bow of Alsace — in the novel but one detail of
an interesting description. The account comes about midway in the book. When the novel was dramatized it became
necessary to make the audience understand, even before the
hero, Jean, enters in Act I, that absorbed in his studies in

[1] *My Best Play.* Edgar Selwyn. *The Green Book Magazine*, March, 1911, pp. 536–537.
[2] *Idem.*

Germany, he has been unaware of the constant friction in the home land between the governing Germans and the Alsatians. Here is the way the dramatist, emotionalizing the description of the novel, turned it into dramatic illustration of Jean's ignorance of the condition of the country. Uncle Ulrich, Bastian, a neighbor, and his daughter, Odile, at sunset are waiting in a wood road for Jean, just arrived from Germany and walking home from the station.

> (*Outside a voice sings as it approaches in the distance.*)
> *The Black Bow of the daughters of Alsace*
> *Is like a bird with spreading wings.*

Ulrich. Ah, look there! Who can be so imprudent as to sing that air of Alsace?
The Voice.
> *It can overpass the mountains.*

Bastian. If it should be he!
The Voice.
> *And watch what goes on there.*

Odile. I am sure it is Jean's voice.
Ulrich. Foolhardy! They will hear him!
The Voice. (*Nearer.*)
> *The Black Bow of the daughters of Alsace —*

Ulrich. Again, and louder than ever!
The Voice.
> *Is like a cross we carry*
> *In memory of those men and women*
> *Whose souls were like our own.*

Ulrich. Jean! Upon my word that young lawyer cannot know the laws. Jean!" [1]

Just at the end of the same act it is necessary to illustrate the constant presence, the activity and alertness of the German forces and the irritation all this means to the Alsatians. In a story much of this would be described by the author. In the play we feel with each of the speakers the irritating presence of the troops, and so have perfect dramatic illustrative action.

[1] *Les Oberlé.* Edmond Haraucourt. *L'Illustration Théâtrale*, Dec. 9, 1905, p. 5.

(They are just starting off when Bastian stops them.)

Bastian. Chut!

Jean. What?

Bastian. (*Softly.*) Listen!

Jean. (*Softly.*) A rolling stone in the ravine.

Ulrich. Another!

Jean. Steps!

Ulrich. Of horses.

Jean. Well?

Ulrich. A patrol!

Jean. (*Moved.*) Ah!

Bastian. The Hussars!

Jean. What are they doing?

Ulrich. They are keeping watch.

Bostian. They are drilling.

Ulrich. Always!

Jean. Ah!

Bastian. Day and night.

Ulrich. Never resting.

Bastian. Perhaps they are trailing some deserter.

Jean. Ah! There are deserters?

Bastian. They won't tell you so in the town.

Odile. But we on the frontiers see them.

Jean. Ah!

Bastian. They who go out by the Grand' fontaine pass this way.

Odile. (*Softly.*) Near our farm. From our house one can see them passing.

Jean. Ah!

Ulrich. Chut!

Jean. I hear the breathing of their horses.

Ulrich. Be still.

Jean. We are doing nothing wrong.

Bastian. Wait.

Ulrich. Down there — wait — lean over.

Jean. I see —

Ulrich. They are coming up.

Bastian. They are going by.

Jean. They have crossed the road.

Ulrich. We can go down for the moment.

Bastian. Ouf!

Jean. It is strange — twenty times, a hundred times in Germany
I have met the patrols of dragoons, or hussars, and admired their
fine form. Here —
Ulrich. Here?
Jean. Only to see them gives me a queer feeling at the heart.
Ulrich. Don't you understand, my dear Jean? There they were
in their own country, here they are in ours. [1]

Early in the first scene of *The Changeling*, by Thomas
Middleton, Beatrice states clearly, and more than once, the
physical repulsion De Flores causes her. Knowing full well,
however, the dramatic value of illustrative action, Middleton
handled the ending of the scene in this way. Beatrice turning to leave the room, starts as she finds De Flores close at
hand.

> *Beatrice.* (*Aside.*) Not this serpent gone yet? (*Drops a glove.*)
> *Vermandero.* Look, girl, thy glove's fallen,
> Stay, stay! De Flores, help a little.
> > (*Exeunt Vermandero, Alsemero and Servant.*)
> *De Flores.* Here, lady. (*Offers her glove.*)
> *Beatrice.* Mischief on your officious forwardness!
> Who bade you stoop? they touch my hand no more:
> There! for the other's sake I part with this;
> > (*Takes off and throws down the other glove.*)
> Take 'em, and draw thine own skin off with 'em.
> > (*Exit with Diaphanta and Servants.*)
> *De Flores.* Here's a favour with a mischief now! I know
> She had rather wear my pelt tanned in a pair
> Of dancing pumps, than I should thrust my fingers
> Into her sockets here.[2]

Here the dramatist makes repulsion clear by illustrative action so emotional that it moves us to keenest sympathy or
dislike for the woman herself. Dramatically speaking, then,
illustrative action is not merely something which illustrates
an idea or character, but it must be an illustration mirroring

---

[1] *Les Oberlé*, p. 7.
[2] *Plays of Thomas Middleton.* Mermaid Series. Chas. Scribner's Sons, New York.

emotion of the persons in the play or creating it in the observer.

What is the relation of illustrative action to dramatic situation? The first is the essence of the second. A dramatic episode presents an individual or group of individuals so moved as to stir an audience to responsive emotion. Illustrative action by each person in the group or by the group as a whole is basal. The glove incident in *The Changeling* concerns both Beatrice and De Flores. Hers is illustrative action when she shrinks from the glove his hand has touched. He shows it when kissing and amorously fondling the glove she has refused. Their illustrative actions make together the dramatic episode of the glove, — which is in turn a part of Scene 1 of the first act of the play. There are the divisions: play, act, scene, episode, and illustrative action. Just as sometimes the development of a single episode may make a scene, or there may be but one scene to an act, there are cases when an illustrative action is a dramatic episode. The ending of Act II of Ostrovsky's *Storm* illustrates this.

Varvara, who has just gone out, has put into the hands of Catherine the key to a gate in the garden hedge. This Varvara has taken without the knowledge of her mother, who is the mother-in-law of Catherine. Just as Varvara goes, she has said that if she meets Catherine's lover, Boris, she will tell him to come to the gate. Catherine, terrified, at first tries to refuse the key, but Varvara insists on leaving it with her.

Catherine. (Alone, the key in her hand.) Oh, what is she doing? What hasn't she courage for? Ah, she is crazy — yes, crazy. Here is what will ruin me. That's the truth! I must throw this key away, throw it far away, into the river, so that it may never be found again. It burns my hand like a hot coal. *(Dreamily.)* This is how we are ruined, people like me! Slavery, that isn't a gay business for any one. How many ideas it puts into our heads. Another would be enchanted with what has happened to me, and would rush on full tilt. How can one act in that way without reflection, without

reason? Misfortune comes so quickly, and afterward there is all
the rest of one's life in which to weep and torment oneself, and the
slavery will be still more bitter. (*Silence.*) And how bitter it is,
slavery! Oh, how bitter it is! Who would not suffer from it? And we
other women suffer more than all the rest. Here am I at this moment battling with myself in vain, not seeing a ray of light, and I
shan't see one. The further I go, the worse it is. And here is this
additional sin that I am going to take on my conscience. (*She
dreams a moment.*) Were not my mother-in-law — she has broken
me: it is she who has made me come to hate this house. I hate its
very walls. (*She looks pensively at the key.*) Ought I to throw it
away? Of course I ought. How did it get into my hands? To se-
duce me to my ruin. (*Listening.*) Some one is coming! My heart
fails me. (*She puts the key into her pocket.*) No! — no one. Why
was I so frightened? And I hid the key — Very well, that's the
way it is to be. It is clear that fate wills it. And after all, where
is the sin in seeing him just once, if at a distance? And if I were
even to talk with him a little, where would the harm be? — But my
husband — Very well, it was he himself who didn't forbid it! Perhaps I shall never have such another chance in all my life. Then I
shall weep and say to myself, "You had a chance to see him and
didn't know how to take advantage of it." What am I saying?
Why lie to myself? I will die for it if necessary, but see him I will.
Whom do I want to deceive here? Throw away the key? No, not
for anything in the world. I keep it. Come what will, I will see
Boris. Ah, if the night would only come more quickly!

Curtain.[1]

Sometimes, even a playwright of considerable experience,
though his mind is full of dramatic material, finds his plotting at a standstill. The trouble is that he has not sifted his
material by means of the purpose he has in mind. When
he does, details of setting, bits of characterization or even
characters as wholes, parts or all of a scene and many ideas
good in themselves but not necessarily connected with his
real subject, will drop out. Many plays of modern realism
have been overloaded with details of setting, with figures, or

[1] *Chefs-d'Œuvres Dramatiques de A. N. Ostrovsky.* E. Durand-Gréville. E. Plon Nourrit
et Cie, Paris.

even scenes really unessential. In a recent play of Breton life
a prominent detail in the setting of a cave was the figurehead
of a ship. Even if one missed noticing this striking detail, its
presence was emphasized by the text. It turned out, however, that the figurehead had nothing to do with the story
or its development, nor was it really needed for any special
color it gave. It should, therefore, have been omitted. No
fault is more common than the use of unnecessary figures.
When Lady Gregory wrote her version of *The Workhouse
Ward*, she wisely cut out the matron, the doorkeeper, and all
the inmates except two. With three figures her play is a
masterpiece. With five actors and voices from off stage, Dr.
Hyde's Gaelic version is not. A one-act play adapted from
the Spanish showed some dozen or more individual parts and
a mob of at least forty. Ultimately, on a small stage, the
plot was done full justice with half that number of individual
parts and the crowd reduced to twenty or less. An amusing
play of mistaken identity had a delightful scene in which an
aunt of the heroine is proposed to by a friend of her youth.
In it, the dramatist, with admirable characterization, set
forth the views on matrimony of many middle-aged women.
Yet the whole scene had nothing whatever to do with the
story of the heroine. Consequently it was ultimately dropped
out. That dramatic ideas must be sifted was shown on
page 75 in the play seemingly about architects' draughtsmen.

Not even when a scene, a bit of dialogue or some other detail, is entirely in character may it always keep its position.
Though a detail or episode must be in character before it is
admitted, it can hold its position only if it is necessary for
the purpose of the play. Time limits everything for the dramatist. The final curtain impending inevitably at the end of
two hours and a half is the dramatist's "sword of Damocles."
It reminds him that in a play, "whatever goes for nothing,

goes for less than nothing" because it shuts out something which, in its place, might be effective. In Tennyson's *Becket* is a fine scene, the washing of the beggars' feet by the Archbishop.[1] It illustrates both customs of the time and a side of Becket's character, yet it contained nothing absolutely necessary to the central purpose of the play. Consequently, as the play must be condensed for acting purposes, Sir Henry Irving cut out the whole scene.

This time limit forces the dramatist, when choosing between two episodes of equal value otherwise, to select that which does more in less space, or to combine desirable parts of the two episodes when possible. In Tennyson's *Becket*, Scene 1 of Act II and Scene 1 of Act III take place in Rosamund's Bower. Henry and Rosamund are the principal speakers in both. There is, too, no marked lapse of time between the scenes, though Tennyson chose to separate them by the "Meeting of the Kings" at Montmirail. Very naturally, therefore, when condensation was necessary, Irving by severe cutting brought these two scenes together as Act II of his version. He not only saved time; he gained in unity of effect. Similarly, Irving brings together the essential parts of Scene 2, Act II, the "Meeting of the Kings," and Scene 3, Act III, "Traitor's Meadow at Freteval," making them the first scene of the third act in his version.

A cluttered play is always a bad play. Such clutter usually comes from including details of setting, characterization or idea, and even whole characters or scenes, not really necessary. Selection with one's purpose clearly in mind is the remedy for such clutter.

Even, however, when a writer has so carefully selected his dramatic episodes that each is one or more bits of illustrative action bearing on the main idea and entirely in character, he may still be short of story. He cannot rouse and main-

---

[1] *Becket*, Act I, Scene 4. Alfred Lord Tennyson. The Macmillan Co., New York.

tain interest moving at haphazard. His central idea must appear in dramatic episodes so ordered as to have sequence, — a beginning, a middle, and an end, — and so emphasized as to have the increasing interest which means movement. He cannot have good story till it has unity of action. When Bulwer-Lytton wrote Macready that he had discovered the heart of his proposed play on Marillac to be Richelieu, note that he speaks of the simplification and the unity resulting: "You will be pleased to hear that I have completed the rough Sketch of the Play in 5 acts — & I hope you will like it. I have taken the subject of Richelieu. Not being able to find any other so original & effective, & have employed somewhat of the story I before communicated to you, but simplified and connected. — *You* are Richelieu, & Richelieu is brought out, accordingly, as the prominent light round which the other satellites move. It is written on the plan of a great Historical Comedy, & I have endeavoured to concentrate a striking picture of the passions & events — the intrigue & ambition of that era — in a familiar point of view." [1]

Thomas Dekker found the source of his *Shoemakers' Holiday* [2] in a pamphlet by Thomas Deloney, *The Pleasant and Princely History of the Gentle-Craft*. [3] This loosely written pamphlet tries to tell three stories supposed to redound to the credit of the shoemakers: that of Prince Hugh and his love for Winifred; that of Crispin and Crispinianus and the brave deeds of the latter in the wars in France; and, finally, that of Simon Eyre, the master shoemaker who rose to be Lord Mayor of London, his wife and his apprentices. What obviously attracted Dekker in the pamphlet was the third story, to which he saw he could give much realism from his knowledge of the shoemakers about Leadenhall. Unfortunately,

---

[1] *Letters of Bulwer-Lytton*, p. 38. Brander Matthews, ed.
[2] *Plays of Thomas Dekker*. Mermaid Series. Chas. Scribner's Sons, New York.
[3] A. F. Lange, ed. Mayer & Müller, Berlin.

the story of Simon Eyre, though it provided him with delightful characters, gave him little variety of incident. Perhaps today a dramatist might make such a play carry almost wholly on the characterization of the shoemaker group. The Elizabethans, however, wanted a complicated story of varied action. Dekker, though he had first-rate romantic material in the story of Crispin and Crispinianus, could hardly weave this in with the story of Eyre, a relatively recent historical figure, for one material called for romantic and the other for realistic treatment. There seemed the deadlock. But Dekker, thinking of this Crispin in love with a princess, who disguised himself as a shoemaker in order to win her hand, remembered the wars of 1588 and English sympathy for the Huguenots involved therein. Therefore he turned Crispin into Lacy, a youth of that period. Lacy is not a prince, but a relative of the Earl of Lincoln, and something of a ne'er-do-well, in love with the Lord Mayor's daughter, Rose. He fears that if he goes to the wars in France, his duty as "chief colonel" of the London Companies, he will lose her. Therefore he sends Askew in his stead and stays in London disguised as one of Eyre's shoemaker apprentices. The purpose of Dekker to write a realistic play of complicated plot has helped him to reshape his material till two stories, as in the case of *The Country Boy*, have become one. Unity appears in materials seemingly as irreconcilable as romance and realism.

There are, however, two weaknesses in this story as now developed: Rose and Lacy, though they appear against the background of the wars, do not connect the apprentices with the enlistment, nor do they afford many scenes of marked dramatic force. Wishing one or two scenes of stronger emotion which at the same time would bring the apprentices into closer connection with the wars, Dekker creates Ralph, Jane, and Hammon. Ralph is one of the shoemakers who, pressed to the war, is torn from his protesting wife and fellow apprentices. In his absence, the citizen Hammon falls in love with Jane. Trying to make her believe that Ralph is dead, he wishes to marry her. Ralph, returning from the war to his former work with Eyre, can find no trace of Jane, for after a slight difference with Margery Eyre, she has disappeared. One day a servant brings Ralph a pair of shoes to be duplicated for a wedding gift. The pair to be copied Ralph recognizes as his parting gift to Jane. Summoning his fellow apprentices to aid him, he goes to the place proposed for the wedding and rescues Jane. Thus some scenes of fine if homely emotion are provided. Wedded love is contrasted with that of Rose and Lacy and with Hammon's courtship, and through Ralph the apprentices are brought closely into connection with the wars.

Many a would-be dramatist suffers, however, not from a superabundance of material bearing on his subject but a dearth of it. Again and again one hears the complaint: "I know who my characters are to be, and I have dramatic situation, but I cannot find my story. I haven't enough dramatic situation to round it out." Just this difficulty troubled Bulwer-Lytton when he was preparing for *Richelieu*. He wrote to Macready:

Many thanks for your letter. You are right about the Plot — it is too crowded & the interest too divided. — But Richelieu would be a splendid fellow for the Stage, if we could hit on a good plot to bring him out — connected with some domestic interest. His wit — his lightness — his address — relieve so admirably his profound sagacity — his Churchman's pride — his relentless vindictiveness and the sublime passion for the glory of France that elevated all. He would be a new addition to the Historical portraits of the Stage; but then he must be connected with a plot in which he would have all the stage to himself, & in which some Home interest might link itself with the Historical. Alas, I've no such story yet & he must stand over, tho' I will not wholly give him up. . . .

. . . Depend on it, I don't cease racking my brains, & something must come at last.[1]

Such difficulty means that a writer forgets or is ignorant of one of the first principles of dramatic composition. When he has three or four good situations which are in character, he should not hunt new situations till he is sure he knows the full emotional possibilities of the situations he already has. To decide after the closest scrutiny of the situations in hand, that others are needed is one thing. On the other hand, the inexperienced workman presents as quickly as possible the climactic moment of the scene he has in mind, and gets away as rapidly as possible to another intense climax. Finding himself, as a result, badly in need of additional dramatic moments, he hunts for situations as situations. Returning triumphantly with some strong emotional effect, he must perforce put the characters of the earlier scenes into these. Usually, as they have no real part in these later scenes, they prove troublesome. Sometimes the new scenes may be so reshaped as to fit the original characters, but usually the result of this method is that the scenes are foisted on the original characters, becoming obvious misfits, or that the original characters are so modified as to fit them. When modified, however, the original characters no longer perfectly fit the original scenes. Driven backward and forward between character and story, the dramatist pursuing this method often gives up the attempt, saying despairingly: "It is no use. My characters will not give me a plot."

The trouble here is that the inexperienced dramatist treats the situation as if its value lay in its most climactic moment. Often, however, there is as much pleasure for the public emotionally in working up to the climax as in the climax itself. To "hold a situation," that is, to get from it the full dramatic possibilities the characters involved offer, a dramatist

[1] *Letters of Bulwer-Lytton*, pp. 36–37. Brander Matthews, ed.

must study his characters in it till he has discovered the
entire range of their emotion in the scene. This will give
him not only many and many a new situation within the
original situation, but the transitional scenes which will
unify situations originally apparently unrelated except as
the same figures appeared in them. For example, consider
this.

A kindly woman in middle life comes in friendliest fashion
to offer to take the daughter of a proud man in great financial straits into her own home. As treated by an inexperienced writer, there was a prompt, clear statement of what the
woman desired, with an immediate passionate denial of the
request by the jealously affectionate father. In this treatment we lose the best of the scene. Really this worldly-wise
woman, talking to such a man, would lead up tactfully to her
proposal. As she led up to it, there would be many dramatic
moments, with much interesting revelation of her own and the
man's character. Caring for the man as she does, and loving
the girl deeply, she would not immediately accept a refusal.
After the man's first denial, as she tried by turns to cajole,
convince or dominate him, there would be strong dramatic
conflict, and, once more, interesting revelation of character.
Given, then, some happening, the nature of the human being
involved in it will affect its look. A second person involved
will affect it even more. Two people, influencing each other
because affected by the same incident will give still a third
look to the original situation. When you have what seems a
good situation, don't rush into another at your earliest opportunity, but instead study it till you know every permu-
tation and combination it holds emotionally for every one
involved, both because the situation affects every character,
and because every character may affect all the others. Then
you will know how to "hold a situation." Said Dumas the
Younger: "Before every situation that a dramatist creates,

he should ask himself three questions. In this situation, what should I do? What would other people do? What ought to be done? Every author who does not feel disposed to make this analysis should renounce the theatre, for he will never become a dramatist." [1] Though every writer may not examine his material by means of such formal categories, he must in some way gain the thorough information about it for which Dumas calls. Then and then only he can select from the results of his thinking that which will best accomplish his purpose in the play.

A one-act play with a very good central situation came to nothing because its author had not grasped the principle just set forth. A young man and a girl, eloping, come to the station of a small settlement. They find no one about, but the door of the ticket office ajar as if the person in charge had stepped out for a moment. They fear that the father and mother of the girl and perhaps another admirer are on their trail. Partly from curiosity and partly from the desire not to be seen till the train comes, they step into the office, closing the door behind them. Then they discover that they are prisoners, for the door can be opened even from their side only by a person with the right key. Just at this point, the father and mother arrive, amazed at finding no trace of the fugitives. They too are puzzled by the absence of the ticket-seller. Just as they start out to find him he appears, apologetic for his absence. He is mildly interested in their story, but as he has seen no young persons, and as he expects the train shortly, he starts to go into his office. Then he discovers the closed door and admits that he went out to look for his key, which he must have dropped somewhere since he opened the station that morning. Here was of course a dramatic situation of large possibilities, but in the play it was

[1] Preface, *Au Public*, to *La Princesse Georges*. *Œuvres*, vol. v. p. 78. Calmann Lévy, Paris.

treated almost as just stated. Of course the sensations of the
two young people cooped up in the ticket office, expecting
the parents, the station agent, and the train, should have
given us a comic scene before any one else appeared. The
effect of the discovery that they are prisoners upon the girl,
the effect upon the young man, the way in which the resulting
emotions of each affect the other, all this must be given if
the potential comedy of the situation inside the ticket office
is to be fully used. The arrival of the father and mother offers
a chance not only for the individual emotions of each and
their effect upon one another, but for the emotion of the
concealed elopers as they hear the familiar voices and understand how enraged the parents are. There is opportunity
for a good scene of some length here before the station
master appears. When he does enter, he should be interesting, not simply for himself, but for the effect he has on
father, mother, girl, and young man, and the new interplay of emotions he causes among them. Add the coming
of the former admirer with evidence he has found that the
elopers have been making for this station; and as the new
complications developed by his coming take shape, let the
train be heard far up the line. Surely here is a group of
very promising situations.

In this play so crowded with dramatic opportunity, its
author found only the most dramatic moments, rushing
rapidly from one to the other. Result, a failure. Any dramatic situation made up of a congeries of minor situations is
like a great desk the pigeon holes of which are crowded with
letters and personal documents. The biographer sitting
down before it first makes himself thoroughly conversant
with all the data. Then he selects for use only what is of
value for the biographical purpose he has in mind. The
people in a situation are, for a dramatist, the human data
he must study till he so completely understands them that he

can differentiate clearly in what they offer between what is
useful for his purposes and what is not.

Even Shakespeare, in his earliest work, had not grasped
the importance of "holding a situation," as a scene in the
First Part of Henry VI shows. He knows how to inform his
audience in Scene 2 of Act II why it is that Talbot visits
the Countess of Auvergne; in the *Whispers* of the next to
the last line of this scene he even prepares for the surprise
Talbot springs upon the Countess in the next scene; but
Scene 3 itself he treats merely for the broad situation and
a few bits of rhetoric.

A Messenger come to the English camp has just asked
which of the men before him is the famous Talbot.

Talbot. Here is the Talbot; who would speak with him?
Messenger. The virtuous lady, Countess of Auvergne,
With modesty admiring thy renown,
By me entreats, great lord, thou wouldst vouchsafe
To visit her poor castle where she lies,
That she may boast she hath beheld the man
Whose glory fills the world with loud report.
Burgundy. Is it even so? Nay, then, I see our wars
Will turn unto a peaceful comic sport,
When ladies crave to be encount'red with.
You may not, my lord, despise her gentle suit.
Tal. Ne'er trust me then; for what a world of men
Could not prevail with all their oratory,
Yet hath a woman's kindness over-rul'd;
And therefore tell her I return great thanks,
And in submission will attend on her.
Will not your honours bear me company?
Bedford. No, truly, 'tis more than manners will;
And I have heard it said, unbidden guests
Are often welcomest when they are gone.
Tal. Well, then, alone, since there's no remedy,
I mean to prove this lady's courtesy.
Come hither, captain. (*Whispers*.) You perceive my mind?
Captain. I do, my lord, and mean accordingly.   (*Exeunt*.)

SCENE 3. *The Countess's castle*

Enter the Countess and her porter

Countess. Porter, remember what I gave in charge;
And when you have done so, bring the keys to me.
  Porter. Madam, I will.   (*Exit.*)
  Countess. The plot is laid. If all things fall out right
I shall as famous be by this exploit
As Scythian Tomyris by Cyrus' death.
Great is the rumour of this dreadful knight,
And his achievements of no less account;
Fain would mine eyes be witness with mine ears,
To give their censure of these rare reports.

Enter Messenger and Talbot

  Messenger. Madam,
According as your ladyship desir'd,
By message crav'd, so is Lord Talbot come.
  Countess. And he is welcome. What! is this the man?
  Mess. Madam, it is.
  Countess.   Is this the scourge of France?
Is this the Talbot, so much fear'd abroad
That with his name the mothers still their babes?
I see report is fabulous and false.
I thought I should have seen some Hercules,
A second Hector, for his grim aspect,
And large proportion of his strong-knit limbs.
Alas, this is a child, a silly dwarf!
It cannot be this weak and writhled shrimp
Should strike such terror to his enemies.
  Tal. Madam, I have been bold to trouble you;
But since your ladyship is not at leisure,
I'll sort some other time to visit you.   (*Going.*)
  Countess. What means he now? Go ask him whither he goes.
  Mess. Stay, my Lord Talbot; for my lady craves
To know the cause of your abrupt departure.
  Tal. Marry, for that she's in a wrong belief,
I go to certify her Talbot's here.

Reënter Porter with keys

  Countess. If thou be he, then art thou prisoner.
  Tal. Prisoner! To whom!

Countess.   To me, blood-thirsty lord;
And for that cause I train'd thee to my house.
Long time, thy shadow hath been thrall to me,
For in my gallery thy picture hangs;
But now the substance shall endure the like,
And I will chain these legs and arms of thine,
That hast by tyranny these many years
Wasted our country, slain our citizens,
And sent our sons and husbands captive.

Tal. Ha, ha, ha!

Countess. Laughest thou, wretch? Thy mirth shall turn to moan.

Tal. I laugh to see your ladyship so fond
To think that you have aught but Talbot's shadow
Whereon to practice your severity.

Countess. Why, art not thou the man?

Tal.   I am indeed.

Countess. Then have I substance too.

Tal. No, no, I am but shadow of myself.
You are deceiv'd, my substance is not here.
For what you see is but the smallest part
And least proportion of humanity.
I tell you, madam, were the whole frame here,
It is of such a spacious, lofty pitch,
Your roof were not sufficient to contain't.

Countess. This is a riddling merchant for the nonce;
He will be here, and yet he is not here.
How can these contrarieties agree?

Tal. That will I show you presently.

> (*Winds his horn. Drums strike up: a peal of ordnance. **The
> gates are forced.***)

Enter Soldiers

How say you, madam? Are you now persuaded
That Talbot is but shadow of himself?
These are his substance, sinews, arms, and strength,
With which he yoketh your rebellious necks,
Razeth your cities and subverts your towns
And in a moment makes you desolate.

Countess. Victorious Talbot! pardon my abuse.
I find thou art no less than fame hath bruited
And more than may be gathered by the shape.

Let my presumption not provoke thy wrath;
For I am sorry that with reverence
I did not entertain thee as thou art.
   Tal. Be not dismay'd, fair lady; nor misconstrue
The mind of Talbot, as you did mistake
The outward composition of his body.
What you have done hath not offended me;
Nor other satisfaction do I crave,
But only with your patience, that we may
Taste of your wine and see what cates you have;
For soldiers' stomachs always serve them well.
   Countess. With all my heart, and think me honoured
To feast so great a warrior in my house.

                         (Exeunt.)

Except for a few lines of rhetoric, could the account in Scene 3 be shortened? The Countess awaits Talbot; he comes; she reviles him in a few lines; he turns to go; she declares him a prisoner; he laughs at her; and as she stands amazed, calls in his forces brought in secret to the castle. When Talbot invites himself and his men to feast at her expense, the Countess immediately agrees. Reading the scene, one recalls the words of Dumas fils: "Any one can relate a dramatic situation: the art lies in preparing it, getting it accepted, making it plausible, especially in untying the knot."[1] Here Shakespeare does not untie the knot; the Countess merely yields. What she feels, what happened thereafter, — all these are omitted. It is merely the situation which counts. Before Talbot comes in, the scene could easily be made to reveal much more of the character of the Countess. When he does enter, the play of wits between them, even as it disclosed character, might provide interesting dramatic conflict. Surely the moment when the Countess thinks Talbot trapped and he coolly jeers at her, is worth more development. Here it is treated so quickly that the surprise in the entrance of the soldiers

[1] Preface to *Le Supplice d'une Femme*. *Œuvres*, vol. v. Calmann Lévy, Paris.

hardly gets its full effect. All this is the work of a tyro, even if he be Shakespeare.

In *Richard II*, there is a scene, not as long as that just quoted, in which the central situation might seem to many people less dramatic than that of Talbot and the Countess, yet note to what a clear and convincing conclusion Shakespeare brings it, how plausible he makes the scene, how thoroughly he prepares it for the largest emotional effect by entering thoroughly into the characters involved.

Enter Aumerle.

Duchess. Here comes my son Aumerle.

York.   Aumerle that was;
But that is lost for being Richard's friend,
And, madam, you must call him Rutland now.
I am in Parliament pledge for his truth
And lasting fealty to the new made king.

Duch. Welcome, my son. Who are the violets now
That strew the green lap of the new come spring?

Aum. Madam, I know not, nor I greatly care not
God knows I had as lief be none as one.

York. Well, bear you well in this new spring of time,
Lest you be cropp'd before you come to prime.
What news from Oxford? Do these jousts and triumphs hold?

Aum. For aught I know, my lord, they do.

York. You will be there, I know.

Aum. If God prevent not, I purpose so.

York. What seal is that, that hangs without thy bosom?
Yea, look'st thou pale? Let me see the writing.

Aum. My lord, 'tis nothing.

York. No matter, then, who see it.
I will be satisfied: let me see the writing.

Aum. I do beseech your grace to pardon me.
It is a matter of small consequence,
Which for some reasons I would not have seen.

York. Which for some reasons, sir, I mean to see.
I fear, I fear, —

Duch. What should you fear?
'Tis nothing but some band, which he has ent'red into
For gay apparel 'gainst the triumph day.

York. Bound to himself! What doth he with a bond
That he is bound to? Wife, thou art a fool.
Boy, let me see the writing.
  Aum. I do beseech you, pardon me. I may not show it.
  York. I will be satisfied; let me see it, I say.
      (He plucks it out of his bosom and reads it.)
Treason! foul treason! Villain! traitor! slave!
  Duch. What is the matter, my lord?
  York. Ho! who is within there?

     Enter a Servant

      Saddle my horse.
God for his mercy, what treachery is here!
  Duch. Why, what is it, my lord?
  York. Give me my boots, I say; saddle my horse.
             (Exit Servant.)
Now, by mine honour, by my life, by my troth,
I will appeach the villain.
  Duch. What is the matter?
  York. Peace, foolish woman.
  Duch. I will not peace. What is the matter, Aumerle?
  Aum. Good mother, have content; it is no more
Than my poor life must answer.
  Duch.   Thy life answer!
  York. Bring me my boots; I will unto the King.

    Reënter Servant with boots

  Duch. Strike him, Aumerle. Poor boy, thou art amaz'd.
— Hence villain! never more come in my sight.
  York. Give me my boots, I say.
  Duch. Why, York, what wilt thou do?
Wilt thou not hide the trespass of thine own?
Have we more sons? Or are we like to have?
Is not my teeming date drunk up with time?
And wilt thou pluck my fair son from mine age,
And rob me of a happy mother's name?
Is he not like thee? Is he not thine own?
  York. Thou fond mad woman.
Wilt thou conceal this dark conspiracy?
A dozen of them here have ta'en the sacrament,
And interchangeably set down their hands,
To kill the King at Oxford.

Duch.   He shall be none;
We'll keep him here; then what is that to him?
    York. Away, fond woman! Were he twenty times my son,
I would appeach him.
    Duch.   Hadst thou groan'd for him
As I have done, thou wouldst be more pitiful.
But now I know thy mind; thou dost suspect
That I have been disloyal to thy bed,
And that he is a bastard, not thy son.
Sweet York, sweet husband, be not of that mind.
He is as like thee as a man may be,
Not like to me or any of my kin,
And yet I love him.
    York. Make way, unruly woman!   (*Exit.*)
    Duch. After, Aumerle! Mount thee upon his horse;
Spur post and get before him to the King,
And beg thy pardon ere he do accuse thee.
I'll not be long behind; though I be old,
I doubt not but to ride as fast as York.
And never will I rise up from the ground
Till Bolingbroke have pardon'd thee. Away, be gone!
                                        (*Exeunt.*)

So far as the situation is concerned we might go directly
from York's "fealty to the new made King" to his "What
seal is that?" omitting some ten lines. We should lose, however, the deft touches which make the discovery all the more
dramatic, — the words of York which show that he has no
idea that his son is really involved in any disloyalty; the affectionate effort of the mother to draw the talk from unpleasant subjects; and the distrait mood of Aumerle. Again,
the discovery of the contents of the seal might be made at
once, but the fifteen intervening lines before York cries
"Treason! foul treason!" increase our suspense by their clear
presentation of the emotions of father, mother, and son.
Once more the situation is held when York does not declare
at once the nature of the treason and the frantic mother
demands again and again the contents of the paper before

Aumerle says bitterly, and in perfect character with his first speeches of the scene,

> "it is no more
> Than my poor life must answer."

Still again we should have the necessary action of the scene perfectly if York, as soon as he has his boots, flung out of the room, to be followed immediately by the Duchess, crying that she will follow him to the King and ask the boy's pardon. However, had Shakespeare's treatment here been that he used in the scene of Talbot and the Countess we should have lacked the perfect portrayal of the mother who loses all sense of right and wrong in fear that her loved child may die. Finally, do we not gain greatly by the characterization of the Duchess in the last lines of the scene? Five times, then, Shakespeare, by entering into his characters, "holds the situation."

The second act of *The Magistrate*,[1] by Sir Arthur Pinero, is in central situation broadly this. Cis Farringdon, represented by his mother to his stepfather, Mr. Posket, as fourteen, because she does not like to admit her own age, is really nineteen and precocious at that. He has brought Mr. Posket to one of his haunts, a supper room in the Hotel des Princes, Meek Street, London, where they are to sup together. As Mr. Posket is a police justice, he has been induced to figure for the evening as "Skinner of the stock exchange." Shortly after the arrival of the two comes word that a frequenter of the restaurant twenty years ago, now returned to London, wants to sup in their chosen room for the sake of old times. Therefore Mr. Posket and Cis are put into an adjoining room. Colonel Lukyn, the returned stranger, and a friend, Captain Vale, enter. Just as they are ordering supper, a note comes to the effect that Mrs. Posket, with a woman

---

[1] Walter H. Baker & Co., Boston; W. Heinemann, London.

friend, is below, begging to speak with her old acquaintance,
Colonel Lukyn. As Mrs. Posket asks a private interview,
Captain Vale is put out on the balcony. With Mrs. Posket
comes her sister Charlotte. We have already learned from
Vale that he is deeply depressed because he thinks Charlotte
no longer cares for him. Mrs. Posket has come to beg
Colonel Lukyn, who knew her before she became a widow,
not to reveal the truth about her age.

Watch now the permutations and combinations the author
develops from this general situation. Cis is hardly in the
room before Isadore presents his bill for past meals. Cis sees
the chance, by borrowing from his stepfather, to settle a long
postponed account. Three figures, moved in turn by shrewdness, trickiness, and gullibility, stir us to amusement, giving
us Situation I. Even as the bill is paid, Cis asks Isadore to
show Mr. Skinner the trick of "putting the silver to bed."
Three people amused or interested by a trick, amuse us —
Situation II. With the coming of the note from Alexander
Lukyn, and the assignment of the room adjoining to Cis and
Mr. Skinner-Posket, there is a hint of future complication
which amuses us — Situation III. Lukyn and Vale entering,
the former sentimental over his memories of the place, and
the latter comically depressed over what he thinks to be the
faithlessness of Charlotte Verrinder, give us Situation IV.
The note saying Mrs. Posket is below with a friend, asking
a private interview, produces Situation V, for it amuses us to
think what may happen with Mr. Posket and Cis just on
the other side of the door. Placing Vale on the balcony leads
to Situation VI, for he goes with amusing regret for the delayed supper.

Up to this point the situations may be declared parts of the
main situation, which must now itself be developed. Just
after Blond, the proprietor, ushers in the ladies, the patter-
ing of rain outside is heard.

Lukyn. Good gracious, Blond! What's that?

Blond. The rain outside. It is cats and dogs.

Lukyn. (*Horrified.*) By George, is it? (*To himself, looking towards window.*) Poor devil! (*To Blond.*) There isn't any method of getting off that balcony is there?

Blond. No — unless by getting on to it.

Lukyn. What do you mean?

Blond. It is not at all safe. Don't use it.

(*Lukyn stands horror-stricken. Blond goes out. Heavy rain is heard.*) — Situation VII.

As Mrs. Posket reveals to Lukyn the complications in which her lie is involving her, voices from the next room, not clearly distinguished by those on the stage, but known to us as the voices of Cis and Mr. Skinner-Posket, are heard — Situation VIII. Just when Lukyn is straining every nerve to get the ladies away so that he may release Vale, Charlotte, overwhelmed by hunger, invites herself to supper — Situation IX. As the two women eat, Lukyn sits in anxious despair, at times forgetful of his guests. This brings Situation X, when Vale reaches out from behind the curtains of the balcony and passes to the absent-minded Lukyn from the buffet the dishes Charlotte desires. When Charlotte, turning suddenly, sees the outstretched arm, we have Situation XI. When Vale reënters, thoroughly irritated and quarrels with Lukyn, we have Situation XII. The reunion of Charlotte and Vale makes the thirteenth. That is, if six initial situations produced the situation when all the characters were upon the stage, Sir Arthur has developed seven new situations from the sixth. Now by adding a fresh complication through some new figures, he develops six more situations.

Just as Lukyn, Mrs. Posket, Charlotte, and Vale are about to leave amicably, Blond rushes in to say that the police are below because the prescribed hour for closing has passed. The names and addresses of all persons found on the premises will be taken — Situation XIV. Lukyn, Vale, Mrs. Posket and Charlotte hide themselves in different parts of the room, putting out the lights. Situation XV is the entrance in the darkness of Blond leading Cis and Mr. Skinner-Posket, in order that the other room may be searched safely. At last, the room where all are hidden is examined by the police. All try to hold their breath, but in vain. The police detect some one breathing — Situation XVI. In the resulting confusion, Cis escapes, dragging his stepfather with him — Situation XVII. The other four when caught, foolishly give false names. Lukyn, thoroughly irritated by the officers, flings one of them aside and attempts to force his way out, when he and his party are promptly arrested for assault — Situation XVIII.

> *Lukyn.* You'll dare to lock us up all night?
> *Messiter.* It's one o'clock now, Colonel — you'll come on first thing in the morning.
> *Lukyn.* Come on? At what court?
> *Messiter.* Mulberry Street.
> *Agatha Posket.* Ah! The Magistrate?
> *Messiter.* Mr. Posket, Mum.
> (*Agatha Posket sinks into a chair, Charlotte at her feet; Lukyn, overcome, falls on Vale's shoulders.*) — Situation XIX.

Five situations of nineteen lead up to the sixth. Seven are developed from that sixth by means of four people. The new complication, the search of the restaurant by the police and the bringing into one room of all the figures, gives us six more situations. Certainly Sir Arthur knows how to "hold a situation."

Act III of *Mrs. Dane's Defence* [1] is just equally divided between preparatory material and the great scene which ebbs and flows about the following situation. Mrs. Dane, in love with Lionel, the adopted son of Sir Daniel Carteret, at the opening of the scene has lied so successfully about her past

[1] The Macmillan Co., New York.

that Sir Daniel, who has been suspicious of her, has been entirely convinced of her innocence. Eager to help her set herself right, he asks in the kindest way for information which may aid him. Trying not to commit herself, Mrs. Dane slips once or twice and all the old suspicions of Sir Daniel are rearoused. He cross-examines her so rigidly that ultimately she breaks down and confesses. Handled by the inexperienced that situation might have been good for four or five pages. As treated by Mr. H. A. Jones, it makes a scene of twenty pages of finest suspense and climax. The situation is well held because every reaction upon it by the two characters has been worked out.

One would hardly think two quarrelsome inmates of a poorhouse, visited by a relative of one of them who wishes to take him away to manage her place, likely to produce a masterpiece of comic drama. Yet it does with Lady Gregory in *The Workhouse Ward*,[1] for she knows Irish character and speech so intimately that minor situation after minor situation develops, through the characters, from the original situation.

Indeed, much of our so-called new drama is but a prolonged holding of a situation stated as the play opens, or clearly before us at the end of Act I. *Chains*[2] of Miss Elizabeth Baker in Act I puts this double situation before us. A young married man without children, though happy enough in his marriage, is so weary of the sordidness of his small means and limited opportunities that he longs to break away, go out to Australia, and when he has made a career for himself, send for his wife. His sister-in-law, a shop girl, equally weary of her life, is weakly thinking of marrying a man she does not love, but who really loves her, in order to escape the grayness of her life. At the end of the play these two are accepting the situations in which we found them. Yet the three acts of the play are full of varied interest for an audi-

[1] *Seven Short Plays.* Maunsel & Co., Dublin.
[2] J. W. Luce & Co., Boston; Sidgwick & Jackson, Ltd., London.

ence, so admirably does the writer discern the situations which her characters will develop from the original situation. *Hindle Wakes*,[1] the best play of Stanley Houghton, is really a study of the way in which a situation which took place before the play began affects three families.

Surely it must now be evident that if a dramatist should in the first place understand perfectly that illustrative action is the core of drama, and must be carefully selected; and secondly that he must, among possible illustrative actions, select those which quickest will produce the largest emotional results; he must also recognize that till he has searched and probed his situations by means of the characters, in the first place he cannot know which are his strongest, and in the second place cannot hope to hold the situations chosen.

Another complaint from the inexperienced dramatist when shaping up his story is that though he sees the big moments in his play, he does not see his way from one to another. That is, transitional scenes are lacking. They will not worry him long, however, if he follows the methods just stated for holding a situation. Let him watch the people who have come into his imagination, first simply as people. Who and what are they? Secondly, what are they feeling and thinking in the situations which have occurred to him? He can't long consider this without deciding what people they must have been in order to be in the situations in question. Hard upon this comes the question: "What will people who have been like these and have passed through this experience do immediately, and thereafter? In the answer to the question, "What have they been?" he finds the transitional scenes which take him back into an earlier episode; in the answer to "What will they become?" the transitional scenes that carry him forward. In the scene cited from *Richard II*

[1] J. W. Luce & Co., Boston; Sidgwick & Jackson, Ltd., London.

the main moments are the home-coming, the discovery of
the traitorous paper, and the departure of the Duke and
Duchess of York. How is the transition from one to the other
to be gained? Through knowledge of the characters, as the
analysis showed. What applies here to transition within a
scene from dramatic moment to dramatic moment applies
equally in transition from scene to scene. Suppose that Sir
Arthur Pinero had as the starting-point of the third act of
The Magistrate the idea that Mrs. Posket should be arrested
under such conditions that she must appear in the court of
her husband when he is as guilty as she. Sir Arthur has decided that they must be in some place like the Hotel des
Princes when it is raided. He has in mind episodes which
will bring them all together at that place. He already sees
clearly the scene of the raid and the arrest. But the place
cannot be raided till late in the evening, and Agatha Posket
is too jealous of her reputation thoughtlessly to stay late
in such a place. What are to be the transitional "scenes"
which, in the first place, shall make us feel that considerable time has passed since Mrs. Posket came to the hotel,
and secondly shall keep us amused? Sir Arthur finds them
through the characters. It is the hunger of self-indulgent
Charlotte which motivates the staying and gives us the
supper "scene." It is the character of Vale which gives
us his quarrel with Lukyn. The love making of Charlotte
and Vale provides another transitional "scene." In other
words, whether one is looking for more episodes or for
transitions from one chosen episode to another, one should
not go far afield hunting episodes as episodes, but should
become acquainted with the characters as closely as possible. They will solve the difficulties.

All this lengthy consideration of selection makes for unity
of action in the story resulting. Some unity of action,
whether the story be slight or complicated, there must be.

Of the three great unities over which there has been endless discussion, Action, Place, and Time, the modern dramatists, as we shall see, treat Place with the greatest freedom, and are constantly inventing devices to avoid the Time difficulty. With the dramatists of the present, as with the dramatists of the past, however, what they write must be a whole, a unit. Some central idea, plan, purpose, whatever we choose to call it, must give the play organic structure. Story is the first step to this. Which gives most pleasure, — a string of disconnected anecdotes and jests; or a series of them given some unity because they concern some man of note, for instance, Abraham Lincoln; or the same series edited till, taken all together, they make Abraham Lincoln, in one or more of his characteristics, clearer than ever before? Does not a large part of our pleasure in biography come from the way in which it co-ordinates and interprets episodes and incidents hitherto not properly inter-related in our minds? Unity of action is, then, of first importance in story.

There is, however, another kind of unity which has not been enough considered, — what may, perhaps, be called artistic unity. Why is it that a play which begins seriously and for most of its course so develops, only to end farcically, or which begins lightly only to become tragic, leaves us dissatisfied? Because the audience finds it difficult to readjust its mood as swiftly as does the author. *The Climbers* [1] and *The Girl With the Green Eyes* [2] of Clyde Fitch are examples in point. The first begins with such dignity and mysteriousness that its lighter moods, after Act I, seem almost trivial. In the second play the very tragic scene of the attempted suicide, after the light comedy touch of the preceding parts, is distinctly jarring. A recent play which for two acts or more seemingly had been dealing with but slightly disguised figures of the political world had a late scene in which one of

[1] The Macmillan Co., New York.   [2] The Macmillan Co., New York.

these politicians, like Manson in *The Servant in the House*,[1]
or The Stranger in *The Passing of the Third Floor Back*,[2]
shadowed the figure of Christ himself. The effect was jarring,
unpleasant, and confusing, mainly because of its suddenness.
It will be noted that in both the plays mentioned, Manson
and The Stranger carry their suggestion from the start.
Should we know how to take Percinet and Sylvette in *The
Romancers* [3] of Rostand did not that opening scene, when
these two, in love with being in love, read *Romeo and Juliet*
together, prepare us for all the later fantasy? A dramatist
will do well, then, to know clearly before he begins to write
whether he wishes his story to be melodrama, tragedy, farce,
or comedy of character or intrigue. Unless he does and in
consequence selects his illustrative material so that he may
give it artistic unity, he is likely to produce a play of so
mixed a genre as to be confusing.

"Just what is tragi-comedy, then?" a reader may ask.
The Elizabethan dramatist frequently offered one serious
and one comic plot, running parallel except when brought
together in the last scene of the play. Technically, however,
tragi-comedy is a form which, although it may contain tragic
elements, is throughout given a general emphasis as comedy
and ends in comedy. We do not have good tragi-comedy
when most of the play is comedy or tragedy, and one scene
or act is distinctly the opposite. Therefore not only unity
of action but artistic unity, unity of genre, should be sought
by the dramatist shaping up his story.

How much story does a play require? This is a difficult
point to settle, but first of all let us clearly understand that
there are great differences in audiences as far as plotting is
concerned. Some periods require more plot than others.
Today we do not demand, as did the audience of Shake-

---

[1] Harper & Bros., New York.   [2] Hurst & Blackett, Ltd., London.
[3] Doubleday & McClure Co., New York.

speare's time, plays containing two or more stories, sometimes scarcely at all connected, sometimes neatly interwoven. Middleton's *The Changeling* [1] contains two almost
independent stories. This is nearly as true of *The Coxcomb* [2]
by Beaumont and Fletcher. On the other hand, in *Much
Ado About Nothing* the Hero-Claudio story, the Beatrice-
Benedict story, and the Dogberry-Verges story are so
deftly interwoven that they are, to all appearances, a unit.
Even as late as thirty years ago one found in many plays
a group of characters for the serious interest and another
for the comic values. Gradually, however, dramatists have
come to get their comic values from people essential to the
serious story, or from a comic emphasis they place on certain aspects of the serious figures of the play. Today is
the time of the single story rather than the interwoven
story. Yet even now, so far as the public of the United
States is concerned, a writer may easily go too far in simplicity, or rather scantiness of story, trusting too much to
admirable characterization. That is why that delightful
play, *The Mollusc*, [3] failed in this country. Many people,
among them the intelligent, declared the play too thin to
give them pleasure. That is, apparently we of the United
States care more in our plays for elaborate stories than
do our English cousins.

Indeed, national taste differs as to the amount of plot
desirable. Both Americans and English care more for plot
than do most of the Continental nations, which are often
satisfied with plays of slight story-value but admirable characterization. Nor is the difference a new one. Writing of
Wycherley's arrangement of Molière's *Misanthrope* in his
Plain Dealer, Voltaire said, "The English author has cor-

1 *Plays of Thomas Middleton*. Mermaid Series. Chas. Scribner's Sons, New York.
2 *Works of Beaumont and Fletcher*, vol. IV. Whalley & Colman, eds. 1811.
3 *The Mollusc*. H. H. Davies. Walter H. Baker & Co., Boston ; W. Heinemann,
London.

rected the only fault of Molière's piece, lack of plot." [1] In the same *Letter on Comedy*, Voltaire brings out clearly what any student of English drama knows, that all through its greatest period it depended far more on complicated story than did the drama of the Continent. Lessing in his *Hamburg Dramaturgy*, speaking of Colman's *The English Merchant*, says it has not action enough for the English critics. "Curiosity is not sufficiently fostered, the whole complication is visible in the first act. We Germans are well content that the action is not richer and more complex. The English taste on this point distracts and fatigues us, we love a simple plot that can be grasped at once. The English are forced to insert episodes into French plays if they are to please on their stage. In like manner we have to weed episodes out of the English plays if we want to introduce them to our stage. The best comedies of Congreve and Wycherley would seem intolerable to us without this excision. We manage better with their tragedies. In part these are not so complex and many of them have succeeded well amongst us without the least alteration, which is more than I could say for any of their comedies." [2]

About all the generalization one may permit one's self here is: For the public of the United States one can at present feel sure that story increases its interest in characterization, however fine. As we shall see in dealing with character, the latter should never be sacrificed to story, but story often ferries a play from the shore of unsuccess to the shore of success. Even today it is not the great poetry, the subtle characterization nor the fine thinking of *Hamlet* which give it large audiences: it is the varied story, full of surprises and suspense.

In another way, *Hamlet* is a case in point. It shows the im-

---

[1] *Lettres sur les Anglais*, Lettre XIX, *Sur la Comédie*, p. 170. A. Basle, 1734.
[2] *Hamburg Dramaturgy*, p. 265. Bohn ed.

possibility of laying down any golden rule as to the amount of story a play should have. Only speaking broadly is it true that different kinds of plays seem to call for different amounts of story. Melodrama obviously does depend on story-happenings often unmotivated and forced on the characters by the will of the dramatist. Romance is almost synonymous with action and we associate with it a large amount of story. The word *Intrigue* in the title "Comedy of Intrigue" at once suggests story. Tragedy and High Comedy, on the other hand, depend for their values on subtle characterization. In these last two forms it would seem that the increasing characterization must, because of the time limit, mean decrease in the amount of story; then *Hamlet*, with its complicated story, occurs to us as by no means a single instance of a play of subtle characterization in complicated story. Farce may be either of character or of situation, but there are also farces in which both situation and character have the exaggerations which distinguish this form from comedy. Comedy of Manners must obviously use much characterization, but it does not preclude a complicated story. Melodrama, then, does call above all else for story. With all the other forms it is in the last analysis the common sense of the dramatist which must tell him how much story to use. He will employ the amount the time limits permit him if he is at the same time to do justice to his characters and to the idea, if any, he may wish to convey. That is, story as we have been watching it develop from the point of departure is, for the dramatist, story in the rough. It is only when it has been proportioned and emphasized so that upon the stage it will produce in an audience the exact emotional effects desired by the dramatist that it becomes plot.

Just as the point of departure for a play comes to a writer as a kind of unconscious selection from among all possible subjects, so we have seen that story takes shape by a similar process of conscious or unconscious selection till it is something with a beginning, a middle, and an end, and clear. Nor does selection stop here. The very necessary proportioning and emphasizing mean, as we shall see, that the dramatist selects, and again selects.

CHAPTER V

FROM SUBJECT TO PLOT: PROPORTIONING THE
MATERIAL: NUMBER AND LENGTH OF ACTS

A DRAMATIST, proportioning his rough story for performance
in the limited space of time the stage permits, faces at once
the question: "How many acts?" If inexperienced, noting
the number of changes of set his story seems to demand he
finds himself in a dilemma: to give an act to each change of
scene is to break the play into many scrappy acts of a few
minutes each; to crowd all his needed scenes into five acts is
to get scenes as scrappy as the eight which make the fifth act
of Shakespeare's *Macbeth* or the ten in Act IV of *Henry VI*,
Part II. In either case, if he gives his numerous scenes adequate treatment, he is likely to find their combined length
forces him beyond the time limit the theatre allows — about
two hours and a half.

Let him rid himself immediately of any feeling that custom or dramatic dignity calls for any preference among three,
four, or five acts. The Elizabethan drama put such a spell
upon the imagination of English-speaking peoples that until
recently the idea was accepted: "Five is dignity, with a
trailing robe, whereas one, two, or three acts would be short
skirts, and degrading."[1] Today a dramatist may plan for
a play of three, four, or five acts, as seems to him best.

Why, if no change of scene be required, is not a play of one
long act desirable? At first sight, there would seem to be a
gain in the unbroken movement. The power of sustained
attention in audiences is, however, distinctly limited. Any
one who has seen a performance of *The Trojan Women*[2] by

[1] *Essay on Comedy*, p. 8. George Meredith. Copyright, 1897, by Chas. Scribner's Sons,
New York.
[2] *The Trojan Women*. Translated by Gilbert Murray. G. Allen & Sons, London.

Euripides, or von Hofmannsthal's *Electra*[1] needs no further proof that though each makes a short evening's entertainment it is exhausting because of uninterrupted movement from start to finish. To plays of one long act most audiences become unresponsive from sheer physical fatigue. Consequently, use has confined one-act plays to subjects that may be treated in fifteen minutes to an hour, with an average length of from twenty to forty-five minutes. Strindberg has stated well the problem which the play in one long act involves: "I have tried," he wrote in his Introduction to *Miss Julia*, "to abolish the division into acts. And I have done so because I have come to fear that our decreasing capacity for illusion might be unfavorably affected by intermissions during which the spectator would have time to reflect and to get away from the suggestive influence of the author-hypnotist. My play will probably last an hour and a half, and as it is possible to listen that length of time, or longer, to a lecture, a sermon, or a debate, I have imagined that a theatrical performance could not become fatiguing in the same time. As early as 1872, in one of my first dramatic experiments, *The Outlaw*, I tried the same concentrated form, but with scant success. The play was written in five acts, and wholly completed, when I became aware of the restless, scattered effect it produced. Then I burned it, and out of the ashes rose a single, well-built act, covering fifty printed pages, and taking an hour for its performance. Thus the form of the present play is not new, but it seems to be my own, and changing æsthetical conventions may possibly make it timely.

"My hope is still for a public educated to a point where it can sit through a whole-evening performance in a single act. But that point cannot be reached without a great deal of experimentation." [2]

---

[1] *Electra.* Von Hofmannsthal. Translated by A. Symons. Brentano, New York.

[2] Introduction to *Miss Julia*. Translated by E. Bjorkman. Copyright, 1912, by Chas. Scribner's Sons, New York.

The difficulty with a play of only two acts is similar. If the piece is to fill an evening, each act must last an hour or more. *The Winter's Tale* is really a two-act play: Act I is the story of *Hermione* and *Leontes*, Act II the story of *Florizel* and *Perdita*, with *Time* as Chorus separating the acts. Division of this play into five acts and use of modern scenery have given it the effect of breaking to pieces midway, where Time speaks. When each of the two parts is played uninterruptedly, as in Mr. Granville Barker's recent revival, this effect disappears and it becomes clear that the original division is artistically right. However, so long is each of the two parts that *The Winter's Tale*, when seen in this way, badly strains the attention of a present-day audience.

Contrastingly, to use more than five acts in the space of two hours and a half is either to carry the performance over into a second day, as with the two-part play of Elizabeth's time — something we cannot now tolerate; or to write such scrappy acts that the frequent shifting of scenery and dropping of the curtain spoil desired illusion. If it be remembered that there is nothing essentially wrong in a play of one, two, six, or even more acts, and that changing tastes or the necessities of particular subjects may in very rare instances make any of these divisions desirable, it can be said that three, four, or five acts are today the normal divisions for plays.

An objection to long plays of one or two acts is that when the piece lasts only an hour and a half, as in the case of *Miss Julia*, the evening must be filled out with something else. In the first place, it is by no means easy to arrange a mixed program in which each play shows to complete advantage. Nor are audiences usually fond of adjusting themselves to new characters and new plots two or three times in an evening. On the professional stage, Barrie's short plays have done something to make the general public more ready to shift their interest to fresh subjects in the course of an evening, but a mixed program of plays is rarely popular except in theatres of the so-called "experimental" class.

The advantage in three acts is that each allows a longer space than does the division into four or five acts in which characterization may develop before the eyes of the audience, or a larger number of illustrative actions bearing on the central purpose of the act may be shown. The offset is that three acts provide only two breaks by which the passing of time may be suggested. Neither four nor three acts have any essential superiority over each other, or over five acts. Five acts, in and of themselves, have no superiority over four or three; nor, as some persons have seemed to think, are they the only divisions in which a drama in verse may be written. Avoidance of awkward changes of scene within an act may compel use of four or five acts rather than three. The more episodes in the story to be dramatized, the more aspects of character to be shown by action, the more acts or scenes the dramatist must use. If long spaces of time must be allowed for because they are part of the story or marked changes of character demand them, the dramatist will need more *entr'acte* space, and, consequently, more acts. It is, then, necessary change of place and passage of time which are the chief factors in determining choice among three, four, or five acts.

For centuries theoretical students of the drama have worried themselves about the two unities: place and time. Practising dramatists, however, have usually found that generalizations in regard to them help little and that in each individual play they must work out the place and time problems for themselves. Practice as to shifting scenes has depended most, and always will, upon whether the physical conditions of the stage permit many real or imagined shifts. The Greek stage, with its fixed background and its chorus nearly always present, forced an attempt at unity of place, though the Greeks often broke through it.

Unity of action was the first dramatic law of the ancients; unity of time and place were mere consequences of the former which they would scarcely have observed more strictly than exigency required had not the combination with the chorus arisen. For since their actions required the presence of a large body of people and this concourse always remained the same, who could go no farther from their dwellings nor remain absent longer than it is customary to do from mere curiosity, they were almost obliged to make the scene of the action one and the same spot and confine the time to one and the same day. They submitted bona fide to this restriction; but with a suppleness of understanding such that in seven cases out of nine they gained more than they lost thereby. For they used this restriction as a reason of simplifying the action and to cut away all that was superfluous, and thus, reduced to essentials, it became only the ideal of an action which was developed most felicitously in this form which required the least addition from circumstances of time and place.

The French, on the contrary, who found no charms in true unity of action, who had been spoilt by the wild intrigues of the Spanish school, before they had learnt to know Greek simplicity, regarded the unity of time and place not as consequences of unity of action, but as circumstances absolutely needful to the representation of an action, to which they must therefore adapt their more complicated and richer actions with all the severity required in the use of chorus, which, however, they had totally abolished. When they found, however, how difficult, nay at times impossible this was, they made a truce with the tyrannical rules against which they had not the courage to rebel. Instead of a single place they introduced an uncertain place, under which we could imagine now this now that spot; enough if the places combined were not too far apart and none required special scenery, so that the scenery could fit the one about as well as the other. Instead of the unity of a day, they substituted unity of duration, and a certain period during which no one spoke of sunrise or sunset, or went to bed, or at least did not go to bed more than once, however much might occur in this space, they allowed to pass as a day.[1]

The Elizabethan author writing, in his public performances, for an audience accustomed to build imaginatively

---

[1] *Hamburg Dramaturgy*, p. 370. Lessing. Bohn ed.

a setting from hints given by properties, signs on the stage, or descriptions in the text, changed the scene at will. Recall the thirteen changes in Act III of *Antony and Cleopatra*.

On the modern stage such frequent change is undesirable for three reasons: the expense of constructing and painting so many scenes; the time consumed in making the changes, which may reduce decidedly the acting time of the play; and the check in sustained interest on the part of the audience caused by these many changes. The growth of the touring system also has led to reduction in the number of scenes, for transportation of numerous and elaborate sets is too expensive. Moreover, the interest in extreme realism has carried us more and more into such scenes of simple or sordid living as call for only one to three sets in a play.

At times it is easy, or at least possible with ingenuity, to have for a play, whatever its length, but one setting. Von Hofmannsthal's *Electra* is an illustration. Another is *The Servant in the House*, a play in five acts by Rann Kennedy.

The scene, which remains unchanged throughout the play, is a room in the vicarage. Jacobean in character, its oak-panelling and beamed-ceiling, together with some fine pieces of antique furniture, lend it an air of historical interest, whilst in all other respects it speaks of solid comfort, refinement, and unostentatious elegance.[1]

Hervieu's *Connais-Toi*, a play of three acts, is another instance of one setting throughout.[2]

Not infrequently it is comparatively simple to confine a play to one set for each act, or even less. *The Great Divide*, by William Vaughn Moody, and *The Weavers*, by Hauptmann, show a new setting for each act. In *The Truth*, by Clyde Fitch, Acts I and II have the same setting: "At *Mrs. Warder's*. An extremely attractive room in the best of taste";

---

[1] P. 13. Harper & Bros., New York.
[2] *Chief Contemporary Dramatists*, pp. 517–546. T. H. Dickinson, ed. Houghton Mifflin Co., Boston.

Acts III and IV are in "*Mr. Roland's* rooms in *Mrs. Cres-pigny's* flat in Baltimore." In the four acts of *The Witching Hour*, by Augustus Thomas, there is a change of set only for Act II.[1] Such reducing of possible settings to two or three for a play of four or five acts requires practice, and, in some cases, decided ingenuity. In present-day use the safest principle is this: a set to an act, if really needed, but no change of set within the act unless there be unavoidable reason for it.

What, then, is the would-be dramatist to do when faced by six or more settings to a five-act play, or two or three settings within what he believes should be an act? Often what seems a necessary early scene is but clumsy exposition: skilful handling would incorporate it with the scene immediately following. Scene 1, Act III, of Dryden's *The Spanish Friar* is in the street. Lorenzo, in friar's habit, meeting the real friar, Dominic, bribes him to introduce him into the chamber of Elvira. The scene is merely the easiest way of making the audience understand why the two men enter together very early in the next scene.

ACT III. SCENE 1. *The Street*
Enter Lorenzo, in Friar's habit, meeting Dominic

Here follow some fifteen speeches in which the arrangements are made. Then:

SCENE 2
Enter Elvira, in her chamber

Elvira. He'll come, that's certain; young appetites are sharp, and seldom need twice bidding to such a banquet; — well, if I prove frail, — as I hope I shall not till I have compassed my design, — never woman had such a husband to provoke her, such a lover to allure her, or such a confessor to absolve her. Of what am I afraid, then? not my conscience that's safe enough; my ghostly

---

1 For all these plays, *idem.*

father has given it a dose of church opium to lull it; well, for sooth-
ing sin, I'll say that for him, he's a chaplain for any court in Christendom.

Enter Lorenzo and Dominic

O father Dominic, what news? How, a companion with you! What
game have you on hand, that you hunt in couples?

    Lorenzo. (*Lifting up his hood.*) I'll show you that immediately.
    Elvira. O my love!
    Lorenzo. My life!
    Elvira. My soul!   (*They embrace.*)
    Dominic. I am taken on the sudden with a grievous swimming
in my head and such a mist before my eyes that I can neither hear
nor see.[1]

All the needed exposition given in Scene 1 could, with
very little difficulty, be transferred to Scene 2. Were the two
men to enter, not to Elvira, but by themselves, they could
quickly make their relationship clear. The conduct and
speech of Elvira could be made to illustrate what she now
states in soliloquy just before the two men enter.

In the original last act [2] of Lillo's *George Barnwell*, the settings are: "A room in a prison," "A dungeon." The whole
act could easily have been arranged to take place in some
room where prisoners could see friends. Today we should
in many cases exchange a number of settings as used in
eighteenth century plays for one setting.

Scenes, which in the original story occurred upstairs or
downstairs, inside or outside a house, may often be easily
interchanged or combined. *The Clod*, by Lewis Beach, a one-
act success of the Washington Square Players, in its first draft
showed a setting both upstairs and downstairs. This un-
sightly arrangement was quickly changed so that all the
action took place in a lower room. At one time Bulwer-
Lytton thought seriously of changing what is now Scene 1,

---

[1] Belles-Lettres Series. W. Strunk, ed. D. C. Heath & Co., Boston and New York.
[2] In the seventh edition, a scene, "The place of execution," is inserted to replace the
original brief final scene which apparently took place in the "room." Belles-Lettres Series
Sir A. W. Ward, ed. D. C. Heath & Co.

Act I, of his *Richelieu,* an interior, to an exterior scene. To Macready he wrote:

Let me know what you mean about omitting altogether the scene at Marion de Lorme's.

Do you mean to have no substitute for it?

What think you of merely the outside of the House? François, coming out with the packet and making brief use of Huguet and Mauprat [who figure in the interior scene]. Remember you wanted to have the packet absolutely given to François.[1]

Greek plays, because of the fixed backing, provide many illustrations of interior scenes brought outdoors:

. . . The dramatic action was necessarily laid in the open air — usually before a palace or temple. . . . In general the dramatists displayed an amazing fertility of invention in this particular, as a few illustrations will suffice to show. In the *Alcestis* Apollo explains his leaving Ametus' palace on the ground of the pollution which a corpse would bring upon all within the house (Euripides' *Alcestis,* 22 f.) and Alcestis herself, though in a dying condition, fares forth to look for the last time upon the sun in heaven (*ibid.* 206). Œdipus is so concerned in the afflictions of his subjects that he cannot endure making inquiries through a servant but comes forth to learn the situation in person (Sophocles' *Œdipus Rex,* 6 f.). Karion is driven out of doors by the smoke of sacrifice upon the domestic altar (Aristophanes' *Plutus,* 821 f.). In Plautus' *Mostellaria* (i, ff.) one slave is driven out of doors by another as the result of a quarrel. Agathon cannot compose his odes in the winter time, unless he bask in the sunlight (Aristophanes' *Thesmophoriazusæ,* 67 f.). The love-lorn Phædra teases for light and air (Euripides' *Hippolytus,* 181). And Medea's nurse apologizes for her soliloquizing before the house with the excuse that the sorrows within have stifled her and caused her to seek relief by proclaiming them to earth and sky (Euripides' *Medea,* 56 ff.).[2]

When it is not easy to see how a number of settings may be cut down, a dramatist should carefully consider this: May episodes happening to the same person or persons

---

[1] *Letters of Bulwer-Lytton to Macready,* xxviii. Brander Matthews, ed.

[2] *The Influence of Local Theatrical Conditions upon the Drama of the Greeks.* Roy C. Flickinger. *Classical Journal,* October, 1911.

in the same settings, but apparently demanding separate treatment because they occur at widely different times, be brought together? The dramatizer of a novel faces many opportunities for this telescoping of scenes. Any one adapting *A Tale of Two Cities*, if he uses Jerry Cruncher, will probably combine the two scenes in his home. To bring together incidents happening to the same person or persons at the same place, but at different times, is the easiest method of cutting down possible scenes.

It is, of course, possible to bring together circumstances which happened at different places at different times, but to the same persons. A notable instance is Irving's compacting of two scenes in Tennyson's *Becket* : he places at Montmirail what is essential in both Scene 2, Act II, Montmirail. "The Meeting of the Kings," and Scene 3, Act III, "Traitor's Meadow at Freteval." It is, indeed, often necessary to transfer a group of people from the exact setting in which an occurrence took place to another which makes possible other important action. In Haraucourt's adaptation of *Les Oberlé*, a dinner party at the Brausigs' is transferred to the home of Jean Oberlé, with his father and mother as hosts. This change permits the adapter to follow the dinner party with episodes which must take place in Jean's home. This group of changes concerns, obviously, bringing to one place events which happened to the same persons at another place, and even at another time.

Sometimes necessary condensation forces a dramatist to bring together at one place what really happened at the same time, but to other people in another place. For instance, the heroine of the play is concealing in the house her Jacobite brother, supposed by the people who have seen him to be the Pretender himself. The Whig soldiery come to search the house. Sitting at the spinet, the girl makes her brother crouch between her and the wall, folding her ample gown around and over him. Then, as the officer and his men minutely search the room, she plays, apparently idly song after song of the day. Just at this time, but at a distance, her lover, a young Whig officer, is eating his heart out with jealousy, because he fears that she is concealing the Pretender through love of him. Why waste time on a separate scene for the lover? Make him the officer in command of the searching troop: then all that is vital in what was his scene can be brought out when what happened to the same people at the same time, but at different places, is made to happen at the same place.

Similarly, what happened to two people in the same place but at different times may sometimes, with ingenuity, be made to happen to one person, and thus time saved.

Finally, what happened to another person at another time, and at another place may at times be arranged so that it will happen to any desired figure. About midway in the novel *Les Oberlé*, Jean and his uncle Ulrich hear the women at the autumn grape-picking sing the song of Alsace. In the play, in the first scene, Jean sings it as he passes from the railway station to his house.[1] Shakespeare, in handling the original sources of *Macbeth*, also illustrates successful combination around one person of incidents or details historically associated with other persons, times, and even places.

Most of the story is taken from Holinshed's account [in the *Historie of Scotland*] of the reigns of Duncan and Macbeth (A.D. 1034–1057), but certain details are drawn from other parts of the chronicle. Thus several points in the assassination of Duncan, like the drugging of the grooms by Lady Macbeth, and the portents described in II, iv., are from the murder of Duncan's ancestor Duffe (A.D. 972); and the voice that called "Sleep no more!" seems to have been suggested by the troubled conscience of Duffe's brother Kenneth, who had poisoned his own nephew.[2]

[1] See p. 83.
[2] Introduction to *Macbeth*. Cambridge ed. Houghton Mifflin Co., Boston.

Marlowe, in his *Edward II*, — a dramatization of a part of Holinshed's *History*, — proves that he perfectly understood all these devices for compacting his material.

The action covers a period of twenty years, from 1307, when Gaveston was recalled, to the death of Edward in 1327. Marlowe's treatment of the story shows a selection and transposing of events in order to bring out the one essential fact of the King's utter incompetence and subjection to unworthy favorites. Gaveston was executed in 1312, and the troubles in Ireland (ii, ii.) and in Scotland (ii, ii.) occurred after his death, but Marlowe shifts both forward in point of time in order to connect them with Gaveston's baleful influence. Warwick died in his bed in 1315, seven years before the battle of Boroughbridge, but Marlowe keeps him alive to have him captured and ordered to execution in retaliation for his killing of Gaveston. At the time the play opens the Earl of Kent was six years old, but Marlowe, needing a counsellor and supporter of the King, used Kent for the purpose. In the play young Spencer immediately succeeds Gaveston as the King's favorite; really the young Hugh le Despenser, who had been an enemy of Gaveston, remained an opponent of Edward's for some six years after Gaveston's death. Historically the Mortimers belong with the Spencers, i.e. to the later part of the reign, but in order to motivate the affair between the Queen and young Mortimer Marlowe transfers them to the beginning of the play and makes them leaders in the barons' councils.[1]

The essential point in all this compacting is: when cumbered with more scenes than you wish to use, determine first which scenes contain indispensable action, and must be kept as settings; then consider which of the other scenes may by ingenuity be combined with them.

Evidently a dramatist must develop great ingenuity and skill in so re-working scenes originally conceived as occurring in widely separated places and times that they may be acted in a single set. As has been said, the audience of the public theatres in Shakespeare's day imaginatively shifted the scene at any hint from text, stage properties, or even signs. With

[1] Introduction to Marlowe's *Edward II*. Tatlock and Martin. The Century Co.

the Restoration came elaborate scenery, a gift from earlier
performances at the English court and from the continental
theatres which the English nobility had attended in their
exile. By means of the "drawn scene" dramatists now
changed rapidly from place to place. In *The Spanish Friar*,
Scene 1 of Act II is "The Queen's ante-chamber." For
Scene 2, "The scene draws, and shows the Queen sitting in
state; Bertram standing next her; then Teresa, etc." These
drawn scenes held the stage until very recently. Painted
on flats which could be pulled off stage from left and right,
these scenes could not be "drawn" without hurting theatrical illusion. If moved in any light, all illusion departed; if
changed in darkness, but not instantaneously, they interfered
with illusion. To overcome these objections there have been
many inventions in recent years — Revolving, Wagon, Sinking Stages.[1] Undoubtedly, these make changes of scene
within the act well-nigh unobjectionable. The difficulty
with them is that most are elaborate and expensive, and
therefore exist in only a few theatres. It is, consequently,
useless to stage a play with them in mind, for on the road
it will not find the conditions of production essential to its
success. Occasionally, as in *On Trial*, some simple, easily
portable device makes these very quick changes possible
even on the road. At present, though invention tries steadily
to make change of scene so swift as to be unobjectionable, it
is wiser to keep to one setting to an act, unless the play will
greatly suffer by so doing, or the change is one which may be
made almost instantaneously when the lights are lowered or
the curtain dropped.

On the other hand, recently dramatists have rather overdone reducing possible settings to the minimum. While a
change of setting within the act always demands justification,
forcing a play of three to five acts into one or two settings

[1] See *Play Production in America*. A. E. Krows. Henry Holt & Co., New York.

when, at a trifling additional cost, a pleasing variety to the
eye and a change of place helpful to the dramatist might have
been provided, is undesirable. Lately there have been signs
that our audiences are growing weary of plays of only one
set, especially when they suspect the play has been thus arranged by skill, rather than necessity. Certainly, the newer
group of dramatists permit themselves changes of scene even
within the act. Act II of *The Silver Box*,[1] by Galsworthy,
shows as Scene 1, "The Jones's lodgings, Merthyr Street"; as
Scene 2, "The Barthwicks' dining-room." In *Hindle Wakes*,[2]
by Stanley Houghton, Scene 1, Act I, is the "Kitchen of the
Hawthorns' house"; Scene 2 is the "Breakfast room of the
Jeffcotes' house." To the preliminary statement of scenes the
dramatist appended words which hint the underlying danger
in all changes of setting, — disillusioning waits:

Note. — The scene for Act I, Scene 1, should be very small, as
a contrast to the room at the Jeffcotes'. It might well be set inside
the other scene so as to facilitate the quick change between Scenes
1 and 2, Act I.

All things considered, it is probably best to repeat the
statement already made: a change of scene within the act is
desirable only when absolutely necessary; a change of scene
with each act is desirable, except when truth to life, expense,
or undue time required for setting it forbid.

What exactly does this constantly repeated word "Scene"
mean? In English theatrical usage today, and increasingly
the world over, it signifies: "a change of setting." All that
happens from one change of set to another change makes a
scene. French usage, based on the Latin, till very recently
always marked off a scene when any person more important
than a servant or attendant entered or left the stage. For
instance, in *Les Petits Oiseaux* of Labiche, known in English
as *A Pair of Spectacles*, four consecutive scenes in Act I,
which throughout has no change of setting read thus:

[1] *Plays*, pp. 33, 42. G. P. Putnam's Sons, New York.   [2] J. W. Luce & Co., Boston.

SCENE 4. *Blandinet, Henriette, Leonce, then Joseph [a servant].*

A scene of some fourteen brief speeches follows, when:

> (*They start to go out, Tiburce appears.*)

SCENE 5. *The same persons, Tiburce*

After a scene of eleven short speeches,

> (*Blandinet goes over to left with Leonce.*)

SCENE 6. *Henriette, Tiburce*

Henriette, who sat down after the entrance of Tiburce, and took up her work again, rises immediately on the exit of Blandinet, folding her work.

Tiburce. (*Approaching her hesitatingly.*) You are not working any longer, Aunt. . . . It's done already?

> (*Henriette bows to him frigidly and goes out at right.*)

SCENE 7. *Tiburce, then François*[1]

What this French use of the word "scene" leads to, when logically carried out so that even servants entering or leaving the stage create a scene, the following from Act IV of *George Barnwell*, will show:

SCENE 5. *To them a Servant*

Thorowgood. Order the groom to saddle the swiftest horse, and prepare himself to set out with speed! — An affair of life and death demands his diligence. (*Exit Servant.*)

SCENE 6. *Thorowgood, Trueman, and Lucy*

Thorowgood. For you, whose behavior on this occasion I have no time to commend as it deserves, I must ingage your farther assistance. Return and observe this Millwood till I come. I have your directions, and will follow you as soon as possible.

> (*Exit Lucy.*)

SCENE 7. *Thorowgood and Trueman*

Thorowgood. Trueman, you I am sure would not be idle on this occasion. (*Exit.*)

SCENE 8

Trueman. He only who is a friend can judge of my distress.

> (*Exit.*)[2]

---

1 *Théâtre Complet*, vol. i. Calmann Lévy, Paris.
2 Belles-Lettres Series. Sir A. W. Ward, ed. D. C. Heath & Co., Boston and New York.

This French division of scenes is, of course, made for the convenience of the dramatist as he composes and for the reader, not for the actor or the audience. Though somewhat copied in the past by English authors, it is now rejected by most stages. Even French dramatists are breaking away from it. Memory of this French usage, however, still affects popular speech: when we speak of any part of an act in which two or more people are on stage, we are very likely to call it their "scene" no matter whether they have come on in a changed setting or not. Obviously if *scene* is to correspond with *setting*, we need another word for what in our practice is the same as the older French *scene*.

Not only do necessary changes in setting make proportioning material into acts and within acts difficult, but the time question also raises many problems. It may be troublesome within the act, between the acts, and at the opening of the play. In the final soliloquy of *Faustus* (p. 35), an hour is supposed to elapse in some thirty lines. Though the Elizabethan, in a case like this, was ready to assist the dramatist, today we are so conscious of time spaces that practically all stage clocks are temporarily out of order, lest they mark too distinctly the discrepancy between pretended and real time.[1] The novelist, in a few lines, tells us of many happenings in a considerable space of time, or writes: "Thus, in idle talk, a full hour passed," and we do not query the supposed passage of time. On the stage, however, when one gossip says to another: "I must be off. I meant to stop a minute, and I have gossiped an hour," auditors who recognize perfectly that the two people have not talked ten minutes are likely to laugh derisively. As has been pointed out,[2] this time difficulty has

[1] Not often does a dramatist succeed in making real and supposed time agree as well as does Sir Arthur Pinero in Act III of *The Gay Lord Quex*. From seven to nine pages of absorbing action come between one chiming of the quarter hour and the next. Though a stopwatch would quickly reveal the somewhat disordered condition of that boudoir clock, an auditor, absorbed in the action of the moment, merely feels his tension increase if he notes the passing of time.

[2] See p. 35.

made it practically impossible to dramatize satisfactorily
Stevenson's *The Sire de Maletroit's Door*. The swiftly-moving
simple story demands the one-act form, but certain marked
changes in feeling, convincing enough when they are said
to come after ten or twelve hours of strong emotion, become,
when they are seen to occur after twenty minutes to an hour,
unconvincing. The central situation may be used, but for
success on the stage the story must be so re-told that the
marked changes in feeling are convincing even when seen.
A dilemma results: lapses of time are handled more easily
in three or four acts than in one act; the moment *The Sire
de Maletroit's Door* is re-cast into three or four acts, it needs
so much padding as to lose nearly all its original values.

When a dramatist faces the need to represent, on stage,
a passage of time which could not in real life be coincident
with the action of the scene, he must (*a*) hypnotize an audience by a long scene of complicated and absorbing emotion into thinking that the required time has passed; or
(*b*) must discover some motive sufficiently strong to account
for a swift change in feeling; (*c*) or must get his person or persons off stage and write what is known as a "Cover Scene."

An audience led through an intense emotional experience
does not mark accurately the passage of time. Make the
emotional experience protracted, as well as absorbing, and
you may imply or even state that any reasonable length of
time has passed. The fearful agony of *Faustus* so grips an
audience that it loses track of the time necessary for the
speech, or would, were it not for the unfortunate emphasis
on the actual time: "Ah, half the hour is passed; 't will all be
passed anon"; "The clock strikes twelve." In *Hamlet*, the
fourth act takes place during the absence of Hamlet in England. By its many intensely moving happenings, it makes an
auditor willing to believe that Hamlet has been absent for a
long time, when in reality he has been on the stage within a

half hour. Such time fillings may, of course, be a portion of a scene, a whole scene, or even a whole act. In most cases, it is quite impossible that the time really requisite and the time of action should coincide. The business of the dramatist is to make the audience feel as if the time had passed — to create an illusion of time.

The second method of meeting the time difficulty, finding motivation of some marked change in character or circumstances which permits it to be as swift as it is on the stage, is best treated in the next chapter.

In *The Russian Honeymoon*,[1] a play once very popular with amateurs, there is bad handling of a time difficulty. The hero, going out in his peasant costume, must return after a few speeches, in full regimentals. A lightning change of costume is, therefore, necessary. More than once this lack of a proper Cover Scene has caused an awkward wait at this point in the play. Mark the absurdly short time Steele, in his *Conscious Lovers* allows Isabella for bringing Bevil Junior on stage. Apparently, the latter and all his group must have been waiting at the end of the corridor.

Isabella. But here's a claim more tender yet — your Indiana, sir, your long lost daughter.

Mr. Sealand. O my child! my child!

Indiana. All-gracious Heaven! Is it possible? Do I embrace my father?

Mr. Sealand. And I do hold thee — These passions are too strong for utterance — Rise, rise, my child, and give my tears their way — O my sister!   (*Embracing her.*)

Isabella. Now, dearest niece, my groundless fears, my painful cares no more shall vex thee. If I have wronged thy noble lover with too hard suspicions, my just concern for thee, I hope, will plead my pardon.

Mr. Sealand. O! make him then the full amends, and be yourself the messenger of joy: Fly this instant! — Tell him all these

---

[1] Eugène Scribe, adopted by Mrs. Burton Harrison. Dramatic Publishing Co., Chicago.

wondrous turns of Providence in his favour! Tell him I have now a daughter to bestow, which he no longer will decline: that this day he still shall be a bridegroom: nor shall a fortune, the merit which his father seeks, be wanting: tell him the reward of all his virtues waits on his acceptance. (*Exit Isabella.*) My dearest Indiana!

(Turns and embraces her.)

Indiana. Have I then at last a father's sanction on my love? His bounteous hand to give, and make my heart a present worthy of Bevil's generosity?

Mr. Sealand. O my child, how are our sorrows past o'erpaid by such a meeting! Though I have lost so many years of soft paternal dalliance with thee, yet, in one day, to find thee thus, and thus bestow thee, in such perfect happiness! is ample! ample reparation! And yet again the merit of thy lover —

Indiana. O! had I spirits left to tell you of his actions! how strongly filial duty has suppressed his love; and how concealment still has doubled all his obligations; the pride, the joy of his alliance, sir, would warm your heart, as he has conquered mine.

Mr. Sealand. How laudable is love, when born of virtue! I burn to embrace him —

Indiana. See, sir, my aunt already has succeeded, and brought him to your wishes.

(*Enter Isabella, with Sir John Bevil, Bevil Junior, Mrs. Sealand, Cimberton, Myrtle, and Lucinda.*)

Sir John Bevil. (*Entering.*) Where! where's this scene of wonder! Mr. Sealand, I congratulate, on this occasion, our mutual happiness.[1]

The inexperienced dramatist sending a servant out for wraps, brings him back so speedily that, apparently, in a well-ordered Fifth Avenue or Newport residence, garments lie all about the house or replace tapestries upon the walls. The speed with which servants upon the stage do errands shows that they have been trained in a basic principle of drama: "Waste no time." A more experienced dramatist, realizing that such speed destroys illusion, writes a brief scene which seems to allow time for the errand.

[1] Mermaid Series. Chas. Scribner's Sons, New York.

The telephone and the automobile have been godsends to the young dramatist. By use of the first, a lover can telephone from the drug-store just around the corner, run all the way in his eagerness, take an elevator, and be on the scene with a speed that saves the young dramatist any long Cover Scene. Of course, if said lover be rich or extravagant enough to own an automobile, the distance from which he may telephone increases as the square of the horse-power of his machine. In the old days, and even today, if the truth be regarded, something must be taking place on the stage sufficient to allow time for a lover, however ardent, to cover the distance between the telephone booth and the house.

Here, however, a dramatist meets his Scylla and Charybdis. He yields to Scylla, if he does not write any such scene; to Charybdis, if he writes such a scene but does not advance his play by it — that is, if he merely marks time. In a recent play, whenever a time space was to be covered, a group of citizens talked. What they said was not uninteresting. The characters were well sketched in. But the scene did not advance the story at all. Bulwer-Lytton faced this difficulty in writing *Money:*

I think in the first 3 acts you will find little to alter. But in Act 4 — the 2 scenes with Lady B. & Clara — and Joke & the Tradesman don't help on the Plot much — they were wanted, however, especially the last to give time for change of dress & smooth the lapse of the theme from money to dinner; you will see if this part requires any amendment.[1]

The principle here is this: Whatever is written to cover a time space, long or short, must help the movement of the play to its climax. It may be said that the fourth act of neither *Macbeth* nor *Hamlet* complies with this statement; but more careful thought will show that in each case the act is very important to the whole story. The title of each play,

---

[1] *Letters of Bulwer-Lytton to Macready*, LXIII. Brander Matthews, ed.

and present-day interest in its characterization rather than its story, make us miss greatly the leading figure, wholly absent in the act. Therefore we hasten to declare, not recognizing that story was of first importance in Shakespeare's day, that because this act is not focused on Macbeth or Hamlet the act in question clogs the general movement.

Otway, in *Venice Preserved*, handles passage of time admirably. Toward the end of the first act, Pierre makes an appointment with Jaffier to meet him that night on the Rialto at twelve. Exit Pierre. Immediately Belvidera enters to Jaffier. Their talk, only about four pages in length, is so passionately pathetic that a hearer loses all accurate sense of time. There is an *entr'acte*, and then a scene between Pierre and Aquilina. Again it is brief, only three and a half pages, but it is dramatic, and complicates the story. Consequently, when Jaffier does meet Pierre on the Rialto, we are quite ready to believe that considerable time has passed and it is now twelve o'clock. Otway has used three devices to cover a time space: an absorbing emotional scene, an *entr'acte*, and a Cover Scene.[1]

All the methods just described have had to do with representing time on stage. When time necessary for the telling of a story may be treated as passing off stage, other devices may be used. Most of them gather about a dropping of the curtain. Recently there has been much use of the curtain to denote, without change of set, the passing of some relatively brief time. When a group of people leave the stage for dinner, the curtain is dropped, to rise again as the group, returning from dinner, take up the action of the play. Just this occurs in Act I of Pinero's *Iris*.[2] Mr. Belasco, in *The Woman*, dropped the curtain at the beginning of a cross examination, to raise it for the next act as the examination

---

1 Belles-Lettres Series. C. F. McClumpha, ed. D. C. Heath & Co., Boston and New York.
2 Walter H. Baker & Co., Boston; W. Heinemann, London.

nears its climax. In *The Silver Box*,[1] dropping the curtain twice in Act I makes it possible to see the Barthwicks' dining-room "just after midnight," "at eight-thirty A.M.," and at "the breakfast hour of Mr. and Mrs. Barthwick." Such curtains, though justifiable, have one serious objection. They bring us back with a jolt from absorbed following of the play to the disturbing truth that we are not looking at life, but at life selectively presented under obvious limitations of the stage. Scene 1 of *The Silver Box*, which began "just after midnight," lasts only a few minutes; yet when the curtain "rises again at once," we are to understand that eight hours have elapsed.

The simplest method of handling time off stage is to treat it as having elapsed between acts or on the dropping of a curtain within an act.[2] In how many, many plays — for instance, Sir Arthur Pinero's early *Lady Bountiful* — has the hero, in whatever length of time between the fourth and fifth acts the dramatist has preferred, become the regenerated figure of the last act! All that is needed in *The Man Who Came Back*, as produced, to change the dope-ridden, degenerating youth into a firm character, even into a landed proprietor, is a sea voyage from San Francisco to Honolulu — and an *entr'acte!* What takes place between acts is far too often — medicinally, morally, dare we say dramatically? — more significant than what we see. Yet why deride this refuge of the dramatist? Such use is merely an extension of what we permit any dramatist who, writing two plays on the same subject or person, implies or states that very many years have elapsed beween the two parts. No one seriously objects when thousands of years are supposed to elapse between the *Prometheus Bound* and the *Prometheus Unbound* of Æschylus.[3] Surely, it is logical to treat spaces between

---

[1] *Plays.* G. P. Putnam's Sons, New York.
[2] Walter H. Baker & Co., Boston; W. Heinemann, London.
[3] Everyman's Library. Plumptre, ed.

acts like spaces between plays on related subjects. The trouble lies, not in the time supposed to have elapsed, but in the changes of character said to have taken place. As long as our drama was primarily story, and not, as it has come to be increasingly, a revealer of character, we were content, if each act contained a thrilling dramatic incident, to be told that this or that had happened between the acts. The early drama did this by the Dumb Show and the Chorus.

ACT II

PROLOGUE

Flourish. Enter Chorus

Chorus. Now all the youth of England are on fire,
And silken dalliance in the wardrobe lies.
Now thrive the armourers, and honour's thought
Reigns solely in the breast of every man.
They sell the pasture now to buy the horse,
Following the mirror of all Christian kings,
With winged heels, as English Mercuries.
For now sits Expectation in the air,
And hides a sword from hilts unto the point
With crowns imperial, crowns, and coronets,
Promis'd to Harry and his followers.
The French, advis'd by good intelligence
Of this most dreadful preparation,
Shake in their fear, and with pale policy
Seek to divert the English purposes.
O England! model to thy inward greatness,
Like little body with a mighty heart,
What mightst thou do, that honour would thee do,
Were all thy children kind and natural!
But see thy fault! France hath in thee found out
A nest of hollow bosoms, which he fills
With treacherous crowns; and three corrupted men,
One, Richard Earl of Cambridge, and the second,
Henry Lord Scroop of Masham, and the third,
Sir Thomas Grey, knight, of Northumberland,
Have, for the gilt of France, — O guilt indeed! —

Confirm'd conspiracy with fearful France;
And by their hands this grace of kings must die,
If hell and treason hold their promises,
Ere he take ship for France, and in Southampton.
Linger your patience on, and we'll digest
The abuse of distance, force a play.
The sum is paid; the traitors are agreed;
The King is set from London; and the scene
Is now transported, gentles, to Southampton.
There is the playhouse now, there must you sit;
And thence to France shall we convey you safe,
And bring you back, charming the narrow seas
To give you gentle pass; for, if we may,
We'll not offend one stomach with our play.
But, till the King come forth, and not till then,
Unto Southampton do we shift our scene. (*Exit.*) *Henry V.*

As audiences, becoming more interested in characterization and less in mere story, grew to expect that each act would show the central figure growing out of the preceding act and into the next, they balked more and more at hearing of changes instead of seeing them. They insisted that the effective forces must work before their eyes. Hence the disappearance of Dumb Show and Chorus. With *Lady Bountiful* [1] the public did not object strongly to what was supposed to happen between the fourth and fifth acts, because it took the whole play as a mere story. But in *Iris*, when the author asked it to accept all the important stages in the moral breakdown of Iris as taking place between the fourth and fifth acts, there was considerable dissent. Contrast the greater satisfactoriness when an auditor can watch important changes, as he may with Sophy Fullgarney in the third act of the *Gay Lord Quex*,[2] or with Mrs. Dane in the fourth act of *Mrs. Dane's Defence.* To assume that a lapse of time stated to have passed in a just preceding *entr'acte*, and a

---

[1] Walter H. Baker & Co., Boston; W. Heinemann, London.
[2] R. H. Russell & Co., New York.

change of environment there, have produced marked difference in character is not today enough. A dramatist may assume that only as much time has passed between acts as he makes entirely plausible by the happenings and characterization of the next act. For any needed statement of what has happened since the close of a preceding act he must depend only on deft exposition within the act in question.

Recent usage no longer insists that acts may not somewhat overlap. "Toward the end of Act II of Eugene Walter's *Paid in Full*, Emma Brooks is disclosed making an appointment with Captain Williams over a telephone. In the next act we are transferred to Captain Williams's quarters, and the dramatic clock has, in the meanwhile, been turned back some fifteen minutes, for presently the telephone bell rings, and the same appointment is made over again. In other words, Act II partly overlaps Act I in time, but the scene is different." [1] There is a similar use in *Under Cover*. At the beginning of the last act, a group, sleepily at cards, is startled by the burglar alarm. The climax of the preceding act was that same alarm.

The most difficult kind of off-stage time to treat comes not within or between the acts. It is the time before the play begins in which events took place which must be known as soon as the play opens, if auditors are to follow the play understandingly. Every dramatist, as he turns from his story to his plot, faces the problem: How plant in the mind of the audience past events and facts concerning the characters which are fundamental in understanding the play. The Chorus and the Dumb Show again were, among early dramatists, the clumsy solution of this problem.

[1] *The Influence of Local Theatrical Conditions upon the Drama of the Greeks.* R. C. Flickinger. *Classical Journal*, October, 1911.

THE PROLOGUE

In Troy, there lies the scene. From isles of Greece
The princes orgillous, their high blood chaf'd,
Have to the port of Athens sent their ships,
Fraught with the ministers and instruments
Of cruel war. Sixty and nine, that wore
Their crownets regal, from the Athenian bay
Put forth toward Phrygia; and their vow is made
To ransack Troy, within whose strong immures
The ravish'd Helen, Menelaus' queen,
With wanton Paris sleeps; and that's the quarrel.
To Tenedos they come,
And the deep-drawing barks do there disgorge
Their warlike fraughtage. Now on Dardan plains
The fresh and yet unbruised Greeks do pitch
Their brave pavilions. Priam's six-gated city,
Dardan, and Timbria, Helias, Chetas, Troien,
And Antenorides, with massy staples
And corresponsive and fulfilling bolts
Spar up the sons of Troy.
Now expectation, tickling skittish spirits,
On one and other side, Troyan and Greek,
Sets all on hazard; and hither am I come
A prologue arm'd, but not in confidence
Of author's pen or actor's voice, but suited
In like conditions as our argument,
To tell you, fair beholders, that our play
Leaps o'er the vaunt and firstlings of those broils,
Beginning in the middle, starting thence away
To what may be digested in a play.
Like or find fault; do as your pleasures are.
Now good or bad; 'tis but the chance of war.[1]

A growing technique led the dramatists from Dumb Show
and Chorus to soliloquy, in order to provide this necessary
preliminary exposition. Is Richard, Duke of Gloucester, at
the opening of *Richard III*, much more than a re-christened
Chorus?

[1] *Troilus and Cressida.*

ACT I. SCENE 1. (*London. A street.*)

Enter Richard, Duke of Gloucester, solus

Gloucester. Now is the winter of our discontent
Made glorious summer by this sun of York;
And all the clouds that lour'd upon our house
In the deep bosom of the ocean buried.
Now are our brows bound with victorious wreaths;
Our bruised arms hung up for monuments;
Our stern alarums chang'd to merry meetings, .
Our dreadful marches to delightful measures.
Grim-visag'd War hath smooth'd his wrinkled front;
And now, instead of mounting barbed steeds
To fright the souls of fearful adversaries,
He capers nimbly in a lady's chamber
To the lascivious pleasing of a lute.
But I, that am not shap'd for sportive tricks,
Nor made to court an amorous looking-glass;
I, that am rudely stamp'd, and want love's majesty
To strut before a wanton ambling nymph;
I, that am curtail'd of this fair proportion,
Cheated of feature by dissembling nature,
Deform'd, unfinish'd, sent before my time
Into this breathing world, scarce half made up,
And that so lamely and unfashionable
That dogs bark at me as I halt by them;
Why, I, in this weak piping time of peace,
Have no delight to pass away the time,
Unless to see my shadow in the sun
And descant on mine own deformity.
And therefore, since I cannot prove a lover
To entertain these fair well-spoken days,
I am determined to prove a villain
And hate the idle pleasures of these days.
Plots have I laid, inductions dangerous,
By drunken prophecies, libels, and dreams,
To set my brother Clarence and the King
In deadly hate the one against the other;
And if King Edward be as true and just
As I am subtle, false, and treacherous,

This day should Clarence closely be mew'd up
About a prophecy, which says that G
Of Edward's heirs the murderer shall be.
Dive, thoughts, down to my soul; here Clarence comes.

Led by Shakespeare, dramatists have come to understand that such information should, if in any way possible, be conveyed not by soliloquy but within the play itself. It should, too, be so incorporated with the text that it is acquired almost unconsciously by an auditor held absorbed by the immediate dramatic action.

Sometimes, however, it is well-nigh impossible thus to incorporate needed exposition with the dramatic action. For instance, a play depicted the fortunes of a Jacobite's daughter. All that is dramatic in her story as a young woman is predetermined by terrible scenes attending the death of her father, when she was a child of six. Somehow the audience must be made to understand very early in the play what these scenes were which made a lasting, intense impression on the child. That the young woman, when twenty, should recall the scenes with such minuteness as to make the audience perfectly understand their dramatic values is hardly plausible. To have some one come out of the past to reawaken the old memories is commonplace, and likely, by long descriptions to clog the movement of the act. Facing this problem, present-day dramatists, avoiding chorus, soliloquy, and lengthy description, have chosen to put such needed material into a division which, because it is preliminary, they have at will distinguished from the other acts as the Induction or more frequently the Prologue. The latter term is a confusing use. Historically, it signifies the single figure or group of figures who, before the curtain, bespeak the favor of the audience for the play to follow. Very rarely, the Prologue partook a little of the nature of Chorus, stating details that must be understood, were the play to have its full effect. Dramatists, feeling that the relation of this introductory division to the other divisions is not so close as are the inter-relations of the other divisions, have called this preliminary action, not *Act I*, but *Prologue*. A similar situation exists for what has been dubbed Epilogue. Historically, a figure from the play just ended, or an entirely new figure, strove, often in lines not written by the dramatist, to point the story or, at least, to win for it the final approval of the audience. Today, when a dramatist wishes to point the meaning of a play which he seems to have brought to a close, or to include it in some larger scheme, he writes what he prefers to call, not an additional act, but an Epilogue.

A dramatist should be very careful that what he calls Prologue or Epilogue is not merely an additional act. An act does not cease to be an act, and become a prologue or an epilogue, because its length is shorter than that usual for an act. True it is that most prologues and epilogues are short, but that is not their distinguishing characteristic. If they are brief, it is because the dramatist wants to move as quickly as possible from his induction or prologue to his main story, or knows that when the play proper is ended, he cannot with his epilogue hold his audience long. Not always, however, are prologues, or epilogues short. That of *Madame Sans Gêne*[1] has the same number of pages as Act II, seventeen. The Prologue of *The Passing of the Third Floor Back*[2] fills some sixty-two pages. The Epilogue of the same play covers fifty-six pages. An act in this play makes seventy-eight pages. In *A Celebrated Case*[3] the Prologue covers twenty-one pages; the subsequent acts run from eight to twelve pages each.

Nor is an act changed into a prologue or epilogue because the space of time between it and the other divisions is

[1] Samuel French, New York.   [2] Hurst & Blackett, Ltd., London.
[3] Penn Publishing Co., Philadelphia.

longer than between any two of them. Does an act cease to be an act and become a prologue or epilogue, when the space of time between it and the other acts is twenty-five years, or should it be thirty? The absurdity of making the use of the words Prologue or Epilogue depend upon the space of time between one division and another is evident. It is true that the Prologue of *Madame Sans Gêne* takes place nineteen years before the three acts which follow, but it concerns the same people. It might equally well be called Act I. *The Passing of the Third Floor Back* might just as correctly be announced as a play in three acts instead of "An idle fancy in a Prologue, a Play, and an Epilogue." Recently *A Successful Calamity* was stated to be in two acts, each preceded by a Prologue. Except for the novel appearance of the statement in the program, it might more correctly have been called a play in four acts. Little except the will of the dramatist settled that the last division of Pinero's *Letty* should be called an Epilogue. It occurs only two years and a half after the preceding act. It presents the same people. Similarly the Prologue to Tennyson's *Becket* might just as well be called Act I, except that this nomenclature would give the play six acts. In the stage version by Henry Irving, the four acts and a Prologue might correctly be called five acts.

The anonymous play, *The Taming of a Shrew*,[1] on which Shakespeare founded his farce-comedy of similar title, shows a good use of Prologue and Epilogue. By a practical joke, *Christopher Sly* the beggar is made to believe he is a Lord. As a part of the joke, the play is acted before him. Now and again, in the course of it, he comments on it. He and his group finish the performance in a sort of Epilogue. When Shakespeare uses Sly, only to let him shortly withdraw for good, the arrangement seems curiously incomplete and unsatisfactory. *Romance*, by Edward Sheldon, shows right use

---

[1] *Shakespeare's Library*, vol. VI. W. C. Hazlitt, ed. Reeves & Turner, London.

of so-called epilogue and prologue. As the curtain falls on the brief prologue, the aged Bishop is telling his grandson the story of his love for the Cavallini. Then the play, which is the Bishop's story, unrolls itself for three acts. In turn they fade into the epilogue, in which the grandson, as the Bishop finishes his story, goes off in spite of it to marry the girl he loves. By means of the epilogue and prologue Mr. Sheldon gains irony and contrast, relates the main play to larger values, and answers the inevitable question of his audience at the end of his third act: What happened to them afterward? Not to have used the so-called epilogue and prologue here would have forced total reconstruction of the material and probably a clumsier result. Such setting of a long play within a very brief play is one of the conditions for the legitimate use of the so-called prologue and epilogue.

Another legitimate use, though perhaps not so clear-cut, is illustrated by the Prologue to *A Celebrated Case*.[1] The play might, perhaps, be written without it, but, if it were, the scene of Act I in which Adrienne recognizes the convict as her father, would be filled with much more exposition, and the present emphasis on the powerful emotions of the moment would be somewhat blurred by the emotions called up by exposition of the past. Clearly, the play gains rather than loses by the presence of the prologue. Obviously the latter stands somewhat apart from the three acts which follow, less definitely related to them than they are to one another. So it may, perhaps, better be called a prologue than an act.

Of course, the distinction between prologue and act is a matter of nomenclature, not of effectiveness in acting. Look at *My Lady's Dress*, by Edward Knobloch. Scene 1, Act I, and Scene 3, Act III, have the same setting, a boudoir, and are more closely related to each other than to the rest of the

[1] Penn Publishing Co., Philadelphia.

play.[1] Indeed, what stands between are one-act plays making the dream of Anne. According to present usage, Mr. Knobloch could have called these scenes Prologue and Epilogue, and treated all that stands between as the play proper. That he did or didn't makes no difference in the acting. The growing use of the two words, Prologue and Epilogue, merely marks an increasing sense of dramatic technique which tries by nomenclature to emphasize for a reader nice differences which the dramatist discerns in the interrelations of his material.

To sum up, there is real significance, though present confusion, in recent use of the words, Prologue and Epilogue. The use rests on a fact: that sometimes a play is best proportioned, when it has at the beginning or end, or both, a brief division related to the story and essential to it, but not so closely related to any act as are the acts to one another. The names Prologue and Epilogue should not, however, be used interchangeably for acts. They should be kept for their historical use — verse or prose spoken in front of the curtain before or at an end of the play, in order to win or intensify sympathy for it. We should find different names for these divisions, — perhaps, Induction and Finale?

What should be the length of an act? There can be no rule as to this. Naturally, the work of the first and last acts differs somewhat from the intervening acts, whether one or three in number. While it is the chief business of the intervening acts to maintain and increase interest already created, the first act must obviously create that interest as swiftly as possible, and the last act bring that interest to a climactic close. The first act, because in it the characters must be introduced, necessary past history stated, and the story well started, is likely to be longer than the other acts. The last act, inasmuch as even at its beginning we are usu-

[1] Drama League Series. Doubleday, Page & Co., New York.

ally not distant from the climax of the play, is most often the shortest division, for as soon as the climax is reached, we should drop the curtain as quickly as possible. A glance at certain notable plays of different periods will show, however, that the length of an act most depends, not on any given rule, but on the skill of the dramatist in accomplishing what he has decided the particular act must do. In the Cambridge edition of Shakespeare's *Lear* (printed in two columns of fine type) the acts run as follows:

Act I..........	$9\frac{1}{2}$ pages
Act II.........	7 pages
Act III........	$6\frac{1}{2}$ pages
Act IV.........	$6\frac{1}{4}$ pages
Act V.........	$5\frac{1}{4}$ pages

Kismet, a play modeled on the Elizabethan, shows this division:

Act I..........	48 pages
Act II.........	33 pages
Act III........	$22\frac{1}{2}$ pages

For three plays of Richard Steele it is possible to give the exact playing-time: [1]

The Funeral		*The Conscious Lovers*		*The Tender Husband*	
Act I.....	30 min.	Act I...	33 min.	Act I ...	25 min.
Act II....	36 min.	Act II ..	28 min.	Act II ..	22 min.
Act III...	20 min.	Act III .	24 min.	Act III .	14 min.
Act IV ...	20 min.	Act IV..	28 min.	Act IV..	15 min.
Act V....	20 min.	Act V...	31 min.	Act V. ..	18 min.
Total, 2 hrs. 6 min.		Total, 2 hrs. 24 min.		Total, 1 hr. 34 min.	

Two recent plays divide thus:

Candida		*The Silver Box*	
Act I......	27 pages	Act I.......	27 pages
Act II.....	24 pages]	Act II......	27 pages
Act III....	21 pages	Act III	21 pages

[1] *Life of Richard Steele*, vol II, p. 368. G. Aitken. Wm. Isbister, London.

The plays just cited are of very different lengths: *Kismet* [1] took nearly three hours in performance; *Candida* [2] and *The Silver Box* [3] are so short that they force a manager, if he is to provide an entertainment of the usual length, to a choice: he must begin his performance late, or allow long waits between the acts, or give a one-act piece with the longer play. Yet it is noteworthy that in all these plays except Steele's, the first is as long as any other act, or longer, and the last act is the shortest. However, the only safe principle is that of Dumas *père* already quoted: "First act clear, last act short, and everywhere interest."

In proportioning the whole material into acts, it should be remembered, of course, that the time allowed for a theatrical performance ranges from two hours to two hours and three quarters. Five to fifteen minutes should be allowed for each *entr'acte* unless the usual waits are to be avoided by some mechanical device. Figure that a double-spaced type-written page takes in acting something more than a minute, though necessary dramatic pauses and "business" make it difficult to estimate exactly the playing time of any page. Speaking approximately, it may be said that a three-act play of one hundred and twenty typewritten pages will fill, with the *entr'actes*, at least two hours and a half. In apportioning the story into acts the first requisite is, then, that the total, even with the necessary waits between acts, shall not exceed the length of time during which the public will be attentive.

The length of each act must in every case be determined by the work in the total which it has to do. Since pre-Shakespearean days, the artistry of the act has been steadily developing. Until *circa*, 1595, what dramatists "strove to do was, not so to arrange their material that its inner relations should be perfectly clear, but to narrate a series of

---

[1] Methuen & Co., Ltd., London.
[2] *Plays Pleasant and Unpleasant..* Brentano, New York.
[3] *Plays.* G. P. Putnam's Sons, New York.

events that did not, of necessity, possess such inner relations. It is much to be doubted whether any thought of
such relations ever entered their heads." [1] Influenced particularly by Shakespeare, the drama from that time has
steadily improved in knowledge of what each act should
do in the sum total, and how it should be done. The act
is "more than a convenience in time. It is imposed by the
limited power of attention of the human mind, or by the
need of the human body for occasional refreshment. A
play with a well-marked, well-balanced act-structure is a
higher artistic organism than a play with no act-structure,
just as a vertebrate animal is higher than a mollusc. In
every crisis of real life (unless it be so short as to be a mere
incident) there is a rhythm of rise, progress, culmination,
and solution. Each act ought to stimulate and temporarily
satisfy an interest of its own, while definitely advancing
the main action." [2] Each act, then, should be a unit of
the whole, which accomplishes its own definite work.

Here is Ibsen's rough apportioning of the work for each
act in a play of which he was thinking.

Do you not think of dramatising the story of Faste? It seems to
me that there is the making of a very good popular play in it. Just
listen!

Act 1. — Faste as the half-grown boy, eating the bread of charity and dreaming of greatness.

Act 2. — Faste's struggle in the town.

Act 3. — Faste's victory in the town.

Act 4. — Faste's defeat and flight from the country.

Act 5. — Faste's return as a victorious poet. He has found himself.

It is a fine adventurous career to depict dramatically. But of
course you would have to get farther away from your story first.

---

[1] *A Note on Act Division as practiced in the Early Elizabethan Drama.* Bulletin of Western
Reserve University.

[2] *Play-Making*, p. 136. Wm. Archer. Small, Maynard & Co., Boston.

You perhaps think this a barbarous and inhuman suggestion. But all your stories have the making of a drama in them.[1]

In *The Princess and the Butterfly*,[2] Act I not only disposes of preliminary necessary exposition, but depicts different kinds of restlessness in a group of women at or nearing middle age. Act II does the same for a group of men, and in the proposed duel provides what later may be made to reveal to Sir George how much Fay Zuliani cares for him. Act III complicates the story by showing that Fay is not the niece of Sir George, and illustrates the growing affection between the Princess and Edward Oriel. Act IV reveals to Sir George and Fay how much each cares for the other. The fifth act shows how Sir George and the Princess, who have tried to be wise and restrained, impulsively and instinctively choose the path of seeming unwisdom but immediate happiness.

In *The Trail of the Torch*,[3] Act I states the thesis of the play and offers the first great sacrifice by Sabine for her daughter, Marie-Jeanne. Sabine gives up Stangy in order to be with Marie-Jeanne, only to find that her daughter is in love with Didier. Act II illustrates that a mother will make every sacrifice for her children: Madame Fontenais, the grandmother, when her daughter Sabine begs her to sacrifice her fortune in order that Marie-Jeanne's anxiety as to the finances of Didier may be set at rest, refuses, thinking to protect Sabine's future. In turn, Sabine, putting aside all pride, calls Stangy back to her, believing that he will give her the aid she desires for Marie-Jeanne. Act III shows the extremes of sacrifice to which a mother may go, — here the forgery, and the sacrifice by Sabine of her mother to her daughter. Act IV illustrates the retribution for Sabine: the revelation by Stangy that, after Sabine sent him away, he married; Marie-Jeanne's announcement to her mother that

[1] *Letters of Henrik Ibsen*, p. 236 ; to Jonas Lie.
[2] Walter H. Baker & Co., Boston; W. Heinemann, London.
[3] P. Hervieu. Drama League Series. Doubleday, Page & Co., New York.

she is to go to America with her father and that Sabine cannot go; and the death of Madame Fontenais caused, at least indirectly, by Sabine.

In all three cases we have only the baldest outline of what the act must do. The illustrative dramatic action by which each act is to accomplish its task is either in hand as part of a clearly defined story in the mind of the dramatist, or must be found immediately. Granted that it has been discovered (see chap. III, pp. 47–72), then as each act is shaped up from this material it should have certain qualities. It should be clear. It should lead the hearer on to the acts which follow: in other words, it should at least maintain an interest already established, and in most cases should increase that interest. To put these requisites more briefly, each act should have clearness and movement. Movement in an act means that, while thoroughly interesting itself, the act leads a hearer on to its immediate successor and, above all, the finale. Good movement depends on clearness and right emphasis. The emphasis in each act and in the whole play should be such that ultimately it accomplishes the purpose of the dramatist. How may these qualities, clearness, right emphasis, and consequent movement be gained?

CHAPTER VI

FROM SUBJECT TO PLOT: ARRANGEMENT FOR CLEARNESS, EMPHASIS, MOVEMENT

THE chief desideratum of a dramatist beginning to arrange his material within a number of acts already decided on is to create interest as promptly as possible. To that end neither striking dialogue nor stirring situation is of prime consequence. Clearness is. When an audience does not understand who the people are with whom the play opens and their relations to one another, no amount of striking dialogue or stirring situation will create lasting interest. The danger for a later public of allusive reference clear enough at one time is shown by the verses sung when the Helstone Furry, or Flower Dance, takes place in Cornwall. Lines once full of meaning are today so out of date as to be meaningless.

From an early hour the place is alive with drums and fifes, and townsmen hoarsely chanting a ballad, the burden of which conveys the spirit of the festival:

> With Hal-an-tow,
> Jolly rumble O,
> And we are up as soon as any day O,
> And for to fetch the Summer home,
> The Summer and the May O;
> For the Summer is a-come O,
> And Winter is a-go O!

The verses of the ballad seem to convey topical allusions that have become traditional. One speaks of Robin Hood and Little John as gone to the fair, and the revellers will go too; another triumphs in the Spaniards eating the gray goose feather while the singers will be eating the roast. Another runs thus quaintly:

God bless Aunt Mary Moses
   With all her power and might O;
And send us peace in merry England
   Both night and day O.
      With Hal-an-tow,
      Jolly rumble O,
And we were up as soon as any day O,
And for to fetch the Summer home,
   The Summer and the May O;
For the Summer is a-come O,
And Winter is a-go O!

Thus singing they troop through the town; if they find anyone at work, they hale him to the river and make him leap across; arrived at the Grammar School they demand a holiday; at noon they go "fadding" into the country, and come back with oak branches and flowers in their hats and caps; then until dusk they dance hand-in-hand down the streets, and through any house, in at any door, out at another; when night falls they keep up the dancing indoors. The character of the dancing is exactly that of the ancient Comus; and the whole spirit of the Cornish Furry is a fair representation of primitive nature festivals, except, of course, that modern devoutness has banished from the flower dance all traces of a religious festival; — unless a trace is to be found in the fact that the dancers at one point make a collection.[1]

The Greek dramatist, staging religious legends, could assume in his audience common knowledge as to the identity and the historic background of his figures which saved him much exposition. Today, readers of his play demand explanatory notes because of these omissions.

The *Choephori*, like the plays of Æschylus generally, consists of scenes from a story taken as known. Some indispensable parts of it are represented only by allusions. Others can scarcely be said to be represented at all. The history of Pylades belongs to the second class; that of Strophius belongs to the first. What is evident is that the author presumes us to be familiar with his conception of

----

[1] *Ancient Classical Drama*, chap. VII, "Elements of Comedy." Moulton. Clarendon Press, Oxford.

both, that as a fact we are not, and that our only way of approaching the play intelligently is by the assumption of some working hypothesis.[1]

Something like the position of these elder dramatists toward exposition is held today by writers of plays on George Washington or Abraham Lincoln. Dealing, as the dramatist ordinarily does, however, with a mixture of historical and fictitious figures or with characters wholly fictitious, he must in most cases carefully inform his audience at the outset who his people are, and what are their relations to one another, where the play is laid, and when.

Examine the first column of what follows: it is not a burlesque, but the beginning of a so-called play. Why is it unsatisfactory?

ORCHIDS

Conservatory of the Strones' house. Natalie is walking about among the flowers and plants, arranging them for the day in the vases on the near-by table.

Natalie. (*To herself.*) O-oh, I'm sleepy this morning. It's very nice to have your fiancé live in the next house, but when he insists on writing his stories and things until two or three in the morning — well, I don't think it's very thoughtful of him. He might realize that his light shines directly across into my eyes and keeps me awake. Oh, dear, Mary's been putting lilies-of-the-valley in all the vases again. I'll not have those everywhere when we've got orchids instead. Flowers don't need

Natalie. (*To herself.*) O-oh, I'm sleepy this morning. It's very nice to have your fiancé live in the next house, but when (Tom) insists on writing his stories and things until two and three in the morning — well, I don't think it's very thoughtful of him. He might realize that his light shines directly across into my eyes and keeps me awake. Oh, dear, (that maid's) been putting lilies-of-the-valley in all the vases again. I'll not have those everywhere when we've got orchids instead.

[1] *The "Choephori" of Æschylus.* Introduction, p. xvi. A. W. Verral. The Macmillan Co., New York.

fragrance anyway; they're just meant to be seen. (*Dumping the wilted lilies in a basket by her side and arranging the newly-cut orchids in their place.*) Tom [Who is Tom — brother or fiancé?] always makes a fuss when I have nothing but orchids, so I suppose Mary put the others about to calm him down. [Who is Mary, then: a maid, a sister, a girl friend, some one engaged to Tom?] Really I've got to speak to him about last night when he comes. The light is bad enough, but I won't have him firing his gun out of the window besides. It must have been at that horrid thin cat that's always clawing Hopeful. [A cat, a dog, or a small sister?] I'm glad *she* [Hopeful or the thin cat?] was locked up indoors if Tom's going to act that way. Oh, dear, these are the wrong shears again. (*Rings bell. Enter maid.*) Mary, bring me the other shears — and Mary, where's Hopeful this morning; I haven't seen her?

Mary. The kitten, Miss Strone?

Natalie. Yes, of course.

Mary. Why — why she hasn't been in this morning. (*Starts away.*)

Natalie. Come back, Mary. Don't run off while I'm speaking to you. Haven't you seen her at all?

Flowers don't need fragrance anyway; they're just meant to be seen. (*Dumping the wilted lilies in a basket by her side and arranging the newly-cut orchids in their place.*)
Tom always makes a fuss when I have nothing but orchids, so I suppose Mary put the others about to calm him down.

Really I've got to speak to (Tom Hammond) about last night, when he comes. The light is bad enough, but I won't have him firing his gun out of the window besides. It must have been at that horrid thin cat that's always clawing Hopeful.
I'm glad (Hopeful) was locked up indoors if Tom's going to act that way (with cats). Oh, dear, these are the wrong shears again. (*Rings bell. Enter maid.*) Mary, bring me the other shears — and Mary, where's Hopeful this morning; I haven't seen her?

Mary. The kitten, Miss Strone?

Natalie. Yes, of course.

Mary. Why — why she hasn't been in this morning. (*Starts away.*)

Natalie. Come back, Mary. Don't run off while I'm speaking to you. Haven't you seen her at all?

Mary. Well — yes, Miss Strone — that is Parkins [another maid, a butler, or a milkman?] found — I mean —

Natalie. (*Impatiently.*) Well?

Mary. The shots last night, Miss Strone — that is we think it was — although she *was* on the *other* side of the garden when Parkins came on her — and there's the wall and the alley between — still, Mr. Hammond was shooting out of the upper windows and —

Natalie. (*Quickly.*) Has anything happened to Hopeful?

Mary. Why — why, Parkins —

(*Enter Parkins.*)

Parkins. (*Quietly.*) I buried her all right just now, Miss Strone. (*Louder.*) Mr. Hammond.

> (*Exit* [*sic.*] *Mary and Parkins, enter Tom Hammond.*)

Mary. Well — yes, Miss Strone — that is (the butler) found — I mean —

Natalie. (*Impatiently.*) Well?

Mary. The shots last night, Miss Strone — that is we think it was — although she *was* on the *other* side of the wall when Parkins came on her — and there's the wall and the alley between — still, Mr. Hammond was shooting out of the upper windows and —

Natalie. (*Quickly.*) Has anything happened to Hopeful?

Mary. Why — why, Parkins —

(*Enter Parkins.*)

Parkins. (*Quietly.*) I buried her all right just now, Miss Strone. (*Louder.*) (Mr. Hammond.)

> (*Exeunt Mary and Parkins, enter Tom Hammond.*)

In the left-hand column practically every one in the cast is unidentified when first mentioned. That is, the text fails in the first essential of clearness: we do not for some time know who the people are and their relations to one another. The very slight changes in the right-hand column do away with this fault.

Identify characters, then, as promptly as possible. Writing, "John Paul Jones enters in full Admiral's uniform," a dramatist often runs on for some time before the text itself reveals the identity of the person who has entered. Except in so far as the costume or make-up presents a well-known historical figure, or information carefully given before the figure enters may reveal identity, every newcomer is an entirely unknown person. He must promptly make clear who he is and his relation to the story. The following opening of a play shows another instance of the vagueness resulting when this identification is not well managed:

ANNE — A PLAY IN TWO ACTS
ACT I

Evening of a June day. John Hathaway's Study. Door at right and at left back. Heavy, old-fashioned library furnishings. Walls lined with shelves of books. General disorder of books to produce the effect of recent using. Large flat-topped desk with a double row of drawers stands at front, half way between center and right wall. Desk is covered with books and loose manuscript. Chair at left front. Stool in front of desk. Other chairs toward back.

When the curtain rises, John Hathaway is seated at desk working. Anne enters at right, bangs the door, and stands with back to it.

Anne. I hate Aunt Caroline. (*She hurries forward to stand at opposite side of desk.*) Oh, I know what you will say — just preach and preach and call me "Anne" and tell me I must ask her pardon. — Why don't you begin?

John. (*Smiling.*) Now, Anne!

Anne. Yes, there's the "Anne." I know the rest without your going on: — "Aunt Caroline is a peculiar woman, but is *most* worthy. Her Puritanism keeps her from understanding your temperament, and you are too young to understand hers, —" and you'll go on preaching and smiling in that horrid way — you always do — and you'll make me see how wrong *I've* been and how saintly *Aunt Caroline* is, and at last I'll slink out of the room like a good little pussy-cat to find Aunt Caroline and beg her pardon. But it won't do *this* time, for I begged her pardon *before* I lost my temper so that you *couldn't* send me back. — Oh, Duke, *can't* we send Aunt Caroline away, and just you and me live here always together. (*She swings round the desk to sit on the stool at his side, her back to him. He turns a little in his chair, letting a hand fall on her shoulder.*) When Dad died, he left me with you because next to me he loved you best in all the world. Hundreds and hundreds of times he told me that. — It would have been very nice, Duke, if Dad hadn't died, wouldn't it?

John. Yes, Nan.

Anne. In just that one thing God has not been quite fair to me. Aunt Caroline tries so hard to make me think I am wrong about it. — I know you think so too, but you never argue about it with me. I like you for that, Duke. You see, if Dad had lived, our kingdom would have been complete. Why! a kingdom's only *half* a kingdom without a king.

John. That's true, — but there are still a few of us left. There's the Prime Minister, and the Countess, and the Slave, every one of them loyal to the Princess. Even the War Department is loyal — in warfare. Perhaps, who knows, some day from out a great foreign land a great king may come riding, and the Princess will place him beside her on the throne — and — live happily ever afterward.

Anne. (*Inattentively.*) Perhaps. Duke, did you ever think that the Prime Minister was very fond of the Countess?

John. Why, I have thought so at times.

Anne. And did you ever think that perhaps the Prime Minister would like to *marry* the Countess?

John. Why, yes, now you mention it, that also has occurred to me.

Anne. Well, why doesn't he?

John. Perhaps the Countess isn't willing.

Who is this "Anne"? What is her last name? Is she the niece of "Duke"? How could we learn from the text that "Duke" is John Hathaway? It is the stage direction which gives us that information. And what are we to do with this whole Burke's Peerage, — the Prime Minister, the Countess, the Slave? The author is depending for identification upon a list of *dramatis personæ* just preceding what has been quoted:

Time, present day.
Characters:
    Anne Chesterfield, "The Princess."
    John Hathaway, Anne's guardian, "The Duke."
    Caroline Hathaway, John's aunt, "Head of the War Department."

Doctor Stirling, a friend, "The Prime Minister."
Katharine Bain, a friend, "The Countess."
Tommy Bain, Katharine's young brother, "The Slave."
Professor Heinrich Adler, "The Foreign Ambassador."
James, a Servant.

Cut out this list of characters; in the stage directions strike out "John Hathaway," substituting "A man"; strike out "Anne," substituting "A young woman." At once it is clear that the dialogue reveals nothing about these people, except that a young woman who speaks is a niece of "Aunt Caroline." Yet these substitutions show what the scene looks like to a man entering the theatre without a program. Whenever such substitution of a type name for that of an individual in the titles prefixed to the speeches leaves the speakers unidentified, it is time to re-phrase the material for greater clearness.

Scenery and costume, of course, may show where the opening or later action of a play takes place. If these make clear the nationality of the speakers, or, at most, the province to which they belong, this is in many instances enough for any audience. In some cases, however, the nature of the plot is so dependent on the customs of a particular community that it is necessary or wise to make the text farther particularize any placing of the play by scenery or costumes. Simple interiors, too, are not always easily identifiable as of this or that province, or even country. If province or country at all determines the action of the piece, the text should help out the setting. One reason why the plays of Synge aroused bitter opposition was that some auditors believed them representations of life anywhere in Ireland and not, as they were meant to be, pictures of the manners of Aran Islanders, a group so isolated as to retain much savagery. Also, if the text is clear as to place, suggestion may take the place of realism in the scenery, thus decreasing expense. The emphasis on place in the opening of *The Rising of the Moon* both permits scenery that merely suggests a quay and plants in the minds of hearers a setting essential to the whole development of the play:

SCENE: *Side of a quay in a seaport town. Some posts and chains. A large barrel. Enter three policemen. Moonlight.*

Sergeant, who is older than the others, crosses the stage to right and looks down steps. The others put down a pastepot and unroll a bundle of placards.

Policeman B. I think this would be a good place to put up a notice. *(He points to a barrel.)*

Policeman X. Better ask him. *(Calls to Sergeant.)* Will this be a good place for a placard? *(No answer.)*

Policeman B. Will we put up a notice here on the barrel?

(No answer.)

Sergeant. There's a flight of steps here that leads to the water. This is a place that should be minded well. If he got down here, his friends might have a boat to meet him; they might send it in here from outside.

Policeman B. Would the barrel be a good place to put a notice up?

Sergeant. It might; you can put it there. *(They paste the notice up.)*

Sergeant. *(Reading it.)* Dark hair — dark eyes, smooth face, height five feet five — there's not much to take hold of in that — It's a pity I had no chance of seeing him before he broke out of jail. They say he's a wonder, that it's he makes all the plans for the whole organization. There isn't another man in Ireland would have broken jail the way he did. He must have some friends among the jailers.

Policeman B. A hundred pounds reward is little enough for the Government to offer for him. You may be sure any man in the force that takes him will get promotion.

Sergeant. I'll mind this place myself. I wouldn't wonder at all if he comes this way. He might come slipping along there *(points to side of quay)* and his friends might be waiting for him there *(points down steps)*, and once he got away it's little chance we'd have of finding him; it's maybe under a load of kelp he'd be in a fishing boat, and not one to help a married man that wants it to the reward.[1]

[1] *The Rising of the Moon*, Lady Gregory. *Contemporary Dramatists.* T. H. Dickinson, ed. Houghton Mifflin Co., Boston.

The period in which the play is supposed to take place, if of importance to the action, needs careful statement. Helped out by setting and costumes, the following shows that the play is taking place at the time of the French Revolution.

At rise of curtain, drums are heard beating, trumpets sounding the charge in the distance. A report of a cannon as the curtain rises.

Jennie. (*R., going up to door C.*) Did you hear that? It must be somewhere near the Rue d'Echelle now.

Julie. (*L. crossing to R.*) My! I'm frightened to death.

Marie. (*Carrots — up C.*) I only hope they won't come fighting down *our* street.

Julie. (*Kneeling.*) Bless us and save us!

Jennie. (*Up C.*) Down our street. What should they come here for? It's the Tuileries and the King they're after.

(*Going to window L.*)

First Neighbor and Omnes. (*At back.*) Of course they are. That's it.

First Woman. (*Up C.*) I tell you they're at the Carrousel.

(*Report of cannon.*)

Marie. It will be a mercy if they don't smash every pane of glass in the shop.

Julie. Well I shan't forget this 10th of August in a hurry.

(*At back a National Guard wounded in the leg supported by two other guards enters at L., is taken into the druggist's shop. All the people move towards the shop.*)[1]

Lapse of time between two acts, if important to the development of the plot, should also be clearly stated. Dramatists like to depend on the programs for such information, but they run the chance that many auditors will not see the printed note. Doubtless a program would give these words from the stage direction at the beginning of the fourth act of Hauptmann's *Lonely Lives:* "Time between 4 and 5 P.M.," but the quick passage of time is so important a fact in the development of the plot that six or seven pages later there is the following dialogue:

---

[1] *Mme. Sans Gêne*, Prologue, Scene 1. Sardou and Moreau. Samuel French, New York.

Braun. (*Looks at telegram.*) It is the six o'clock train that **Mr.** Vockerat is coming by? What o'clock is it now?

Mrs. Vockerat. Not half-past four yet.

Braun. (*After a moment of reflection.*) Has there been no change in the course of the week?

Mrs. Vockerat. (*Shakes her head hopelessly.*) None.

Braun. Has she given no hint of any intention to go?

In *The Galloper,* by Richard Harding Davis, what the audience hears will place the play in a hotel at Athens, even if the scenery does not:

Before the curtain rises one hears a drum-and-fife corps playing a lively march, and the sound of people cheering. This comes from the rear and to the left, and continues after the curtain is up, dying away gradually as though the band, and the regiment with it, had passed and continued on up the street.

Anstruther is discovered seated on the lower right-end corner of the table, with his right foot resting on the chair at that corner. He is reading the Paris "New York Herald" and smoking a cigarette. He is a young man of good manner and soldierly appearance. He wears gray whipcord riding breeches, tan riding boots, and Norfolk jacket of rough tweed. His slouch hat, with a white puggaree wrapped round it, lies on the table beside him. Griggs stands at the edge of the French window looking off left. In his hand he holds a notebook in which he takes notes. He is supposed to be watching the soldiers who are passing. He is a pompous little man of about forty with eyeglasses. He wears a khaki uniform similar to that of an officer of the British army, with the difference that the buttons are of bone. His left chest is covered with ribbons of war medals. Hewitt, a young man with a pointed beard and moustache, stands to the left of Griggs, also looking off left. He wears a khaki coat made like a Norfolk jacket, khaki riding breeches, and canvas United States Army leggings and tan shoes. On the table are his slouch hat and the khaki-colored helmet of Griggs.

Captain O'Malley enters right. He is a dashing young Irishman, in the uniform of an officer of the Greek Army. He halts to right of Anstruther and salutes.

Capt. O'Malley. Pardon, I am Captain O'Malley of the Foreign **Legion.** Am I addressing one of the foreign war correspondents?

---

[1] *Lonely Lives,* Act IV. *The Dramatic Works of Gerhart Hauptmann,* vol. III, p. 265. Ludwig Lewisohn, ed. B. W. Huebsch, New York.

Capt. Anstruther. Yes.

Capt. O'Malley. (*Showing him a visiting card.*) Pardon, is this your card?

Capt. Anstruther. (*Reading card.*) "Mr. Kirke Warren." No.

Capt. O'Malley. Do you know if Mr. Warren is in this hotel?

Capt. Anstruther. I couldn't tell you. We arrived in Athens only last night.

Capt. O'Malley. (*Saluting and moving off left.*) I thank you.

(*He exits left.*) [1]

But the dramatist prefaced this with a careful description of the setting. What has just been quoted shows that the dramatist risked no chance that what would probably identify this setting, — "Greek letters of gilt" on the picture frames, and the distant view of the Acropolis, — might fail him. He added what has just been quoted.

This scene shows the interior of the reading room in the Hotel Angleterre at Athens. It is large, cheerful-looking, and sunny, with a high ceiling. Extending nearly across the entire width of the rear wall is a French window, which opens upon the garden of the hotel. Outside it are set plants in green tubs, and above it is stretched a striped green-and-white awning. To the reading room the principal entrance is through a wide door set well down in the left wall. It is supposed to open into the hall of the hotel. Through this door one obtains a glimpse of the hall, where steamer trunks and hatboxes are piled high upon a black-and-white tiled floor. In the right wall there is another door, also well down on the stage. It is supposed to open into a corridor of the hotel. Below it against the wall are a writing desk and chair. A similar writing desk is placed against the rear wall between the right wall and the French window. On the left of the stage, end-on to the audience, is a long library table over which is spread a dark-green baize cloth. On top of it are ranged periodicals and the illustrated papers of different countries. Chairs of bent wood are ranged around this table, one being placed at each side of the lower end. Of these two, the chair to the left of the table is not farther from the left door than five feet. The walls of the room are colored a light, cool gray in distemper, with a black oak wainscot about four feet high. On the walls are hung photographs of

---

[1] *Farces,* "The Galloper," Act I. Richard Harding Davis. Copyright, 1906, by Chas. Scribner's Sons, New York.

the Acropolis and of classic Greek statues. On the black frames hold-
ing these photographs appear the names of shopkeepers in Greek letters
of gilt. The floor is covered with a gray crash. The back drop, seen
through the French window, shows the garden of the hotel, beyond that
the trees of a public park, and high in the air the Acropolis. The light
is that of a bright morning in May.

The test in deciding whether the place and the time should
be stated is not, "Has it been given in the program?" nor,
"May it with ingenuity be guessed from the settings and
costumes?" but, first, "Does place or time, or do both at
all determine the action of the piece?" secondly, "Will any
intelligent observer be vague as to place or time, as the play
develops?" If the answer to either of these questions is yes,
it is wisest to make these matters clear in the text.

Far more troublesome than merely identifying the characters or emphasizing the place and time of the play is showing the relations of the characters to one another. This usually requires exposition of past history which must be clearly
understood if the play is to have its full emotional effect.
More than one reader has been disposed to believe the theory
that *Macbeth*, as we know it, is a cut stage version because,
when Lady Macbeth first enters, she seems less prepared for
and less clearly related to the other figures than is Shakespeare's custom.

SCENE 5. *Inverness. Macbeth's castle*

Enter Lady Macbeth, alone, with a letter

Lady Macbeth. (*Reads.*) "They met me in the day of success;
and I have learn'd by the perfect'st report, they have more in them
than mortal knowledge. When I burn'd in desire to question them
further, they made themselves air, into which they vanish'd.
Whiles I stood rapt in the wonder of it, came missives from the
King, who all-hail'd me, 'Thane of Cawdor'; by which title, before, these weird sisters saluted me, and referr'd me to the coming
on of time, with 'Hail, King thou shalt be!' This I have thought

good to deliver thee, my dearest partner of greatness, that thou
mightst not lose the dues of rejoicing, by being ignorant of what
greatness is promis'd thee. Lay it to thy heart, and farewell."
Glamis thou art, and Cawdor; and shalt be
What thou art promis'd. Yet do I fear thy nature;
It is too full o' the milk of human kindness
To catch the nearest way. Thou wouldst be great,
Art not without ambition, but without
The illness should attend it. What thou wouldst highly,
That wouldst thou holily; wouldst not play false,
And yet wouldst wrongly win. Thou'dst have, great Glamis,
That which cries, "Thus thou must do, if thou have it";
And that which rather thou dost fear to do
Than wishest should be undone. Hie thee hither
That I may pour my spirits in thine ear,
And chastise with the valour of my tongue
All that impedes thee from the golden round
Which fate and metaphysical aid doth seem
To have thee crown'd withal.

The Dumb Show, Chorus, and Soliloquy are now outworn devices for setting forth necessary initial expository
facts. Today any experienced dramatist knows that such
preliminary exposition demands the art which conceals art,
for an audience resents a mere recital of necessary facts.
Examine the first act of Schnitzler's *The Lonely Way*.[1] All of
it is interesting for characterization and statement of facts
essential to an understanding of the play, but it does not
grip the attention as do the other acts where drama, not exposition, is of first consequence.

Early steps in advance on the Chorus were the butler and
the maid servant, garrulously talking of what each must
have known ever since he came into his position. A closely
related form is unbosoming oneself to a male or female confidant.

[1] *The Lonely Way*, etc. *Three Plays by Arthur Schnitzler*. Translated by E. Björkman.
Mitchell Kennerley.

ACT I

(Enter Hippolytus, Theramenes.)

Hippolytus. My mind is settled, dear Theramenes,
And I can stay not more in lovely Troezen.
In doubt that racks my soul with mortal anguish,
I grow ashamed of such long idleness.
Six months and more my father has been gone,
And what may have befallen one so dear
I know not, nor what corner of the earth
Hides him.

    Theramenes. And where, prince, will you look for him?
Already, to content your just alarm,
Have I not cross'd the seas on either side
Of Corinth, ask'd if aught were known of Theseus
Where Acheron is lost among the Shades,
Visited Elis, doubled Toenarus,
And sail'd into the sea that saw the fall
Of Icarus? Inspired with what new hope,
Under what favor'd skies think you to trace
His footsteps? Who knows if the king, your father,
Wishes the secret of his absence known?
Perchance, while we are trembling for his life,
The hero calmly plots some fresh intrigue,
And only waits till the deluded fair —

    Hippolytus. Cease, dear Theramenes, respect the name
Of Theseus. Youthful errors have been left
Behind, and no unworthy obstacle
Detains him. Phædra long has fix'd a heart
Inconstant once, nor need she fear a rival.
In seeking him I shall but do my duty,
And leave a place I dare no longer see.

    Theramenes. Indeed! When, prince, did you begin to dread
These peaceful haunts, so dear to happy childhood,
Where I have seen you oft prefer to stay,
Rather than meet the tumult and the pomp
Of Athens and the court? What danger shun you,
Or shall I say what grief?

    Hippolytus. That happy time
Is gone, and all is changed, since to these shores

The gods sent Phædra.
   Theramenes. I perceive the cause
Of your distress. It is the queen whose sight
Offends you. With a step-dame's spite she schemed
Your exile soon as she set eyes on you.
But if her hatred is not wholly vanish'd,
It has at least taken a milder aspect.
Besides, what danger can a dying woman,
One too who longs for death, bring on your head?
Can Phædra, sick'ning of a dire disease
Of which she will not speak, weary of life
And of herself, form any plots against you?
   Hippolytus. It is not her vain enmity I fear;
Another foe alarms Hippolytus.
I fly, it must be owned, from Aricia,
The soul survivor of an impious race.
   Theramenes. What! You become her persecutor too!
The gentle sister of the cruel sons
Of Pallas shared not in their perfidy;
Why should you hate such charming innocence?
   Hippolytus. I should not need to fly, if it were hatred.
   Theramenes. May I, then, learn the meaning of your flight? [1]

Another device is an intensely inquisitive stranger just returned from foreign parts who listens with patience not always shared by an auditor to any needed preliminary exposition.

The Opportunity,[2] by James Shirley, shows an ingenious adaptation of the device of the inquisitive stranger newly come to some city. Aurelio, a gentleman of Milan, coming to Urbino with his friend Pisauro, is mistaken for Borgia, who has been banished from Urbino. As one person after another, greeting Aurelio as Borgia, naturally talks to him of his past, his family, and what is to be expected of him now that he is returned, they identify and relate clearly to one another the chief people whom Aurelio is to meet in the play.

---

[1] *Phædra*, Act 1. Racine. Translated by R. B. Boswell. *Chief European Dramatists.* Houghton Mifflin Co., Boston.
[2] *Works*, vol. 3. W. Gifford and Dyce. Murray, London.

A hearer would take in almost unconsciously the needed exposition, so amused would he be at the increasing bewilderment of Aurelio.

Such ways and means as these three — the servant, the confidant, the stranger — Buckingham ridiculed in the late seventeenth century in his *Rehearsal:*

Enter Gentleman-Usher and Physician

Physician. Sir, by your habit, I should guess you to be the Gentleman-Usher of this sumptuous palace.

Usher. And by your gait and fashion,. I should almost suspect you rule the healths of both our noble Kings, under the notion of Physician.

Physician. You hit my function right.

Usher. And you mine.

Physician. Then let's embrace.

Usher. Come.

Physician. Come.

Johnson. Pray, sir, who are those so very civil persons?

Bayes. Why, sir, the Gentleman-Usher and Physician of the two Kings of Brentford.

Johnson. But, pray, then, how comes it to pass that they know one another no better?

Bayes. Phoo! that's for the better carrying on of the plot.[1]

Another method, talking back to people off stage, as one enters, in such a way as to bring out necessary facts, Terence both used and ridiculed centuries ago. This is his use of the device:

Enter Mysis

Mysis. (*Speaking to the housekeeper within.*) I hear, Archilis, I hear: Your orders are to fetch Lesbia. On my word she's a drunken reckless creature, not at all a fit person to take charge of a woman in her first labour: am I to fetch her all the same? (*Comes forward.*)[2]

---

[1] *The Rehearsal*, Act I. The Duke of Buckingham. Bell's *British Theatre*, vol. XV. London, 1780.

[2] *The Lady of Andros*, Act I. Terence. Translated by J. Sargeaunt. The Macmillan Co., New York; W. Heinemann, London.

In the last lines of the following he ridicules this very use:

Re-enter Lesbia

Lesbia. (*Speaking through the doorway.*) So far, Archilis, the usual and proper symptoms for a safe delivery, I see them all here. After ablution give her the drink I ordered and in the prescribed quantity. I shall be back before long. (*Turning round.*) Lor' me, but a strapping boy is born to Pamphilus. Heaven grant it live, for the father's a noble gentleman and has shrunk from wronging an excellent young lady. (*Exit.*)

Simo. For example now, wouldn't any one who knew you think you were at the bottom of this?

Davus. Of what, sir?

Simo. Instead of prescribing at the bedside what must be done for the mother, out she plumps and shouts it at them from the street.[1]

Lately the telephone, the stenographer, and most recently the dictaphone have seemed to puzzled dramatists the swift road to successful initial exposition. To all these human or unhuman aids some overburdened soul has felt free to say anything the audience might need to hear. Probably this use of the telephone has come to stay, for daily there is proof that nothing is too intimate for it. There are, however, more ambitious workers who, weary of servants, confidants, telephones, stenographers, and dictaphones, want to set forth necessary information so naturally that no one may question whether it might have come out in this way. Also, they want the information to be so interestingly conveyed that an auditor thinks of what is happening rather than merely of the facts.

In the first act of *The Second Mrs. Tanqueray,*[2] the audience must hear a narrative setting forth Aubrey Tanqueray's position in society, his first marriage, his relations with his daughter, and the nature of his proposed second marriage. What complicates the task is that the narrative must be

[1] *The Lady of Andros*, Act III.
[2] Walter H. Baker & Co., Boston; W. Heinemann, London.

told to old friends, so that much of it is to them well known.
What device will make the narrative, under the circumstances, plausible? Here is where a modern dramatist sighs
for the serviceable heralds, messengers, and chorus of plays
of decades long past or for the freer methods in narrative of
the novelist. How easy to tell much of this in your own person, as have Thackeray or Meredith, in comparison with
stating it through another so placed that he will be glad to
hear again much which he already knows! The necessity
creates with Sir Arthur the device of the little supper party
in Aubrey Tanqueray's chambers in the Albany, to which he
has invited four of his oldest friends. The moment chosen
for the opening of the play is when the old friends, over the
coffee, fall quite naturally into reminiscent vein. What helps
to freer exposition is their chance to talk of Cayley Drummle,
who, even yet, though bidden, has not appeared. Before the
chat is over and Cayley enters, much needed information is
in the minds of the audience. Cayley brings news of a terrible *mésalliance* in a family known to all the supper party.
In his efforts to advise and comfort the distracted mother he
has been kept from the meeting of old friends. The news
leads Aubrey Tanqueray to avow his quixotic scheme for a
second marriage. Through the contrasting comments of the
friends, even through their reservations, the audience becomes perfectly informed as to the view the world will take
of this second marriage. Indeed, as the supper party breaks
up, all the audience requires in order to listen intelligently
to the succeeding acts, is a chance to see Paula herself. Her
impulsive visit to Tanqueray, just after the supper party
ends, provides the information needed, for in it her character
is sketched in broadly as it will be filled out in detail in the
succeeding acts. Evidently device, the ingenious discovery
of a plausible reason for exposition necessary in a play, is
basal in the best stage narrative. Without it, character is

sacrificed to mere necessary exposition; with it, the spectator, absorbed by incident or characterization, learns unconsciously that without which he cannot intelligently and
sympathetically follow the story of the play. In other words,
successful discovery of devices for such exposition clearly
means that disguising which is essential to the best narrative
in drama.

The first quality of good expository device is clearness.
Secondly, it should be an adequate reason for the exposition it
contains: i.e., it must seem natural that the facts should come
out in this way. Thirdly, and of the utmost importance, the
device must be something so interesting in itself as to hold
the attention of an auditor while necessary facts are insinu-
ated into his mind. Lastly, the device should permit this
preliminary exposition to be given swiftly. It is hard to conceal exposition as such if the movement is as slow as in the
first two scenes of Act I of *The Journey of Papa Perrichon.*

ACT I

*The Lyons railway station at Paris. At the back, a turn-stile open-
ing on the waiting-rooms. At the back, right, a ticket window. At the
back, left, benches, a cake vender; at the left, a book stall.*

SCENE 1. *Majorin, A Railway Official, Travelers, Porters*

Majorin. (Walking about impatiently.) Still this Perrichon doesn't
come! Already I've waited an hour. . . . Certainly it is today
that he is to set out for Switzerland with his wife and daughter.
(*Bitterly.*) Carriage builders who go to Switzerland! Carriage
builders who have forty thousand pounds a year income! Carriage
builders who keep their carriages! What times these are! While I,
— I am earning two thousand four hundred francs . . . a clerk,
hard-working, intelligent, always bent over his desk. . . . Today I
asked for leave . . . I said it was my day for guard duty. . . . It is
absolutely necessary that I see Perrichon before his departure. . . .
I want to ask him to advance me my quarter's salary. . . . Six hundred francs! He is going to put on his patronizing air . . . make himself important . . . a carriage builder! It's a shame! Still he

doesn't come! One would say that he did it on purpose! (*Addressing a porter who passes, followed by travelers.*) Monsieur, at what time does the train start for Lyons?

Porter. (*Brusquely.*) Ask the official. (*He goes out at the left.*)

Majorin. Thanks ... clodhopper! (*Addressing the official who is near the ticket window.*) Monsieur, at what time does the through train start for Lyons?

The Official. (*Brusquely.*) That doesn't concern me! Look at the poster. (*He points to a poster in the left wings.*)

Majorin. Thanks. ... (*Aside.*) The politeness of these corporations! If ever you come to my office, you ... ! Let's have a look at the poster. ... (*He goes out at the left.*)

SCENE 2. *The Official, Perrichon, Madame Perrichon, Henriette*

(*They enter at the right*)

Perrichon. Here we are! Let's keep together! We couldn't find each other again. ... Where is our baggage? (*Looking to the right; into the wings.*) Ah, that's all right! Who has the umbrellas?

Henriette. I, papa.

Perrichon. And the carpet bag? The cloaks?

Madame Perrichon. Here they are!

Perrichon. And my panama? It has been left in the cab! (*Making a movement to rush out and checking himself.*) Ah! No! I have it in my hand! ... Phew, but I'm hot!

Madame Perrichon. It is your own fault! ... You hurried us, you hustled us! ... I don't like to travel like that!

Perrichon. It is the departure which is tiresome ... once we are settled! ... Stay here, I am going to get the tickets. ... (*Giving his hat to Henriette.*) There, keep my panama for me. ... (*At the ticket window.*) Three, first class, for Lyons! ...

The Official. (*Brusquely.*) Not open yet! In a quarter of an hour!

Perrichon. (*To the official.*) Ah! pardon me! It is the first time I have traveled. ... (*Returning to his wife.*) We are early.

Madame Perrichon. There! When I told you we should have time. You wouldn't let us breakfast!

Perrichon. It is better to be early! ... one can look about the station! (*To Henriette.*) Well, little daughter, are you satisfied? ... Here we are, about to set out! ... A few minutes yet, and then, swift as the arrow of William Tell, we rush toward the Alps! (*To his wife.*) You brought the opera glasses?

Madame Perrichon. Of course!

Henriette. (*To her father.*) I'm not criticizing, papa, but it is now two years, at least, since you promised us this trip.

Perrichon. My daughter, I had to sell my business. . . . A merchant does not retire from business as easily as his little daughter leaves boarding school. . . . Besides, I was waiting for your education to be ended in order to complete it by revealing to you the splendid spectacle of nature!

Madame Perrichon. Are you going on in that strain?

Perrichon. What do you mean?

Madame Perrichon. Phrase-making in a railway station!

Perrichon. I am not making phrases. . . . I'm improving the child's mind. (*Drawing a little notebook from his pocket.*) Here, my daughter, is a notebook I've bought for you.

Henriette. For what purpose?

Perrichon. To write on one side the expenses, and on the other the impressions.

Henriette. What impressions?

Perrichon. Our impressions of the trip! You shall write, and I will dictate.

Madame Perrichon. What! You are now going to become an author?

Perrichon. There's no question of my becoming an author . . . but it seems to me that a man of the world can have some thoughts and record them in a notebook!

Madame Perrichon. That will be fine, indeed!

Perrichon. (*Aside.*) She is like that every time she doesn't take her coffee!

A Porter. (*Pushing a little cart loaded with baggage.*) Monsieur, here is your baggage. Do you wish to have it checked?

Perrichon. Certainly! But first, I am going to count them . . . because, when one knows the number . . . One, two, three, four, five, six, my wife, seven, my daughter, eight, and for myself, nine. We are nine.

Porter. Put it up there!

Perrichon. (*Hurrying toward the back.*) Hurry!

Porter. Not that way, this way!   (*He points to the left.*)

Perrichon. All right! (*To the women.*) Wait for me there! We mustn't get lost!   (*He goes out running, following the porter.*)[1]

---

1 *Théâtre Complet*, vol. ii. Calmann Lévy, Paris.

The first scene undoubtedly helps to create the atmosphere
of a large railway station, but everything in it could be
brought out in what is now Scene 2. Even the way in which
Majorin is passed from one employee to the other could be
transferred to Perrichon. Every fact in Majorin's soliloquy
is either repeated in the scenes which follow, or could easily
be brought out in them.

What has made necessary this swifter preliminary exposition is, probably, the growing popularity of three or four acts
as compared with five. Less space has forced a swifter movement. Contrast, in the five-act piece *Une Chaine* [1] by Scribe,
the slow exposition in a first act of thirty-two pages with the
perfectly adequate re-statement in six and a half pages in the
one-act adaptation by Sidney Grundy, *In Honour Bound.* [2]

It is easy, however, to overload a first act with what seems
needed exposition but is not. Careful consideration may
show that some part may be postponed for "later exposition." Here is the history which lies behind Act I of Sudermann's *Heimat*, or *Magda.* [3] The famous singer, Dall'Orto,
who was Magda Schwartze, has returned to her native place
for a music festival. Ten years before she was driven from
home by her father, an army officer, because she would not
marry the man of his choice, Pastor Hefferdingt. Going to
Berlin to train her voice, she was betrayed by young von
Keller, a former acquaintance. After six months he deserted her. A child was born to whom she is passionately devoted. Von Keller is now a much respected citizen of the
home town, who lives in awe of public opinion. He and
Magda have not met since their Berlin days and he does not
know there was a child. Since his return to the town he has
kept away from the Schwartzes. Hefferdingt has remained
single, devoting himself to good works. Magda's father

---

[1] *Théâtre*, vol. ii. Michel Lévy frères, Paris.   [2] Walter H. Baker & Co., Boston.
[3] *Magda*, translated by A. E. A. Winslow. Lamson, Wolffe & Co., Boston.

nearly lost his mind from an apoplectic shock when he learned of her flight, but he has won back some part of his health through the wise and tender aid of Hefferdingt. There has been no communication between Magda and her family in the ten years. Now the younger sister Marie is engaged to the nephew of von Keller, Max, but the young people have not enough money to marry. They have been hoping that an aunt, Franziska, who caused Magda much unhappiness in the old days, will aid them. The narrow life of the town and the subservience of the Schwartzes to it had much to do with the rebelliousness of Magda as a girl. Through hard work and much bitter experience, she has won a supreme place in the world of music. She has developed a somewhat cynical philosophy of life which calls for complete self-expression, at any cost to others. She craves sight of her family again, and especially of Marie, a mere child when Magda left home.

Somewhere in the course of the play an audience must learn all these facts. How many of them must be set forth in Act I, and how many may be set apart for "later exposition"? Sudermann decided to postpone till Act II any detailed statement of the past relations between Magda and Hefferdingt. In Act I we learn only that he wished to marry Magda, and that there is anger in the family because of the way in which she refused him. What that was is not stated. Thus by giving mystery to these past relations of Magda and Hefferdingt, curiosity and interest are aroused and suspense created.

Of Magda's relations with von Keller we really learn nothing in Act I. We are, it is true, made to suspect that his admitted meeting with her in Berlin covers more than he is willing to reveal, and that his avoidance of the Schwartzes means something, but we learn nothing clearly until Act III. Not till then do we know a child was born and is still alive.

In other words, postponing detailed exposition of these matters provides the most important scene of Act II, that of
Hefferdingt and Magda, and the central scene of Act III
between von Keller and Magda. Note that deciding what
shall be preliminary and what later exposition has much to
do here, as always, with creating Suspense, a subject which
will be treated under Movement. A difficult task for the
dramatist is this determining what in the historical background of his play must be treated as preliminary exposition,
and what may be postponed for later treatment, when the
real action of the play is well under way.

Even when it is clear just what must go into preliminary
exposition the ordering of the details chosen is very important. Look again at *Magda*. It is love for Marie which, in
large part, draws Magda to her home, and at first keeps her
there. The love affair which Magda fled from seemed to her
conventional. Sudermann opens his play, therefore, with a
picture of the thoroughly conventional engagement of Max
and Marie, but remembering that the sooner a dramatist
creates interest the better, he starts with the mysterious
bouquet, far too expensive if sent by Max to Marie and
wholly unacceptable if sent by any one else. When Max,
entering, says that the flowers are not from him, there is
a chance to emphasize two points of importance: the lovers'
lack of money, and their fear of gossip. Meantime the fact
has been planted that there is a music festival in the town.
As the two young people talk of their need and the people
who might help them, we learn that the father thinks Magda's
departure was for some reason a "blot" on the family, and
that Hefferdingt wished to marry her. The call of von Keller
shows that since his return home he has been distant toward
the Schwartzes; that he is afraid of public opinion; and that
he met Magda in Berlin, "but only for a moment, on the
street." With the entrance of the father and mother we have

the petty social ambitions of the latter, and the tyrannical attitude of the former toward his family. The scene with von Klebs and Beckmann not only illustrates social conditions in the town, but begins to connect Dall'Orto with the lost daughter by showing the extraordinary interest of Hefferdingt in meeting the singer. The coming of Aunt Franziska with her announcement that the Dall'Orto is Magda ends the preliminary exposition, for with the arrival of Hefferdingt and his effort to bring Magda home, the real action of the play begins. Obviously much thought and care have gone into the re-ordering of these details, so that the facts which must be first understood are stated first and so that there shall be growing interest through the creation of more and more suspense.

In one of the early drafts of *Rosmersholm*, the opening page ran as follows. Note that there is no mention of any "white horses."

(*Mrs. Rosmer is standing by the farthest window, arranging the flowers. Madam Helset enters from the right with a basket of table linen.*)

Madam Helset. I suppose I had better begin to lay the tea-table, ma'am?

Mrs. Rosmer. Yes, please do. He must soon be in now.

Madam Helset. (*Laying the cloth.*) No, he won't come just yet; for I saw him from the kitchen —

Mrs. Rosmer. Yes, yes —

Madam Helset. — on the other side of the millpond. At first he was going straight across the foot-bridge; but then he turned back —

Mrs. Rosmer. Did he?

Madam Helset. Yes, and then he went all the way round. Ah, it's strange about such places. A place where a thing like that has happened — there —. It stays there; it isn't forgotten so soon.

Mrs. Rosmer. No, it is not forgotten.

Madam Helset. No, indeed it isn't. (*Goes out to the right.*)

Mrs. Rosmer. (*At the window, looking out.*) Forget. Forget, ah!

Madam Helset. (In the doorway.) I've just seen the rector, ma'am. He's coming here.

Mrs. Rosmer. Are you sure of that?

Madam Helset. Yes, he went across the millpond.

Mrs. Rosmer. And my husband is not at home.

Madam Helset. The tea is ready as soon as you want it.

Mrs. Rosmer. But wait; we can't tell whether he'll stay.

Madam Helset. Yes, yes.   *(Goes out to the right.)*

Mrs. Rosmer. (Goes over and opens the door to the hall.) Good afternoon; how glad I am to see you, my dear Rector![1]

In this version the "white horses" appear, definitely explained, after some sixteen pages:

Rosmer. . . . My former self is dead. I look upon it as one looks upon a corpse.

Mrs. Rosmer. Yes, but that is just when these white horses appear.

Rosmer. White horses? What white horses?

   (Madam Helset brings in the tea-urn and puts it on the table.)

Mrs. Rosmer. What was it you told me once, Madam Helset? You said that from time immemorial a strange thing happened here whenever one of the family died.

Madam Helset. Yes, it's true as I'm alive. Then the white horse comes.

Rosmer. Oh, that old family legend —

Mrs. Rosmer. In it comes when the night is far gone. Into the courtyard. Through closed gates. Neighs loudly. Launches out with its hind legs, gallops once round and then out again and away at full speed.

Madam Helset. Yes, that's how it is. Both my mother and my grandmother have seen it.

Mrs. Rosmer. And you too?

Madam Helset. Oh, I'm not so sure whether I've seen anything myself. I don't generally believe in such things. But this about the white horse — I do believe in that. And I shall believe in it till the day of my death. Well, now I'll go and —   *(Goes out to the right.)*[2]

In the final draft, Ibsen put the "white horses" into his

---

[1] *From Ibsen's Workshop*, pp. 271–272. Translated by A. G. Chater. Copyright, 1911, by Chas. Scribner's Sons, New York.

[2] *Idem*, pp. 288–289.

opening page. The beginning of this draft emphasizes particularly a grim, unexplained tragedy. The most mysterious touch in the new arrangement is given by the "white horses," here treated referentially, not in definite explanation.

(*Sitting-room at Rosmersholm; spacious, old-fashioned, and comfortable.*)
(*Rebecca West is sitting in an easy chair by the window and crocheting a large white woolen shawl, which is nearly finished. Now and then she looks out expectantly through the leaves of the plants. Soon after, Madam Helseth enters from the right.*)

Madam Helseth. I suppose I'd better begin to lay the table, Miss?

Rebecca West. Yes, please do. The Pastor must soon be in now.

Madam Helseth. Do you feel the draught, Miss, where you're sitting?

Rebecca. Yes, there is a little draught. Perhaps you had better shut the window.

(*Madame Helseth shuts the door into the hall, and then comes to the window.*)

Madam Helseth. (*About to shut the window, looks out.*) Why, isn't that the Pastor over there?

Rebecca. (*Hastily.*) Where? (*Rises.*) Yes, it's he. (*Behind the curtain.*) Stand aside, don't let him see us.

Madam Helseth. (*Keeping back from the window.*) Only think, Miss, he's beginning to take the path by the mill again.

Rebecca. He went that way the day before yesterday, too. (*Peeps out between the curtains and the window frame.*) But let us see whether —

Madam Helseth. Will he venture across the foot-bridge?

Rebecca. That's what I want to see. (*After a pause.*) No, he's turning. He's going by the upper road again. (*Leaves the window.*) A long way round.

Madam Helseth. Dear Lord, yes. No wonder the Pastor thinks twice about setting foot on *that* bridge. A place where a thing like that has happened —

Rebecca. (*Folding up her work.*) They cling to their dead here at Rosmersholm.

Madam Helseth. Now *I* would say, Miss, that it's the dead that clings to Rosmersholm.

Rebecca. (*Looks at her.*) The dead?

Madam Helseth. Yes, it's almost as if they couldn't tear themselves away from the folk that are left.

Rebecca. What makes you fancy that?

Madam Helseth. Well, if it weren't for that, there would be no white horse, I suppose.

Rebecca. Now what *is* all this about the white horse, Madam Helseth?

Madam Helseth. Oh, I don't like to talk about it. And, besides, you don't believe in such things.

Rebecca. Do *you* believe in them?

Madam Helseth. (*Goes and shuts the window.*) Now you're making fun of me, Miss. (*Looks out.*) Why, isn't that Mr. Rosmer on the mill path again —?

Rebecca. (*Looks out.*) That man there? (*Goes to the window.*) No, it's the Rector!

Madam Helseth. Yes, so it is.

Rebecca. How glad I am! You'll see, he's coming here.

Madam Helseth. He goes straight over the foot-bridge, *he* does, and yet she was his sister, his own flesh and blood. Well, I'll go and lay the table then, Miss West.

> (*She goes out to the right. Rebecca stands at the window for a short time; then smiles and nods to some one outside. It begins to grow dark.*)

Rebecca. (*Goes to the door on the right.*) Oh, Madam Helseth, you might give us some little extra dish for supper. You know what the Rector likes best.

Madam Helseth. (*Outside.*) Oh yes, Miss, I'll see to it.

Rebecca. (*Opens the door to the hall.*) At last! How glad I am to see you, my dear Rector.[1]

How a dramatist opens his play is, then, very important. He is writing supposedly for people who, except on a few historical subjects, know nothing of his material. If so, as soon as possible, he must make them understand: (1) who his people are; (2) where his people are; (3) the time of the play; and (4) what in the present and past relations of his characters causes the story. Is it any wonder that Ibsen,

---

[1] *Ibsen's Prose Dramas,* vol. v, Walter Scott, London; Chas. Scribner's Sons, New York.

when writing *The Pillars of Society*, said: "In a few days I shall have the first act ready; and that is always the most difficult act of the play"?[1]

What has just been said as to ordering the details in preliminary exposition is equivalent to saying: Decide where, in this exposition, you will place your emphasis. What a dramatist is trying to do will not be clear throughout his play unless he knows how properly to emphasize his material, for it is above all else emphasis which reveals the meaning of a play. Right emphasis depends basally on knowing what exactly is the desired total effect of the piece, — a picture, a thesis, a character study, or a story. Remember that Dumas fils said: "You cannot very well know where you should come out, when you don't know where you are going." Often, too, a play is either meant to set people thinking of undesirable social conditions, or to state a distinct thesis. With these two kinds particularly in mind, Mr. Galsworthy has said: "A drama must be shaped so as to have a spire of meaning."[2]

Whatever we make prominent by repetition, by elaborate treatment, by the position given it in an act or in the play as a whole, or by striking illustration, we emphasize, for it stays in the memory and shapes the meaning of a play for an auditor. In *Othello*, why does Shakespeare bring forward Iago at the end of an act as chorus to his own villainy? In order that the audience may not go astray as to the purposes of Iago and the general meaning of the play. Hence the soliloquies: "Thus do I ever make my fool my purse," as well as "And what's he, then, that says I play the villain?" It might almost be said that good drama consists in right selection of necessary illustrative action and in right emphasis.

Even though the general exposition of a play be clear, it

---

[1] *Letters of Henrik Ibsen*, p. 291. Fox, Duffield & Co., New York.
[2] *Some Platitudes concerning Drama. Atlantic Monthly*, December, 1909.

is sure, without well-handled emphasis, to leave a confused effect. When a play runs away with its author, its emphasis is always bad. The cause of this trouble usually is that the author drifts or rushes on, as the case may be, lured by an idea which he tries to present dramatically; or by the development of some character who, for the moment, possesses his imagination; or by the handling of some scene of large dramatic possibilities. In a recent play meant to illustrate amusingly a series of situations arising from the gossip of a small town, Act I so ended that a reader could not tell whether the school principal, a woman dentist, or the atmosphere of gossip was meant to be of prime importance. Nor was this poor emphasis ever corrected anywhere. Result: a confusing play.

A story-play in some respects of great merit failed in its total effect because the author never really knew whether it was a study of the deterioration of a young man's character or of a mother's self-sacrificing and redeeming love, a mere story-play, or a drama intended to drive home a central idea which, apparently, always eluded the author. Fine realism of detail, good characterization in places, and genuine if scattered interest could not carry this play to success.

In another play, Act I ended with the failure of a well-intentioned friend to take a child from her father for her better bringing-up. Apparently, we were entering upon a study of parental affection. In Act II, however, this interest practically disappeared, and we were asked to give all our attention to the way in which a son-in-law was bringing ruin upon this same parent. In Act III, another cause for anxiety on the part of the parent appeared, the other disappearing. At the end of the play, however, we were expected to understand that the fond parent was in sight of calm weather. Proper emphasis which would have brought out the central idea illustrated by each of the acts was missing.

In *The Trap*, a four-act play developed from a vaudeville sketch, lack of good emphasis went far to spoil an interesting play. In the original sketch, a woman, induced by lies of the villain, comes to the apartment of a man who has at one time been in love with her. She is determined to know whether what the villain has told her is true or not. All is a trap which the villain has set for her. From it the astuteness and quick decision of her former admirer rescue her. In the vaudeville sketch, it was the former lover who was the active person, — advising, scheming, and controlling the situation. When this was made over, in Act I the heroine was the central figure; in Act II the villain took this position away from her; in Act III the hero, as in the original sketch, had the centre of the stage; in Act IV there was an attempt to bring the heroine back into prominence, but she divided interest with the hero. As a result of this uncertain emphasis, the play seemed intended for the heroine but taken away from her by the greater human appeal of the hero. Just as the lecturer keeps clear from start to finish the main theme of his discourse and the bearing upon it of the various divisions of the work, the dramatist keeps his main purpose clear and also the relations to it of scenes and acts. This he does by well-handled emphasis. Othello, for instance, must have some proof which the audience will believe conclusive for him of Desdemona's infidelity. This is the handkerchief which Iago tells Othello that Desdemona gave to Cassio. Notice the iteration with which this handkerchief is impressed upon the attention of the public just before it is used as conclusive proof of Desdemona's guilt.

> *Othello.* I have a pain upon my forehead here.
> *Desdemona.* Faith, that's with watching; 'twill away again:
> Let me but bind it hard, within this hour
> It will be well.

Othello. Your napkin is too little;   (*Lets fall her napkin.*)
Let it alone. Come, I'll go in with you.
    Desdemona. I am very sorry that you are not well.

                    (*Exeunt Othello and Desdemona.*)

    Emilia. I am glad I have found this napkin;
This was her first remembrance from the Moor.
My wayward husband hath a hundred times
Woo'd me to steal it; but she so loves the token,
For he conjur'd her she should ever keep it,
That she reserves it evermore about her
To kiss and talk to. I'll have the work ta'en out,
And give it to Iago. What he will do with it
Heaven knows, not I;
I nothing but to please his fantasy.

                    (*Re-enter Iago*)

    Iago. How now! what do you here alone?
    Emilia. Do not you chide; I have a thing for you.
    Iago. A thing for me? It is a common thing —
    Emilia. Ha!
    Iago. To have a foolish wife.
    Emilia.   Oh, is that all? What will you give me now
For that same handkerchief?
    Iago. What handkerchief?
    Emilia. What handkerchief!
Why, that the Moor first gave to Desdemona;
That which so often you did bid me steal.
    Iago. Hast stolen it from her?
    Emilia. No, faith; she let it drop by negligence,
And, to the advantage, I, being here took't up.
Look, here it is.
    Iago. A good wench; give it me.
    Emilia. What will you do with't, that you have been so earnest
To have me filch it?
    Iago. (*Snatching it.*) Why, what is that to you?
    Emilia. If it be not for some purpose of import,
Give't me again. Poor lady, she'll run mad
When she shall lack it.
    Iago. Be not acknown on't; I have use for it,
Go, leave me.   (*Exit Emilia.*)

I will in Cassio's lodging lose this napkin,
And let him find it. Trifles light as air
Are to the jealous confirmations strong
As proofs of holy writ; this may do something.
The Moor already changes with my poison,
Dangerous conceits are, in their natures, poisons,
Which at the first are scarce found to distaste,
But with a little act upon the blood,
Burn like the mines of sulphur.[1]

Five times the handkerchief is mentioned. The first time the action is such that Othello specially notices the handkerchief. The second time we find another reason why the Moor should specially remember the handkerchief, and learn that Iago wants it for some reason of his own. The third time appears the iteration,

. . . that same handkerchief?

    Iago. What handkerchief?
    Emilia. What handkerchief!

and emphasis on the ideas already stated:

    Emilia. Why, that the Moor first gave to Desdemona;
    That which so often you did bid me steal.

The next time, the action, as Iago snatches the handkerchief and Emilia tries to get it back, holds it before our attention. Finally, Iago, left alone, tells us his malicious scheme in regard to it. Surely, after all this, the audience has been properly prepared for the scenes in which Iago deceives and enrages Othello by means of this very handkerchief.

In the first few minutes of the play, *Lady Windermere's Fan*, the attention of the audience is drawn to the fan:

    Lady Windermere. My hands are all wet with these roses. Aren't they lovely? They came up from Selby this morning.
    Lord Darlington. They are quite perfect. (*Sees a fan lying on the table.*) And what a wonderful fan! May I look at it?

---

[1] *Othello*, Act III, Scene 3.

Lady Windermere. Do. Pretty, isn't it! It's got my name on it, and everything. [Note the emphasis here.] I have only just seen it myself. It's my husband's birthday present to me. You know today is my birthday?

Lord Darlington. No? Is it really? [1]

Just before the close of the first act, it is with this fan that Lady Windermere points her threat against Mrs. Erlynne:

Lady Windermere. (*Picking up fan.*) Yes, you gave me this fan today; it was your birthday present. If that woman crosses my threshold I shall strike her across the face with it.

That Lady Windermere owns a fan; that it bears her name; that, as a gift chosen by her husband and recently given her, he must recognize it on sight: all these important facts have been planted by neat emphasis when Act I ends. Even in Act II, the fan is kept before the public. Just before Mrs. Erlynne enters, we have:

Lady Windermere. Will you hold my fan for me, Lord Darlington? Thanks.

. . . .

Lady Windermere. (*Moves up.*) Lord Darlington, will you give me back my fan, please? Thanks. . . . A useful thing, a fan, isn't it?

When Mrs. Erlynne enters, Lady Windermere "clutches at her fan, then lets it drop on the floor":

Lord Darlington. You have dropped your fan, Lady Windermere. (*Picks it up and hands it to her.*)

Such careful emphasizing makes sure that Lord Windermere's instant recognition of the significance of finding the fan in Lord Darlington's rooms, in the critical scene of the third act, will be immediately shared by any audience.

Mr. Augustus Thomas, in Act II of *As a Man Thinks*, wishes his audience to feel instantly the full significance of

---

[1] *Lady Windermere's Fan*, Act i. Oscar Wilde. J. W. Luce & Co., Boston.

the opera libretto picked up by Hoover, as he watches Elinor enter the apartment of De Lota. Therefore, earlier in the act he emphasizes as follows:

Elinor. (*To Burril.*) Here's a libretto of Aida. Find that passage of which you spoke.
Burril. There were several.
Mrs. Seelig. Our coffee won't interfere with your cigars.
De Lota. Do you mind?
Elinor. This room is dedicated to nicotine. (*To Mrs. Seelig.*) Besides, we're going to take Dr. De Lota to the piano.
De Lota. Are you?
Elinor. (*To Vedah.*) Aren't we?
Vedah. We are.
Burril. Here's one place. (*His pencil breaks.*) Ah!
Clayton. (*Offering a pencil attached to his watch chain.*) Here.
Burril. (*Giving libretto to Clayton.*) Just mark that passage — "My native land," etc. (*To Elinor.*) Now follow that when Aida sings Italian and note how the English stumbles.[1]

Two pages later, as Elinor goes out to the automobile, in order that the audience may see the libretto of which we have heard so much pass into the hands of De Lota, we have this:

Elinor. Take this for me. (*Hands libretto to De Lota.*)

Later in the act, when Judge Hoover is telling Clayton that he saw some woman with De Lota as he was entering the apartment, the dialogue runs:

Clayton. You spoke to him?
Hoover. *Called* to him.
Clayton. Called?
Hoover. Yes — I was forty feet away.
Clayton. Had your nerve with you.
Hoover. The girl dropped something — I thought it was a fan.
Clayton. Well?
Hoover. 'Twasn't — but that's why I called De Lota.

[1] Duffield & Co., New York.

Clayton. How do you know it wasn't?

Hoover. I picked it up.

Clayton. What was it?

Hoover. A libretto.

Clayton. What libretto?

Hoover. Don't know — but grand opera — I remember that and libretto —

Clayton. You threw it away?

Hoover. No — kept it.

Clayton. Where is it?

Hoover. Overcoat pocket.

Clayton. (*Pause.*) I'd like to see it. Think I could have some fun with De Lota.

Hoover. (*Going up the hallway.*) My idea too — fun and word ɟf caution. (*Gets coat and returns, feeling in pocket for libretto.*)

Clayton. Caution — naturally.

Hoover. Here it is. (*Reads.*) Aida.

Clayton. (*Taking libretto savagely.*) Aida — let me see it.

Hoover. What's the matter? (*Puts coat on a chair.*)

Clayton. (*In sudden anger, throws book.*) The dog! Damn him — damn both of them!

Hoover. What is it? Sée here — Who's with Dick?

Clayton. Not his mother — no! (*Points to libretto on the floor.*) Marked. *I* did that myself, not an hour ago, and gave it to her.

Hoover. To Elinor?

Clayton. (*Calling as he rushes to the hall.*) Sutton! Sutton!

Hoover. Hold on, Frank — there's some mistake.

Clayton. Get me a cab — never mind — I'll take Seelig's machine. (*Disappears.*) Here! Doctor Seelig says to take me to —
(*He goes out. Door bangs.*)

Sutton enters from the dining-room

Sutton. Is Master Dick in danger, sir?

Hoover. (*Nervously.*) I don't know, Sutton. Where's his mother?

Sutton. Opera, sir.

Hoover. With whom?

Sutton. Mr. De Lota.

Because of the emphasis given the libretto in the first quotation, the audience's suspicions are roused at the same time as Clayton's and his emotions are theirs. Yet, even in this last scene, note the care of Mr. Thomas to make all absolutely clear. He does not stop when Hoover says "A libretto," and "Of grand opera," but he lets the audience see the same libretto which passed from Elinor to De Lota pass from Hoover to Clayton, the latter identifying it in his cry, "Aida." That there may be absolutely no doubt in the evidence piling up against Elinor, he has Clayton point to the marked place with the words: "I did that myself."

Emphasis, as in these three instances, may come on some detail — handkerchief, fan, libretto — which is to be made important later in the development of the plot. It may come within a scene or act, or at the end of either to emphasize a part or the whole of the scene or act. The soliloquies of Iago referred to on page 183 are of this sort. Emphasis may stress little by little or with one blow what the play means. The significance of the whole play *Strife* — the utter uselessness of the conflict chronicled — is thus emphasized in the last lines of the play:

Harness. A woman dead; and the two best men both broken!

Tench. (*Staring at him — suddenly excited.*) D'you know, sir — these terms, they're the *very same* we drew up together, you and I, and put to both sides before the fight began? All this — all this — and — and what for?

Harness. (*In a slow, grim voice.*) That's where the fun comes in!
    (*Underwood without turning from the door makes a gesture of assent.*)
          The curtain falls [1]

The Second Mrs. Tanqueray [2] illustrates the play in which emphasis little by little brings out the meaning of the whole piece. Examine even the first act. It is full of the feeling: "It cannot nor it will not come to good." Tanqueray himself says frankly, "My marriage is not even the conventional sort of marriage likely to satisfy society." Drummle com-

[1] *Plays.* G. P. Putnam's Sons, New York.
[2] Walter H. Baker & Co., Boston; W. Heinemann, London.

ing in declares that George Orreyed is "a thing of the past," because he has married Mabel Hervey. The group of old friends show anxiety, and it is clear that to the mind of Cayley Drummle Tanqueray is but repeating the rash step of Orreyed. The whole act prepares for the finale of the play.

Hervieu's *The Trail of the Torch* shows the emphasis which strikes one hard blow and leaves to the rest of the play illustration of what has been clearly stressed. About one third of the way through Act I, Maravon explains to Sabine the thesis which the entire play illustrates:

Sabine. (Pointing to the two who have just gone.) Ah, my dear Maravon, what an absurd friend I have there!

Maravon. Mme. Gribert, you mean?

Sabine. Haven't you noticed that she is beginning to look like a governess? I suppose it's because she has been doing a governess' work for so long that she has ceased to have any personal existence. She no longer cares to possess anything of her own, everything belongs to her daughter, and her husband works his fingers to the bone to pay for Beatrice's dresses, while Beatrice lords it over both of them in a way that is beginning to be just a trifle odious.

Maravon. I'm afraid I don't agree with you, Madame. With naïvely natural beings, like these, I enjoy watching the family wheels function with such simplicity. People of this kind conform to the law which begins by demanding of the mother the flesh of her flesh, often her beauty, her health, and, if need be, her life, for the formation of the child. And then, for the profit of the newer generation, Nature exerts herself to despoil the old. She exacts without stint from the parents in the shape of labors, anxieties, expenses, gifts, and sacrifices, all of their vital forces to equip, arm, and decorate their sons and daughters who are descending into the plain of the future. Take my own case, for instance. There was the question of my son's position in life. Didier was able to persuade me very quickly that my property would be better placed, for the future, in his hands. To show you that Mme. Gribert and her daughter are merely following out a tradition of the remotest antiquity, if you can endure the pedantry of an old college professor, I will give you an example from the classics.

Sabine. Oh! Please do.

Maravon. You have probably never heard of the "Lampado-phories," have you? Well, on certain solemn occasions the citizens of Athens placed themselves at regular intervals, forming a sort of chain through the city. The first one lighted a torch at an altar, ran to the second and passed to him the light, and he to a third who ran to the fourth and so on, from hand to hand. Each one of the chain ran onward without ever looking back and without any idea except to keep the flame alight and pass it on to the next man. Then, breathlessly stopping, each saw nothing but the progress of the flaming light, as each followed it with his eyes, his then use-less anxiety, and superfluous vows. In that Trail of the Torch has been seen a symbol of all the generations of the earth, though it is not I, but my very ancient friend Plato, and the good poet Lucretius, who made the analogy.

Sabine. That is not at all my idea of family relations. From my point of view, receiving life entails as great an obligation as giving it. There is a certain sort of link which makes the obligations counter balance. Since Nature has not made it possible for chil-dren to bring themselves into the world, of their own accord, I say that it was her intention to impose upon them a debt to those who give them life.

Maravon. They absolve that debt by giving life in turn to their children.

Sabine. They absolve it by filial piety which has been the in-spiration of many deeds of heroism as you seem to forget.[1]

A recent editor of Hauptmann's *Gabriel Schilling's Flight* writes of it: "His analysis is projected creatively in the char-acters of the two women — Evelyn Schilling and Hanna Elias. What is it, in these women, that — different as they are — menaces the man and the artist Schilling? It is a pas-sion for possession, for absorption, a hunger of the nerves rather than of the heart. These modern women have aban-doned the simple and sane preoccupations of their grand-mothers; the enormous garnered nervous energy that is no longer expended in household tasks and in childbearing strikes itself, beak and clawlike, into man. But man has not

---

[1] *The Trail of the Torch*, Paul Hervieu. Translated by J. H. Haughton. Drama League Series, vol. XII. Doubleday Page & Co., New York.

changed. His occupations are not gone. He cannot endure
the double burden. That is why Gabriel Schilling, rather
than be destroyed spiritually by these tyrannies and exac-
tions, seeks a last refuge in the great and cleansing purity
of the sea.

'The modern malady of love is nerves.'"[1]

It is possible that all this may be derived from the play,
but the Berlin audience which watched its first night left
the theatre bewildered in more than one respect. There were
a half-dozen opinions as to what this ugly story of a very
weak man was meant to signify. Was it simply the tale of
a weak man? Was it meant to show, as Professor Lewisohn
thinks, that creation in an artist not naturally weak at first
may be killed if he is pursued by women selfish in their love?
Does the ending, however, show that Hanna is entirely selfish? Does the play signify that the man who chooses to follow women rather than his art is lost? Why is there so much
emphasis on the awesomeness of Nature on the island? Have
these conditions of Nature anything to do with Schilling's
death? If so, do they not mitigate the effect upon him of the
women? Lack of well-placed emphasis made *Gabriel Schilling's Flight* a failure, interesting as were the questions it
raised and masterly as is much of its characterization.

Too often young dramatists forget that the beginning and
the ending of acts and plays emphasize even when the author
does not so intend. As in real life, it is first and final impressions, rather than intermediate, which count most. An able
young dramatist complained that though he wished one of
his characters to dominate Act I she certainly failed to do
this. The trouble was that an attractive old gardener, the
character who took the act away from the young woman,
opened the play attractively characterized and closed Act I

[1] *The Dramatic Works of Gerhart Hauptmann*, vol. vi, Introduction, p. xi, Ludwig Lewisohn, ed. B. W. Huebsch, New York.

with effective speech and pantomime, when the woman was busy only with unimportant pantomime. The prominence unintentionally given to the old gardener emphasized him at the expense of the young woman.

For the value of openings in emphasizing the meaning of the whole play, see Tennyson's *Becket* as originally written, and as rearranged by Sir Henry Irving.[1] Tennyson's *Becket* begins with Henry and the future Archbishop at chess, talking of matters in state and church.

PROLOGUE

A Castle in Normandy. Interior of the hall. Roofs of a city seen through windows. Henry and Becket at chess.

Henry. So then our good Archbishop Theobald
Lies dying.
Becket. I am grieved to know as much.
Henry. But we must have a mightier man than he
For his successor.
Becket. Have you thought of one?
Henry. A cleric lately poison'd his own mother,
And being brought before the courts of the Church,
They but degraded him. I hope they whipt him.
I would have hang'd him.
Becket. It is your move.
Henry. Well — there. (*Moves.*)
The Church in the pell-mell of Stephen's time
Hath climb'd the throne and almost clutched the crown;
But by the royal customs of our realm
The Church should hold her baronies of me,
Like other lords amenable to law.
I'll have them written down and made the law.
Becket. My liege, I move my bishop.
Henry. And if I live,
No man without my leave shall excommunicate
My tenants or my household.
Becket. Look to your king.

[1] The Macmillan Co. publish both forms.

Henry. No man without my leave shall cross the seas
To set the Pope against me — I pray your pardon.
Becket. Well — will you move?
Henry.   There.   (*Moves.*)
Becket.   Check — you move so wildly.
Henry. There then!   (*Moves.*)
Becket.   Why — there then, for you see my bishop
Hath brought your king to a standstill. You are beaten.
Henry. (*Kicks over the board.*) Why, there then — down go
             bishop and king together.
I loathe being beaten; had I fixt my fancy
Upon the game I should have beaten thee,
But that was vagabond.
Becket.   Where, my liege? With Phryne,
Or Lais, or thy Rosamund, or another?
Henry My Rosamund is no Lais, Thomas Becket;
And yet she plagues me too — no fault in her —
But that I fear the Queen would have her life.
Becket. Put her away, put her away, my liege!
Put her away into a nunnery!
Safe enough there from her to whom thou art bound
By Holy Church. And wherefore should she seek
The life of Rosamund de Clifford more
Than that of other paramours of thine?
Henry. How dost thou know I am not wedded to her?
Becket. How should I know?
Henry.   That is my secret, Thomas.
Becket. State secrets should be patent to the statesman
Who serves and loves his king, and whom the king
Loves not as statesman, but true lover and friend.
Henry. Come, come, thou art but deacon, not yet bishop,
No, nor archbishop, nor my confessor yet.
I would to God thou wert, for I should find
An easy father confessor in thee.

Irving, transposing, takes us at once into the plotting of
the Queen against Becket because of her hatred for Rosamund and Becket's supposed protection of the King's mistress. A secondary interest in Tennyson's presentation becomes by this shifting first interest with Irving.

PROLOGUE

SCENE 1. *A Castle in Normandy. Eleanor. Fitz Urse*

Eleanor. Dost thou love this Becket, this son of a London merchant, that thou hast sworn a voluntary allegiance to him?

Fitz Urse. Not for my love toward him, but because he hath the love of the King. How should a baron love a beggar on horseback, with the retinue of three kings behind him, outroyaltying royalty?

Eleanor. Pride of the plebeian!

Fitz Urse. And this plebeian like to be Archbishop!

Eleanor. True, and I have an inherited loathing of these black sheep of the Papacy. Archbishop? I can see farther into man than our hot-headed Henry, and if there ever come feud between Church and Crown, and I do not charm this secret out of our loyal Thomas, I am not Eleanor.

Fitz Urse. Last night I followed a woman in the city here. Her face was veiled, but the back methought was Rosamund — his paramour, thy rival. I can feel for thee.

Eleanor. Thou feel for me! — paramour — rival! No paramour but his own wedded wife! King Louis had no paramours, and I loved him none the more. Henry had many and I loved him none the less. I would she were but his paramour, for men tire of their fancies; but I fear this one fancy hath taken root, and borne blossom too, and she, whom the King loves indeed, is a power in the State. Follow me this Rosamund day and night, whithersoever she goes; track her, if thou can'st, even into the King's lodging, that I may (*clenches her fist*) — may at least have my cry against him and her, — and thou in thy way shouldst be jealous of the King, for thou in thy way didst once, what shall I call it, affect her thine own self.

Fitz Urse. Ay, but the young filly winced and whinnied and flung up her heels; and then the King came honeying about her, and this Becket, her father's friend, like enough staved us from her.

Eleanor. Us!

Fitz Urse. Yea, by the blessed Virgin! There were more than I buzzing round the blossom — De Tracy — even that flint De Brito.

Eleanor. Carry her off among you; run in upon her and devour her, one and all of you; make her as hateful to herself and to the King as she is to me.

Fitz Urse. I and all should be glad to wreak our spite on the rose-

faced minion of the King, and bring her to the level of the dust, so
that the King —

Eleanor. If thou light upon her — free me from her! — let her
eat it like the serpent and be driven out of her paradise!

The story of Nathan Hale might be made into a play
with patriotism as its dominant idea, a close character study
of Hale himself, or little more than a love story. Notice the
way in which with Clyde Fitch the close of the acts steadily
emphasizes the love story as the central interest. The first
scene is in the school room where Hale is the teacher of
Alice Adams.

(*Hale goes toward Alice with his arms outstretched to embrace her;
Alice goes into his arms — a long embrace and kiss; a loud tapping on
a drum outside startles them.*)

Hale. The Tory meeting!

Alice. Fitzroy will be back. I don't want to see him!

Hale. Quick — we'll go by the window! (*Putting a chair under
the window he jumps onto chair; then leans in the window and holds
out his hands to Alice, who is on the chair.*) And if tomorrow another
drum makes me a soldier —?

Alice. It will make me a soldier's sweetheart!

Hale. Come.

> (*She goes out of the window with his help, and with loud
> drum tattoo and bugle call, the stage is left empty and the
> curtain falls.*)

The second act at Colonel Knowlton's house closes on
Hale's decision to serve his country as a spy:

Alice. (*In a whisper.*) You *will* go?

Hale. I must.

Alice. (*A wild cry.*) Then I hate you!

Hale. And I *love you* and always will so long as a heart beats in
my body. (*He wishes to embrace her.*)

Alice. No!

> (*She draws back her head, her eyes blazing, she is momenta-
> rily insane with fear and grief, anger and love. Hale bows
> his head and slowly goes from the room. Alice, with a faint
> heartbroken cry, sinks limply to the floor, her father hurry-
> ing to her as the curtain falls.*)

This is the close of Act III.

Fitzroy. Look!

> (*And he bends Alice's head back upon his shoulder to kiss her on the lips.*)

Hale. Blackguard!

> (*With a blow of his right arm he knocks Cunningham on the head, who, falling, hits his head against the pillar of the porch and is stunned. Meanwhile, the moment he has hit Cunningham, Hale has sprung upon Fitzroy, and with one hand over his mouth has bent his head back with the other until he has released Alice. Hale then throws Fitzroy down and seizing Alice about the waist dashes off with her to the right, where his horse is. Fitzroy rises and runs to Cunningham, kicks him to get his gun, which has fallen under him.*)

Fitzroy. Get up! Get up! You fool!

> (*Horse's hoofs heard starting off.*)

Third Picket's Voice. (*Off stage.*) Who goes there?

Fitzroy. (*Stops, looks up, and gives a triumphant cry.*) Ah, the picket! They're caught! They're caught!

Hale. Returning with Alice Adams on private business.

Picket. The password.

Hale. "Love!"

Fitzroy. Damnation! Of course he heard! (*Runs off right, yelling.*) Fire on them! Fire! For God's sake, fire!

> (*A shot is heard, followed by a loud defiant laugh from Hale, and echoed "Love," as the clatter of the horse's hoofs dies away, and the curtain falls.*)

Act IV has a double ending: the closing of the love story and the execution. The chief interest thus far created for the audience could end with the parting of the lovers.

(*The soldiers sing the air of what is now called "Believe Me If All Those Endearing Young Charms." Hale stands listening for the sound of Alice's coming. The Sentinel retires to the farther corner of the tent, and stands with arms folded, his back towards Hale. Tom comes on first, bringing Alice. As they come into Hale's presence, Alice glides from out of Tom's keeping, and her brother leaves the two together. They stand looking at each other a moment without moving and then both make a quick movement to meet. As their arms touch in the commencement of their embrace, they remain in that position a few moments, looking into each other's eyes. Then they embrace, Hale clasping her tight in his arms and pressing a long kiss upon her lips. They remain a few moments in this position, silent and immovable. Then they slowly loosen their arms — though not altogether discontinuing the embrace — until they take their first position and again gaze into each other's faces. Alice sways, about to fall, faint from the effort to control her emotions, and Hale gently leads her to the tree stump at right. He kneels beside her so that she can rest against him with her arms about his neck. After a moment, keeping her arms still tight about him, Alice makes several ineffectual efforts to speak, but her quivering lips refuse to form any words, and her breath comes with difficulty. Hale shakes his head with a sad smile, as if to say, "No, don't try to speak. There are no words for us." And again they embrace. At this moment, while Alice is clasped again tight in Hale's arms, the Sentinel, who has his watch in his hand, slowly comes out from the tent. Tom also re-enters, but Alice and Hale are oblivious. Tom goes softly to them and touches Alice very gently on the arm, resting his hand there. She starts violently, with a hysterical taking-in of her breath, and an expression of fear and horror, as she knows this is the final moment of parting. Hale also starts slightly, rising, and his muscles grow rigid. He clasps and kisses her once more, but only for a second. They both are unconscious of Tom, of everything but each other. Tom takes her firmly from Hale, and leads her out, her eyes fixed upon Hale's eyes, their arms outstretched toward each other. After a few paces she breaks forcibly away from Tom, and with a wild cry of "No! No!" locks her hands about Hale's neck. Tom draws her away again and leads her backward from the scene, her lips dry now and her breath coming in short, loud, horror-stricken gasps. Hale holds in his hand a red rose she wore on her breast, and thinking more of her than of himself, whispers, as she goes, "Be brave! be brave!" The light is being slowly lowered, till, as Alice disappears, the stage is in total darkness.)*

The second ending merely connects the play more closely with history.

Colonel Rutger's Orchard, the next morning. The scene is an orchard whose trees are heavy with red and yellow fruit. The centre tree has a heavy dark branch jutting out, which is the gallows; from this branch all the leaves and the little branches have been chopped off; a heavy coil

*of rope with a noose hangs from it, and against the trunk of the tree
leans a ladder. It is the moment before dawn, and slowly at the back
through the trees is seen a purple streak, which changes to crimson as
the sun creeps up. A dim gray haze next fills the stage, and through this
gradually breaks the rising sun. The birds begin to wake, and suddenly
there is heard the loud, deep-toned, single toll of a bell, followed by a
roll of muffled drums in the distance. Slowly the orchard fills with
murmuring, whispering people; men and women coming up through
the trees make a semicircle amongst them, about the gallows tree,
but at a good distance. The bell tolls at intervals, and muffled drums
are heard between the twittering and happy songs of birds. There is
the sound of musketry, of drums beating a funeral march, which gets
nearer, and finally a company of British soldiers marches in, led by
Fitzroy, Nathan Hale in their midst, walking alone, his hands tied
behind his back. As he comes forward the people are absolutely silent,
and a girl in the front row of the spectators falls forward in a dead faint.
She is quickly carried out by two bystanders. Hale is led to the foot of
the tree before the ladder. The soldiers are in double lines on either side.*

Fitzroy. (*To Hale.*) Nathan Hale, have you anything to say?
We are ready to hear your last dying speech and confession!

> (*Hale is standing, looking up, his lips moving slightly, as if
> in prayer. He remains in this position a moment, and
> then, with a sigh of relief and rest, looks upon the sym-
> pathetic faces of the people about him, with almost a smile
> on his face.*)

Hale. I only regret that I have but one life to lose for my country!

> (*Fitzroy makes a couple of steps toward him; Hale turns
> and places one foot on the lower rung of the ladder, as the
> curtain falls.*)[1]

Watch, then, the beginning and the ending of scenes and
acts, lest an unconscious and undesired emphasis result.

An important means of emphasis is contrast — in character, situation, and even dialogue. Melodrama has always
rested, in large part, for its definite emotional appeals on
sharply contrasted characters—the spotless hero, the double-
dyed villain, the adventuress, and the heroine so innocent

---

[1] *Nathan Hale*, Act IV, Scene 2. Clyde Fitch. Little, Brown & Co., Boston.

of the world as to provide unlimited dramatic situations. Recall the impetuous Julia and the gentle Sylvia of *The Two
Gentlemen of Verona*. If it be said that such direct contrasting
of dissimilar figures belongs more to the earlier plays of dramatists, this is not true. In *The Gay Lord Quex*,[1] contrast
of the old and the young roués, Quex and Bastling, helps to
make clear and to emphasize the point of the play. *The
Princess and the Butterfly*[2] largely depends upon contrast, —
among the restless women of Act I, the restless men of Act
II, between the Princess and Sir George, between the love
of Fay Zuliani for Sir George and that of Edward for the
Princess.

Contrast in situation was a great reliance with the Elizabethans and, even when very crudely used, remains popular
with the American public today. So much pleasure did the
Elizabethan derive from contrasted situation that he was willing to have it worked up as a separate sub-plot, at times very
slightly connected with the main plot. Take *The Changeling* of Middleton: the titular part, written for comic value,
deals with scenes in a madhouse; the other intensely tragic
plot of De Flores and Beatrice-Joanna is but slightly connected with it. Think of the grave-diggers in *Hamlet*, just
before the burial of Ophelia, and, above all, consider in *Macbeth* the consummate use of a contrasting scene, in the porter at the gate just after the murder of Duncan.

It is a sense of the value of contrasting situation which
produces the best dramatic irony. When in Scene 2, Act I,
of *Hindle Wakes*, we listen to Alan Jeffcote's father and
mother planning for his marriage, the fine dramatic irony
comes from the contrast we feel with the facts of his conduct, known to us from the preceding scene, which may
make his marriage impossible. Dramatic irony depends on
a preceding planting in the minds of the auditors of infor-

[1] Walter H. Baker & Co., Boston; W. Heinemann, London.   [2] *Idem.*

mation which makes what is true contrast sharply with what the characters of the particular scene suppose to be true. Contrast, then, underlies dramatic irony. An audience, feeling the dramatic irony of a scene, is put into a state of suspense as to how and when the blow they anticipate will fall. Evidently, then, emphasis by means of contrast, when it results in dramatic irony, makes for dramatic suspense.

Contrast may be used effectively in dialogue. The modern dramatist sometimes overdoes this use. Because he has observed that the greatest suffering of the strongest natures rarely finds expression in rich or varied speech, he tries to discover words which in their feebleness, their inappositeness, or their unexpected commonplaceness, contrast sharply with what a hearer feels is the intensity of the emotion behind them. This has given us in recent drama some dialogue unnatural in its tameness. This kind of contrast, however, when handled with real understanding, is extremely effective. In the parting of Laurie and the heroine in *Iris*,[1] the very commonplaceness of the details of which they talk shows that they do not dare to speak of what is really in their minds, and makes the best preparation for the sudden loosing of emotion by Iris in what would be ordinarily a simple request: "Close the jalousies!"

Except in our recent revival of Moralities for the delectation of moral Broadway, we are growing away dramatically from mere contrasting of types of character and from plays in which a serious and a comic plot are but loosely connected. Yet dramatists will always find contrast highly useful in emphasizing points of characterization and important values in the story. Moreover, any trained dramatist knows that when his audience has been somewhat exhausted by laugh-

[1] Pp. 143–45. R. H. Russell, New York. Also published by Walter H. Baker & Co., Boston.

ter or tears, a scene of contrasting emotional value is of the highest importance. By changing the focus of interest, it renews the power of response exhausted in the just preceding scene. As has been pointed out again and again, though it may be true that the drunken porter in *Macbeth* was funnier for an Elizabethan public than he is today, nevertheless his coming breaks the tension of the terrible murder scene and makes it possible even now to turn to fresh horrors with surer responsiveness. There is no space here to go into any satisfactory analysis of the basal relations between the serious and the comic, but every competent actor knows that frequently, if the full desired comic values are to appear, it is necessary to play a part, or all the parts, with great seriousness, even in a piece meant to be broadly comic for the audience. This is true not merely in some of Shaw's plays, — *Man and Superman, You Never Can Tell*, etc., but in many old farces and even in burlesque. In the contrast the audience makes between the seriousness of the characters in what they do and say and the attitude the dramatist creates toward them lie the real comic values. Often it is only on the flint of the serious that one may strike the most brilliant spark of the comic.

Emphasis is needed not only to keep clear the development of the story and its thesis, if there be any, but also to determine and maintain the dramatic form in which it is cast — farce, comedy, melodrama, and tragedy. If an audience is kept long in the dark as to whether the dramatist is thinking of his material seriously or with amusement, or if they feel at the end that the story has been told with no coördinating emphasis to determine whether it is farce or comedy or tragedy, they are confused and likely to hold back part of their proper responsiveness. As has been pointed out, it is more than doubtful whether the scene of the attempted suicide in what is otherwise a genuine comedy of character, *The*

Girl with the Green Eyes,[1] did not seriously hurt the effectiveness of the play for a great many people.

Here, again, beginnings and endings are of the utmost consequence. Notice the extreme care of Maeterlinck, at the outset of *Pelleas and Melisande*[2] to create a mood for his play. One is prepared for the tragic and the mysterious by the opening scene of the handmaidens washing the mysterious stain from the palace steps. An auditor has not heard ten speeches of Synge's *Riders to the Sea*[3] before he knows that the dramatist is dealing seriously with grim matters, that, in all probability, the play is a tragedy. Look at Rostand's *The Romancers*.[4] It is to be a graceful telling of a jest played upon two sentimental children by two fond fathers. The author must make clear early in the play that what may be tragic enough for the young people is to be fantastic comedy for any hearers. Could anything be better than the opening: these two children, on the wall between their homes, so reading *Romeo and Juliet* together that it is obvious that they are in love with being in love, nothing more? There is the perfect emphasis which establishes early the attitude of the dramatist toward his material, in this case making the play poetic comedy. Can any one feel much doubt what form of drama is *The Importance of Being Earnest?*[5] The first few pages show that dialogue is to count heavily as such. Evidently the mood is comic. As evidently, there is exaggeration. Thus we move from initial farce to the more broadly farcical mourning for the death of the supposititious Earnest and to the fateful black handbag. If the ending of *The Romancers* be played as it was in London, with the speakers of the last lines gradually fading from sight in the dimming lights,

[1] Act IV, Scene 2. The Macmillan Co.
[2] *Contemporary Dramatists*. Houghton Mifflin Co., Boston.
[3] J. W. Luce & Co., Boston.
[4] Translated by May Hendee. Doubleday, McClure & Co., New York.
[5] *Plays of Oscar Wilde*, vol. II. J. W. Luce & Co., Boston.

surely that emphasis must mean to the audience that it has been seeing a fantasy.[1]

However, as has been said, danger lurks in these places of easy emphasis, the beginning and the ending, for at times something effective in itself swings the emphasis the wrong way. In *Masks and Faces*.[2] two generations have shed tears over the woes of Triplet as meant for "real life," only to be somewhat rebuffed when, just before the final curtain, all the characters step out of the play for the "Epilogue," and so stamp it as "only a story after all."

In brief, unless some special purpose is subserved thereby, an audience should not long be left in the dark as to the form in which the dramatist thinks he has cast his play. He who treats his material in many different moods runs the chance of confusing his hearers. Only by sure and well-placed emphasis can he keep his chosen form clear. Particularly is this true in the mixed forms, tragi-comedy and farce-comedy. Only well-placed emphasis will carry an audience through these with just the result desired by the dramatist.

How decide what to emphasize? Tom Taylor, despising the intelligence of audiences of his day, used to say, "When you have something to say to an audience, tell them you are going to say it. Tell them you're saying it. Tell them you've said it. Then, perhaps, they'll understand it." Truth probably lies between this and the statement of a dramatist of today, "I am re-writing a play originally composed some ten years ago. Do you know what I am doing? I am cutting and condensing, because the intervening years have taught me that I may suggest where I thought I must explain in full, and state but once what I thought I must repeat. Audiences are far quicker than ten years ago I supposed them to be." Till the training of the dramatist gives him a kind

---

[1] *The Fantasticks*, pp. 145–146. Translated by George Fleming. R. H. Russell, New York.

[2] Samuel French, New York.

of sixth sense which tells him what in his plot needs emphasis for his public, he must depend on the comments of really intelligent hearers to whom he reads the manuscript and, above all, on retouching his play after the first performances.

It is not enough, however, by clearness and right emphasis to maintain interest: as the play develops, the interest should if possible be increased. Either to maintain or to increase interest means that a hearer must be led on from scene to scene, act to act, absorbed while the curtain is up and, between the acts, eager for it to rise again. Such attention given a play means that it has a third essential quality, movement. The plays of tyro dramatists today are often sadly lacking in good movement.

Good movement rests, first of all, on clearness; secondly, on right emphasis; and thirdly, on something already mentioned in connection with both clearness and right emphasis, — suspense. This means a straining forward of interest, a compelling desire to know what will happen next. Whether a hearer is totally at a loss to know what will happen, but eager to ascertain; partly guesses what will take place, but deeply desires to make sure; or almost holds back so greatly does he dread an anticipated situation, he is in a state of suspense, for be it willingly or unwillingly on his part, on sweeps his interest.

There should be good movement within the scene, the act, and even the play as a whole. It is, however, easily checked. If scenes or characters not essential are allowed place within a play, it has been shown on pages 87–89 that this may interfere with either clearness or good emphasis. They will hurt the movement of the play. Closely related as a possible danger are necessary scenes not well placed. Often shifting part of a scene or act makes all the difference between sustained and interrupted suspense. For example, a young man, after some quarrelsome words, threatens to shoot his sister.

As they stand facing each other, steps are heard outside. A group which enters brings about an amusing scene. Good as it is, it may kill the suspense created by those two tense figures, if it switches interest wholly or in large part from them. If it does, any effective picking up the scene between the angry brother and sister, when the visitors go out, may be impossible. On the other hand, so write the scene that the audience, never diverted in its attention to those two figures, feels that the moment the visitors leave the quarrel will be resumed with greater intensity just because of the interruption: then there will be no loss of tension. Just here lies the important point: suspense once created must never be allowed to lapse so long as to be lost. A scene for contrast or to renew the power of desired emotional response in the audience or to develop part of a correlated story may be introduced, but always what is put between something which makes the audience strain forward and its goal should leave it as eager, and preferably more eager for the solution.

A shift in order may do much to increase suspense. When Ibsen transferred Rosmer's confession, which is very necessary to the play, from Act II to the end of Act I, he greatly added to the suspense created by the first act. To put it differently, he greatly accelerated the movement of the play. An audience, knowing that Rosmer is "an apostate from the faith of his fathers," eagerly desires to see what will happen to him in such surroundings as those made clear in Act I. In the earlier version, a reader learns that there are mysteries which the play will probably solve, but has nothing on which to focus his attention as a compelling element of suspense.

Any one knows that when an actor fails to come on at the right moment, unless quick-witted actors invent dialogue or action, the stage "waits" for the actor. There is something which exactly corresponds to this in the text of plays. Henry

Le Barron comes to call on Madge Ellsworth. The maid, after showing him into the library, goes to find her mistress. "*Meanwhile Henry looks idly at the books on the table till Madge enters.*" Unless Madge, perfectly sure that Henry would call at this hour, is waiting just outside the door, some action is needed on the stage to cover the time space until she can enter naturally. It is true that looking at the books fills the time for Henry, but it does not sustain for the audience interest already created in him or the story. When nothing is taking place on the stage, something is taking place in the audience which greatly concerns the dramatist: it is slipping away from him because it is losing interest. For contrast, suppose that Henry sits restlessly only a moment, then with a sigh picks up a book, tries to read, falls to dreaming, and holds the book so that we may see he is reading it upside down. He tries another book in vain. He starts three or four times, thinking that the door is about to open. He absent-mindedly examines a piece of bric-à-brac. He starts forward eagerly the moment Madge enters. Now we are interested, because he is either exhibiting emotions the cause of which we understand, emotions which lead us to expect an interesting scene between him and Madge, or his conduct sets us guessing as to what can lie ahead between the two. In the first illustration, the play lacks movement; in the second, commonplace as it is, the movement does not cease.

At times it helps suspense not only to shift the order of details but to separate two elements of suspense, treating them separately in well correlated groups. In *Hamlet*, Q1, the soliloquy, "To be, or not to be" precedes the meeting of Ophelia and Hamlet, part of Hamlet's tricking of Polonius, and the coming of Rosencrantz and Guildenstern. The greater part of the befuddling of Polonius then follows. The players enter and plan with Hamlet the performance of *The Mousetrap*. Hamlet, left alone, bursts into the solilo-

quy, "Why what a dunghill idiot slave am I!" Q2 rearranges
thus: Polonius and Hamlet; Rosencrantz and Guildenstern;
Polonius returning to announce the players; the planning
for *The Mousetrap;* Hamlet left alone crying, "Oh what a
rogue and peasant's slave am I!" Here all the details bearing on the play are gathered together. Next come the King
and Queen with their plot to try out Hamlet by means of
Ophelia. The soliloquy, "To be, or not to be" follows this.
Then Hamlet and Ophelia have the scene "To a nunnery go!"
Instead of jumbling two elements of suspense, — probable
results of the play planned by Hamlet and of the Ophelia-
Hamlet interest, — each is given added suspense by separate treatment. In Q1, as we shift from one to the other, each
weakens the other or is momentarily blocked by it. Rearranged, the very order of the details in each part makes not
only for clearer but stronger suspense.[1]

Today a plot made up of two or three but slightly related stories is far less popular than in the days of Queen
Elizabeth. Our public demands that such stories shall be so
correlated within the play as to be mutually helpful. This
desire results not from innate niceness of feeling for unity
of design but from dislike of a distribution of interests which
interferes with the suspense each story creates. Though it is,
of course, possible perfectly to maintain suspense in plays
of interwoven plots — the plays of Shakespeare and many
writers since prove this — it is far more difficult than main-
taining suspense in a play of single plot. Quite possibly this
is the chief reason for the great popularity today of plays
of single plot: they are both easier to follow and easier to
write.

A related fault which interferes with suspense is the "stage
wait" treated on page 209. As has also been pointed out,
there is danger in transitional scenes meant to cover a time

---

[1] *The Devonshire Hamlets,* pp. 34–46. Sampson Low, Son & Co., London.

space or to shift the interest of an audience. If they accomplish either purpose and do not advance the plot, they really fail. Bulwer-Lytton met this difficulty in writing *Money:*

> I think in the first 3 acts you will find little to alter. But in Act 4 — the 2 scene with Lady B. & Clara — & Joke & the Tradesman don't help on the Plot much — they were wanted, however, especially the last to give time for change of dress & smooth the lapse of the theme from money to dinner; you will see if this part requires any amendment.[1]

Also exposition, undoubtedly necessary but delayed too long, may so clog an act as to weaken or kill it. In a play set in what was once a fashionable dining-room, but is now the fitting-room of a dressmaker, the scene is not placed for some time. Finally, a figure entering makes clear the supposed setting, but for this the action on stage has to be broken off.

The increasing popularity of a play of three or four acts as compared with five has almost wholly done away with another destroyer of suspense — the explanatory and adjusting last act. In it, intelligent auditors who knew from the close of the fourth act how the story must end were expected to watch with interest final disposition of the characters. Dramatists of the eighties and nineties turned from this use slowly. For proof examine the last act of *The Hypocrites*, by H. A. Jones, in other respects a play well away from the older methods of technique. Now, both the older and the younger generation of dramatists expect to carry suspense as near the end of the play as they possibly can. Letting an audience anticipate something of the end of a play is all very well, but when it foresees just what is going to happen and has no farther interest, except to learn whether it happens exactly as anticipated, suspense and even attention cease. In that

[1] *Letters of Bulwer-Lytton to Macready*, LXIII. Brander Matthews, ed.

case an audience begins to gather its belongings for departure. Something held back which cannot surely be anticipated is the very basis of suspense.

It follows from what has just been said that there can never be perfect suspense when the plot ends an act or more before the final curtain. It is vain to try to start new interests in order to create fresh suspense. Unless the latter part of a play grows out of the first, at least as much as the Perdita-Florizel story grows out of that of Leontes and Hermione, there can be no good suspense. When it seems necessary to tack on new material because all suspense is ended, do not add: rewrite.

It has often been said that surprise — springing something unexpectedly upon an audience — is better than suspense. Lessing said of the comparative value of surprise and suspense:

For one instance where it is useful to conceal from the spectator an important event until it has taken place there are ten and more where interest demands the very contrary. By means of secrecy a poet effects a short surprise, but in what enduring disquietude could he have maintained us if he had made no secret about it! Whoever is struck down in a moment, I can only pity for a moment. But how if I expect the blow, how if I see the storm brewing and threatening for some time about my head or his? For my part none of the personages need know each other if only the spectator knows them all. Nay I would even maintain that the subject which requires such secrecy is a thankless subject, that the plot in which we have to make recourse to it is not as good as that in which we could have done without it. It will never give occasion for anything great. We shall be obliged to occupy ourselves with preparations that are either too dark or too clear, the whole poem becomes a collection of little artistic tricks by means of which we effect nothing more than a short surprise. If on the contrary everything that concerns the personages is known, I see in this knowledge the source of the most violent emotions. Why have certain monologues such a great effect? Because they acquaint me with the secret intentions of the speaker and this confidence at once fills me with hope or fear. If the condition of the personages is unknown, the spectator cannot interest himself more vividly in the action than the personages. But the interest would be doubled for the spectator if light is thrown on the matter, and he feels that action and speech would be quite otherwise if the personages knew one another.

Only then I shall scarcely be able to await what is to become of them when I am able to compare that which they really are with that which they do or would do.[1]

Look at the quotation from the *First Part of Henry VI* on Pp. 97–100. Talbot whispers to the Captain, and leaves us guessing what he means to do at his meeting with the Countess of Auvergne. In like manner the Countess merely refers to the plot she has laid with her Porter. We never know just what was the plan of the Countess. We get only a momentary sensation, surprise, when Talbot's soldiers force their way in. Suppose we had been allowed to know the plans of the Countess, and they had seemed very dangerous for Talbot. Then, as she played with him, sure of her position, there would have been more suspense than in Shakespeare's text, because an audience would have been wondering, not merely "What is the blow Talbot will strike?" but "Can any blow he will strike overcome the seemingly effective plans of the Countess?" Suppose we had been allowed to know the plans of both. Then, as we watched the Countess playing her scheme off against the plan of Talbot, of which she would be unaware, might there not easily be even more suspense? At every turn of their dialogue we should be wondering: "Why does not Talbot strike now? Can he save the situation, if he delays? With all this against him, can he save it in any case?" In the use of surprise, the dramatist depends almost entirely on his situation. Suspense permits him to elaborate his situation by means of the characters in it. In other words, surprise is situation, suspense is characterization.

On this matter recent words of William Archer seem final:

[1] *Hamburg Dramaturgy*, p. 377. Lessing. Bohn, ed.

Curiosity [I said] is the accidental relish of a single night; whereas the essential and abiding pleasure of the theatre lies in foreknowledge. In relation to the characters of the drama, the audience are as gods looking before and after. Sitting in the theatre, we taste, for a moment, the glory of omniscience. With vision unsealed, we watch the gropings of purblind mortals after happiness and smile at their stumblings, their blunders, their futile quests, their misplaced exultations, their groundless panics. To keep a secret from us is to reduce us to their level, and deprive us of our clairvoyant aloofness. There may be a pleasure in that too; we may join with zest in the game of blind-man's-buff; but the theatre is in its essence a place where we are privileged to take off the bandage we wear in daily life, and to contemplate, with laughter or with tears, the blindfold gambols of our neighbors.[1]

What is basal in suspense is, of course, that an audience shall feel for some person or persons of the play just the degree of sympathy the dramatist desires. Unless their sympathy is as keen as his, the scene must fall short emotionally. For instance, in a play produced some years ago author and actors expected the audience to sympathize throughout with a mother. At the climax of one of the acts she was left on-stage in an agonized state of mind because her husband, who hates her illegitimate child, has left the stage with threats to kill it. The actress wrote of the first night: "In that scene I might as well have recited the alphabet for all the audience cared for my emotion. Their sympathy made them live, not with me, but with the defenceless child who at any moment might be murdered off-stage by the cruel father." Suspense for the audience there certainly was, but not of the kind intended. It was necessary to rewrite the scene.

Evidently, what happens off-stage may, by its greater interest for the audience, kill the effect of what is passing on-stage. What the dramatist dares not try to represent on-stage because of its mechanical difficulty or horror, he tries to carry off by vivid and even terrifying description. By

[1] *Play-Making*, pp. 171–172. William Archer. Small, Maynard & Co., Boston.

making the audience see the off-stage action through the eyes of the person most affected, or by portraying vividly his emotions when another describes the action to him, dramatists endeavor to lose none of their desired suspense. The point to remember is that the moment the off-stage action becomes of more importance than the emotions caused by that action for persons on-stage, the real centre of interest has been shifted, the desired suspense is gone, and the scene must be rewritten. Suspense in a play is rightly handled, then, when it is promptly created to the extent desired by the dramatist; carries on with increasing intensity from act to act; and reaches its climax at or just before the final curtain.

Climax is, therefore, an integral part of suspense. The point of greatest intensity reached in an incident, scene, act, or play is the moment of climax. Climax is not the result of theory but comes from long observation of audiences. A scene or act which breaks off or declines in interest towards its close never delights an audience as does a scene or act which closes with its strongest emotional effect. Look at the ending of *The Troublesome Raigne of King John, Part I*. Though King John declares himself "the joyfulst man alive," the audience does not so sympathize with him that his delight is a fitting climax to the play. Rather do they so keenly sympathize with Prince Arthur and even the lords who have been outraged by Arthur's proposed death that they want to know more of him and them.

> *Hubert.* My lord, attend the happie tale I tell,
> For heauens health send Sathan packing hence
> That instigates your Highnes to despaire.
> If Arthurs death be dismall to be heard,
> Bandie the newes for rumors of vnthruth:
> He liues my Lord, the sweetest youth aliue,
> In health, with eyesight, not a hair amisse.
> This hart tooke vigor from this froward hand,
> Making it weake to execute your charge.

Iohn. What, liues he! Then sweete hope come home agen,
Chase hence despaire, the purueyor for hell.
Hye Hubert, tell these tidings to my Lords
That throb in passions for yong Arthurs death:
Hence Hubert, stay not till thou hast reueald
The wished newes of Arthurs happy health.
I go my selfe, the joyfulst man aliue
To storie out this new supposed crime.   (*Exeunt.*)[1]

The author, though he got from this a suspense which
carried his audience over to the performance of Part II on
the next day, missed any real climax for Part I.

Inexperienced playwrights, in spite of good characterization and dialogue, frequently do not understand the value
and the nature of real climax. Consequently, an audience
feels that any interest it has given is cheated in the end. The
following scenario, though its feebleness can hardly be
traced solely to lack of climax, illustrates what is meant.

THE DÉBUTANTE

Characters:

Major Worthington, an American financier;
Emil Richter, a young poet;
Dr. Van Metre, } who do "team work" for the hand of *Kitty.*
Willy Squeam, }
Kitty Worthington, the *débutante.*
Mme. Cavanaugh King, a widow, *Kitty's* aunt.

SCENE: *Den, off the ballroom of Major Worthington's home. Music from the ballroom is heard intermittently during the action.*

DISCOVERED: *A group of guests who chatter and pass out, leaving Squeam and Van Metre. They talk of the attractions of Kitty, the
débutante, and make a wager as to who will win out. Each agrees to
back the other up in case of failure. They go off as Mrs. King and
Major Worthington enter. She reproves her brother for looking tired
and uninterested on this occasion of his daughter's "coming out."*

---

[1] *The Troublesome Raigne of King Iohn,* pp. 279-280; *Shakespeare's Library,* vol. v. Reeves
& Turner, London.

At length, exhausted by his sister's flippancy, he tells her that they are financially ruined, and that the crash will come on the morrow. Mrs. King is distracted, but they both brighten as Kitty enters in a whirl. She is radiantly happy, and hugs one and then the other, then both. Enter Richter, a stalwart young westerner, who does not know how to dance. They congratulate him on his little volume of verses which has just been published. After promising to sit out a dance with him, Kitty sends him off to talk with Miss Smithkins. He picks up a rose which Kitty has dropped and goes off with it. Enter Dr. Van Metre and Squeam. Exeunt Major Worthington and Mrs. King. Van Metre and Squeam take turns in proposing to Kitty. Enter Mrs. King, to whom Squeam finds himself making violent love, mistaking her for Kitty. He starts to bolt, but she lays hold of him, and they go off together. Kitty and Van Metre go off to dance, she laughing at his ardent protestations. Enter Major. He takes out a revolver from his writing desk, and puts it back as some dancers pass through. Enter Emil, and the two exeunt arm-in-arm. Enter Mrs. King and Kitty. Mrs. King bluntly tells Kitty their financial straits, and adds that Kitty must give up any sentimental feelings she has for Richter, and must, if she gets the chance, accept Van Meter or Squeam on the spot. With this, she hastily departs, leaving Kitty in tears. The tears turn to dimples the moment Richter appears, and she tries to shock him into a dislike for her. Nevertheless, he makes a clumsy effort at proposing which is interrupted by Van Metre, then Squeam, then both, who insist on taking her to supper. She dismisses them. (Soft music.) Richter proposes, and Kitty refuses him, telling him the reason frankly, as her aunt has just given it to her. He reprimands her for having mercenary motives, and makes an eloquent plea for the equality of men. Enraged, she leaves the room, but quickly returns and throws herself into his arms. Enters Mrs. King hastily, and says they may go right on embracing, as the Major has just received a telegram stating that he has won out in a law suit involving millions of dollars' worth of iron mines. Enter the Major hilarious. Enter Squeam and Van Meter. They shake hands and declare the wager off. Enter the dancers from a cotillion figure. They are arrayed in grotesque paper hats and bonnets and garlands of paper flowers. They circle about Kitty and Richter, and pelt them with paper flowers. Exeunt. Tableau: Kitty and Richter looking into firelight.

Curtain.

Obviously, though some slight suspense has been created

as to the possible solution of Kitty's difficulties, the proposed play goes all to pieces the moment Mrs. King enters with her news. When an audience knows that had the dramatist so willed, the fateful telegram might have arrived at any moment in the play other than the point chosen, it is likely to vote unanimously that the telegram should have been received before the curtain was ever rung up. Except in amateur performances arranged for admiring friends, there is no hope that such a fizzle can be covered by introducing dancers to make a pretty picture and a pseudo-climax.

Climax is, then, whatever in action, speech, pantomime, or thought (whether conveyed or suggested) will produce in an audience the strongest emotion of the scene, act, or play.

The means to climax range from mere action to quiet speech, from pure theatricality to lifelike subtlety. The poisoned cup, the fatal duel, indeed, the general slaughter at the end of *Hamlet* make a tremendous climax of action. Mere action, however, does not necessarily give climax. The writer of the scenario just quoted, missing a real climax, tried to offset this by the gay dance. Whether a dance, parade, or tableau is a genuine climax depends on whether it illustrates attainment of that in regard to which suspense has been created. No mere dance in costume, no spectacular parade or brilliant tableau is ever an adequate substitute for a climax which brings to the greatest intensity emotionalized interest already awakened in an audience. Such climax by action may, then, be as purely theatrical as in *revues*, much musical comedy, or pure melodrama, or as simple and true as in Heijermans' *The Good Hope*. The women, Joe and Kneirtje, are left alone, wild with anxiety for their fisherman-lover and son. A storm rages outside.

Jo. (*Beating her head on the table.*) The wind! It drives me mad, mad!

Kneirtje. (Opens the prayerbook, touches Jo's arm. Jo looks up, sobbing passionately, sees the prayerbook, shakes her head fiercely. Again wailing, drops to the floor, which she beats with her hands. Kneirtje's trembling voice sounds.) O Merciful God! I trust! With a firm faith, I trust.

(The wind races with wild lashings about the house.)
Curtain.[1]

Climax may come through surprise, as the discussion of suspense shows (pp. 212–214). Such surprise may be theatrical, as in *Home*[2] where it is obviously an arranged effect, or genuinely dramatic because justified by the preceding characterization, as in *The Clod*.

(Mary goes to the cupboard; returns to the table with the salt. Almost ready to drop, she drags herself to the window nearer back, and leans against it, watching the Southerners like a hunted animal. Thaddeus sits nodding in the corner. The Sergeant and Dick go on devouring food. The Sergeant pours the coffee. Puts his cup to his lips, takes one swallow; then, jumping to his feet and upsetting his chair as he does so, he hurls his cup to the floor. The crash of china stirs Thaddeus. Mary shakes in terror.)

Sergeant. (Bellowing and pointing to the fluid trickling on the floor.) Have you tried to poison us, you God damn hag?

> *(Mary screams, and the faces of the men turn white. It is like the cry of the animal goaded beyond endurance.)*

Mary. (Screeching.) Call my coffee poison, will ye? Call me a hag? I'll learn ye! I'm a woman, and ye're drivin' me crazy.

> *(Snatches the gun from the wall, points it at the Sergeant, and fires. Keeps on screeching. The Sergeant falls to the floor. Dick rushes for his gun.)*

Thaddeus. Mary! Mary!

Mary. (Aiming at Dick, and firing.) I ain't a hag. I'm a woman, but ye're killin' me.

> *(Dick falls just as he reaches his gun. Thaddeus is in the corner with his hands over his ears. Mary continues to pull the trigger of the empty gun. The Northerner is motionless for a moment; then he goes to Thaddeus, and shakes him.)*

---

[1] *The Good Hope,* Act III. Herman Heijermans. *The Drama,* November, 1912.
[2] See pp. 29–30.

Northerner. Go get my horse, quick!

> (*Thaddeus obeys. The Northerner turns to Mary. She gazes at him, but does not understand a word he says.*)

Northerner. (*With great fervor.*) I'm ashamed of what I said. The whole country will hear of this, and you.

> (*Takes her hand, and presses it to his lips; then turns and hurries out of the house. Mary still holds the gun in her hand. She pushes a strand of gray hair back from her face, and begins to pick up the fragments of the broken coffee cup.*)

Mary. (*In dead, flat tone.*) I'll have to drink out the tin cup now.

> (*The hoof-beats of the Northerner's horse are heard.*)
> *Curtain.*[1]

Note the wholly unexpected turn after the final speech of the Northerner. Yet this surprise merely rounds out the characterization of Mary.

This kind of climax by surprise recalls one of the principles in acting which Joseph Jefferson laid down for himself: "Never anticipate a strong effect; in fact, lead your audience by your manner, so that they shall scarcely suspect the character capable of such emotion; then when some sudden blow has fallen, the terrible shock prepares the audience for a new and striking phase in the character; they feel that under these new conditions you would naturally exhibit the passion which till then was not suspected." [2]

Before the present insistence on reality held sway, it was possible to close a play of pretended truth to life with a tag. Here is the quiet ending of *Still Waters Run Deep* (1855):

Potter. My dear boy, you astonish me! But, however, there's an old proverb that says that "All is not gold that glitters."

Mildmay. Yes, and there is another old proverb and one much more to the purpose that says, "Still waters run deep."

The convention which made that sort of ending desirable

[1] *Washington Square Plays; The Clod.* Lewis Beach. Drama League Series, No. xx. Doubleday, Page & Co., New York.

[2] *The Autobiography of Joseph Jefferson,* pp. 210–211. Century Co., New York.

has passed. However, today another convention, — the quiet ending, — might make it possible to end this same play with the speech just preceding the two quoted.

Potter. John Mildmay the master of this house? Emily, my dear, has your aunt been — I mean has your aunt lost her wits?

Mrs. Mildmay. No, she has found them, papa, as I have done, thanks to dear John. Ask his pardon, papa, as we have, for the cruel injustice we have done him.

Potter. Oh, certainly, if you desire it. John Mildmay, I ask your pardon — Jane and Emily say I ought; though what I have done, or what there is to ask pardon for —

Mildmay. Perhaps you'll learn in time. But we're forgetting dinner — Langford, will you take my wife? (*He does so.*) Markham, you'll take Mrs. Sternhold? [1]

Add to this, "They all go out to dinner," and you have one of the "quiet endings" dear to the hearts of some recent dramatists. These writers, after an act has swept to a strong emotional height, add some very quiet ending such as going out to dinner or the conventional farewells of the group assembled, as if for some reason either were more artistic than to close on the moment of strong emotion. This is bad. On the other hand, if the quiet ending carries characterization, or irony, to point the scene, act, or play, or really illustrates the meaning, this and not the absence of strong emotion or physical action is what gives both real value and genuine climax. For instance, at the end of Act I of *Monsieur Poirier's Son-in-Law,* by Augier, this is the dialogue:

Enter a Servant.

Servant. Dinner is served.

Poirier. (*To the Servant.*) Bring up a bottle of 1811 Pomard — (*To the Duke.*) The year of the comet, Monsieur le duc — fifteen francs a bottle! The king drinks no better. (*Aside to Verdelet.*) You mustn't drink any — neither will I!

Gaston. (*To the Duke.*) Fifteen francs, bottle to be returned when empty!

[1] The DeWitt Publishing House, New York.

Verdelet. (Aside to Poirier.) Are you going to allow him to make
fun of you like that?
  Poirier. (Aside to Verdelet.) In matters of this sort, you must
take your time. *(They all go out.)*

Curtain.[1]

Here it is not the quietude but the particularly apt, humor-
ous illustration of Poirier's character which gives climax.
In *The Amazons*, too, what could better illustrate acceptance
of the usual by all the group who have been fighting against
it than the sedate and utterly commonplace exeunt?

Lady Castlejordan. Lord Tweenwayes —
  *(Tweenwayes comes with great dignity to Lady Castlejordan.
  The girls fall back.)*
Lady Castlejordan. Lord Litterly — Lady Noeline. Monsieur de
Grival — Lady Wilhelmina. Mr. Minchin — Lady Thomasin.
  (The couples are formed, and all go out sedately.)[2]

When quiet speech sums up the whole meaning of a scene
or play, it too gives climax. Ann's words at the end of *Man
and Superman*, "John you are still talking," make a fine
ironic climax. Irony, whether quiet or decidedly dramatic, is
a very effective means to climax. At the end of Act II, Herod,
in the play of that name by Stephen Phillips, has ordered
Mariamne killed. Completely infatuated by her, he has done
this only when her enemies have forced him to believe that
she is utterly false. Almost instantly his love overwhelms his
mistrust. He tries to revoke his word, crying,

  Yet will I not be bound, I will break free,
  She shall not die — she shall not die — she shall not —

News of the triumph he has longed for interrupts:

Enter Attendant.

  Attendant. O king, the Roman eagles! See!
  A cry. (Without.)   From Rome!

  [1] *Monsieur Poirier's Son-in-Law*, Act I. Emile Augier. Translated by B. H. Clark.
A. Knopf, New York.
  [2] *The Amazons*, Act III. Sir Arthur Pinero. Walter H. Baker & Co., Boston.

Enter Roman Envoy and Suite.

Envoy. O king, great Cæsar sent us after you,
But, though we posted fast, you still outran us.
Thus then by word of mouth great Cæsar greets
Herod his friend. But he would not confine
That friendship to the easy spoken word,
And hear I bear a proof of Cæsar's faith.
Herein is added to thy boundaries
Hippo, Samaria and Gadara,
And high-walled Joppa, and Anthedon's shore,
And Gaza unto these, and Straton's towers.   *(Moves down.)*
Here is the scroll, with Cæsar's own hand signed.
    Herod. (*Taking the scroll — at foot of steps.*) Mariamne, hear you
this? Mariamne, see you?   *(Turns to look at scroll.)*
                (Servant enters and moves down to Gadias down L.)
                        (He goes up the stairs.)
Hippo, Samaria and Gadara,
And high-walled Joppa, and Anthedon's shore,
And Gaza unto these, and Straton's towers.
    Servant. (*Aside to Gadias.*) O sir, the queen is dead!
    Gadias. (*Aside to Pheroras, Cypros, and Salome.*) The queen is
dead!
    Herod. Mariamne, hear you this? Mariamne, see you?
                (Repeating the words, and going up steps.)
Hippo, Samaria and Gadara,
And high-walled Joppa, and Anthedon,   *(As he moves up.)*
And Gaza unto these, and Straton's towers! [1]

The perfect climax lies in the irony of the fact that all
Herod most desires as ruler comes to him at just the moment
when he has killed the thing that most he loved.

At the end of Act III of *Chains*, by Elizabeth Baker,
everybody — the father-in-law and mother-in-law, Percy,
the brother-in-law, and Sybil, a pretty but useless bit of
femininity — has been making Charlie entirely miserable
because no one can understand that his expressed desire to
try his fortunes in Australia and then send for his wife,

---

[1] *Herod, A Tragedy*, Act. ii. Stephen Phillips. John Lane, New York.

Lily, is not a pretext for abandoning her. Percy, with next to nothing a year, is just engaged to Sybil. Foster wants to marry Margaret, Charlie's sister-in-law, who is dissatisfied with her lot.

Enter Lily, dressed for going out, also Mrs. Massey. Lily goes round, kissing and shaking hands, with a watery smile and a forced tearful cheerfulness.

Charley. (Without going all around and calling from the door.) Good night, all!   *(Exeunt Lily and Charley.)*

Mrs. Massey. Well, I must say —

Percy. O, let's drop it, mother. Play something, Maggie.

Maggie. I don't want to.

Mrs. Massey. Walter would like to hear something, wouldn't you, Walter?

Foster. If Maggie feels like it.

Maggie. She doesn't feel like it.

Massey. Be as pleasant as you can, my girl — Charley's enough for one evening.

> *(Maggie goes to the piano and sitting down plays noisily, with both pedals on, the chorus, "Off to Philadelphia.")*

Mrs. Massey. Maggie, it's Sunday!

Maggie. I forgot!

Mrs. Massey. You shouldn't forget such things — Sybil, my dear —

Sybil. I don't play.

Massey. Rubbish! Come on!

> *(Sybil goes to the piano and Percy follows her.)*

Percy. (Very near to Sybil and helping her to find the music.) Charley is a rotter! What d'ye think he was telling me the other day?

Sybil. I don't know.

Percy. Told me to be sure I got the right girl.

Sybil. Brute!

Percy. What do you think I said? Darling!

> *(Kisses her behind music.)*

Massey. (Looking around.) Take a bigger sheet.

> *(Sybil sits at piano quickly and plays the chorus to "Count Your Many Blessings." To which they all sing:)*

Count your many blessings, count them one by one,
Count your blessings, see what God has done.
Count your blessings, count them one by one,
And it will surprise you what the Lord has done.[1]

Is not the irony of this group of unsatisfied or dissatisfied people singing " Count your many blessings," fully climactic?

Not quietness of speech or action, then, but appropriateness makes any of these approved endings climactic and artistic.

There can hardly be any question that the original ending of *Still Waters Run Deep* is theatrical in the sense that it is climactic only by the dramatic convention of its time. Except when theatricality is intentionally part of the artistic design, it is, of course, undesirable. Rostand, letting the figures in *The Romancers* comment on their own play as a kind of epilogue, has a really artistic though theatrical climax.

Sylvette. (*Summoning the actors about her.*) And now we five —
if Master Straforel please —
Let us expound the play in which we've tried to please.
      (*She comes down stage and addresses the audience, marking
      time with her hand.*)
Light, easy rhymes; old dresses, frail and light;
Love in a park, fluting an ancient tune.   (*Soft music.*)
   Bergamin. A fairy-tale quintet, mad as Midsummer-night.
   Pasquin. Some quarrels. Yes! — but all so very slight!
   Straforel. Madness of sunstroke; madness of the moon!
A worthy villain, in his mantle dight.
   Sylvette. Light, easy rhymes; old dresses, frail and light;
Love in a park, fluting an ancient tune.
   Percinet. A Watteau picture — not by Watteau, quite;
Release from many a dreary Northern rune;
Lovers and fathers; old walls, flowery-bright;
A brave old plot — with music — ending soon.

1 J. W. Luce & Co., Boston; Sidgwick & Jackson, Ltd., London.

Sylvette. Light, easy rhymes; old dresses, frail and light.
  (*The stage gradually darkens; the last lines are delivered in
  voices that grow fainter as the actors appear to fade away
  into mist and darkness.*)
                          Curtain.[1]

So light the finale, as in London, that the figures fade
from sight till only their voices are faintly heard, and theatricality helps to place the play as a mere bit of fantasy. On
the other hand, there is something like genuine theatricality at the end of Sudermann's *Fritzschen.* Fritz is going to
his death in a prospective duel with a man who is an unerr-
ing shot. Though the others present suspect or know the
truth, his mother thinks he is going to new and finer fortunes.
Isn't the following the real climax?

Fritz. (*Stretching out his hand to her cheerfully.*) Dear Ag—
(*Looks into her face, and understands that she knows. Softly, ear-
nestly.*) Farewell, then.
Agnes. Farewell, Fritz!
Fritz. I love you.
Agnes. I shall always love you, Fritz!
Fritz. Away, then, Hallerpfort! Au revoir, papa! Au revoir!
Revoir!   (*Starts for the door on the right.*)
Frau von Drosse. Go by the park, boys — there I have you
longer in sight.
Fritz. Very well, mamma, we will do it! (*Passes with Haller-
pfort through the door at the centre; on the terrace, he turns with a cheer-
ful gesture, and calls once more.*) Au Revoir! (*His voice is still au-
dible.*) Au revoir!
                (*Frau von Drosse throws kisses after him, and waves her
                handkerchief, then presses her hand wearily to her heart
                and sighs heavily.*) [2]

Because the history of the theatre shows that the contained appeal always moves an audience, Sudermann adds

---

[1] *The Fantasticks*, Act III. Edmond Rostand. Translated by Geo. Fleming. R. H. Russell & Co., New York.
[2] *Morituri, Fritzschen,* Herman-Sudermann. Translated by Archibald Alexander. Copyright, 1910, by Chas. Scribner's Sons, New York.

one more touch of misery as the mother dwells on her dream
of the night before:

> (*Agnes hurries to her, and leads her to a chair, then goes over
> to the Major, who, with heaving breast, is lost in thought.*)
> *Frau von Drosse.* Thank you, my darling! — Already, I am quite
> well again! . . . God, the boy! How handsome he looked! And so
> brown and so healthy. . . . You see, I saw him exactly like that
> last night. . . . No, that is no illusion! And I told you how the
> Emperor led him in among all the generals! And the Emperor
> said — (*More softly, looking far away with a beatific smile.*) And
> the Emperor said —
>
> Curtain.[1]

Though a new twist is given our emotions, is not something
lost to the artistry of the play?

If the means to climax be various, the ways in which it
may elude a writer are several. If an audience foresees it,
much of the value of climax, perhaps all, disappears. Bulwer-
Lytton, in writing *Money*, recognized this:

> And principally with regard to Act 5 I don't feel easy. The first
> idea suggested by you & worked on by me was of course to carry
> on Evelyn's trick to the last — & bring in the creditors &c when it
> is discovered that he is as rich as ever. I so made Act 5 at first.
> But . . . the trick was so palpable to the audience that having been
> carried thro' Acts 3 & 4, it became stale in Act 5 — & the final dis-
> covery was much less comic than you w^d suppose.[2]

If anticipating a climax will impair it for an audience, repetition may kill it. In the civic masque, *Caliban*,[3] as performed, many of the historical scenes were introduced in
the same way: Ariel asked his master, Prospero, what he
should show him next, and at his bidding summoned the
episode. No variety in phrasing could surmount the monotony of this. There was consequent loss in suspense and
climax.

[1] *Idem.*
[2] *Letters of Bulwer-Lytton to Macready*, Brander Matthews, ed.
[3] Doubleday, Page & Co., New York.

It is easy, also, to miss possible climax by using more at a given point than is absolutely necessary. Sometimes it is wiser to postpone part or all of thoroughly desirable material for later treatment. In the novel, *Les Oberlé*,[1] father and daughter sympathize with the Germans, mother and son with the old French tradition. In patriarchal fashion, the half-paralytic grandfather, as head of the house, keeps the keys. When a young German officer, favored by the daughter, asks her hand, feeling becomes intense and strained between the parents and the brother and the sister. Suddenly the old paralytic enters, half-supported by his attendant. Furious to think of his granddaughter as the wife of a German he cries, with a superb gesture of dismissal, "Clear out! This is my house!" (*Va t'en! Ici chez moi!*) The dramatizer saw that with the accompanying action of all concerned, especially the silent going of the German suitor, "Ici chez moi" made a sufficient climax. Therefore, with a touch of real genius, he saved the "Va t'en" for a climax to a totally different scene. Later in the play, Jean, who has determined to escape across the French boundary rather than serve longer in the German army, has been locked in his room by his outraged father. As usual, after the house has been locked up for the night, the keys have been handed to the old, half-paralytic grandfather, who lies sleepless in a room near Jean's. Learning from Uncle Ulrich what has occurred, the grandfather totters into the living-room with his keys. Unlocking Jean's door, with a fine gesture of affection, and command toward the outer door, he cries to Jean, "Va." Here the dramatist gets two fine climaxes where the novelist gained but one.

Sometimes a very effective climax at a given point should be postponed because it will be even more effective later,

---

[1] *Les Oberlé*. René Bazin. Dramatized by E. Haraucourt. L'Illustration Théâtrale, December 9, 1905, p. 14.

and if given the first position would check preferable movement in the play. At the end of Act IV of *Magda* (*Heimat*) by Sudermann, we seem all ready for a scene in which Magda confesses the truth about her past life to her father.

Schwartze. Magda, — I want Magda.

Marie. (*Goes to the door and opens it.*) She's coming now, — down the stairs.

Schwartze. So! (*Pulls himself together with an effort.*)

Marie. (*Clasping her hands.*) Don't hurt her!

    (*Pauses with the door open. Magda is seen descending the stairs. She enters in travelling dress, hat in hand, very pale but calm.*)

Magda. I heard you call, father.

Schwartze. I have something to say to you.

Magda. And I to you.

Schwartze. Go in, — into my room.

Magda. Yes, father.

    (*She goes to the door left. Schwartze follows her. Marie, who has drawn back frightened to the dining-room, makes an unseen gesture of entreaty.*) [1]

Now, any interview between Magda and her father will both unduly lengthen an act already long and bring the play well into its final climax. Stopping the act here creates superb suspense. Starting a new act under slightly different conditions keeps all the suspense created by Act IV and intensifies it by new details. The new act gives us the chance easily to introduce von Keller, who is needed if the play is to be more than another treatment of the erring daughter confessing her sin to her father. Just through him comes emphasis which gives special meaning to the play. Therefore, we gain by postponing the full confession from the end of Act IV till well toward the end of Act V.

Evidently, climax rests on (*a*) right feeling for order in presenting ideas; (*b*) a correct sense of what is weaker and what is stronger in phrasing emotions; and (*c*) just appreciation of

---

[1] *Magda.* Translated by C. E. A. Winslow. Lamson, Wolffe & Co., Boston.

the feeling of the audience toward the emotions presented.
For both clearness and climax it is usually a wise rule to consider but one idea at a time. In the following illustration,
column 1 shows confusion, because three subjects — the fan,
the greeting, and the compliment of Lady Windermere —
are started at the same time. In column 2, quoted from
Miss Anglin's acting version of *Lady Windermere's Fan*,
treating each of these subjects in its natural sequence brings
both clearness and climax.

Parker. Mrs. Erlynne.

(*Lord Windermere starts.
Mrs. Erlynne enters, very
beautifully dressed and
very dignified. Lady Win-
dermere clutches at her
fan, then lets it drop on the
floor. She bows coldly to
Mrs. Erlynne, who bows
to her sweetly in turn, and
sails into the room.*)

Lord Darlington. You have
dropped your fan, Lady Windermere.

(*Picks it up and hands it to
her.*)

Mrs. Erlynne. (*C.*) How do
you do again, Lord Windermere?
How charming your sweet wife
looks! Quite a picture!

Lord Windermere. (*In a low
voice.*) It was terribly rash of
you to come!

Mrs. Erlynne. (*Smiling.*) The
wisest thing I ever did in my
life. And, by the way, you must
pay me a good deal of attention
this evening.

Parker. Mrs. Erlynne.

(*Lord Windermere starts.
Mrs. Erlynne enters, very
beautifully dressed, and
very dignified. Lady Win-
dermere clutches at her
fan, then lets it drop on the
floor. She bows coldly to
Mrs. Erlynne, who bows
to her sweetly in turn,
and sails into the room.*)

Mrs. Erlynne. (*C.*) How do
you do again, Lord Windermere?

Lord Darlington. You have
dropped your fan, Lady Windermere.

(*Picks it up, and hands it to
her.*)

Lord Windermere. (*In a low
voice.*) It was terribly rash of
you to come!

Mrs. Erlynne. (*Smiling.*) The
wisest thing I ever did in my life.
How charming your sweet wife
looks! Quite a picture! And, by
the way, you must pay me a good
deal of attention this evening.[1]

[1] *Lady Windermere's Fan*, Act II. Oscar Wilde. Acting version as arranged by Miss Margaret Anglin.

In the next extract, note that omission of "I want to live childless still" and shifting the position of the words "For twenty years, as you say, I have lived childless" permit an actress to work up to the strongest climax of the speech, when spoken, "They made me suffer too much." Miss Anglin, trained by years of experience to great sensitiveness to the emotional values of words, has here arranged the sentences better than the author himself.

Lord Windermere. What do you mean by coming here this morning? What is your object? (*Crossing L. C. and sitting.*) *Mrs. Erlynne.* (*With a note of irony in her voice.*) To bid goodbye to my dear daughter, of course. (*Lord Windermere bites his underlip in anger. Mrs. Erlynne looks at him, and her voice and manner become serious. In her accents as she talks there is a note of deep tragedy. For a moment she reveals herself.*) Oh, don't imagine I am going to have a pathetic scene with her, weep on her neck and tell her who I am, and all that kind of thing. I have no ambition to play the part of mother. Only once in my life have I known a mother's feelings. That was last night. They were terrible — they made me suffer — they made me suffer too much. For twenty years, as you say, I have lived childless — I want to live childless still.

Lord Windermere. What do you mean by coming here this morning? What is your object? (*Crossing L. C. and sitting.*) *Mrs. Erlynne.* (*With a note of irony in her voice.*) To bid goodbye to my dear daughter, of course. (*Lord Windermere bites his underlip in anger. Mrs. Erlynne looks at him, and her voice and manner become serious. In her accents as she talks there is a note of deep tragedy. For a moment she reveals herself.*) Oh, don't imagine I am going to have a pathetic scene with her, weep on her neck and tell her who I am, and all that kind of thing. I have no ambition to play the part of mother. For twenty years, as you say, I have lived childless. Only once in my life have I known a mother's feelings. That was last night. They were terrible — they made me suffer — they made me suffer too much.[1]

[1] *Idem,* Act IV. Acting version as arranged by Miss Margaret Anglin.

When an eighteenth-century manager, in his production of *The School for Scandal*, had colored fire set off in the wings as the falling screen revealed Lady Teazle, he failed of his intended effect because he thought that for his audience the falling of the screen was climactic. Really, of course, the enjoyment of the audience, as it listens to the dialogue, knowing that Lady Teazle overhears, is the chief source of pleasure. It is the dismay of Sir Peter, when he sees who is really behind the screen, which makes the climax. That dismay is not greater against a background of red fire. Crowded with action as the end of *Hamlet* is, we close it in acting, not on the fatal wounding of Hamlet, but either on his words, "The rest is silence," or as the soldiers of Fortinbras march out with Hamlet's body on their shields. Experience has proved that a stronger climax for an audience lies in those words or in seeing the procession which passes among the kneeling courtiers, stronger than from all the noisy emotions which have just preceded. In brief, except when we feel sure that we have made our feeling as to the emotions of a scene or act the public's, it is they who must determine where the climax lies. Where it rests we must in all cases of doubt decide from our past experience of the public and present observation of it.

From all these illustrations it must be clear that the only rule for finding climax is: Understand clearly the audience for which you intend your play; create in it the sympathetic relation toward your characters you wish; then you may be sure that what seems to you a climax for your scene will be so for your audience.

Movement depends, then, on clearness, unity, emphasis, and a right feeling for suspense and climax. This movement may be steadily upward, as in the last scene of *Hamlet*, or it may have the wave-like advance found in Sigurjónsson's *Eyvind of the Hills* [1] or Sir Arthur Pinero's *The Gay Lord*

---

[1] *Eyvind of the Hills*, J. Sigurjónsson. American Scandinavian Society, New York.

Quex. The emotional interest in each of these sweeps up to a pure climax, drops back part way for a fresh start, and then advances to a stronger climax.

Granted that a would-be playwright understands the proportioning of his work and the correct development of it for clearness, emphasis and movement, he is ready to repeat the words of Ibsen: "I have just completed a play in five acts, that is to say, the rough draft of it. Now comes the elaboration, the more energetic individualization of the persons, and their modes of expression." [1] He is ready to perfect his characterization and dialogue.

1 *From Ibsen's Workshop*, p. 8. Copyright, 1911, by Chas. Scribner's Sons, New York.

CHAPTER VII

CHARACTERIZATION

In drama, undoubtedly the strongest immediate appeal to the general public is action. Yet if a dramatist is to communicate with his audience as he wishes, command of dialogue is indispensable. The permanent value of a play, however, rests on its characterization. Characterization focuses attention. It is the chief means of creating in an audience sympathy for the subject or the people of the play. "A Lord," "A Page," in a pre-Shakespearean play usually was merely a speaker of lines and little, if at all, characterized. When Robert Greene or his contemporaries adapted such sources for their stage, with sure instinct for creating a greater interest in their public, they changed these prefixes to "Eustace," "Jacques," "Nano," etc. Merely changing the name from type to individual called for individualization of character and usually brought it. Indeed, in drama, individualization is always the sign of developing art. In any country, the history of modern drama is a passing, under the influence of the audience, from abstractions and personifications, through type, to individualized character. In the Trope, cited p. 17, one Mary cannot be distinguished from another. In a later form it is not a particular unguent seller who meets the Maries on the way to the tomb, but a type, — Unguent Seller. When a writer of a Miracle Play first departed a little from the exact actions and dialogue of the Bible, it was to add abstractions — Justice, Virtue, etc. — or types: soldiers, shepherds, etc. From these he moved quickly or slowly, as he was more or less endowed dramatically, to figures individualized from types, such as the well-characterized shepherds of the Second Towneley Play. The Morality illustrates this same evolution even more clearly. Beginning with the pure abstractions of *Mundus et Infans* or *Mankind* it passes through type characterization in *Lusty Juventus* or *Hyckescorner* to as well individualized figures as Delilah and Ishmael in *The Nice Wanton*.[1] Abstractions permit an author to say what he pleases with the least possible thought for characterization. Type presents characteristics so marked that even the unobservant cannot have failed to discern them in their fellow men. Individualization differentiates within the types, running from broad distinctions to presentation of very subtle differences. Because individualization moves from the known to the less known or the unknown, it is harder for an audience to follow than type characterization, and far more difficult to write. However, he who cannot individualize character must keep to the broader kinds of melodrama and farce, and above all to that last asylum of time-honored types — musical comedy.

Fundamentally, type characterization rests on a false premise, namely, that every human being may be adequately represented by some dominant characteristic or small group of closely related characteristics. All the better recent drama emphasizes the comic or tragic conflict in human beings caused by many contradictory impulses and ideas, some mutually exclusive, some negativing others to a considerable extent, some apparently dormant for a time, yet ready to spring into great activity at unforeseen moments. Ben Jonson carried the false idea to an extreme when he wrote of his "humour" comedies:

> In every human body,
> The choler, melancholy, phlegm, and blood,
> By reason that they flow continually

[1] For all of these except *Hyckescorner* see *Specimens of Pre-Shakespearean Drama.* J. M. Manly. 2 vols. Ginn & Co., Boston. For *Hyckescorner* see *The Origin of the English Drama.* Vol. I. T. Hawkins, ed. Clarendon Press, Oxford.

In some one part and are not continent,
Receive the name of humours. Now thus far
It may, by metaphor, apply itself
Unto the general disposition:
As when some one peculiar quality
Doth so possess a man that it doth draw
All his affects, his spirits and his powers,
In his confluctions, all to run one way,
This may be truly said to be a humour.[1]

Were Ben Jonson's physiology sound, we should have, not occasional cranks and neurotics as now, but a race of nothing else. Today modern medical science has proved the bad physiology of his words, and dramatists have followed its lead.

What gave the type drama its great hold, in the Latin comedy of Plautus and Terence, in Ben Jonson and other Elizabethans, what keeps it alive today in the less artistic forms — broad farce, pure melodrama — is fourfold. Type characterization, exhibiting a figure wholly in one aspect, or through a small group of closely related characteristics, is easy to understand. Secondly, it is both easy to create, and, as Ben Jonson's great following between 1605 and 1750 proves, even easier to imitate. Thirdly, farce and melodrama, indeed all drama depending predominantly on mere situation, may succeed, though lacking individualization of character, with any audience which, like the Roman or the Elizabethan, gladly hears the same stories or sees the same figures handled differently by different writers. Much in the plays of Reade, Tom Taylor, and Bulwer-Lytton [2] which passed, in the mid-nineteenth century, for real life, depending as it did on a characterization which barely rose above type, was only thinly disguised melodrama. The recent increasing response of the public to

---

[1] *Induction, Every Man in His Humour.* Mermaid Series or Everyman's Library.
[2] See *Two Loves and a Life, The Ticket of Leave Man, The Lady of Lyons.* All published by Samuel French, New York.

better characterization in both farce and melodrama has
tended to lift the former into comedy, the latter into story-
play and tragedy. Just here appears a fourth reason for the
popularity of characterization by types. Though entertaining plays may be presented successfully with type characterization only, no dramatist with inborn or acquired ability
to characterize, can hold consistently to types. Observation, interpretative insight, or a flash of sympathy will advance him now and again, as Jonson was advanced more
than once, to real individualization of character. Contrast
the thoroughly real Subtle, Face, and Doll of *The Alchemist*[1]
with the types, Ananias and Sir Epicure Mammon; contrast the masterly, if very brief, characterization of Ursula
in *Bartholomew Fair*[2] with the mere type of Zeal-of-the-Land
Busy. An uncritical audience responding to the best
characterization in a play, overlooks the merely typical
quality of the other figures. That is, the long vogue of types
upon the stage rests upon ease of comprehension, entire
adequacy for some crude dramatic forms, ease of imitation,
and a constant tendency in a dramatist of ability to rise
to higher levels of characterization. Now that we are more
and more dissatisfied with types in plays making any claim
to realism, the keen distinction first laid down by Mr.
William Archer in his *Play-Making* becomes essential. If
type presents a single characteristic or group of intimately
related characteristics, "character drawing is the present-
ment of human nature in its commonly recognized, understood, and accepted aspects; psychology is, as it were, the
exploration of character, the bringing of hitherto unsur-
veyed tracts within the circle of our knowledge and comprehension."[3] Mr. Galsworthy in *The Silver Box* and *Justice*

---

[1] Belles-Lettres Series. F. E. Schelling, ed. D. C. Heath & Co.; Mermaid Series, vol. III, or Everyman's Library.

[2] Mermaid Series, vol. II. Chas. Scribner's Sons, New York.

[3] *Play-Making*, pp. 376, 378. Small, Maynard & Co., Boston.

Mr. Archer regards as a drawer of character; in *Strife*[1] as a psychologist. He holds Sir Arthur Pinero a character-izer of great versatility who becomes a psychologist in some of his studies of feminine types — in Iris, in Letty, in the heroine of *Mid-Channel*.[2] By this distinction, most good drama shows character drawing; only the great work, psychology.

Drama which does not rise above interest in its action rests, as has been said, on the idea that most people are simple, uncomplicated, and easy to understand. Great drama depends on a firm grasp and sure presentation of complicated character, but of course a dramatist has a perfect right to say that, though he knows his hero — Cyrano de Bergerac, for instance — may have had many character-istics, it is enough for the purpose of his play to represent the vanity, the audacity, and the underlying tenderness of the man. It is undeniable, too, that particular characteris-tics of ours may be so strong that other characteristics will not prevent them from taking us into sufficient dramatic complications to make a good play. In such a case, the dramatist who is not primarily writing for characterization will present the characteristics creating his desired situations, and let all others go. Conversely, he who cares most for characterization will try so to present even minor qualities that the perfect portrait of an individual will be recognized. Often, however, the happenings of a play may seem to an audience incompatible, that is, the character in one place may seem to contradict himself as presented elsewhere. Just here is where the psychologist in the dramatist, step-ping to the front, must convince his audience that there is only a seeming contradiction. Otherwise, the play falls promptly to the level of simple melodrama or farce. That

[1] *Plays.* Chas. Scribner's Sons, New York.
[2] Walter H. Baker & Co., Boston; W. Heinemann, London.

is, the character-drawer paints his portrait, knowing that, if it is well done, its life-likeness will at once be recognized. The psychologist, knowing that the life-likeness will not be readily admitted, by illustrative action throws light on his character till his point is won. Our final judgment of characterization must depend on whether the author is obviously trying to present a completely rounded figure or only chosen aspects.

Thus the old statement, "Know thyself," becomes for the dramatist "Know your characters as intimately as possible." Too many beginners in play-writing who care more for situation than for character, sketch in a figure with the idea that they may safely leave it to the actor to "fill out the part." When brought to book they say: "I felt sure the actor in his larger experience, catching my idea — you do think it was clearly stated, don't you? — would fill it out perfectly, and be glad of the freedom." Were modesty the real basis for this kind of work, there might be good in it; but what really lies behind it are two great foes of good dramatic writing: haste or incompetence. The interest and the delight of a dramatist in studying people should lie in accurate conveying to others of their contradictions, their deterioration or growth as time passes, the outcropping of characteristics in them for which our observation has not prepared us. Nobody who really cares for characterization wants somebody else to do it for him. Nobody who has really entered into his characters thoroughly will for a moment be satisfied to sketch broad outlines and let the actor fill in details. Rarely, however, does the self-deceived author of such slovenly work deceive his audience. It meets at their hands the condemnation it deserves. Such an author assumes that in all the parts of his play, actors of marked ability and keen intelligence will be cast. Only in the rarest cases does that happen. Many actors may not see the full significance of the outlines. Others, whether they see them or not, will develop a character so as to get as swiftly as possible effects not intended by the author but for which they, as actors, are specially famous. Such a playwright must, then, contend, except in specially fortunate circumstances, against possible dullness, indifference, and distortion. It is the merest common sense so to present characters that a cast of average ability, or a stage manager of no extraordinary imagination may understand and represent them with at least approximate correctness, rather than so to write that only a group of creative artists can do any justice to the play. Clear and definitive characterization never hampers the best actors: for actors not the best it is absolutely necessary unless intended values are to be blurred.

It frequently happens that a writer whose dialogue is good and who has enough dramatic situations finds himself unable to push ahead. He knows broadly what he wants a scene to be, but somehow cannot make his characters move freely and naturally in it. Above all, the minor transitional scenes prove strangely difficult to write. Of course a scene or act may be thus clogged because the writer is mentally fagged. If, when a writer certainly is not tired, or when, after rest, he cannot with two or three sustained attempts develop a scene, the difficulty is not far to seek. In real life do we surely find out about people at our first, second, or even third meeting? Only if the people are of the simplest and most self-revelatory kind. The difficulty in these clogged scenes usually is that the author is treating the situation as if it were not the creation of the people in it, and as if a skilful writer could force any group of people into any situation. As Mr. Galsworthy has pointed out, " character is situation." [1] The latter exists because some one is what he

[1] *Some Platitudes Concerning Drama, Atlantic Monthly,* December, 1909.

is and so has inner conflict, or clashes with another person, or with his environment. Change his character a little and the situation must change. Involve more people in it, and immediately their very presence, affecting the people originally in the scene, will change the situation. In the left-hand column of what follows, the Queen, though she has one speech, in no way affects the scene: the situation is treated for itself, and barely. In the right-hand column, the Queen becomes an individual whose presence affects the speeches of the King and Hamlet. Because she is what she is, Hamlet addresses to her some of the lines which in the first version he spoke to the King: result, a scene far more effective emotionally.

King. And now princely Sonne Hamlet,
What meanes these sad and melancholy moodes?
For your intent going to Wittenberg,
Wee hold it most unmeet and unconvenient,

Being the Joy and halfe heart of your mother.
Therefore let mee intreat you stay in Court,
All Denmarkes hope our coosin and dearest Soone

King. But now my Cosin Hamlet, and my sonne.
Ham. A little more than kin, and lesse then kind.
King. How is it that the clowdes still hang on you.
Ham. Not so much my Lord, I am too much in the sonne.
Queene. Good Hamlet cast thy nighted colour off
And let thine eye looke like a friend on Denmarke,
Doe not forever with thy vailed lids
Seeke for thy noble Father in the dust,
Thou know'st 'tis common all that lives must die,
Passing through nature to eternitie.
Ham. I Maddam, it is common.
Quee. If it be

Ham. My lord, 'tis not the sable sute I weare:
No nor the teares that still stand in my eyes,
Nor the distracted haviour in the visage,
Nor all together mixt with outward semblance,
Is equall to the sorrow of my heart,
Him have I lost I must of force forgoe,
These but the ornaments and sutes of woe.

King. This shewes a loving care in you, Sonne Hamlet,
But you must thinke your father lost a father,
That father dead, lost his, and so shalbe untill the
Generall ending.   Therefore cease laments,
It is a fault gainst heaven, fault gainst the dead,
A fault gainst nature, and in reasons
Common course most certaine,
None lives on earth, but hee is borne to die.

Why seemes it so perticuler with thee.
Ham. Seemes Maddam, nay it is, I know not seemes,
Tis not alone my incky cloake coold mother
Nor customary suites of solembe blacke
Nor windie suspiration of forst breath
No, nor the fruitfull river in the eye,
Nor the dejected havior of the visage
Together with all formes, moodes, chapes of griefe
That can denote me truely, these indeede seeme,
For they are actions that a man might play
But I have that within which passes showe
These but the trappings and the suites of woe.
King. Tis sweete and commendable in your nature Hamlet,
To give these mourning duties to your father
But you must knowe your father lost a father,
That father lost, lost his, and the surviver bound
In filliall obligation for some tearme
To do obsequious sorrowe, but to persever
In obstinate condolement, is a course
Of impious stubbornes . . . etc.

Que. Let not thy mother loose her praiers Hamlet, Stay here with us, go not to Wittenberg. *Ham.* I shall in all my best obay you madam.	*Queé.* Let not thy mother loose her prayers Hamlet, I pray thee stay with us, goe not to Wittenberg. *Ham.* I shall in all my best obay you Madam.[1]

Inexperienced dramatists too often forget that a character who is simply one of several in a scene may not act as he would alone.

Mr. Macready's Bentevole is very fine in its kind. It is natural, easy, and forcible. Indeed, we suspect some parts of it were too natural, that is, that Mr. Macready thought too much of what his feelings might dictate in such circumstances, rather than of what the circumstances must have dictated to him to do. We allude particularly to the half significant, half hysterical laugh and distorted jocular leer, with his eyes towards the persons accusing him of the murder, when the evidence of his guilt comes out. Either the author did not intend him to behave in this manner, or he must have made the other parties on the stage interrupt him as a self-convicted criminal.[2]

Stevenson clearly recognized this truth:

I have had a heavy case of conscience of the same kind about my Braxfield story. Braxfield — only his name is Hermiston — has a son who is condemned to death; plainly there is a fine tempting fitness about this; and I meant he was to hang. But now, on considering my minor characters, I saw there were five people who would — in a sense who must — break prison and attempt his rescue. They are capable, hardy folks, too, who might very well succeed. Why should they not, then? Why should not young Hermiston escape clear out of the country? and be happy if he could with his — But soft! I will betray my secret or my heroine.[3]

When a scene clogs, don't hold the pen waiting for the impulse to write: don't try to write at all. Study the situation, not for itself, but for the people in it. "The Dramatist who depends his characters to his plot," says Mr. Gals-

[1] *The Devonshire Hamlets*, Act I, pp. 9–10.
[2] *Dramatic Essays*. William Hazlitt.
[3] *The Stage in America*, pp. 81–82. N. Hapgood. The Macmillan Co.

worthy, "instead of his plot to his characters, ought himself to be depended." [1] If a thorough knowledge of the characters in the particular situation does not bring a solution, study them as the scene relates itself to what must precede in characterization. More than once a dramatist has found that he could not compose some scene satisfactorily till he had written carefully the previous history of the important character or characters. The detailed knowledge thus gained revealed whether or not the characters could enter the desired situation, and if so, how. Pailleron, author of *Le Monde où l'on s'ennuie* declared that, in his early drafts, he always had three or four times the material in regard to his *dramatis personæ* ultimately used by him.

Intimate knowledge of his characters is the only safe foundation for the ambitious playwright. It is well-nigh useless to ask managers and actors to pass finally on a mere statement of a situation or group of situations, without characterization. All they can say is: "Bring me this again as an amplified scenario, or a play, which shows me to what extent the people you have in mind give freshness of interest to this story, which has been used again and again in the drama of different nations, and I will tell you what I will do for you." Reduce any dramatic masterpiece to simple statement of its plot and the story will seem so trite as hardly to be worth dramatization. For instance: a man of jealous nature, passionately in love with his young wife, is made by the lies and trickery of a friend to believe that his wife has been intriguing with another of his friends. The fact is that the calumniator slanders because he thinks his abilities have not been properly recognized by the husband and he has been repulsed by the wife. In a fury of jealousy the husband kills his innocent wife and then himself. That might be recognized as the story of any one of

---

[1] *Some Platitudes Concerning Drama, Atlantic Monthly,* December, 1909.

fifty French, German, Italian, English, or American plays of the last hundred years. It is, of course, the story of *Othello* — a masterpiece because Shakespeare knew Othello, Iago, Desdemona, and Cassio so intimately that by their interplay of character upon character they shape every scene perfectly. In other words, though a striking dramatic situation is undoubtedly dramatic treasure trove, whether it can be developed into anything fresh and contributive depends on a careful study of the people involved. What must they be to give rise to such a situation — not each by himself, but when brought together under the conditions of the scene? Even if a writer knows this, he must work backward into the earlier history of his people before he can either move through the particular scene or go forward into other scenes which should properly result from it.

Far too often plays are planned in this way. A writer thinks of some setting that will permit him a large amount of local color — a barroom, a dance hall, the wharf of an incoming ocean liner. Recognizing or not that most of this local color is unessential to the real action of the play, he does see that one or two incidents which are necessary and striking may be set against this background. Knowing broadly, how he wants to treat the scene, instead of studying the main and minor characters in it till he knows them so intimately that he can select from a larger amount of material than he can possibly use, he moves, not where the characters lead him, but whither, *vi et armis*, he can drive them. Rarely to him will come the delightful dilemma, so commonly experienced by the dramatist who really cares for character, when he must choose between what he was going to do and the scene as developed by the creatures of his imagination who, as they become real, take the scene away from him and shape it to vastly richer results.[1]

[1] See the quotation from Stevenson, p. 243, as to *Weir of Hermiston.*

When the dramatist interested only in situation shapes the acts preceding his most important scene, he searches simply for conditions of character which will permit this important scene to follow. Result: earlier acts, largely of exposition and talk, or of illustrative action slight and unconvincing because characters forced into a crucial situation can hardly reveal how they brought themselves to it. There is no middle way for the dramatist who seeks truth in character-ization. Given a situation, either it must grow naturally out of the characters in it, or the people originally in the mind of the author must be remodeled till they fit naturally into the situation. In the latter case, all that precedes and follows the central situation must be re-worked, not as the dramatist may wish, but as the remodeled characters permit. A critic met a well-known dramatist on the Strand. The dramatist looked worried. "What's the matter," queried the critic, "anything gone wrong?" "Yes. You remember the play I told you about, and that splendid situation for my hero-ine?" "Yes. Well?" "Well! She won't go into it, con-found her, do the best I can." "Why make her?" "Why? Because if I don't there's an end to that splendid situation." "Well?" "Oh, that's just why I'm bothered. I don't want to give in, I don't want to lose that situation; but she's right, of course she's right, and the trouble is I know I've got to yield."

At first sight the problem may seem different in an histori-cal play, for here a writer is not creating incident but is often baffled by the amount of material from which he must select, — happenings that seem equally dramatic, speeches that cry out to be transferred to the stage, and delightful bits of illustrative action. Yet, whether his underlying purpose is to convey an idea, depict a character, or tell a story, how can he decide which bits among his material make the best illustrative action before he has minutely studied the im-

portant figures? Above all others, the dramatist working
with history is subject to the principles of characterization
already laid down. Lessing stated the whole case suc-
cinctly:

Only if he chooses other and even opposed characters to the
historical, he should refrain from using historical names, and
rather credit totally unknown personages with well-known facts
than invent characters to well-known personages. The one mode
enlarges our knowledge or seems to enlarge it and is thus agreeable.
The other contradicts the knowledge that we already possess and
is thus unpleasant. We regard the facts as something accidental, as
something that may be common to many persons; the characters
we regard as something individual and intrinsic. The poet may
take any liberties he likes with the former so long as he does not
put the facts into contradiction with the characters; the characters
he may place in full light but he may not change them, the smallest
change seems to destroy their individuality and to substitute in
their place other persons, false persons, who have usurped strange
names and pretend to be what they are not.[1]

There is, however, a contrasting danger to insufficient
characterization. Any one profoundly interested in character may easily fill a scene with delicate touches which nevertheless swell the play to undue length. When careful examination of a play which is too long makes obvious that no act
or scene can be spared in whole or in part, and that the
dialogue is nowhere wordy or redundant, watch the best
characterized scenes to discover whether something has not
been conveyed by two strokes rather than one. If so, choose
the better. Watch the scenes also lest delicate and sure
touches of characterization may have been included which,
delightful though they be, are not absolutely necessary to
our understanding of the character. If so, select what most
swiftly yet clearly gives the needed information. Over-
detail in characterization is the reason why certain modern

---

[1] *Hamburg Dramaturgy*, p. 324. Lessing. Bohn ed.

plays have sagged, or hitched their way to a conclusion, instead of producing the effect desired by the author.

For ultimate convincingness no play can rise above the level of its characterization. The playwright who works for only momentary success may doubtless depend upon the onward rush of events, in a play of strong emotion, to blind his audience to lack of motivation in his characters. John Fletcher is the great leader of these opportunists of the theatre. Evadne, in *The Maid's Tragedy*,[1] killing the King, is a very different woman from the Evadne who gladly became his mistress. Nor are the reproaches and exhortations of her brother Melantius powerful enough to change a woman of her character so swiftly and completely. An audience, absorbed in the emotion of the moment, may overlook such faults of characterization in the theatre. As it reviews the play in calmer mood, however, it ranks it, no matter how poetic as a whole or how well characterized in particular scenes, not as a drama which interprets life, but as mere entertainment. Even perfect characterization of some figures, when the chief are mere puppets, cannot make us accept the play as more than pure fiction. In Thomas Heywood's *A Woman Killed with Kindness* and *English Traveler*,[2] if the erring wives and their lovers were only as well characterized as the fine-spirited husbands, the servants, and youths like Young Geraldine, the plays might hold the stage today. Doubtless the actor's art in the days of Elizabeth and James gave to villains like Wendoll and women like Mrs. Frankford enough verisimilitude to make the plays far more convincing than they are in the reading. But try as we may, we cannot understand from the text either of these characters. Their motivation is totally inadequate; that is, their conduct seems not to grow out of their

[1] Belle-Lettres Series. A. H. Thorndike, ed. D. C. Heath & Co., Boston and New York.
[2] Mermaid Series for both plays. Chas. Scribner's Sons, New York.

characters. Rather, they are the creatures of any situation into which the dramatist wishes to thrust them.

This need of motivation may be fundamental, that is, the characters may seem to an audience unconvincing from the start; or may be evident in some insufficiently explained change, transition in character; or may appear only in the last scene of the play, where characters hitherto consistent are made to act in a way which seems to the audience improbable. When Nathaniel Rowe produced his *Ambitious Stepmother* in 1700, Charles Gildon bitterly attacked it as unconvincing in its very fundamentals.

Mirza is indeed a Person of a peculiar Taste; for a Cunning Man to own himself a Rogue to the Man he shou'd keep in ignorance, and whom he was to work to his ends, argues little pretence to that Name; but he laughs at *Honesty*, and professes himself a Knave to one he wou'd have honest to him. . . .

In the second Act, he talks of *Memnon's* having recourse to Arms, of which Power we have not the least Word in the first: All that we know is, that he returns from Banishment on a day of Jubilee, when all was Safe and Free. . . .[1]

For similar reasons, Mr. Eaton criticises unfavorably *The Fighting Hope:*

One of the best (or the worst) examples of false ethics in such a play is furnished by *The Fighting Hope*, produced by Mr. Belasco in the Autumn of 1908, and acted by Miss Blanche Bates. In this play a man, Granger, has been jailed, his wife and the world believe for another man's crime. The other man, Burton Temple, is president of the bank Granger has been convicted of robbing. A district attorney, hot after men higher up, is about to reopen the case. It begins to look bad for Temple. Mrs. Granger, disguised as a stenographer, goes to his house to secure evidence against him. What she secures is a letter proving that not he, but her husband, was after all the criminal.

Of course this letter is a knockout blow for her. She realizes that the "father of her boys" is a thief, that the man she would send

---

[1] *A New Rehearsal, or Bays the Younger.* Charles Gildon. 1714–15.

to jail (and with whom you know the dramatist is going to make her finally fall in love) is innocent. Still, in her first shock, her instinct to protect the "father of her boys" persists, and she burns the letter.

So far, so good, but Mrs. Granger is represented as a woman of fine instincts and character. That she should persist in cooler blood in her false and immoral supposition that her boys' name will be protected or their happiness preserved — to say nothing of her own — by the guilt of two parents instead of one, is hard to believe. Yet that is exactly what the play asks you to believe, and it asks you to assume that here is a true dilemma. A babbling old house-keeper, whose chief use in the house seems to be to help the plot along, after the manner of stage servants, tells Mrs. Granger that she must not atone for her act by giving honest testimony in court, that of course she must let an innocent man go to jail, to "save her boys' name."

It would be much more sensible should Mrs. Granger here strike the immoral old lady, instead of saving her blows for her cur of a husband, in the last act, who, after all, was the "father of her boys." But she listens to her. She appears actually in doubt not only as to which course she will pursue, but which she should pursue. She is intended by the dramatist as a pitiable object because on the one hand she feels it right to save an innocent man (whom she has be-gun to love), and on the other feels it her duty to save her sons' happiness by building their future on a structure of lies and deceit. And she reaches a solution, not by reasoning the tangle out, not by any real thought for her boys, their general moral welfare, not by any attention to principles, but simply by discovering that her hus-band has been sexually unfaithful to her. Further, he becomes a cad and charges her with infidelity. Then she springs upon him and beats him with her fists, which is not the most effective way of convincing an audience that she was a woman capable of being torn by moral problems.

Of course as the play is written, there is no moral problem. The morality is all of the theatre. It belongs to that strange world behind the proscenium, wherein we gaze, and gazing sometimes utter chatter about "strong situations," "stirring climaxes," and the like, as people hypnotized. There might have been a moral problem if Mrs. Granger, before she discovered her husband's guilt, had been forced to fight a rising tide of passion for Temple in her own heart. There might have been a moral problem after the discovery and her first hasty, but natural, destruction of the letter, if she had felt that her desire to save Temple was prompted by a passion still illicit, rather than by justice. But no such real problems were presented. The lady babbles eternally of "saving her boys' good name," while you are supposed to weep for her plight. Unless you have checked your sense of reality in the cloak room, you scorn her perceptions and despise her standards. How much finer had she continued to love her husband! But he, after all, was only the "father of her boys." [1]

It is insufficiently motivated characterization which Mr. Eaton censures in *The Nigger:*

Obviously, the emotional interest in this play is — or should be, rather — in the tragedy of the proud, ambitious Morrow, who wakes suddenly to find himself a "nigger," an exile from his home, and hopes, from his sweetheart and his dreams. Yet, as Mr. Sheldon has written it, and as it was played by Mr. Guy Bates Post in the part of Morrow, and by the other actors, the play is most poignant in its moments of sheer theatrical appeal, almost of melodrama, such as the suspense of the cross-examination of the old mammy and her cry of revelation, or the pursuit of the fugitive in act one. Between his interest in the suspense of his story and in the elucidation of the broader aspects of the negro question in the South, Mr. Sheldon neglected too much his chief figure, as a human being. Unless the figures live and suffer for the audience, unless their personal fate is followed, their minds and hearts felt as real, the naturalistic drama of contemporary life can have but little value, after all. That is what makes its technique so difficult and so baffling. From the moment when Morrow learned of his birth, he became a rather nebulous figure, not suffering so much as listening to theories which were only said by the dramatist to have altered his character and point of view. [2]

Perhaps it would be more strictly accurate to say that the comment on *The Nigger* points to inadequate treatment of character changing as the play progresses. The favorite place of many so-called dramatists for a change of character

[1] *At the New Theatre,* pp. 189–192. W. P. Eaton. Small, Maynard & Co., Boston.
[2] *Idem,* pp. 47–48.

is in their vast silences between the acts. There, the authors expect us to believe that marked and necessary changes take place. They show us in clear-cut dramatic action the good character before he became bad and after he has become bad, but for proof that the changes took place, we must look off stage in the *entr'acte*. Read *Lady Bountiful* and note that between the last and the next to the last acts large changes have taken place in the main characters. *Iris* would be a far greater play than it is could we have seen how its central figure passes from the taking of the check book to the state of mind which makes her accept Maldonado's apartment. Contrast with these plays the thoroughly motivated change in the Sergeant of *The Rising of the Moon* or of Nora in *A Doll's House.*

Where American plays too frequently break down is in what may be called the logic of character. Even when actions have been properly motivated up to the last act or scene, this is handled in such a way as rather to please the audience than to grow inevitably out of what has preceded. Rumor has it that when *Secret Service* was produced in one of the central cities of New York State, the hero at the end chose his country rather than the girl. The public, with that fine disregard in the theatre for the values it places on action outside, disapproved. Promptly, the ending was so changed that the two lovers could be started on that sure road to happiness ever after which all men know an engagement is — upon the stage. In a play such as *Secret Service*, planned primarily to entertain, such a shift may be pardonable, but even in such a case it must be done with skill if it is not to jar. *The Two Gentlemen of Verona* in some fifty lines at its close shows Proteus madly in love with Silvia, and Valentine longing for her also; Valentine threatening the life of Proteus when he discovers the latter's perfidy, but forgiving him instantly when Proteus merely asks pardon;

and Proteus, when he discovers that the page who has been
following him is Julia, turning instantly away from Silvia
to her. Here is faulty characterization in two respects: each
change is not sufficiently motived; each does not accord with
the characterization of Proteus and Valentine in the earlier
scenes.

> *Proteus.* Nay, if the gentle spirit of moving words
> Can no way change you to a milder form,
> I'll woo you like a soldier, at arms' end,
> And love you 'gainst the nature of love, — force ye.
>   *Silvia.* O heaven!
>   *Pro.*   I'll force thee yield to my desire.
>   *Valentine.* Ruffian, let go that rude uncivil touch,
> Thou friend of an ill fashion!
>   *Pro.*   Valentine!
>   *Val.* Thou common friend, that's without faith or love,
> For such is a friend now! Treacherous man,
> Thou hast beguil'd my hopes! Nought but mine eye
> Could have persuaded me. Now I dare not say
> I have one friend alive; thou wouldst disprove me.
> Who should be trusted now, when one's right hand
> Is perjured to the bosom? Proteus,
> I am sorry I must never trust thee more,
> But count the world a stranger for thy sake.
> The private wound is deepest. O time most accurst,
> 'Mongst all foes that a friend should be the worst!
>   *Pro.* My shame and guilt confounds me.
> Forgive me, Valentine; if hearty sorrow
> Be a sufficient ransom for offence,
> I tender't here; I do as truly suffer
> As e'er I did commit.
>   *Val.*   Then I am paid;
> And once again I do receive thee honest.
> Who by repentance is not satisfied
> Is nor of heaven nor earth, for these are pleas'd.
> By penitence the Eternal's wrath's appeas'd;
> And, that my love may appear plain and free,
> All that was mine in Silvia I give thee.
>   *Julia.* O me unhappy!   (*Swoons.*)

Pro. Look to the boy.

Val. Why, boy! why, wag! how now! What's the matter? Look up; speak.

Jul. O good sir, my master charg'd me to deliver a ring to Madame Silvia, which, out of my neglect, was never done.

Pro. Where is that ring, boy?

Jul. Here 'tis; this is it.

Pro. How? let me see!

Why this is the ring I gave to Julia.

Jul. O, cry you mercy, sir, I have mistook;

Pro. But how cam'st thou by this ring? At my depart
I gave this unto Julia.

Jul. And Julia herself did give it me;
And Julia herself hath brought it hither.

Pro. How! Julia!

Jul. Behold her that gave aim to all thy oaths,
And entertain'd 'em deeply in her heart.
How oft hast thou with perjury cleft the root!
O Proteus let this habit make thee blush!
Be thou asham'd that I have took upon me
Such an immodest raiment, if shame live
In a disguise of love.
It is the lesser blot, modesty finds,
Women to change their shapes than men their minds.

Pro. Than men their minds! 'tis true. O heaven! were man
But constant, he were perfect. That one error
Fills him with faults; makes him run through all the sins.
Inconstancy falls off ere it begins.
What is Silvia's face, but I may spy
More fresh in Julia's with a constant eye?

Val. Come, come, a hand from either.
Let me be blest to make this happy close;
'Twere pity two such friends should be long foes.

Pro. Bear witness, Heaven, I have my wish for ever.

Jul. And I mine.

Similar inconsistencies are in many modern plays. A dramatist has a particularly striking scene which he wishes to make the climax of his play. Into it he forces his figures regardless. Lessing made fun of this fault.

... In another still worse tragedy where one of the principal characters died quite casually, a spectator asked his neighbor, "But what did she die of?" — "Of what? Of the fifth act," was the reply. In very truth the fifth act is an ugly evil disease that carries off many a one to whom the first four acts promised a longer life.[1]

Or it may be, as in the case of Shakespeare just cited, that a dramatist feels certain changes of character are necessary if the play is to end as promptly as it must. Such changes, therefore, he brings about even if it means throwing character or truth to the winds. English and American plays of the 1880 and 1890 periods show many instances of theatrically effective endings either forced upon the characters or only one of several possible endings — and not the most probable. According to the conventions of the time, any young woman who had parted with her virtue, no matter what the circumstances, must make reparation by death. This usually came from some wasting but not clearly diagnosed disease. There was not always a clear distinction between inanition and inanity. A similar convention usually saved from death the male partners of these "faults," provided they indulged at the right moment in self-repentant speeches. Sir Arthur Pinero, writing what he regarded as the logical ending of *The Profligate*, was forced by the sentimentality of his public to keep Dunstan Renshaw alive. Here are the two endings:

THE ENDING AS ACTED

Dunstan. (*He is raising the glass to his lips when he recoils with a cry of horror.*) Ah! stop, stop! This is the deepest sin of all my life — blacker than that sin for which I suffer! No, I'll not! I'll not! (*He dashes the glass to the ground.*) God, take my wretched life when You will, but till You lay Your hand upon me, I will live on! Help me! Give me strength to live on! Help me! Oh, help me!

[1] *Hamburg Dramaturgy*, p. 238. Bohn ed.

(*He falls on his knees and buries his face in his hands. Leslie enters softly, carrying a lamp which she places on the sideboard; then she goes to Dunstan.*)

Leslie. Dunstan! Dunstan!

Dunstan. You! You!

Leslie. I have remembered. When we stood together at our prayerless marriage, my heart made promises my lips were not allowed to utter. I will not part from you, Dunstan.

Dunstan. Not — part — from me?

Leslie. No.

Dunstan. I don't understand you. You — will — not — relent? You cannot forget what I am!

Leslie. No. But the burden of the sin you have committed I will bear upon my shoulders, and the little good that is in me shall enter into your heart. We will start life anew, always seeking for the best that we can do, always trying to repair the worst that we have done. (*Stretching out her hand to him.*) Dunstan! (*He approaches her as in a dream.*) Don't fear me! I will be your wife, not your judge. Let us from this moment begin the new life you spoke of.

Dunstan. (*He tremblingly touches her hand as she bursts into tears.*) Wife! Ah, God bless you! God bless you, and forgive me!

(*He kneels at her side, and she bows her head down to his.*)

Leslie. Oh, my husband!

THE ENDING AS PRINTED

Dunstan. Fool! Fool! Why couldn't you have died in Florence? Why did you drag yourself here all these miles — to end it *here?* I should have known better — I should have known better. (*He takes a phial from his pocket and slowly pours some poison into a tumbler.*) When I've proved that I could not live away from her, perhaps she'll pity me. I shall never know it, but perhaps she'll pity me then. (*About to drink.*) Supposing I am blind! Supposing there is some chance of my regaining her. Regaining her! How dull sleeplessness makes me! How much could I regain of what I've lost! Why, *she knows me* — nothing can ever undo that — *she knows me.* Every day would be a dreary, hideous masquerade; every night a wakeful, torturing retrospect. If she smiled, I should whisper to myself — " yes, yes, that's a very pretty pretence, but — *she knows you !* " The slamming of a door would shout it, the creaking of a stair would murmur it " *she knows you !* " And when she thought herself alone, or while she lay in her sleep, I should be always stealthily spying for that dreadful look upon her face, and I should find it again and again as I see it now — the look which cries out so plainly "Profligate! you taught one good woman to believe in you, but now *she knows you!*" No, no—no, no! (*He drains the contents of the tumbler.*) The end — the end. (*Pointing towards the clock.*) The hour at which we used to walk together in the garden at Florence — husband and wife — lovers. (*He pulls up the window-blind and looks out.*) The sky — the last time — the sky. (*He rests drowsily against the piano.*) Tired — tired. (*He walks rather unsteadily to the table.*) A line to Murray. (*Writing.*) A line to Murray — telling him — poison — morphine — message — (*The pen falls from his hand and his head drops forward.*) The light is going out. I can't see. Light—I'll finish this when I wake — I'll rest. (*He staggers to the sofa and falls upon it.*) I shall sleep tonight. The voice has gone. Leslie — wife — reconciled —

(*Leslie enters softly and kneels by his side.*)

Leslie. Dunstan, I am here. (*He partly opens his eyes, raises himself, and stares at her; then his head falls back quietly. Leslie's face averted.*) Dunstan, I have returned to you. We are one and we will make atonement for the past together. I will be your Wife, not your Judge — let us from this moment begin the new life you spoke of. Dunstan! (*She sees the paper which has fallen from his hand, and reads it.*) Dunstan! Dunstan! No, no! Look at me! Ah! (*She catches him in her arms.*) Husband! Husband! Husband! [1]

It is of course true, as M. Brieux maintains in regard to the two endings of his early play, *Blanchette*,[2] that sometimes more than one ending may be made plausible. Consequently he changed a tragic close to something more pleasing to his audience. Belief grows, however, that when a play has been begun and developed with a tragic ending in mind, this cannot with entire convincingness be changed to something else unless the play is rewritten from the start. There is inevitableness in the conduct on the stage of the creatures of our brains even as with people of real life. So strongly does Sir Arthur Pinero feel this as the

---

[1] Walter H. Baker & Co., Boston; W. Heinemann, London.
[2] P. V. Stock, Paris. Published in translation by J. W. Luce & Co., Boston.

result of his long experience that, though he changed the
ending of *The Big Drum* in 1915 in accordance with public
demand, he restored the original version when printing the
play. He says in his Preface:

The Big Drum is published exactly as it was written, and as it
was originally performed. At its first representation, however, the
audience was reported to have been saddened by its "unhappy
ending." Pressure was forthwith put upon me to reconcile Philip
and Ottoline at the finish, and at the third performance of the play
the curtain fell upon the picture, violently and crudely brought
about, of Ottoline in Philip's arms.

I made the alteration against my principles and against my
conscience, and yet not altogether unwillingly. For we live in de-
pressing times; and perhaps in such times it is the first duty of a
writer for the stage to make concessions to his audience and,
above everything, to try to afford them a complete, if brief, distraction from the gloom which awaits them outside the theatre.

My excuse for having at the start provided an "unhappy" ending is that I was blind enough not to regard the ultimate break
between Philip and Ottoline as really unhappy for either party.
On the contrary, I looked upon the separation of these two people
as a fortunate occurrence for them both; and I conceive it as a piece
of ironic comedy which might not prove unentertaining that the
falling away of Philip from his high resolves was checked by the
woman he had once despised and who had at last grown to know
and to despise herself.

But comedy of this order has a knack of cutting rather deeply,
of ceasing, in some minds, to be comedy at all; and it may be said
that this is what has happened in the present instance. Luckily
it is equally true that certain matters are less painful, because less
actual, in print than upon the stage. The "wicked publisher"
therefore, even when bombs are dropping round him, can afford
to be more independent than the theatrical manager; and for this
reason I have not hesitated to ask my friend Mr. Heinemann to
publish *The Big Drum* in its original form.[1]

What Ibsen thought of the ultimate effect of changing an
ending to accord with public sentiment, these words about
A Doll's House show:

---

[1] Walter H. Baker & Co., Boston; W. Heinemann, London.

At the time when *A Doll's House* was quite new, I was obliged to give my consent to an alteration of the last scene for Frau Hedwig Niemann-Raabe, who was to play the part of Nora in Berlin. At that time I had no choice. I was entirely unprotected by copyright law in Germany, and could, consequently, prevent nothing. Besides, the play in its original, uncorrupted form was accessible to the German public in a German edition which was already printed and published. With its altered ending it had only a short run. In its unchanged form it is still being played.[1]

Dumas fils was even more severe in his strictures:

If at the second performance you are ready to modify your central idea, your development or your conclusion to please the public whom the night before you were pretending to teach something fresh, you may be, perhaps, an ingenious worker in the theatre, an adroit impresario, a facile inventor; you will never be a dramatist. You can make mistakes in details of execution; you have no right to make a mistake in the logic of your play, its co rrelations of emotions and acts, and least of all, in their outcome.[2]

Characterization, then, should be watched carefully in its fundamentals, all changes, and especially for its logical outcome. Long ago, Diderot summed up the subject thus:

One can form an infinitude of plans on the same subject and developed around the same characters. But the characters being once settled, they can have but one manner of speaking. Your figures will have this or that to say according to the situation in which you may have placed them, but being the same human beings in all the situations, they will not, fundamentally, contradict themselves.[3]

How may we know whether our motivation is good or not? First of all, it must be clear. If an audience cannot make out why one of our characters does what he is doing, from that moment the play weakens. It is on this ground that William Archer objected to the *Becket* of Tennyson:

---

[1] *Letters of Henrik Ibsen*, p. 437.
[2] *Au Public, La Princesse Georges.* Calmann Lévy, Paris.
[3] *Œuvres*, vol. VII, p. 320. Garnier Frères, Paris.

"Some gents," says the keeper, in *Punch,* to the unsuccessful sportsman, "goes a-wingin' and a-worritin' the poor birds; but you, sir — you misses 'em clane and nate!" With the like delicate tact criticism can only compliment the poet on the "clane and nate" way in which he has missed the historical interest, the psychological problem, of his theme. What was it that converted the Becket of Toulouse into the Becket of Clarendon — the splendid warrior-diplomatist into the austere prelate? The cowl, we are told, does not make the monk; but in Lord Tennyson's psychology it seems that it does. Of the process of thought, the development of feeling, which leads Becket, on assuming the tonsure, to break with the traditions of his career, with the friend of his heart and with his own worldly interest — of all this we have no hint. The social and political issues involved are left equally in the vague. Of the two contending forces, the Church and the Crown, which makes for good, and which for evil? With which ought we to sympathize? It might be argued that we have no right to ask this question, and that it is precisely a proof of the poet's art that he holds the balance evenly, and does not write as a partisan. But as a matter of fact this is not so. The poet is not impartial; he is only indefinite. We are evidently intended to sympathize, and we *do* sympathize, with Becket, simply because we feel that he is staking his life on a principle; but what that principle precisely is, and what its bearings on history and civilization, we are left to find out for ourselves. Thus the intellectual opportunity, if I may call it so, is missed "clane and nate."[1]

Contrast the third, fourth, and fifth acts of *Michael and His Lost Angel* [2] with the first and second. So admirable is the characterization of Acts I and II that a reader understands exactly what Audrie and Michael are doing and why. In the other acts, though what they are doing is clear, why the Audrie and Michael of the first two acts behaved thus is by no means clear and plausible. Indeed, plausibility and clearness go hand in hand as tests of motivation. Accounting for the deeds of any particular character is easy if the conduct rests on motives which any audience will immedi-

[1] *The Theatrical World for 1893,* pp. 46–47. W. Archer. Walter Scott, Ltd., London.
[2] The Macmillan Co., New York.

ately recognize as both widespread and likely to produce
the situation. It is just here, however, that national taste
and literary convention complicate the work of the dramatist. An American, watching a performance of *Simone* [1]
by M. Brieux, hardly understood the loud protests which
burst from the audience when the heroine, at the end of the
play, sternly denounced her father's conduct. To him, it
seemed quite natural that an American girl should assume
this right of individual judgment. The French audience
felt that a French girl, because of her training, would not,
under the circumstances, thus attack her father. M. Brieux
admitted himself wrong and changed the ending. It is this
fact, that conduct plausible for one nation is not always
equally plausible for another, which makes it hard for an
American public to understand a goodly number of the
masterpieces of recent Continental dramatic literature.

What literary convention may do in twisting conduct
from the normal, the pseudo-classic French drama of Corneille and Racine, and its foster child, the Heroic Drama of
England, illustrate. Dryden himself points out clearly the
extent to which momentary convention among the French
deflected the characters in their tragedies from the normal:

> The French poets . . . would not, for example, have suffer'd
> Cleopatra and Octavia to have met; or, if they had met, there must
> only have passed betwixt them some cold civilities, but no eagerness
> of repartee, for fear of offending against the greatness of their char-
> acters, and the modesty of their sex. This objection I foresaw, and
> at the same time contemn'd; for I judg'd it both natural and prob-
> able that Octavia, proud of her new-gain'd conquest, would search
> out Cleopatra to triumph over her; and that Cleopatra, thus at-
> tack'd, was not of a spirit to shun the encounter: and 'tis not un-
> likely that two exasperated rivals should use such satire as I have
> put into their mouths; for, after all, tho' the one were a Roman, and
> the other a queen, they were both women.

∘ ⋅ ⋅ ⋅ ⋅ ⋅ ⋅ ⋅ ⋅ ⋅ ⋅ ⋅ ⋅ ⋅ ⋅

[1] P. V. Stock, Paris.

Thus, their Hippolytus is so scrupulous in point of decency that he will rather expose himself to death than accuse his stepmother to his father; and my critics I am sure will commend him for it: but we of grosser apprehensions are apt to think that this excess of generosity is not practicable, but with fools and madmen. This was good manners with a vengeance; and the audience is like to be much concern'd at the misfortunes of this admirable hero; but take Hippolytus out of his poetic fit, and I suppose he would think it a wiser part to set the saddle on the right horse, and choose rather to live with the reputation of a plain-spoken, honest man, than to die with the infamy of an incestuous villain. In the meantime we may take notice that where the poet ought to have preserv'd the character as it was deliver'd to us by antiquity, when he should have given us the picture of a rough young man, of the Amazonian strain, a jolly huntsman, and both by his profession and his early rising a mortal enemy to love, he has chosen to give him the turn of gallantry, sent him to travel from Athens to Paris, taught him to make love, and transformed the Hippolytus of Euripides into Monsieur Hippolyte.[1]

One of the chief elements in the genius of Shakespeare is his power to transcend momentary conventions, fads, and theories, and to discern in his material, whether history or fiction, eternal principles of conduct. Thus he wrote for all men and for all time. In *Love's Labor's Lost* he wrote for a special audience, appealing to its ideas of style and humor. In *Twelfth Night* he let his characters have full sway. Which is the more alive today?

Nor is it only the literary conventions of an audience which affect the problem of plausibility set an author. The French public of 1841 which came to the five-act play of Eugène Scribe, *Une Chaine*,[2] asked, not a convincing picture of life, but mere entertainment. Therefore they accepted insufficient motivation and artificiality in handling the scenes. Louise, the wife, discovering from words of her

---

[1] *Selected Dramas of John Dryden*, p. 230. Preface, *All for Love*. G. R. Noyes, ed. Scott, Foresman & Co., New York.
[2] *Théâtre*, vol. II. Michel Lévy Frères, Paris.

husband as she enters the room that her former lover, Emmeric, now prefers Aline to her, sits down and dashes off a signed letter releasing him. Just why is not clear. In order that she may do this writing unobserved by her husband, two characters must, for some time, be so managed as to stand between him and her. In order that the husband may never know she has been in love with Emmeric, the letter must be kept out of his hands, and read only by the guardian of Aline, Clerambeau. All this requires constant artifice. Sidney Grundy made a one-act adaptation of *Une Chaine* called *In Honor Bound*.[1] In this, Lady Carlyon, waking from sleep on the divan in her husband's study, hears, unobserved by Philip and Sir George, the young man's admission that he no longer cares for her. When her cry reveals her, Sir George, her husband, thinking her unwell, goes to bring her niece, Rose, to her aid. Lady Carlyon learns promptly from Philip that the guardian of the girl he is engaged to demands a letter releasing him from any former entanglement. Lady Carlyon, to cover her chagrin, with seeming willingness writes and signs a letter. Thus the writing takes place when the husband is off stage, and the evident chagrin of Lady Carlyon motivates it better. The relation of the husband to the letter is also handled better than in the original. He, unlike St. Geran, strongly suspects that his wife has cared for the younger man. Lady Carlyon is unaware that Sir George is the guardian in question and that the girl is her niece, Rose. Consequently she lets slip that Philip possesses the desired letter. Sir George demands it as his right, noting her disturbance when she learns that her husband is involved in the situation. When Philip refuses to surrender the letter, Sir George courteously permits him to read it aloud. Just before the signature is reached, he stops Philip, asking him if the letter is signed. When Philip

[1] Walter H. Baker & Co., Boston.

admits that it is, Sir George insists on having the letter, then, without looking at it, burns it at the lamp with words of sympathy for the writer. All this turns the husband in this scene from a mere lay figure into a character, and greatly lessens the artificiality of the original. By means of better characterization a motivation fundamentally more plausible is provided. Why? Because an English audience of 1880–90 expected much more probability in a play than did a French or English audience of 1841.

Of course, conduct initially unconvincing may be so treated as to become entirely satisfactory. One of the delights in characterization is so preparing for an exhibition of character likely to seem unreal of itself that when it is presented it is accepted either at once or before the scene closes. Any motive which a dramatist can make acceptable to his audience is ultimately just as good as one accepted unquestioningly. Shylock's demand for the pound of flesh is in itself unplausible enough — the act of one demented or insane. But Shakespeare's emphasis on his racial hate lends it possibility. His presentation of the other people in the play as accepting the bond with the minimum of question makes it seem probable. If a would-be dramatist were to rule out as material not to be treated whatever at the outset seems improbable or impossible, think what our drama would lose: such plays as *Faust, Midsummer Night's Dream, The Blue Bird,* and even *Hamlet.*

Repeatedly in treating plausibility it has been implied or stated that what is said or done must be " in character." This suggests another test of good motivation. What happens must be plausible, not only in that it accords with known human experience, but with what has been done by the character in preceding portions of the play. In *The Masqueraders,* when Sir Brice and David stake Dulcie and her child against the fortune of the latter, and let all turn upon a game of cards, a reader is skeptical, for even if it be admitted that Sir Brice might do this, it does not accord with what we know of David from the earlier scenes of the play.

> (*Exit Dulcie. The two men are left alone. Another slight pause. Sir Brice walks very deliberately up to David. The two men stand close to each other for a moment or two.*)

Sir Brice. You've come to settle your little account, I suppose?

David. I owe you nothing.

Sir Brice. But I owe you six thousand pounds. I haven't a penny in the world. I'll cut you for it, double or quits.

David. I don't play cards.

Sir Brice. You'd better begin.

> (*Rapping on the table with the cards.*)

David. (*Very firmly.*) I don't play cards with *you*.

Sir Brice. And I say you shall.

David. (*Very stern and contemptuous.*) I don't play cards with you. (*Going towards door; Sir Brice following him up.*)

Sir Brice. You refuse?

David. I refuse.

Sir Brice. (*Stopping him.*) Once for all, will you give me a chance of paying back the six thousand pounds that Lady Skene has borrowed from you? Yes or no?

David. No.

Sir Brice. No?

David. (*Very emphatically.*) No. (*Goes to door, suddenly turns round, comes up to him.*) Yes. (*Comes to the table.*) I *do* play cards with you. You want my money. Very well. I'll give you a chance of winning all I have in the world.

Sir Brice. (*After a look of astonishment.*) Good. I'm your man. Any game you like, and any stakes.

David. (*Very calm, cold, intense tone all through.*) The stakes on my side are some two hundred thousand pounds. The stakes on your side are — your wife and child.

Sir Brice. (*Taken aback.*) My wife and child.

David. Your wife and child. Come — begin!

> (*Points to the cards.*)

Sir Brice. (*Getting flurried.*) My wife and child? (*Puts his hand restlessly through his hair, looks intently at David. Pause.*) All right. (*Pause. Cunningly.*) I value my wife and child very highly.

David. I value them at all I have in the world. (*Pointing to the cards.*) Begin!

Sir Brice. You seem in a hurry.

David. I believe I haven't six months to live. I want to make the most of those six months. If I have more I want to make the most of all the years. Begin!

Sir Brice. (*Wipes his face with his handkerchief.*) This is the first time I've played this game. We'd better arrange conditions.

David. There's only one condition. We play till I'm beggared of every farthing I have, or till you're beggared of them. Sit down!

Sir Brice. (*Sits down.*) Very well. (*Pause.*) What game?

David. The shortest.

Sir Brice. Simple cutting?

David. What you please. Begin!

Sir. Brice. There's no hurry. I mean to have a night's fun out of this.

David. Look at me. Don't trifle with me! I want to have done with you. I want them to have done with you. I want to get them away from you. Quick! I want to know now — now — this very moment — whether they are yours or mine. Begin.

Sir Brice. (*Shuffles the cards.*) All right. What do we cut for?

David. Let one cut settle it.

Sir Brice. No. It's too much to risk on one throw.

David. One cut. Begin.

Sir Brice. It's too big. I can't. (*Gets up, walks a pace or two.*) I like high play, but that's too high for me. (*David remains at back of table, very calm ; does not stir all through the scene ; Sir Brice walking about.*) No, by Jove! I'll tell you what I'll do. Three cuts out of five. Damn it all! I'm game! Two out of three. By Jove, two out of three! Will that do?

David. So be it! Shuffle. Sit down!

> (*Sir Brice sits down ; begins shuffling the cards. All through the scene he is nervous, excited, hysterical, laughing. David as cold as a statue.*)[1]

An almost similar situation in a play set in a remote part of the West, *Believe Me, Xantippe*, is more convincing. A loutish beast agrees to gamble for a woman he is kidnapping with a young adventurer who sees at the moment no other way to save her from the other man's clutches. The scene

---

[1] The Macmillan Co., New York. Act III.

is not at all improbable for either man. In *The Princess and the Butterfly*, all the preceding acts are but a preparation for what the world will call the unreason, in the last act, of the marriages of Sir George and the Princess Pannonia, — of middle age with youth. Their final conduct would seem unplausible were it not entirely in keeping with their characters as carefully developed in the earlier parts of the play. *The Rising of the Moon* of Lady Gregory shows a final situation for the Police Sergeant which, at the opening of the play, would seem impossible for him. In a few pages, however, the dramatist so develops the character that we are perfectly ready to accept his sacrifice of the "hundred pounds reward" which he so coveted at the outset.

Motivation should not, however, be allowed to obtrude itself, but should be subordinated to the emotional purpose of the scene. The modern auditor prefers to gather it almost unconsciously as the action of the play proceeds rather than to have it emphasized for him, as does Iago, at the end of several acts of *Othello*. Another instance of this frank motivation among the Elizabethans may be found in the soliloquy from *The Duchess of Malfi:*

> *Cardinal.* The reason why I would not suffer these
> About my brother is because at midnight
> I may with better privacy convay
> Julias body, to her owne lodging. O, my conscience!
> I would pray now: but the divell takes away my heart
> For having any confidence in praier.
> About this hour I appointed Bosola
> To fetch the body: when he hath serv'd my turne,
> He dies.[1]

Good motivation, then, must be clear; either plausible naturally or made so by the art of the dramatist; should in each particular instance comport with the preceding actions and speech of the character; and should not be so stressed

[1] Belles-Lettres Series, p. 373. M. W. Sampson, ed. D. C. Heath & Co., Boston.

as to draw attention away from the emotional significance of the scene.

It is by well-motived characterization that drama passes from melodrama to story-play and so to tragedy; or, from the broadest farce or extravaganza through low comedy to high. As long as we care little what the people in our play are, and greatly for comic or serious happenings, we may string situations together almost at will. The moment that our figures come alive, as has been pointed out, selection in our possible material has begun. Some of the incidents in our melodrama or broad farce will drop out as wholly impossible for these figures which have come to life. Others must be modified if the figures are to take part in them. Give a melodrama sustaining, convincing characterization and it must at least turn into a story-play, something which after a mingling of the serious and the comic does not end tragically. So characterize in a story with a serious ending that the tragic result develops inevitably from the sequence of preceding scenes, and tragedy is born. Watch the way in which Shakespeare lifts the Hubert and Arthur scene of the old play of *King John* by the infused characterization. In the old play the author presents us with puppets depending for their effect on the contained horror of the scene. Shakespeare creates a winsome, brave young prince, and a very human Hubert. The scene moves us, not simply from our dread of physical torture, but because of our growing intense sympathy for the lad who is fighting for his life.

ACT IV. SCENE 1. *North-ampton. A Room in the castle*

Enter Hubert de Burgh with three men

Enter Hubert and two Attendants

Hub. My masters, I have shewed you what warrant I have of this attempt; I perceive

Hub. Heat me these irons hot, and look thou stand Within the arras: when I strike my foot

by your heavie countenances,
you had rather be otherwise im-
ployed, and for my owne part,
I would the King had made
choyce of some other executioner; onely this is my comfort,
that a King commaunds, whose
precepts neglected or omitted,
threatneth torture for the de-
fault. Therefore in briefe, leave
me, and be readie to attend the
adventure: stay within that
entry, and when you hear me
crie, God save the King, issue
sodainly foorth, lay handes on
Arthur, set him in his chayre,
wherein (once fast bound) leave
him with me to finish the rest.
Attendants. We goe, though
loath.   (*Exeunt.*)
Hub. My Lord, will it please
your Honour to take the bene-
fite of the faire evening?

Enter Arthur to Hubert de Burgh

Arth. Gramercie Hubert for
   thy care of me,
In or to whom restraint is newly
   knowen,
The joy of walking is small benefit,
Yet will I take thy offer with
   small thankes,
I would not loose the pleasure
   of the eye.
But tell me curteous Keeper if
   you can,
How long the King will have me
   tarrie here.
Hub. I know not Prince, but
   as I gesse, not long.

Upon the bosom of the ground,
   rush forth,
And bind the boy, which you
   shall find with me,
Fast to the chair: be heedful.
   Hence, and watch.
1. Attend. I hope, your warrant will bear out the deed.
Hub. Uncleanly scruples: fear
   not you: look to't. —
            (*Exeunt Attendants.*)
Young lad, come forth; I have
   to say with you.

Enter Arthur

Arth. Good morning, Hubert.
Hub.   Good morrow,
   little prince.
Arth. As little prince (having
   so great a title
To be more prince,) as may be.
   — You are sad.
Hub. Indeed I have been mer-
   rier.
Arth. Mercy on me!
Methinks nobody should be sad
   but I:
Yet, I remember, when I was in
   France,
Young gentlemen would be as
   sad as night,
Only for wantonness. By my
   christendom,
So I were out of prison and kept
   sheep,
I should be as merry as the day
   is long;
And so I would be here, but that
   I doubt
My uncle practises more harm
   to me:

God send you freedome, and God save the King.

(*They issue forth.*)

Arth. Why now sirs, what may this outrage meane?

O help me Hubert, gentle Keeper helpe;

God send this sodaine mutinous approach

Tend not to reave a wretched guiltless life.

Hub. So sirs, depart, and leave the rest for me.

Arth. Then Arthur yeeld, death frowneth in thy face,

What meaneth this? Good Hubert plead the case.

Hub. Patience yong Lord, and listen words of woe,

Harmful and harsh, hells horror to be heard:

A dismall tale fit for a furies tongue.

I faint to tell, deepe sorrow is the sound.

Arth. What, must I die?

Hub. No newes of death, but tidings of more hate,

A wrathfull doome, and most unluckie fate:

Deaths dish were daintie at so fell a feast,

Be deafe, heare not, its hell to tell the rest.

Arth. Alas, thou wrongst my youth with words of feare,

Tis hell, tis horror, not for one to heare:

What is it man if needes be don,

Act it, and end it, that the paine were gon.

He is afraid of me and I of him.

Is it my fault that I was Geffrey's son?

No, indeed, is't not; and I would to heaven,

I were your son, so you would love me, Hubert.

Hub. (*Aside.*) If I talk to him, with his innocent prate

He will awake my mercy, which lies dead:

Therefore I will be sudden, and dispatch.

Arth. Are you sick, Hubert? you look pale today.

In sooth, I would you were a little sick;

That I might sit all night, and watch with you:

I warrant I love you more than you do me.

Hub. (*Aside.*) His words do take possession of my bosom. —

Read here, young Arthur,

(*Showing a paper.*)

(*Aside.*) How now, foolish rheum!

Turning dispiteous torture out of door?

I must be brief; lest resolution drop

Out at mine eyes in tender womanish tears.—

Can you read it? Is it not fair writ?

Arth. Too fairly, Hubert, for so foul effect.

Must you with hot irons burn out both mine eyes?

Hub. Young boy, I must.

Hub. I will not chaunt such dolour with my tongue,
Yet must I act the outrage with my hand.
My heart, my head, and all my powers beside,
To aide the office have at once denide.
Peruse this Letter, lines of treble woe,
Reade ore my charge, and pardon when you know.

Hubert, these are to commaund thee, as thou tendrest our quiet in minde, and the estate of our person, that presently upon the receipt of our commaund, thou put out the eies of Arthur Plantaginet.

Arth. Ah, monstrous damned man! his very breath infects the elements.
Contagious venyme dwelleth in his heart;
Effecting meanes to poyson all the world.
Unreverent may I be to blame the heavens
Of great injustice, that the miscreant
Lives to oppresse the innocents with wrong.
Ah, Hubert! makes he thee his instrument,
To sound the tromp that causeth hell triumph?
Heaven weepes, the Saints do shed celestiall teares,

Arth. And will you?
Hub. And I will.
Arth. Have you the heart? When your head did but ache,
I knit my handkerchief about your brows,
(The best I had, a princess wrought it me,)
And I did never ask it you again:
And with my hand at midnight held your head,
And, like the watchful minutes to the hour,
Still and anon cheer'd up the heavy time,
Saying, What lack you? and, Where lies your grief?
Or, What good love may I perform for you?
Many a poor man's son would have lain still,
And ne'er have spoken a loving word to you;
But you at your sick service had a prince.
Nay you may think my love was crafty love,
And call it cunning: do, an if you will.
If heaven be pleas'd that you will use me ill,
Why, then you must. — Will you put out mine eyes?
These eyes that never did, nor never shall
So much as frown on you?
Hub. I have sworn to do it,
And with hot irons must I burn them out.

They feare thy fall, and cyte
    thee with remorse,
To knock thy conscience, mov-
    ing pitie there,
Willing to fence thee from the
    range of hell,

Hell, Hubert, trust me all the
    plagues of hell
Hangs on performance of this
    damned deede.
This seale, the warrant of the
    bodies blisse,
Ensureth Satan chieftaine of
    thy soule:
Subscribe not Hubert, give not
    Gods part away,
I speake not only for eyes priv-
    iledge,
The chiefe exterior that I would
    enjoy:
But for they perill, farre be-
    yond my paine,
Thy sweetes soules losse, more
    than my eyes vaine lack:
A cause internall, and eternall
    too,
Advise thee Hubert, for the case
    is hard,
To loose salvation for a Kings
    reward.
    Hub. My Lord, a subject
    dwelling in the land
Is tyed to execute the Kings
    commaund.
    Arth. Yet God commaunds
    whose power reacheth fur-
    ther,

    Arth. Ah! none but in this
    iron age would do it.
The iron of itself, though heat
    red-hot,
Approaching near these eyes
    would drink my tears,
And quench this fiery indigna-
    tion,
Even in the matter of mine in-
    nocence:
Nay, after that, consume away
    in rust,
But for containing fire to harm
    mine eye.
Are you more stubborn hard
    than hammered iron?
An if an angel should have come
    to me,
And told me Hubert should put
    out mine eyes,
I would not have believ'd him;
    no tongue but Hubert's.
    Hub. Come forth. (*Stamps.*)

*Re-enter Attendants, with Cord,
    Irons, &c.*

Do as I bid you do.
    Arth. Oh! save me, Hubert,
    save me! my eyes are out,
Even with the fierce looks of
    these bloody men.
    Hub. Give me the iron, I say,
    and bind him here.
    Arth. Alas! what need you
    be so boisterous-rough?
I will not struggle; I will stand
    stone-still.
For heaven's sake, Hubert, let
    me not be bound.
Nay, hear me Hubert: drive
    these men away,

That no commaund should stand in force to murther.

Hub. But that same Essence hath ordained a law,
A death for guilt, to keepe the world in awe.

Arth. I pleade, not guiltie, treasonlesse and free.

Hub. But that appeale, my Lord, concernes not me.

Arth. Why thou art he that maist omit the perill.

Hub. I, if my Soveraigne would remit his quarrell.

Arth. His quarrell is unhallowed false and wrong.

Hub. Then be the blame to whom it doth belong.

Arth. Why thats to thee if thou as they proceede,
Conclude their judgement with so vile a deede.

Hub. Why then no execution can be lawfull,
If Judges doomes must be reputed doubtfull.

Arth. Yes where in forme of Lawe in place and time,
The offended is convicted of the crime.

Hub. My Lord, my Lord, this long expostulation,
Heapes up more griefe, than promise of redresse;
For this I know, and so resolude I end,
That subjects lives on Kings commaunds depend.
I must not reason why he is your foe,

And I will sit as quiet as a lamb;
I will not stir nor wince, nor speak a word,
Nor look upon the iron angerly.
Thrust but these men away, and I'll forgive you,
Whatever torment you do put me to.

Hub. Go, stand within: let me alone with him.

1. Attend. I am best pleas'd to be from such a deed.
(*Exeunt Attendants.*)

Arth. Alas! I then have chid away my friend:
He hath a stern look, but a gentle heart. —
Let him come back that his compassion may
Give life to yours.

Hub. Come, boy, prepare yourself.

Arth. Is there no remedy?

Hub. None but to lose your eyes.

Arth. O heaven! — that there were but a mote in yours,
A grain, a dust, a gnat, a wandering hair,
Any annoyance in that precious sense!
Then, feeling what small things are boisterous there,
Your vile intent must needs seem horrible.

Hub. Is this your promise? go to; hold your tongue.

Arth. Hubert, the utterance of a brace of tongues

But doo his charge since he com-
maunds it so.
Arth. Then doo thy charge,
and charged be thy soule
With wrongfull persecution don
this day.
You rowling eyes, whose super-
ficies yet
I doo behold with eyes that Na-
ture lent:
Send foorth the terror of your
Moovers frowne,
To wreake my wrong upon the
murtherers
That rob me of your faire re-
flecting view:
Let hell to them (as earth they
wish to me)
Be darke and direfull guerdon
for their guylt,
And let the black tormenters of
deepe Tartary
Upbraide them with this
damned enterprise,
Inflicting change of tortures on
their soules.
Delay not Hubert, my orisons
are ended,
Begin I pray thee, reave me of
my sight:
But to performe a tragedie in-
deede,
Conclude the period with a mor-
tal stab.
Constance farewell, tormenter
come away,
Make my dispatch the Tyrants
feasting day.
Hub. I faint, I feare, my conscience bids desist:

Must needs want pleading for a
pair of eyes:
Let me not hold my tongue; let
me not, Hubert:
Or Hubert, if you will, cut out
my tongue.
So I may keep mine eyes. O!
spare mine eyes;
Though to no use, but still to
look on you.
Lo! by my troth, the instrument
is cold,
And would not harm me.
Hub. I can
heat it, boy.
Arth. No, in good sooth; the
fire is dead with grief,
Being create for comfort, to be
us'd
In undeserv'd extremes: see else
yourself;
There is no malice in this burning coal;
The breath of heaven hath
blown his spirit out,
And strew'd repentant ashes on
his head.
Hub. But with my breath I
can revive it, boy.
Arth. And if you do, you will
but make it blush,
And glow with shame of your
proceedings, Hubert:
Nay, it, perchance, will sparkle
in your eyes;
And like a dog that is com-
pell'd to fight,
Snatch at his master that doth
tarre him on.
All things that you should use
to do me wrong,

Faint did I say? fear was it that
  I named:
My King commaunds, that war-
  rant sets me free:
But God forbids, and he com-
  mandeth Kings,
That great Commaunder coun-
  terchecks my charge,
He stayes my hand, he maketh
  soft my heart.
Goe cursed tooles, your office is
  exempt,
Cheere thee young Lord, thou
  shalt not loose an eye,
Though I should purchase it
  with losse of life.
Ile to the King and say his will
  is done,
And of the langor tell him thou
  art dead,
Goe in with me, for Hubert was
  not borne
To blinde those lampes that
  nature pollisht so.
  Arth. Hubert, if ever Arthur
  be in state,
Looke for amends of this received gift,
I tooke my eyesight by thy
  curtesie,
Thou lentst them me, I will not
  be ingrate.
But now procrastination may
  offend
The issue that thy kindness
  undertakes:
Depart we Hubert, to prevent
  the worst.   (*Exeunt.*)[1]

Deny their office: only you do
  lack
That mercy, which fierce fire,
  and iron, extends,
Creatures of note for mercy-
  lacking uses.
  Hub. Well, see to live; I will
  not touch thine eyes
For all the treasures that thine
  uncle owes:
Yet I am sworn, and I did pur-
  pose, boy,
With this same very iron to
  burn them out.
  Arth. O! now you look like
  Hubert; all this while
You were disguised.
  Hubert.   Peace! no more.
  Adieu.
Your uncle must not know but
  you are dead:
I'll fill these dogged spies with
  false reports;
And pretty child, sleep doubt-
  less, and secure,
That Hubert for the wealth of
  all the world
Will not offend thee.
  Arth.   O heaven! —
I thank you, Hubert.
  Hub. Silence! no more. Go
  closely in with me;
Much danger do I undergo for
  thee.   (*Exeunt.*)

---

[1] *Shakespeare's Library*, vol. v, pp. 267–271. W. C. Hazlitt, ed.

For further illustration of Shakespeare's clear understanding that the emotions of well-characterized figures are
better means of controlling an audience than a merely
horrific situation, study his handling of the ghost scene in
Richard III or *Julius Cæsar* in contrast with similar places
in *Hamlet*. What most transmuted the *Ur-Hamlet* of Thomas
Kyd into one of the greatest tragedies of all time was the
characterization Shakespeare put into it. Certainly, characterization makes for dramatists the stepping-stones on
which they may rise from dead selves to higher things.

How may all this needed characterization best be done?
A dramatist should not permit himself to describe his characters, for in his own personality he has no proper place in
the text. There the characters must speak and act for themselves. There has been, however, an increasing tendency
lately to describe the *dramatis personæ* of the play in programs, either in the list of characters or in a summary of the
plot. Some writers apparently assume that every auditor
reads his program carefully before the curtain goes up.
Such an assumption is false: more than that it is lazy, incompetent, and thoroughly vicious, putting a play on the
level with the motion pictures, which cannot depend wholly
on themselves but would often be wholly vague without
explanatory words thrown upon the canvas. Nor can the
practice of the older dramatists like Wycherley and Shadwell, who often prefixed to their printed plays elaborate
summaries describing the *dramatis personæ*, be cited as a
final defense.

Sir William Belfond, a Gentleman of above 3,000 per annum, who
in his youth had been a spark of the town, but married and retired into the country, where he turned to the other extreme,
rigid and morose, most sordidly covetous, clownish, obstinate,
positive, and froward.

Sir Edward Belfond, his Brother, a merchant, who by lucky hits
had gotten a great estate, lives single, with ease and pleasure,

reasonably and virtuously. A man of great humanity and gentleness and compassion towards mankind; well read in good books possessed with all gentleman-like qualities.

Belfond, Senior, eldest son to Sir William; bred after his father's rustic, swinish manner, with great rigour and severity; upon whom his father's estate is entailed; the confidence of which makes him break out into open rebellion to his father, and become lewd, abominably vicious, stubborn, and obstinate.

Belfond, Junior, second Son to Sir William; adopted by Sir Edward, and bred from his childhood by him, with all tenderness, and familiarity, and bounty, and liberty that can be, instructed in all the liberal sciences, and in all gentlemanlike education. Somewhat given to women, and now and then to good fellowship, but an ingenious, well-accomplished gentleman: a man of honour, and of excellent disposition and temper.

Truman, his friend, a man of honour and fortune.

Cheatly, a rascal, who by reason of debts dares not stir out of Whitefriars, but there inveigles young heirs in tail, and helps them to goods and money upon great disadvantages; is bound for them, and shares with them, till he undoes them. A lewd, impudent, debauched fellow, very expert in the cant about town.

Shamwell, cousin to the Belfonds, an heir, who being ruined by Cheatly, is made a decoy-duck for others; not daring to stir out of Alsatia, where he lives. Is bound with Cheatly for heirs, and lives upon them a dissolute, debauched life.

Captain Hackum, a blockheaded bully of Alsatia; a cowardly, impudent, blustering fellow; formerly a sergeant in Flanders, run from his colours, retreated into Whitefriars for a very small debt, where, by the Alsatians, he is dubbed a captain; marries one that lets lodgings, sells cherry brandy, and is a bawd.

Scrapeall, a hypocritical, repeating, praying, psalm-singing, precise fellow, pretending to great piety, a godly knave, who joins with Cheatly, and supplies young heirs with goods and money.

Attorney to Sir William Belfond, who solicits his business and receives all his packets.

Lolpoop, a North-country fellow, servant to Belfond, Senior, much displeased at his master's proceedings.[1]

---

[1] *Squire of Alsatia.* Mermaid Series. G. Saintsbury, ed. Chas. Scribner's Sons, New York.

It is more than doubtful if anything so elaborate could be found in the manuscripts of Wycherley and Shadwell. Their purpose was doubtless the same as that of certain modern dramatists who, with a view to making plays less difficult for those unaccustomed to reading them, greatly amplify the stage directions before their plays go to print. Mr. Granville Barker in the manuscripts of his plays is particularly frugal of stage directions, but in the printed form of *The Madras House*,[1] practically the whole history of Julia is given in the opening stage direction:

Julia started life — that is to say, left school — as a genius. The head mistress had had two or three years of such dull girls that really she could not resist this excitement. Watercolour sketches were the medium. So Julia was dressed in brown velveteen, and sent to an art school, where they wouldn't let her do watercolour drawing at all. And in two years she learnt enough about the trade of an artist not ever to want to do those watercolour drawings again. Julia is now over thirty, and very unhappy. Three of her watercolours (early masterpieces) hang on the drawing-room wall. They shame her, but her mother won't have them taken down. On a holiday she'll be off now and then for a solid day's sketching; and as she tears up the vain attempt to put on paper the things she has learnt to see, she sometimes cries. It was Julia, Emma, and Jane who, some years ago, conspired to present their mother with that intensely conspicuous cosy corner. A cosy corner is apparently a device for making a corner just what the very nature of a corner should forbid it to be. They beggared themselves; but one wishes that Mr. Huxtable were more lavish with his dress allowances, then they might at least have afforded something not quite so hideous.

Such characterizing is an implied censure on the ability of most readers to see the full significance of deft touches in the dialogue. If not, then it is necessary because some part of it is not given in the text as it should be, or it is wholly unnecessary and undesirable, for the text, repeating all this detail, will be wearisome to an intelligent reader. The safest principle is, in preparing a manuscript for acting, to keep

[1] Mitchell Kennerley, New York.

stage directions to matters of setting, lighting, essential movements, and the intonations which cannot, by the utmost efforts of the author, be conveyed by dialogue.[1] In this last group belong certain every-day phrases susceptible of so many shadings that the actor needs guidance. In the last line of this extract from the opening of Act III of *Mrs. Dane's Defence*, the "tenderly" is necessary.

> *Enter Wilson right, announcing Lady Eastney. Enter Lady Eastney. Exit Wilson.*
>
> *Lady Eastney.* (*Shaking hands.*) You're busy?
> *Sir Daniel.* Yes, trying to persuade myself I am forty — solely on your account.
> *Lady Eastney.* That's not necessary. I like you well enough as you are.
> *Sir Daniel.* (*Tenderly.*) Give me the best proof of that.

Notice that the statement just formulated as to stage directions reads, "cannot be conveyed," not "may not." Cross the line, and differences between the novel and the play are blurred, for the author runs a fair chance of omitting exposition needed in the text and of writing colorless dialogue. A recently published play prefaces not only every speech, but even parts of the speeches with careful statements as to how they should be given, even when the text is perfectly clear. Nothing is left to the imagination, and the text is often emotionally colorless.

Let it be remembered, then, that the stage direction is not a pocket into which a dramatist may stuff whatever explanation, description, or analysis a novelist might allow himself, but is more a last resort to which he turns when he cannot make his text convey all that is necessary.

The passing of the soliloquy and the aside[2] makes the dramatist of today much more limited than were his prede-

[1] For illustration of good work, see pp. 25–26, 36, 49, 162, 174, 181, 190.
[2] See for discussion of these, pp. 382–96.

cessors in letting a character describe itself. Today everything depends on the naturalness of the self-exposition. The
vainglorious, the self-centered, the garrulous will always talk
of themselves free'y. The reserved, the timid, and persons
under suspicion will be sparing of words. When the ingenuity of the dramatist cannot make self-exposition plausible,
the scene promptly becomes unreal. The point to be remembered is, as George Meredith once said, that "The verdict
is with the observer." Not what seems plausible to the
author but what, as he tries it on auditors, proves acceptable, may stand.

Description of one character by another is usually more
plausible than the method just treated. Even here, however, the test remains plausibility. It requires persuasive
acting to make the following description of Tartuffe perfectly natural. There is danger that it will appear more the
detailed picture the dramatist wishes to place in our minds
than the description the speaker would naturally give his
listeners:

> *Orgon.* Ah! If you'd seen him, as I saw him first,
> You would have loved him just as much as I.
> He came to church each day, with contrite mien,
> Kneeled, on both knees, right opposite my place,
> And drew the eyes of all the congregation,
> To watch the fervor of his prayers to heaven;
> With deep-drawn sighs and great ejaculations.
> He humbly kissed the earth at every moment;
> And when I left the church, he ran before me
> To give me holy water at the door.
> I learned his poverty, and who he was,
> By questioning his servant, who is like him,
> And gave him gifts; but in his modesty
> He always wanted to return a part.
> "It is too much," he'd say, "too much by half;
> I am not worthy of your pity." Then,
> When I refused to take it back, he'd go,
> Before my eyes, and give it to the poor.

At length Heaven bade me take him to my home,
And since that day, all seems to prosper here.
He censures nothing, and for my sake
He even takes great interest in my wife;
He lets me know who ogles her, and seems
Six times as jealous as I am myself.
You'd not believe how far his zeal can go:
He calls himself a sinner just for trifles;
The merest nothing is enough to shock him;
So much so, that the other day I heard him
Accuse himself for having, while at prayer,
In too much anger caught and killed a flea.[1]

The scene in which Melantius draws from his friend
Amintor (*The Maid's Tragedy*, Act III, Scene 2) admission
of his wrongs, shows admirable use of both kinds of description
— of oneself and of another person.

 Melantius.   You may shape, Amintor,
Causes to cozen the whole world withall,
And you yourselfe too; but tis not like a friend
To hide your soule from me. Tis not your nature
To be thus idle: I have seene you stand
As you were blasted midst of all your mirth;
Call thrice aloud, and then start, faining joy
So coldly! — World, what doe I here? a friend
Is nothing! Heaven, I would ha told that man
My secret sinnes! Ile search an unknowne land,
And there plant friendship; all is withered here.
Come with a complement! I would have fought,
Or told my friend a lie, ere soothed him so.
Out of my bosome!
 Amintor. But there is nothing.
 Mel.   Worse and worse! farewell.
From this time have acquaintance, but no friend.
 Amin. Melantius, stay; you shall know what that is.
 Mel. See; how you plaid with friendship! be advis'd
How you give cause unto yourselfe to say
You ha lost a friend.

[1] *Tartuffe*, Act I. *Chief European Dramatists.* Brander Matthews, ed. Houghton Mifflin Co., Boston.

Amin. Forgive what I ha done;
For I am so oregone with injuries
Unheard of, that I lose consideration
Of what I ought to doe. — Oh! — Oh!
Mel. Doe not weepe.
What ist? May I once but know the man
Hath turn'd my friend thus!
Amin. I had spoke at first,
But that —
Mel. But what?
Amin. I held it most unfit
For you to know. Faith, doe not know it yet.
Mel. Thou seest my love, that will keepe company
With thee in teares; hide nothing, then, from me;
For when I know the cause of thy distemper,
With mine old armour Ile adorn myselfe,
My resolution, and cut through my foes,
Unto thy quiet, till I place thy heart
As peaceable as spotless innocence.
What is it?
Amin. Why, tis this — it is too bigge
To get out — let my teares make way awhile.
Mel. Punish me strangely, Heaven, if he escape
Of life or fame, that brought this youth to this.[1]

The cry with which Electra turns to her peasant husband
in the play of Euripides is perhaps as fine an instance as
there is of natural description by one person of her relations
to another.

Peasant. What wouldst thou now, my sad one, ever fraught
With toil to lighten my toil? And so soft
Thy nurture was! Have I not chid thee oft,
And thou wilt cease not, serving without end?
Electra. (*Turning to him with impulsive affection.*) O friend,
my friend, as God might be my friend,
Thou only hast not trampled on my tears.
Life scarce can be so hard, 'mid many fears
And many shames, when mortal heart can find
Somewhere one healing touch, as my sick mind

---

[1] Act III, Scene 2. Belles-Lettres Series. A. H. Thorndike, ed. D. C. Heath & Co.

Finds thee. . . . And should I wait thy word, to endure
A little for thine easing, yea, or pour
My strength out in thy toiling fellowship?
Thou hast enough with fields and kine to keep;
'Tis mine to make all bright within the door.
'Tis joy to him that toils, when toil is o'er,
To find home waiting, full of happy things.
    Peasant. If so it please thee, go thy way.[1]

Unquestionably, however, the best method of characterization is by action. In the first draft of Ibsen's *A Doll's House*, Krogstad uses with his employer Helmar, because he is an old school fellow, the familiar "tu." This under the circumstance illustrates his tactlessness better than any amount of description. When Helmar is irritated by this familiarity, his petty vanity is perfectly illustrated. Any one who recalls the last scene of *Louis XI* as played by the late Sir Henry Irving remembers vividly the restless, greedily moving fingers of the praying King. They told far more than words. The way in which Mrs. Lindon, throughout the opening scene of Clyde Fitch's *The Truth*,[2] touches any small article she finds in her way perfectly indicates her fluttering nervousness.

At Mrs. Warder's. . . . A smart, good-looking man-servant, Jenks, shows in Mrs. Lindon and Laura Fraser. The former is a handsome, nervous, overstrung woman of about thirty-four, very fashionably dressed; Miss Fraser, on the contrary, a matter-of-fact, rather commonplace type of good humor — wholesomeness united to a kind of sense of humor. . . .

Mrs. Lindon nervously picks up check-book from the writing-table, looks at it but not in it, and puts it down. . . .

She opens the cigar box on the writing-table behind her and then bangs it shut. . . .

She picks up stamp box and bangs it down.

Rises and goes to mantel, looking at the fly-leaves of two books on a table which she passes.

---

[1] Act i. Tr. Gilbert Murray. Geo. Allen & Sons, London.   [2] The Macmillan Co., N.Y.

Does not the action of this extract from Middleton's
A Chaste Maid in Cheapside help most in depicting the
greed and dishonesty of Yellowhammer, as well as the
humor and ingenuity of the suitor?

> *Touchwood junior.* (*Aside.*) 'Twere a good mirth now to set
>   him a-work
> To make her wedding-ring; I must about it:
> Rather than the gain should fall to a stranger,
> 'Twas honesty in me t' enrich my father.
>   *Yellowhammer.* (*Aside.*) The girl is wondrous peevish. I fear
>   nothing
> But that she's taken with some other love,
> Then all's quite dashed: that must be narrowly looked to;
> We cannot be too wary in our children. —
> What is't you lack?
>   *Touch. jun.* O, nothing now; all that I wish is present:
> I'd have a wedding-ring made for a gentlewoman
> With all speed that may be.
>   *Yel.* Of what weight, sir?
>   *Touch. jun.* Of some half ounce, stand fair
> And comely with the spark of a diamond;
> Sir, 'twere pity to lose the least grace.
>   *Yel.* Pray, let's see it. (*Takes stone from Touchwood junior.*)
> Indeed, sir 'tis a pure one.
>   *Touch. jun.* So is the mistress.
>   *Yel.* Have you the wideness of her finger, sir?
>   *Touch. jun.* Yes, sure, I think I have her measure about me:
> Good faith, 'tis down, I cannot show it to you;
> I must pull too many things out to be certain.
> Let me see — long and slender, and neatly jointed;
> Just such another gentlewoman — that's your daughter, sir?
>   *Yel.* And therefore, sir, no gentlewoman.
>   *Touch. jun.* I protest.
> I ne'er saw two maids handed more alike;
> I'll ne'er seek farther, if you'll give me leave, sir.
>   *Yel.* If you dare venture by her finger, sir.
>   *Touch. jun.* Ay, and I'll bide all loss, sir.
>   *Yel.* Say you so, sir?
> Let us see. — Hither, girl.

Touch. jun. Shall I make bold
With your finger, gentlewoman?
Moll. Your pleasure, sir.
Touch. jun. That fits her to a hair, sir.
(*Trying ring on Moll's finger.*)

Yel. What's your posy, now, sir?
Touch. jun. Mass, that's true: posy? i'faith, e'en thus, sir:
"Love that's wise
Blinds parents' eyes."
Yel. How, how? if I may speak without offence, sir, I hold
my life —
Touch. jun. What, sir?
Yel. Go to, — you'll pardon me?
Touch. jun. Pardon you? ay, sir.
Yel. Will you, i' faith?
Touch. jun. Yes, faith, I will.
Yel. You'll steal away some man's daughter: am I near you?
Do you turn aside? you gentlemen are mad wags!
I wonder things can be so warily carried,
And parents blinded so: but they're served right,
That have two eyes and were so dull a' sight.
Touch. jun. (*Aside.*) Thy doom take hold of thee!
Yel. Tomorrow noon
Shall show your ring well done.
Touch. jun. Being so, 'tis soon. —
Thanks, and your leave, sweet gentlewoman.
Moll. Sir, you're welcome. —
(*Exit Touchwood junior.*)

O were I made of wishes, I went with thee![1]

Could any description or analysis by the author or another
character paint as perfectly as does the action of the following lines the wistful grief of the child pining for his mother?

Enter Giovanni, Count Lodovico.

Francisco. How now, my noble cossin! what, in blacke?
Giovanni. Yes, unckle, I was taught to imitate you
In vertue, and you must imitate mee
In coloures of your garments: my sweete mother
Is —

[1] Mermaid Series. Vol. i, Act. i, Scene 1. Chas. Scribner's Sons, New York.

Fran. How? where?

Giov. Is there; no, yonder; indeed, sir, Ile not tell you,
For I shall make you weepe.

Fran.   Is dead.

Giov. Do not blame me now,
I did not tell you so.

Lodovico.   She's dead, my lord.

Fran. Dead!

Monticelso. Blessed lady; thou art now above thy woes!
Wilt please your lordships to withdraw a little?

                              (*Exeunt Ambassadors.*)

Giov. What do the deade do, uncie? do they eate,
Heare musicke, goe a hunting, and bee merrie,
As wee that live?

Fran. No, cose; they sleepe.

Giov.   Lord, Lord, that I were dead!
I have not slept these six nights. When doe they wake?

Fran. When God shall please.

Giov.   Good God let her sleepe ever!
For I have knowne her wake an hundredth nights,
When all the pillow, where she laid her head,
Was brine-wet with her teares. I am to complaine to you, sir.
Ile tell you how they have used her now shees dead:
They wrapt her in a cruell fould of lead,
And would not let me kisse her.

Fran.   Thou didst love her.

Giov. I have often heard her say she gave mee sucke,
And it would seeme by that shee deerely lov'd mee
Since princes seldome doe it.

Fran. O, all of my poore sister that remaines!
Take him away, for Gods sake!

                    (*Exeunt Giovanni, Lodovico, and Marcello.*)[1]

In brief, then, understand your characters thoroughly,
but do not, in your own personality, describe them anywhere. Let them describe themselves, or let other people
on the stage describe or analyze them, when this is naturally
convincing or may be made plausible by your skill. Trust,

[1] *Vittoria Corambona*, Act III, Sc. 2. Webster. Belles-Lettres Series. M. W. Sampson, ed.
D. C. Heath & Co., Boston and New York.

however, above all, to letting your characters live before
your audience the emotions which interest you, thus making
them convey their characters by the best means of communication between actor and audience — namely, action.

In the chapter (VI) dealing with clearness in exposition
the extreme importance of identifying the characters for
the audience has been carefully treated.[1] Closely connected
with this identifying is the matter of entrances and exits.

The characterizing value of exits and entrances is usually
little understood by the inexperienced dramatist. Yet in
real life, men and women cannot enter or leave a room without characterization. Watch the people in a railroad car
as it nears the terminus. The people who rise and stand in
the aisles are clearly of different natures from those who
remain quietly seated till the train reaches its destination.
The twenty or thirty standing wait differently and leave
the car with different degrees of haste, nervousness or antici-
pation. Those who remain seated differ also. Some are
absorbed in conversation, oblivious of the approaching station; others, somewhat ostentatiously, watch the waiters in
the aisles with amused contempt. Study, therefore, exits
and entrances. Very few will be found negative in the sense
that they add nothing to the knowledge of the characters.
How did Claude enter in the following extract from a recent
play? Claude, it should be said, has been mentioned just
in passing, as a suitor of Marna. Other matters, however,
have been occupying attention.

Enter Claude

Claude. (*Sitting beside her on the settle.*) I thought I should
not see you tonight.
Marna. I wondered if you would come.

Claude must really have entered in character — quickly,
impetuously, or ardently. He may have paused an instant

[1] See pp. 154–161.

on the threshold; he may have dashed in, leaving the door ajar; he may have closed it cautiously; he may have come in through the window. And how did they get to the settle? The author may know all this, but he certainly does not tell. He should visualize his figures as he writes, seeing them from moment to moment as they move, sit, or stand. Otherwise, he will miss much that is significant and characterizing in their actions.

In a play that was largely a study of a self-indulgent, self-centred youth, to the annoyance of all he is late at the family celebration of his cousin's birthday. Sauntering in, he meets a disappointing silence. Looking about, he says, "Nobody has missed me." And then, as all wait for his excuses, he shifts the burden of speech to his mother with the words, "Hasn't her ladyship anything to say?" Surely this entrance characterizes.

Illusion disappears, also, when people needed on the stage, from taxi-cab drivers to ambassadors, are apparently waiting just outside the door. A play of very interesting subject-matter became almost ridiculous because whenever anybody was needed, he or she was apparently waiting just outside one of the doors. As some of these were persons involved in affairs of state and others supposedly lived at a distance, their prompt appearance partook of wizardry. People should not only come on in character, but after time enough has been allowed or suggested to permit them to come from the places where they are supposed to have been.

How much the entrance of a character should be prepared for must be left to the judgment of the dramatist. Whatever is needed to make the entrance produce the effect desired must be planted in the minds of the audience before the character appears. Phormio, in Terence's play of that name, does not appear before the second act. His entrance is undoubtedly held back both to whet curiosity to the utmost before he appears, and in order to set forth clearly the tangle of events which his ingenuity must overcome. Magda, in Sudermann's *Heimat*, also appears first in the second act. This is not done because some leading lady wished to make as triumphant an entrance as possible, an inartistic but time-honored reason in some plays, but because, till we have lived with Magda's family in the home from which she was driven by her father's narrowness and inflexibility, we cannot grasp the full significance of her character in this environment when she returns. Usually, of course, a character of importance does appear in the first act, but naturalness first and theatrical effectiveness second determine the point at which it is proper that a character should appear. The supposed need in the audience for detailed information, slight information, or no information as to a figure about to enter must decide the amount of perliminary statement in regard to him. If possible, a character enters, identifies himself, and places himself with regard to the other persons involved in the action as nearly as possible at one and the same time. The more important the character, the more involved the circumstances which we must understand before he can enter properly, the greater the amount of preliminary preparation for him. In *Phormio*[1] and *Heimat* (or *Magda*) this preparation fills an act; in Tartuffe it fills two acts. More often bits here and there prepare the way, or some one passage of dialogue, as in the introduction of Sir Amorous La-Foole in Ben Jonson's *Epicœne*.[2]

Dauphine. We are invited to dinner together, he and I, by one that came thither to him, Sir La-Foole.

Clerimont. I, that's a precious mannikin!

Daup. Do you know him?

[1] *Chief European Dramatists.* Brander Matthews, ed. Houghton Mifflin Co., Boston.
[2] Act I, Scene 1. Mermaid Series, vol. III, or Everyman's Library.

Cler. Ay, and he will know you too, if e'er he saw you but once, though you should meet him at church in the midst of prayers. He is one of the braveries, though he be none of the wits. He will salute a judge upon the bench, and a bishop in the pulpit, a lawyer when he is pleading at the bar, and a lady when she is dancing in a masque, and put her out. He does give plays and suppers, and invite his guests to them, aloud, out of his window, as they ride by in coaches. He has a lodging in the Strand for the purpose: or to watch when ladies are gone to the china-houses, or the Exchange, that he may meet them by chance, and give them presents, some two or three hundred pounds' worth of toys, to be laughed at. He is never without a spare banquet, or sweetmeats in his chamber for their women to alight at, and come up to for bait.

Daup. Excellent! he was a fine youth last night; but now he is much finer! what is his Christian name? I have forgot.

Re-enter Page

Cler. Sir Amorous La-Foole.
Page. The gentleman is here below that owns that name.
Cler. 'Heart, he's come to invite me to dinner, I hold my life.
Daup. Like enough: prithee, let's have him up.
Cler. Boy, marshall him.

In Scene 1, Act I, of *Becket*, as written by Lord Tennyson, we have:

Enter Rosamund de Clifford, flying from Sir Reginald Fitz Urse, drops her veil

Becket. Rosamund de Clifford!
Rosamund. Save me, father, hide me — they follow me — and I must not be known.

Sir Henry Irving arranged this for the stage as follows:

Enter Rosamund de Clifford. Drops her veil

Rosamund. Save me, father, hide me.
Becket. Rosamund de Clifford!
Rosamund. They follow me — and I must not be known.

There are real values in these seemingly slight changes. With a rush and in confusion, Rosamund enters. As it is her first appearance in the play, it is of the highest importance that she be identified for the audience. If Becket gives her name as she enters, it may be lost in her onward rush. If entering, she speaks the line, "Save me, father, hide me," she centers attention on him and he may fully emphasize the identification in, "Rosamund de Clifford!" Note as bearing on what has already been said in regard to unnecessary use of stage direction that Irving cut out "flying from Sir Reginald Fitz Urse." He knew that Rosamund's speeches and her action would make the fleeing clear enough, and that the scene immediately following with Fitz Urse would show who was pursuing her. Entrances, when well handled, therefore, must be in character, prepared for, and properly motivated.

Exits are just as important as entrances. The exit of Captain Nat in *Shore Acres* has already been mentioned under pantomime. Mark the significance of the exit of Hamlet in the ghost scene, as he goes with sword held out before him. The final exit of Iris in Pinero's play is symbolic of her passing into the outer and under world.

Maldonado. You can send for your trinkets and clothes in the morning. After that, let me hear no more of you. (*She remains motionless, as if stricken.*) I've nothing further to say.
    (*A slight shiver runs through her frame and she resumes her walk. At the door, she feels blindly for the handle; finding it, she opens the door narrowly and passes out.*)

The absurdities in which the ill-managed exit or entrance may land us, Lessing shows amusingly:

Maffei often does not motivate the exits and entrances of his personages: Voltaire often motivates them falsely, which is far worse. It is not enough that a person says why he comes on, we ought also to perceive by the connection that he must therefore come. It is not enough that he say why he goes off, we ought to see subsequently that he went on that account. Else, that which the poet places in his mouth is mere excuse and no cause. When, for example, Eurykles goes off in the third scene of the second act, in order, as he says, to assemble the friends of the queen, we ought to hear afterwards about these friends and their assemblage. As, however, we hear nothing of the kind, his assertion is a schoolboy "Peto veniam exeundi," the first falsehood that occurs to the boy. He does not go off in order to do what he says; but in order to return a few lines on as the bearer of news which the poet did not know how to impart by means of any other person. Voltaire treats the ends of acts yet more clumsily. At the close of the third act, Polyphontes says to Merope that the altar awaits her, that all is ready for the solemnizing of their marriage and he exits with a "Venez, Madame." But Madame does not come, but goes off into another coulisse with an exclamation, whereupon Polyphontes opens the fourth act, and instead of expressing his annoyance that the queen has not followed him into the temple (for he had been in error, there was still time for the wedding) he talks with his Erox about matters he should not ventilate here, that are more fitting conversation for his own house, his own rooms. Then the fourth act closes — exactly like the third. Polyphontes again summons the queen into the temple, Merope herself exclaims, "Courons nous vers le temple où m'attend mon outrage"; and says to the chief priests who come to conduct her thither, "Vous venez à l'autel entraîner la victime." Consequently we must expect them inside the temple at the beginning of the fifth act, or are they already back again? Neither; good things will take time. Polyphontes has forgotten something and comes back again and sends the queen back again. Excellent! Between the third and fourth, between the fourth and fifth acts nothing occurs that should, and indeed, nothing occurs at all, and the third and fourth acts only close in order that the fourth and fifth may begin.[1]

At the end of Act II of *The Princess and the Butterfly* the exits are as important as any part of the text. Note particularly the last.

Denstroude. (*On the steps, pausing and looking back.*) You cycle at Battersea tomorrow morning?
Mrs. St. Roche. It's extremely unlikely.
Denstroude. I shall be there at ten. Don't be later.

[1] *Hamburg Dramaturgy*, pp. 367–368. Bohn ed.

(He kisses his hand to her and departs. She stands quite still, thinking. A Servant enters, crosses to the billiard-room, and proceeds to cover up the billiard-table. She walks slowly to the ottoman and sits, looking into the fire. St. Roche reappears and comes down the steps. She does not turn her head. He goes to the table and mixes some spirits and water.)

St. Roche. (*As he mixes the drink.*) What d'ye think — what d'ye think that silly, infatuated feller's goin' to do?

Mrs. St. Roche. Demailly?

St. Roche. (*Glancing toward the billiard-room.*) Sssh! (*With a nod.*) Um!

> *(He comes to her, bringing her the tumbler in which he has mixed the drink.)*

Mrs. St. Roche. (*Taking the tumbler, her eyes never meeting his.*) Well, what is he going to do?

St. Roche. Marry that low woman.

Mrs. St. Roche. (*Callously.*) Great heavens! the fool!

St. Roche. Yes. Shockin', ain't it?

Mrs. St. Roche. (*Putting the glass to her lips, with a languid air.*) She has blinded him, I suppose, with some story or other; or he would hardly have committed the outrage, tonight, of presenting her to me.

St. Roche. (*Returning to the table and mixing a drink for himself.*) That's it — blinded him. And yet it's almost incomprehensible how a feller can be as blind as all that. Why, the very man-in-the-street —

> *(The Servant switches off the lights in the billiard-room, and comes out from the room.)*

St. Roche. (*To the man.*) I'll switch off the lights here.

> *(The Servant goes out.)*

Mrs. St. Roche. Well, you had better let him know that he mustn't attempt to come to this house again.

St. Roche. Poor chap!

Mrs. St. Roche. We can't be associated, however remotely, with such a disgraceful connection.

St. Roche. Of course, of course. (*Coming down, glass in hand.*) I could tell you things I've heard about this Mrs. Ware —

Mrs. St. Roche. (*Rising.*) Please don't! I want no details concerning a person of her world.

> (*She ascends the steps slowly, carrying her cloak and her tumbler — without looking back.*)

Goodnight.

> St. Roche. (*With a wistful glance at her.*) Goodnight.
>
> (*She departs. He stands for a little while contemplating space; then he switches off the light. The room remains partially illumined by the fire-glow. He turns to examine the fire. Apparently assured on that point, he walks, still carrying his tumbler, to the door which is in the centre wall; where, uttering a little sigh as he opens the door, he disappears.*)[1]

The passages quoted (pp. 268–275) from *The Troublesome Reign of King John* and Shakespeare's play show crude and perfect handling of exits and entrances. In the old play the murderers merely enter and go out again as ordered. In Shakespeare they enter at the moment which makes them the climactic touch in the terror of Arthur and the audience. When Hubert orders them to go, it is the first sign that he may relent.

The inexperienced dramatist is almost always wasteful in the number of characters used. An adaptation of a Spanish story called for a cast of about a dozen important figures and some sixty supernumeraries as soldiers and peasants — all this in a one-act play. It meant very little labor to cut the soldiery to a few officers and some privates, and the peasantry to some six or eight people. Ultimately, the total cast did not contain a quarter as many people as the original, yet nothing important had been lost. Rewriting a play often is, and should be, a "slaughter of the innocents." Don't use unneeded people. You must provide them with dialogue, and as the play goes on, some justification for existence. The manager must pay them salaries. First of all, get rid of entirely unnecessary people. They usually hold over from the story as originally heard or read. For

---

[1] Samuel French, New York; W. Heinemann, London.

instance, a recent adaptation used from the original story a blinking dwarf sitting silent, forever watchful, at a table in the restaurant where the story was placed. His smile simply emphasized the cynicism of the story enacted in his sight. He was in no way necessary to the telling of the story, — and so he disappeared in the final form of the play. One is constantly tempted to bring in some figure for purposes of easy exposition only to find that one must either bind him in with the story as it develops, or drop him out of sight the moment his expository work is done. The trouble with such figures is that they are likely to give false clues, stirring a hearer to interest in them or their apparent relation to the story, when nothing is to come of one or the other. Usually a little patience and ingenuity will give this needed exposition to some character or characters essential to the plot. In a recent play of Breton life during the Chouan War, an attractive peasant boy was introduced in order to plant in the minds of the audience certain ideas as to immediate conditions of the war, and the relation of the woman to whom he is talking with the Prince, his leader. Wishing to show the devotion of the Prince's followers, the author had the boy talk much of his own loyalty to his leader. Just there was the false clue. Every auditor expected his loyalty to lead to something later in the play; but the youth, having told his tale, disappeared for good. It took very little time to discover that all the young man told could perfectly well be made clear in one preceding scene between the woman and her son, and two of the other scenes immediately following, between the woman and the young Prince. It is these unnecessary figures who are largely responsible for the scenes already spoken of in chapter IV which clog the movement of a play.

Sometimes, too, similar figures at different places in a play do exactly or nearly the same work, — servants for instance. When it does not interfere with verisimilitude, give the tasks to one person rather than two, or two rather than three. That is, use only people absolutely needed. Sometimes these carelessly introduced figures stray through a play like an unquiet spirit. In *The Road to Happiness* one character, Porter, was of so little importance that most of the time, when on the stage, he had nothing to do. When really acting, it was largely in pantomime, or with speech that, not effectively, reiterated what some one else was saying. He existed really for two scenes. In the first act he might just as well have been talked about as shown, and in the second act what he did could well have been done by one of the other important characters. When any character in a play shows a tendency not to get into the action readily; when for long periods he is easily overlooked by the author; it is time to consider whether he should not be given the *coup de grâce*.

Today we are fortunately departing from an idea somewhat prevalent in the middle of the nineteenth century, that a figure once introduced into a play should be kept there until the final curtain. That is exalting technique, and the so-called "well-made" play, above truth to life. When a character is doing needed work, use him when and as long as he would appear in real life, and no longer. Use each character for a purpose, and when it is fulfilled, drop him. Naturalness and theatrical economy are the two tests: the greater of these is naturalness.

All that has been said comes to this. Know your characters so intimately that you can move, think, and feel with them, supplied by them with far more material than you can use in any one play. See that they are properly introduced to the audience; that they are clearly and convincingly presented. Do not forget the importance of entrances and exits. Cut out all unnecessary figures.

There follow three bits of characterization from very different types of play: Sir John Vanbrugh's *The Provoked Wife*, a comedy of manners; G. B. Shaw's farce-comedy, *You Never Can Tell;* and Eugène Brieux's thesis play, *The Cradle*. The first scene aims merely to present vividly the riotous and drunken squire. The second, while characterizing William, aims to illustrate that contentment lies in doing that to which one is accustomed, under accustomed conditions. The third not only characterizes; it shows that no law of man can wholly give a woman to a second husband when common anxiety with the first husband for the child of their marriage draws them together. Note in all three the use of action as compared with description or analysis; the connotative value of the phrasings; the succint sureness.

THE PROVOKED WIFE

ACT IV. SCENE, *Covent Garden*

Enter Lord Rake, Sir John, &c., with Swords drawn

Lord Rake. Is the Dog dead?

Bully. No, damn him, I heard him wheeze.

Lord Rake. How the Witch his Wife howl'd!

Bully. Ay, she'll alarm the Watch presently.

Lord Rake. Appear, Knight, then; come you have a good Cause to fight for, there's a Man murder'd.

Sir John. Is there? Then let his Ghost be satisfy'd, for I'll sacrifice a Constable to it presently, and burn his body upon his wooden Chair.

Enter a Taylor, with a Bundle under his Arm

Bully. How now; what have we here? a Thief.

Taylor. No, an't please you, I'm no Thief.

Lord Rake. That we'll see presently: Here; let the General examine him.

Sir John. Ay, ay, let me examine him, and I'll lay a Hundred Pound I find him guilty in spite of his Teeth — for he looks — like a — sneaking Rascal.

Come, Sirrah, without Equivocation or mental Reservation, tell me of what opinion you are, and what Calling; for by them — I shall guess at your Morals.

Taylor. An't please you, I'm a Dissenting Journyman Taylor.

Sir John. Then, Sirrah, you love Lying by your Religion, and Theft by your Trade: And so, that your Punishment may be suitable to your Crimes — I'll have you first gagg'd — and then hang'd.

Taylor. Pray, good worthy Gentlemen, don't abuse me; indeed I'm an honest Man, and a good Workman, tho I say it, that shou'd not say it.

Sir John. No words, Sirrah, but attend your Fate.

Lord Rake. Let me see what's in that Bundle.

Taylor. An't please you, it is the Doctor of the Parish's Gown.

Lord Rake. The Doctor's Gown! — Hark you, Knight, you won't stick at abusing the Clergy, will you?

Sir John. No. I'm drunk, and I'll abuse anything — but my Wife; and her I name — with Reverence.

Lord Rake. Then you shall wear this Gown, whilst you charge the Watch: That tho the Blows fall upon you, the Scandal may light upon the Church.

Sir John. A generous Design — by all the Gods — give it me.
                                    (*Takes the Gown, and puts it on.*)

Taylor. O dear Gentlemen, I shall be quite undone, if you take the Gown.

Sir John. Retire, Sirrah; and since you carry off your Skin — go home, and be happy.

Taylor. (*Pausing.*) I think I had e'en as good follow the Gentleman's friendly Advice; for if I dispute any longer, who knows but the Whim may take him to case me? These Courtiers are fuller of Tricks than they are of Money; they'll sooner cut a Man's Throat, than pay his Bill.   (*Exit Taylor.*)

Sir John. So, how d'ye like my Shapes now?

Lord Rake. This will do to a Miracle; he looks like a Bishop going to the Holy War. But to your Arms, Gentlemen, the Enemy appears.

Enter Constable and Watch

Watchman. Stand! Who goes there? Come before the Constable.

Sir John. The Constable's a Rascal — and you are the Son of a Whore.

Watchman. A good civil answer for a Parson, truly!

Constable. Methinks, Sir, a Man of your Coat might set a better Example.

Sir John. Sirrah, I'll make you know — there are Men of my Coat can set as bad Examples — as you can, you Dog you.

> (*Sir John strikes the Constable. They knock him down, disarm him, and seize him. Lord Rake &c. run away.*)

Constable. So, we have secur'd the Parson however.

Sir John. Blood, and Blood — and Blood.

Watchman. Lord have mercy upon us! How the wicked Wretch raves of Blood. I'll warrant he has been murdering some body tonight.

Sir John. Sirrah, there's nothing got by Murder but a Halter: My Talent lies towards Drunkenness and Simony.

Watchman. Why that now was spoke like a Man of Parts, Neighbours; it's pity he should be so disguis'd.

Sir John. You lye — I'm not disguis'd; for I am drunk barefac'd.

Watchman. Look you here again — This is a mad Parson, Mr. Constable; I'll lay a Pot of Ale upon's Head, he's a good Preacher.

Constable. Come, Sir, out of Respect to your Calling, I shan't put you into the Round house; but we must secure you in our Drawing-Room till Morning, that you may do no Mischief. So, come along.

Sir John. You may put me where you will, Sirrah, now you have overcome me — But if I can't do Mischief, I'll think of Mischief — in spite of your Teeth, you Dog you. (*Exeunt.*)[1]

YOU NEVER CAN TELL

ACT IV

Waiter. (*Entering anxiously through the window.*) Beg pardon, ma'am; but can you tell me what became of that — (*He recognizes Bohun, and loses all his self-possession. Bohun waits rigidly for him to pull himself together. After a pathetic exhibition of confusion, he recovers himself sufficiently to address Bohun weakly, but coherently.*) Beg pardon, sir, I'm sure, sir. Was — was it you, sir?

Bohun. (*Ruthlessly.*) It was I.

Waiter. (*Brokenly.*) Yes, sir. (*Unable to restrain his tears.*) You

[1] *Plays.* Vol. i. J. Tonson, London, 1730.

in a false nose, Walter! (*He sinks faintly into a chair at the table.*) I beg your pardon, ma'am, I'm sure. A little giddiness —

Bohun. (*Commandingly.*) You will excuse him, Mrs. Clandon, when I inform you that he is my father.

Waiter. (*Heartbroken.*) Oh, no, no, Walter. A waiter for your father on the top of a false nose! What will they think of you?

Mrs. Clandon. (*Going to the waiter's chair in her kindest manner.*) I am delighted to hear it, Mr. Bohun. Your father has been an excellent friend to us since we came here.   (*Bohun bows gravely.*)

Waiter. (*Shaking his head.*) Oh, no, ma'am. It's very kind of you — very ladylike and affable indeed, ma'am; but I should feel at a great disadvantage off my own proper footing. Never mind my being the gentleman's father, ma'am: it is only the accident of birth, after all, ma'am. (*He gets up feebly.*) You'll excuse me, I'm sure, having interrupted your business.

> (*He begins to make his way along the table, supporting himself from chair to chair, with his eye on the door.*)

(*Bohun.*) One moment. (*The waiter stops, with a sinking heart.*) My father was a witness of what passed to-day, was he not, Mrs. Clandon?

Mrs. Clandon. Yes, most of it, I think.

Bohun. In that case we shall want him.

Waiter. (*Pleading.*) I hope it may not be necessary, sir. Busy evening for me, sir, with that ball: very busy evening indeed, sir.

Bohun. (*Inexorably.*) We shall want you.

Mrs. Clandon. (*Politely.*) Sit down, won't you?

Waiter. (*Earnestly.*) Oh, if you please, ma'am, I really must draw the line at sitting down. I couldn't let myself be seen doing such a thing, ma'am: thank you, I am sure, all the same.

> (*He looks round from face to face wretchedly, with an expression that would melt a heart of stone.*)

Gloria. Don't let us waste time. William only wants to go on taking care of us. I should like a cup of coffee.

Waiter. (*Brightening perceptibly.*) Coffee, miss? (*He gives a little gasp of hope.*) Certainly, miss. Thank you, miss: very timely, miss, very thoughtful and considerate indeed. (*To Mrs. Clandon, timidly, but expectantly.*) Anything for you, ma'am?

Mrs. Clandon. Er — oh, yes: it's so hot, I think we might have a jug of claret cup.

Waiter. (*Beaming.*) Claret cup, ma'am! Certainly ma'am.

Gloria. Oh, well, I'll have claret cup instead of coffee. Put some cucumber in it.

Waiter. (*Delightedly.*) Cucumber, miss! yes, miss. (*To Bohun.*) Anything special for you, sir? You don't like cucumber, sir.

Bohun. If Mrs. Clandon will allow me — syphon, Scotch.

Waiter. Right, sir. (*To Crampton.*) Irish for you, sir, I think sir? (*Crampton assents with a grunt. The waiter looks enquiringly at Valentine.*)

Valentine. I like the cucumber.

Waiter. Right, sir. (*Summing up.*) Claret cup, syphon, one Scotch, and one Irish?

Mrs. Clandon. I think that's right.

Waiter. (*Perfectly happy.*) Right ma'am. Directly, ma'am. Thank you.

> (*He ambles off through the window, having sounded the whole gamut of human happiness, from the bottom to the top in a little over two minutes.*) [1]

THE CRADLE (LE BERCEAU)

ACT I. SCENE 9

[Laurence and Raymond, her first husband, meet by chance by the sick bed of their little boy, M. de Girieu, the second husband, who is madly jealous of Raymond, and of Laurence's love for her boy, has just refused Raymond's request to be allowed to watch by the child till he is out of danger. Resting confidently on the control over Laurence and the boy which the laws give him, M. de Girieu is sure he can keep his wife and her former husband apart.]

Long silent scene. The door of little Julien's room opens softly. Laurence appears with a paper in her hand. The two men separate, watching her intently. She looks out for a long time, then shuts the door, taking every precaution not to make a noise. After a gesture of profound grief, she comes forward, deeply moved, but tearless. She makes no more gestures. Her face is grave. Very simply she goes straight to Raymond.

[1] *Plays Pleasant and Unpleasant.* Brentano, New York.

Raymond. (*Very simply to Laurence.*) Well?

Laurence. (*In the same manner.*) He has just dropped asleep.

Ray. The fever?

Lau. Constant.

Ray. Has the temperature been taken?

Lau. Yes.

Ray. How much?

Lau. Thirty-nine.

Ray. The cough?

Lau. Incessant. He breathes with difficulty.

Ray. His face is flushed?

Lau. Yes.

Ray. The doctor gave you a prescription?

Lau. I came to show it to you. I don't thoroughly understand this.

> (*They are close to each other, examining the prescription which Raymond holds.*)

Ray. (*Reading.*) "Keep an even temperature in the sick room."

Lau. Yes.

Ray. "Wrap the limbs in cotton wool, and cover that with oiled silk." I am going to do that myself as soon as he wakes. Tell them to warn me.

Lau. What ought he to have to drink? I forgot to ask that, and he is thirsty.

Ray. Mallow.

Lau. I'm sure he doesn't like it.

Ray. Yes, yes. You remember when he had the measles.

Lau. Yes, yes. How anxious we were then, too!

Ray. He drank it willingly. You remember perfectly?

Lau. Yes, of course I remember. Some mallow then. Let us read the prescription again. I have n't forgotten anything? Mustard plasters. The cotton wool, you will attend to that. And I will go have the drink made. "In addition — every hour — a coffee-spoonful of the following medicine."

> (*The curtain falls slowly as she continues to read. M. de Girieu has gone out slowly during the last words.*) [1]

Finally, contrast the treatment by John Webster and Robert Browning of the same dramatic situation. Which is the clearer, which depends more on illustrative action?

[1] P. V. Stock, Paris.

Enter Antonio

Duchess.   I sent for you; sit downe:
Take pen and incke, and write: are you ready?
    Antonio.   Yes.
    Duch. What did I say?
    Ant. That I should write some-what.
    Duch.   Oh, I remember:
After this triumph and this large expence,
It's fit (like thrifty husbands) we enquire,
What's laid up for tomorrow.
    Ant. So please your beauteous excellence.
    Duch.   Beauteous?
Indeed I thank you: I look yong for your sake.
You have tane my cares upon you.
    Ant.   I'le fetch your grace
The particulars of your revinew and expence.
    Duch. Oh, you are an upright treasurer: but you mistooke,
For when I said I meant to make enquiry
What's layd up for tomorrow, I did meane
What's layd up yonder for me.
    Ant.   Where?
    Duch.   In heaven.
I am making my will (as 'tis fit princes should
In perfect memory), and I pray sir, tell me
Were not one better make it smiling, thus,
Then in deepe groanes, and terrible ghastly lookes,
As if the guifts we parted with procur'd
That violent distraction?
    Ant.   Oh, much better.
    Duch. If I had a husband now, this care were quit:
But I intend to make you over-seer.
What good deede shall we first remember? say.
    Ant. Begin with that first good deede began i' th' world,
After man's creation, the sacrament of marriage.
I'ld have you first provide for a good husband:
Give him all.
    Duch.   All?
    Ant.   Yes, your excellent selfe.
    Duch. In a winding sheete?
    Ant.   In a cople.

Duch. St. Winifrid, that were a strange will!

Ant. 'Twere strange if there were no will in you
To marry againe.

Duch. What doe you thinke of marriage?

Ant. I take't, as those that deny purgatory,
It locally containes or heaven or hell;
There's no third place in't.

Duch. How doe you affect it?

Ant. My banishment, feeding my mellancholly,
Would often reason thus —

Duch. Pray let's heare it.

Ant. Say a man never marry, nor have children,
What takes that from him? onely the bare name
Of being a father, or the weake delight
To see the little wanton ride a cock-horse
Upon a painted sticke, or heare him chatter
Like a taught starling.

Duch. Fye, fie, what's all this?
One of your eyes is blood-shot; use my ring to't.
They say 'tis very soveraigne; 'twas my wedding-ring,
And I did vow never to part with it,
But to my second husband.

Ant. You have parted with it now.

Duch. Yes, to helpe your eye-sight.

Ant. You have made me starke blind.

Duch. How?

Ant. There is a sawcy and ambitious divell
Is dauncing in this circle.

Duch. Remoove him.

Ant. How?

Duch. There needs small conjuration, when your finger
May doe it: thus, is it fit?

Ant. What sayd you? (*He kneeles.*)

Duch. Sir,
This goodly roofe of yours is too low built;
I cannot stand upright in't, nor discourse,
Without I raise it higher: raise yourselfe,
Or if you please, my hand to help you: so.

Ant. Ambition, madam, is a great man's madnes,
That is not kept in chaines and close-pentoomes,
But in fair lightsome lodgings, and is girt

With the wild noyce of pratling visitants,
Which makes it lunatique, beyond all cure.
Conceive not I am so stupid but I ayme
Whereto your favours tend: but he's a foole
That (being a cold) would thrust his hands i' th' fire
To warme them.

  Duch.   So, now the ground's broake,
You may discover what a wealthy mine
I make you lord of.

  Ant.   Oh my unworthiness!

  Duch. You were ill to sell your selfe:
This darkning of your worth is not like that
Which trades-men use i' th' city; their false lightes
Are to rid bad wares off: and I must tell you,
If you will know where breathes a compleat man
(I speake it without flattery), turne your eyes,
And progresse through your selfe.

  Ant. Were there nor heaven, nor hell,
I should be honest: I have long serv'd vertue,
And nev'r tane wages of her.

  Duch.   Now she paies it.
The misery of us that are borne great,
We are forc'd to woe, because none dare woe us:
And as a tyrant doubles with his words,
And fearefully equivocates, so we
Are forc'd to expresse our violent passions
In ridles and in dreames, and leave the path
Of simple vertue, which was never made
To seeme the thing it is not. Goe, go brag
You have left me heartlesse; mine is in your bosom:
I hope 'twill multiply love there. You doe tremble:
Make not your heart so dead a peece of flesh,
To feare, more then to love me. Sir, be confident,
What is't distracts you? This is flesh and blood, sir;
'Tis not the figure cut in allablaster
Kneeles at my husbands tombe. Awake, awake, man,
I do here put off all vaine ceremony,
And onely doe appeare to you a yong widow
That claimes you for her husband, and like a widow,
I use but halfe a blush in't.

Ant.   Truth speake for me,
I will remaine the constant sanctuary
Of your good name.[1]

This is Browning's version:

Duchess. Say what you did through her, and she through
      you —
The praises of her beauty afterward!
Will you?
Valence. I dare not.
Duch.   Dare not?
Val.   She I love
Suspects not such a love in me.
Duch.   You jest.
Val. The lady is above me and away.
Not only the brave form, and the bright mind,
And the great heart combine to press me low —
But all the world calls rank divides us.
Duch.   Rank!
Now grant me patience! Here's a man declares
Oracularly in another's case —
Sees the true value and the false, for them —
Nay, bids them see it, and they straight do see.
You called my court's love worthless — so it turned:
I threw away as dross my heap of wealth,
And here you stickle for a piece or two!
First — has she seen you?
Val.   Yes.
Duch.   She loves you, then.
Val. One flash of hope burst; then succeeded night:
And all's at darkest now. Impossible!
Duch. We'll try: you are — so to speak — my subject yet?
Val. As ever — to the death.
Duch.   Obey me, then!
Val. I must.
Duch.   Approach her, and . . . no! first of all
Get more assurance. "My instructress," say,
"Was great, descended from a line of kings,
"And even fair" — (wait why I say this folly) —

---

[1] *The Duchess of Malfi*, Act 1, Sc. 2. Webster. Belles-Lettres Series. M. W. Sampson, ed.
D. C. Heath & Co., Boston and New York.

"She said, of all men, none for eloquence,
"Courage, and (what cast even these to shade)
"The heart they sprung from, — none deserved like him
"Who saved her at her need: if she said this,
"Why should not one I love, say?"
    Val.   Heaven — this hope —
Oh, lady, you are filling me with fire!
    Duch. Say this! — nor think I bid you cast aside
One touch of all the awe and reverence;
Nay, make her proud for once to heart's content
That all this wealth of heart and soul's her own!
Think you are all of this, — and, thinking it,
. . . (Obey!)
    Val.   I cannot choose.
    Duch.   Then, kneel to her!
                (*Valence sinks on his knee.*)
I dream!
    Val. Have mercy! yours, unto the death, —
I have obeyed. Despise, and let me die!
    Duch. Alas, sir, is it to be ever thus?
Even with you as with the world? I know
This morning's service was no vulgar deed
Whose motive, once it dares avow itself,
Explains all done and infinitely more,
So, takes the shelter of a nobler cause.
Your service names its true source, — loyalty!
The rest's unsaid again. The Duchess bids you,
Rise, sir! The Prince's words were in debate.
    Val. (*Rising.*) Rise? Truth, as ever, lady, comes from you!
I should rise — I who spoke for Cleves, can speak
For Man — yet tremble now, who stood firm then.
I laughed — for 'twas past tears — that Cleves should starve
With all hearts beating loud the infamy,
And no tongue daring trust as much to air:
Yet here, where all hearts speak, shall I be mute?
Oh, lady, for your sake look on me!
On all I am, and have, and do — heart, brain,
Body and soul, — this Valence and his gifts!
I was proud once: I saw you, and then sank,
So that each, magnified a thousand times,
Were nothing to you — but such nothingness,

Would a crown gild it, or a sceptre prop,
A treasure speed, a laurel-wreath enhance?
What is my own desert? But should your love
Have . . . there's no language helps here . . . singled me, —
Then — oh, that wild word "then!" — be just to love,
In generosity its attribute!
Love, since you pleased to love! All's cleared — a stage
For trial of the question kept so long:
Judge you — Is love or vanity the best?
You, solve it for the world's sake — you, speak first
What all will shout one day — you, vindicate
Our earth and be its angel! All is said.
Lady, I offer nothing — I am yours:
But, for the cause' sake, look on me and him,
And speak!
    Duch. I have received the Prince's message:
Say, I prepare my answer!
    Val.   Take me, Cleves! (*He withdraws.*) [1]

The formula for the would-be dramatist so far as his
people are concerned is this: A play which aims to be real in
depicting life must illustrate character by characterization
which is in character.

[1] *Colombe's Birthday*, Act IV, Scene 1. Robert Browning. Belles-Lettres Series
A. Bates, ed. D. C. Heath & Co., Boston and New York.

CHAPTER VIII

DIALOGUE

MODERN dramatic dialogue had beginnings far from realistic. It originated, as the Latin tropes show, in speeches given in unison and to music — a kind of recitative. What was the aim of this earliest dramatic dialogue? It sought to convey, first, last, and always, the facts of the episode or incident represented: "Whom seek ye here, O Christians? Jesus of Nazareth, the Crucified, O Heavenly Ones." And that is what good dramatic dialogue has always done, is doing, and must always do as its chief work — state clearly the facts which an auditor must understand if the play is to move ahead steadily and clearly. Already enough has been said (chapter VI, pp. 154–183) as to the need of clear preliminary and later exposition to show how axiomatic is the statement that the chief purpose of good dialogue is to convey necessary information clearly.

Even, however, when dialogue is clear in its statement of needed information, it may still be confusing for reader or hearer. What is the trouble with the text in the left-hand column — from an early draft of a play dealing with John Brown and his fortunes?

SCENE: *The Prison at Harper's Ferry*

Brown. Mary! I'm glad to see you, Mary.

(*For a few seconds, silence.*)

Mrs. Brown. (*Crying out.*) Oh, my dear husband, it is a hard fate.

Brown. (*Strong in his composure.*) Well, well, Mary, let

Brown. Mary! I'm glad to see you, Mary.

(*For a few seconds, silence.*)

Mrs. Brown. (*Crying out.*) Oh, my dear husband, it is a hard fate. It's been so long since I heard your voice.

Brown. (*Strong in his com-*

us be cheerful. We must all
bear it the best we can.

(*Stroking her hair.*)

Mrs. Brown. Oh! You to go
from me forever.

(*Sinks her head on his breast
again.*)

Brown. It must be, — and all
is for ᵗhe best. There, there.

(*Pats her head in an effort
to comfort her.*)

Mrs. Brown. But our poor
children, John.

Brown. Those that have died
are at peace in the next world.
(*She breaks out weeping again.*)
Come, come, dry your tears; sit
down and tell me about those at
home. (*He tries to lead her to
chair on right of table, but she
checks her grief and seats herself.
He goes slowly back to the other
chair.*) It weakens me to stand.
Now tell me about home.

Mrs. Brown. It's a sad place.
We couldn't believe the first
reports about you and the
boys being taken prisoners. We
couldn't believe you had *failed.*
Then a New York paper came.
We sat by the fire in the living room. There was Watson's
widow —

Brown. Poor Isabel, with her
little Freddie.

Mrs. Brown. And William
Thompson's widow, our Ruth,
and Annie, and Oliver's
widow —

Brown. Poor Martha. When
the time came it was hard for

posure.) Well, well, Mary, let
us be cheerful. We must all
bear it the best we can.

(*Stroking her hair.*)

Mrs. Brown. Oh! You to go
from me forever.

(*Sinks her head on his breast
again.*)

Brown. It must be, — and
all is for the best. There, there.

(*Pats her head in an effort
to comfort her.*)

Mrs. Brown. (*After a mo-
ment's silence.*) Do they treat
you well here, John?

Brown. Like Joseph, I have
gained favor in the sight of the
prison-keeper. He is a most humane gentleman — never mistreats or tries to humiliate me.

Mrs. Brown. May God bless
such a man. Do you sleep any,
John?

Brown. Like a child, — all
night in peace.

Mrs. Brown. I am glad of
that. I worried about it. Are
the days long and lonesome?

Brown. All hours of the day
glorious thoughts come to me.
I am kept busy reading and
answering letters from my
friends. I have with me my
Bible, here. (*Placing his hand
on the leather-bound volume at
the end of the table.*) It is of infinite comfort. I never enjoyed
life more than since coming to
prison. I wish all my poor family were as composed and as
happy.

her to leave the farm house and Oliver behind. She kind of felt that she wouldn't see him any more.

Mrs. Brown. We said almost nothing while Salmon read. We felt in our blindness God had been unfaithful to you and the boys.

Brown. My dear wife, you must keep up your spirits. Don't blame God. He has taken away my sword of steel, but He has given me the sword of the Spirit.

Mrs. Brown. (Looking up into his face with almost a sad smile upon hers.) That sounds just like you, John. Oh, it's been so long since I heard your voice.

Brown. Tell me more about the family.

Mrs. Brown. Owen doesn't dare come home yet.

Brown. Do you know where he is?

Mrs. Brown. Hiding among friends in Ohio. Poor boy, he is called all kinds of vile names, just for being with you.

Brown. For the cause we have all suffered much in the past; we shall have to in the future. We should rejoice at his escape.

Mrs. Brown. I do, John, but O, poor Oliver and Watson! We shall never see them again.

Brown. Not in this world, but we shall meet together in that other world where they do not

Mrs. Brown. But our poor children, John. Poor Oliver and Watson. We shall never see them again.

Brown. Those that have died are at peace. *(She breaks out weeping again.)* But we shall meet together in that other world where they do not shoot and hang men for loving justice and desiring freedom for all men. Come, come, dry your tears. Sit down and tell me about those at home. *(He tries to lead her to chair on right of table, but she checks her grief and seats herself. He goes slowly back to the other chair.)* It weakens me to stand. Now, tell me about home, for that will give me comfort, Mary. No man can get into difficulties too big to be surmounted if he has a firm foothold at home.

Mrs. Brown. It's a sad place. We couldn't believe the first reports about you and the boys being taken prisoners. *We wouldn't* believe you had failed.

Brown. I have been a great deal disappointed in myself for not keeping to my plan.

Mrs. Brown. You made a mistake only in judging how much you could do.

Brown. I acted against my better judgment.

Mrs. Brown. But after taking the arsenal, why didn't you flee to the mountains, as we thought you would?

Brown. The delay was my

shoot and hang men for loving justice and desiring freedom for all men.

Mrs. Brown. Yes, and they *did die* for a great and good cause!   (*Said with spirit.*)

Brown. Some day all the people of the earth will say that.   (*A moment's silence.*)

Mrs. Brown. Do they treat you well here, John?

Brown. Like Joseph, I have gained favor in the sight of the prison-keeper. He is a most humane gentleman — never mistreats or tries to humiliate me.

Mrs. Brown. May God bless such a man. Do you sleep any, John?

Brown. Like a child, — all night in peace.

Mrs. Brown. I'm glad of that. I worried about it. Are the days long and lonesome?

Brown. All hours of the day glorious thoughts come to me. I am kept busy reading and answering letters from my friends. I have with me my Bible, here. (*Placing his hand on the leather-bound volume at the end of the table.*) It is of infinite comfort. I never enjoyed life more than since coming to prison. I wish all my poor family were as composed and as happy.

Mrs. Brown. We have become more and more resigned.

Brown. Do any feel disgrace or shame?

mistake. But in God's greater and broader plan maybe it was infinitely better. It was foreordained to work out that way, determined before the world was made.

Mrs. Brown. His ways are mysterious and wonderful.

(*A slight pause as both think.*)

Brown. How did you first get the news?

Mrs. Brown. A New York paper came. We sat by the fire in the living room. There was Watson's widow —

Brown. Poor Isabel, with her little Freddie.

Mrs. Brown. And William Thompson's widow, our Ruth, and Annie, and Oliver's widow —

Brown. Poor Martha. When the time came, it was hard for her to leave the farm house and Oliver behind. She kind of felt she wouldn't see him any more.

Mrs. Brown. We said almost nothing while Salmon read. We felt in our blindness God had been unfaithful to you and the boys.

Brown. My dear wife, you must keep up your spirits. Don't blame God. He has taken away my sword of steel, but He has given me the sword of the Spirit.

Mrs. Brown. (*Looking up into his face with almost a sad smile upon hers.*) That sounds just like you, John. We have become more and more resigned.

Mrs. Brown. Not one, John. You are, in our eyes, a noble martyr. The chains on your legs bind our hearts all the closer to you.

Brown. That gives me comfort, Mary. No man can get into difficulties too big to be surmounted, if he has a firm foothold at home.

Mrs. Brown. You made a mistake only in judging how much you could do.

Brown. I have been a great deal disappointed in myself for not keeping to my plan. I acted against my better judgment.

Mrs. Brown. But after taking the arsenal, why didn't you flee to the mountains, as we thought you would?

Brown. The delay was my mistake. But in God's greater and broader plan, maybe it was infinitely better. It was foreordained to work out that way, determined before the world was made.

Mrs. Brown. His ways are mysterious and wonderful.

(*Avis comes in.*)

Brown. Do any feel disgrace or shame?

Mrs. Brown. Not one, John. You are, in our eyes, a noble martyr. The chains on your legs bind our hearts all the closer to you.

Brown. Tell me more about the family.

Mrs. Brown. Owen doesn't dare come home yet.

Brown. Do you know where he is?

Mrs. Brown. Hiding among friends in Ohio. Poor boy, he is called all kinds of vile names, just for being with you.

Brown. For the cause we have all suffered much in the past; we shall have to in the future. We should rejoice at his escape.

Mrs. Brown. I do, John. And Oliver and Watson *did die* for a great and good cause!

(*Said with spirit.*)

Brown. Some day, all the people of the earth will say that.

(*Avis comes in.*)

There are several faults in the original dialogue, but perhaps the chief is not regarding the principle that clearness dramatically consists, not merely in stating needed facts, but in so stating them that interest is not allowed to lapse. The original dialogue was scrappy, lacking sequence, not so much of thought as of emotion. If it be said that at such a moment talk is often fitful, it must be remembered that our time-limits forbid giving every word said in such a scene.

We must present merely its essentials. Only in that way may a play, a condensed presentation of life, hope to give a total effect for a scene equal to that of the original. The re-ordered dialogue of the right-hand column seeks merely to bring together ideas really closely related, and to move, in a way in keeping with the characters, from lesser to stronger emotion. With the disappearance of the scrappy effect, is not the result clearer? Even now, the dialogue might well be condensed and made emotionally more significant.

If we let the dialogue of a play merely state necessary facts, what is the result? At the worst, something like the left-hand column. Two young women, one the married hostess and the other the friend of her girlhood, are opening their morning mail on the piazza. Serena, the hostess, has known nothing of the engagement of Elise to Teddy.

ORIGINAL	REVISION
Elise. (*Looking up from her letters.*) Is he coming?	*Elise.* Is he coming?
Serena. I don't know yet, but I wish he were still in South Africa. If he does come, I don't know what will happen. There's a letter from Aunt Deborah.	*Serena.* I don't know yet, but I wish he were still in South Africa. Look at this: (*Showing letter.*) A letter from Aunt Deborah.
Elise. Yes? What does she want?	*Elise.* Yes?
Serena. Did you know she had a terrible quarrel with Teddy just before he went to South Africa?	*Serena.* Aunt Deborah had a terrible quarrel with Teddy just before he went!
Elise. I had a vague idea of it. It must all be made up now and they'll be delighted to meet here.	*Elise.* Oh, that must be all made up now.
Serena. No, she won't. She says she's sure she'll have a shock if she sees him and very gladly accepts our kind invitation because so she can avoid meeting him.	*Serena.* Listen! (*Reading from letter.*) "If I see that man I'll have a shock," and (*with a despairing gesture*) she very gladly accepts our invitation!

From the left-hand column we surely do learn that a before-mentioned Teddy has been in South Africa; that he and a certain Aunt Deborah have quarreled; and that though she particularly does not wish to meet Teddy, she is coming, as he is, to visit at this house — three important points. Like everyday speech, the quoted dialogue lacks compactness. Let us first, therefore, cut out all that is not absolutely necessary. We do not need, in the first speech of Elise, anything more than the query, "Yes?" The inflection will give the rest. In the second speech of Serena we can cut "to South Africa," for we have already mentioned where Teddy has been. In the second speech of Elise, it is the words "It must be all made up now" that are important. What precedes and what follows may be omitted. Similarly, in the first and second speeches of Serena, it is the first and the third sentences which are important. The second, if given, really anticipates an effect which will be stronger later. If we change the second speech from a query to an assertion or an exclamation, we shall gain and slightly condense. It will then read, "Aunt Deborah had a terrible quarrel with Teddy just before he went!" Because we have cut the last speech of Elise, the first sentence of the next speech of Serena becomes unnecessary. It will be necessary, however, to re-phrase what remains of this final speech, so hard is it to deliver. The revised dialogue may still be poor enough, but it says all the original did in less space — that is condensation. The effect is better because we have cut out some parts, and have slightly changed others. That is selection. The slight changes have been made in order to make the sequence of ideas clearer, to suggest emotion more clearly, or to make the dialogue natural — and all that means the beginning of characterization. The final word on this dialogue is, however, that even now either speaker could utter the words of the other, and that is all wrong. Clearly, then, even in stating facts, dialogue may be bad, indifferent, and good.

The following opening of a Japanese No drama shows that even more trained writers may write dialogue with no virtue except its clearness:

TWO HEARTS

A drama by J. Mushakoji

SCENE: *A forest glade on the nobleman's estate. A cross for crucifixion in the foreground. Two men A and B standing on either side of the cross holding spears.*

A. That fellow has behaved foolishly!

B. Yes, and the girl also.

A. It was certain that they would be killed when found out.

B. And nothing could prevent the discovery.

A. Our master is extremely indignant.

B. There has not been one person crucified since the present lord succeeded.

A. Although the stewards have assured him that it is the established law of the land, the present master has never given permission for the punishment of criminals by crucifixion and fire. But now he has announced that he will kill them in this manner, and we are commissioned to carry out the disagreeable duty.

B. Even though we refused to obey the command at first and requested him to excuse us he would not listen to our petition.

A. The master must have been very fond of this young girl.

B. Yes. Rumour has it that he became attached to her while the late mistress was still living.

A. He did not care very much for his wife. Anyway, she was too inferior to be his companion.

B. It was said that he did not grieve over her death.

A. And I have heard that the girl fainted when her mistress died.

B. She must have been a favourite among the other attendants who accompanied the lady when she became the wife of the lord.

A. She was clever and pretty and had a strong character.

B. Why did the girl fall in love with that fellow, I wonder?

A. He is the kind of a man a woman admires.

B. And because the girl loved him he now receives such severe punishment.

A. We can never tell. What seems good luck may mean unexpected misfortune.

B. She would have been happier if she had obeyed the master's will instead of rejecting him.

A. Probably she did not like him.

B. But he seemed to care a great deal for her.

A. It may not be right to say so, but his decision seems to have been taken because of his jealousy.

B. Yes, that is true. I wonder why he has commanded us to prepare only one cross.

A. Perhaps it is his plan to save one of them.

B. I don't think that could be done very well.

A. But some one said the master told the girl that he would save her life if she would only desert the young man for him.

B. That may be so. Perhaps he intends to crucify the young man first in the presence of the girl so as to break her obstinate spirit and thus gain her love.

A. That may be so.

B. It is said that the young man has already repented of his love for the girl. But she was not at all frightened when the punishment was announced and she was informed that she was to be crucified. The man, on the contrary, at once turned white and almost fainted when he heard the judgment passed upon him.

A. But a woman is much braver in love affairs than a man.

B. You speak as though you had had experience!

A. Ha! Ha! Ha!

B. Perhaps the master wishes to kill the young man in as cruel a manner as possible.

A. Hush! The lord is here! We are now obliged to remain silent and witness a living drama.

B. And we have a dreadful task to perform.[1]

Though this omits nothing in the way of necessary information, how colorless it is! When we note how perfectly either A or B could speak the lines of the other, we see where the difficulty lies. The lines lack all characterization. The history of the drama shows that while the facts of a

[1] *The Far East*, June 6, 1914, p. 295.

play may be interesting in themselves, they are much more interesting to an audience which hears them as they present themselves to well-defined characters of the story. It is axiomatic that sympathy quickens interest. Take a much better known illustration of the same point. The left-hand column gives the opening lines of the first quarto, *Hamlet.* The right-hand column shows the opening of the second quarto.

Enter two Centinels	*Enter Barnardo and Francisco, two Centinels*
1. Stand: who is that?	*Barnardo.* Whose there?
2. Tis I.	*Francisco.* [Nay answere me.] Stand and unfolde your selfe.
	Bar. Long live the King.
	Fran. Barnardo.
	Bar. Hee.
1. O you come most carefully upon your watch.	*Fran.* You come most carefully upon your houre.
	Bar. Tis now strooke twelfe, get thee to bed Francisco.
	Fran. For this relief much thanks, [tis bitter cold,] And I am sick at heart.
	Bar. Have you had quiet guard?
	Fran. [Not a mouse stirring.]
	Bar. Well, good night:
2. And if you meete Marcellus and Horatio, The partners of my watch, bid them make haste.	If you doe meete Horatio and Marcellus, The rivals of my watch, bid them make hast.
1. I will: See who goes there.	
Enter Horatio and Marcellus	*Enter Horatio and Marcellus*
	Fran. I think I heare them, stand ho, who is there?
Horatio. Friends to this ground.	*Horatio.* Friends to this ground.

Marcellus. And leegemen to the Dane,

O farewell honest souldier, who hath relieved you?
1. Barnardo hath my place, give you good night.

Marcellus. And Leedgemen to the Dane,
Fran. Give you good night.

Mar. O, farewell honest souldiers, who hath relieved you?
Fran. Barnardo hath my place; give you good night.
(*Exit Francisco.*)[1]

The first of these extracts, without question gives the necessary facts of the changing of the watch. It busies itself only with this absolutely necessary action. The second quarto identifies the speakers, and, by a different phrasing with additional lines, both characterizes them and gives the scene atmosphere. Study the re-phrasings and bracketed additions of the second scene — "Nay answere me," "Tis bitter cold," "Not a mouse stirring" — and note that this dialogue gains over the first in that it interests by what it adds as much as by the essential action.

A second quotation from *Hamlet* in the two quartos illustrates the same point even better. The text in the left-hand column, merely stating the facts necessary to the movement of the scene, leaves to the actor all characterizing of Montano, and gives the player of Corambis only the barest hints. The second quarto text, in the right-hand column, makes Polonius so garrulous that he cannot keep track of his own ideas; shows his pride in his would-be shrewdness; indeed, rounds him out into a real character. It even makes Reynaldo a man who does not yield at once, but a person of honorable instincts who is overborne. Can there be any question which scene holds the attention better?

[1] *The Devonshire Hamlets*, pp. 1-2.

Enter Corambis and Montano

Corambis. Montano; here, these letters to my sonne,
And this same money with my blessing to him,
And bid him ply his learning good Montano.

Montano. I will my lord.
Cor. You shall do very well Montano, to say thus,

I knew the gentleman, or know his father
To inquire the manner of his life,
And thus; being amongst his acquaintance,
You may say, you saw him at such a time, marke you mee,

Enter old Polonius, with his man or two

Polonius. Give him this money and these notes Reynaldo.
Reynaldo. I will my Lord.
Pol. You shall doe marviles wisely good Reynaldo
Before you visite him to make inquire
Of his behaviour.
Rey. My Lord, I did intend it.
Pol. Mary well said, very well said; look you sir,
Enquire me first what Danskers are in Parris,
And how, and who, what meanes and where they keepe,
What companie, at what expence, and finding
By this encompasment, and drift of question
That they doe know my sonne, come you more neerer
Then your particular demands will tuch it,
Take you as t'were some distant knowledge of him,
As thus, I know his father, and his friends,
And in part him, doe you marke this, Reynaldo?
Rey. I, very well my Lord.
Pol. And in part him, but you may say, not well,
But y'ft be he I meane, hee's very wilde,
Adicted so and so, and there put on him

At game, or drincking, swearing, or drabbing,
You may go so farre.
Mon. My Lord, that will im-
peach his reputation.
Cor. I faith not a whit, no
not a whit,

What forgeries you please,
marry none so ranck
As may dishonour him, take
heede of that,
But sir, such wanton, wild, and
usuall slips
As are companions noted and
most knowne
To youth and libertie.
Rey. As gaming my Lord.
Pol. I, or drinking, fencing,
swearing,
Quarrelling, drabbing, you may
go so far.
Rey. My Lord, that would
dishonour him.
Pol. Fayth as you may season
it in the charge.
You must not put another scan-
dell on him,
That he is open to incontinencie,
That's not my meaning, but
breath his faults so quently
That they may seeme the taints
of libertie,
The flash and out-breake of a
fierie mind,
A savagenes in unreclamed
blood
Of generall assault.
Rey. But my good Lord.
Pol. Wherefore should you
do this?
Rey. I my Lord, I would
know that.
Pol. Marry, sir, heer's my
drift,
And I believe it is a fetch of wit,
You laying these slight sallies
on my sonne
As t'were a thing a little soyld
with working,

Marke you, your partie in converse, him you would
sound
Having ever seene in the pre-
nominat crimes
The youth you breath of guiltie,
be assur'd

Now happely hee closeth with
you in the consequence,
As you may bridle it not dis-
parage him a iote.

He closes with you in this consequence,
Good sir, (or so,) or friend, or
gentleman,
According to the phrase, or the
addition
Of man and country.
Rey. Very good my Lord.
Pol. And then sir, doos a
this, a doos, what was I
about to say?

What was I about to say,

By the masse I was about to say
something,
Where did I leave?

Mon. He closeth with you in
the consequence.

Rey. At closes in the consequence.[1]

Even the dialogue, which with broad characterization
states necessary facts clearly, is by no means so effective as
dialogue so absorbing by its characterization that we assim-
ilate the facts unconsciously. Contrast the opening of *The
Good Natur'd Man* with that of *Hindle Wakes*. The first is
so busy in characterizing an absent but important figure
that it presents the two speakers only in the broadest way.
That is, exposition exists here as its only excuse for being.
In *Hindle Wakes*, the rapid development of an interesting
situation through two characters who as individuals become
more distinct and interesting with every line, probably
conceals from most auditors or readers the fact that seven
important bits of information are given before Fanny enters.

[1] *The Devonshire Hamlets*, pp. 26-27.

ACT I

SCENE — *An apartment in Young Honeywood's house*
Enter Sir William Honeywood, Jarvis

Sir William. Good Jarvis, make no apologies for this honest bluntness. Fidelity like yours is the best excuse for every freedom.

Jarvis. I can't help being blunt, and being very angry, too, when I hear you talk of disinheriting so good, so worthy a young gentleman as your nephew, my master. All the world loves him.

Sir Will. Say, rather, that he loves all the world; that is his fault.

Jarv. I'm sure there is no part of it more dear to him than you are, tho' he has not seen you since he was a child.

Sir Will. What signifies his affection to me, or how can I be proud of a place in a heart where every sharper and coxcomb find an easy entrance?

Jarv. I grant you that he's rather too good natur'd; that he's too much every man's man; that he laughs this minute with one, and cries the next with another; but whose instructions may he thank for all this?

Sir Will. Not mine, sure? My letters to him during my employment in Italy taught him only that philosophy which might prevent, not defend his errors.

Jarv. Faith, begging your honour's pardon, I'm sorry they taught him any philosophy at all; it has only served to spoil him. This same philosophy is a good horse in the stable, but an arrant jade on a journey. For my own part, whenever I hear him mention the name on't, I'm always sure he's going to play the fool.

Sir Will. Don't let us ascribe his faults to his philosophy, I entreat you. No, Jarvis, his good nature rises rather from his fears of offending the importunate, than his desire of making the deserving happy.

Jarv. What it arises from, I don't know. But to be sure, everybody has it that asks it.

Sir Will. Ay, or that does not ask it. I have been now for some time a concealed spectator of his follies, and find them as boundless as his dissipation.

Jarv. And yet, faith, he has some fine name or other for them all. He calls his extravagance generosity; and his trusting everybody, universal benevolence. It was but last week he went security for a fellow whose face he scarce knew, and that he call'd an act of exalted mu-mu-munificence; ay, that was the name he gave it.

Sir Will. And upon that I proceed, as my last effort, tho' with very little hopes to reclaim him. That very fellow has just absconded, and I have taken up the security. Now, my intention is to involve him in fictitious distress, before he has plunged himself into real calamity. To arrest him for that very debt, to clap an officer upon him, and then let him see which of his friends will come to his relief.[1]

ACT I. SCENE 1

The scene is triangular, representing a corner of the living-room of No. 137, Burnley Road, Hindle, a house rented for about 7s. 6d. a week. In the left-hand wall, low down, there is a door leading to the scullery. In the same wall, but further away from the spectator, is a window looking on to the backyard. A dresser stands in front of the window. About half-way up the right-hand wall is the door leading to the hall or passage. Nearer, against the same wall, a high cupboard for china and crockery. The fire-place is not visible, being in one of the walls not represented. However, down in the L. corner of the stage is an arm-chair, which stands by the hearth. In the middle of the room is a square table, with chairs on each side. The room is cheerful and comfortable. It is nine o'clock on a warm August evening. Through the window can be seen the darkening sky, as the blind is not drawn. Against the sky an outline of roof tops and mill chimneys. The only light is the dim twilight from the open window. Thunder is in the air. When the curtain rises, Christopher Hawthorn, a decent, white-bearded man of nearly fifty, is sitting in the arm-chair, smoking a pipe. Mrs. Hawthorn, a keen, sharp-faced woman of fifty-five, is standing, gazing out of the window. There is a flash of lightning and a rumble of thunder far away.

Mrs. Hawthorn. It's passing over. There'll be no rain.
Christopher. Ay! We could do with some rain.

(There is a flash of lightning.)

Chris. Pull down the blind and light the gas.
Mrs. H. What for?
Chris. It's more cozy-like with the gas.
Mrs. H. You're not afraid of the lightning?
Chris. I want to look at that railway guide.
Mrs. H. What's the good. We've looked at it twice already. There's no train from Blackpool till half-past ten, and it's only just on nine now.

---

[1] Act I, Scene 1. Belles-Lettres Series. Austin Dobson, ed. D. C. Heath & Co.

Chris. Happen we've made a mistake.

Mrs. H. Happen we've not. Besides, what's the good of a railway guide? You know trains run as they like on Bank Holiday.

Chris. Ay! Perhaps you're right. You don't think she'll come round by Manchester!

Mrs. H. What would she be doing coming round by Manchester?

Chris. You can get that road from Blackpool.

Mrs. H. Yes. If she's coming from Blackpool.

Chris. Have you thought she may not come at all?

Mrs. H. (*Grimly.*) What do you take me for?

Chris. You never hinted.

Mrs. H. No use putting them sort of ideas into your head.

(*Another flash and a peal of thunder.*)

Chris. Well, well, those are lucky who haven't to travel at all on Bank Holiday.

Mrs. H. Unless they've got a motor car, like Nat Jeffcote's lad.

Chris. Nay, *he's* not got one.

Mrs. H. What? Why I saw him with my own eyes setting out in it last Saturday week after the mill shut.

Chris. Ay! He's gone off these Wakes with his pal George Ramsbottom. A couple of thick beggars, those two!

Mrs. H. Then what do you mean telling me he's not got a motor car?

Chris. I said he hadn't got one of his own. It's his father's. You don't catch Nat Jeffcote parting with owt before his time. That's how he holds his lad in check, as you might say.

Mrs. H. Alan Jeffcote's seldom short of cash. He spends plenty.

Chris. Ay! Nat gives him what he asks for, and doesn't want to know how he spends it either. But he's *got* to ask for it first. Nat can stop supplies any time if he's a mind.

Mrs. H. That's likely, isn't it?

Chris. Queerer things have happened. You don't know Nat like I do. He's a bad one to get across with.

(*Another flash and gentle peal. Mrs. H. gets up.*)

Mrs. H. I'll light the gas.

(*She pulls down the blind and lights the gas.*)

Chris. When I met Nat this morning he told me that Alan had telegraphed from Llandudno on Saturday asking for twenty pounds.

Mrs. H. From Llandudno?

Chris. Ay! Reckon he's been stopping there. Run short of brass.

Mrs. H. And did he send it?

Chris. Of course he sent it. Nat doesn't stint the lad. (*He laughs quietly.*) Eh, but he *can* get through it, though!

Mrs. H. Look here. What are you going to say to Fanny when she comes?

Chris. Ask her where she's been?

Mrs. H. Ask her where she's been. Of course we'll do that. But suppose she won't tell us?

Chris. She's always been a good girl.

Mrs. H. She's always gone her own road. Suppose she tells us to mind our own business?

Chris. I reckon it *is* my business to know what she's been up to.

Mrs. H. Don't you forget it. And don't let her forget it either. If you do, I promise you I won't.

Chris. All right. Where's that post-card?

Mrs. H. Little good taking heed of that.

(*Christopher rises and gets a picture post-card from the dresser.*)

Chris. (*Reading.*) She'll be home before late on Monday. Lovely weather. (*Looking at the picture.*) North Pier, Blackpool. Very like, too.

Mrs. H. (*Suddenly.*) Let's have a look. When was it posted?

Chris. It's dated Sunday.

Mrs. H. That's nowt to go by. Any one can put the wrong date. What's the postmark? (*She scrutinizes it.*) "August 5th, summat P.M." I can't make out the time.

Chris. August 5th. That was yesterday all right. There'd only be one post on Sunday.

Mrs. H. Then she was in Blackpool till yesterday, that's certain.

Chris. Ay!

Mrs. H. Well, it's a mystery.

Chris. (*Shaking his head.*) Or summat worse.

Mrs. H. Eh? You don't think *that*, eh?

Chris. I don't know what to think.

Mrs. H. Nor me neither.

(*They sit silent for a time. There is a rumble of thunder, far away. After it has died away, a knock is heard at the front door. They turn and look at each other. Mrs. Hawthorn rises and goes out in silence. In a few moments, Fanny Hawthorn comes in, followed by Mrs. Hawthorn.*)[1]

[1] *Hindle Wakes*, Stanley Houghton. J. W. Luce & Co., Boston; Sidgwick & Jackson, Ltd., London.

What usually keeps a writer from passing to well characterized dialogue from dialogue merely clear as to essential facts is that he is so bound to his facts that he sees rather than feels the scene. The chief trouble with the dialogue of the John Brown play was an attempt to keep so close to historical accounts of the particular incident that sympathetic imagination was benumbed. One constantly meets this fault in the earlier Miracle Plays before writers had come to understand that audiences care more for the human being in the situation than for the situation itself, and that only by representing a situation not for itself but as felt by the people involved can it be made fully interesting. At the left is a speech of Mary in *The Crucifixion* of the York Cycle; at the right is her speech in the Hegge or so-called Coventry Plays.

Mary. Alas! for my sweet son, I say,
That dolefully to deed thus is dight,
Alas! for full lovely thou lay
In my womb, this worthely wight
Alas! that I should see this sight
Of my son so seemly to see,
Alas! that this blossom so bright
Untruly is tugged to this tree, Alas!
My lord, my life,
With full great grief,
Hanges as a thief,
Alas! he did never trespass.[1]

Mary. O my son, my son! my darling dear!
What have I defended [offended] thee?
Thou hast spoke to all of those that be here,
And not a word thou speakest to me.
To the Jews thou art full kind,
Thou hast forgiven all here misdeed;
And the thief thou hast in mind,
For once asking mercy heaven is his meed.
Ah! my sovereign lord, why wilt thou not speak
To me that am thy mother in pain for thy wrong?
Ah, heart, heart why wilt thou not break?
That I were out of this sorrow so strong! [2]

[1] *York Plays*, p. 363. L. T. Smith, ed. Clarendon Press, Oxford.
[2] *Ludus Coventriæ*, p. 322. J. O. Halliwell, ed. Shakespeare Society.

The writer of the Hegge speech had discovered long before Ralph Waldo Emerson that the secret of good dialogue is "truth carried alive into the heart by passion." The second requisite, then, of good dialogue is that it must be kindled by feeling, made alive by the emotion of the speaker. For the would-be dramatist the secret is so to know his characters that facts are not mere facts, but conditions moving him because they move the characters he perfectly understands. As he interprets between character and audience, he must be like Planchette or the clairvoyant, the creature of another's will, whose ideas and emotions rather than his own he tries with all the power that is in him to convey. In brief, then, though it is absolutely necessary that dialogue give the facts as to what happens, who the people are, their relations to one another, etc., it is better dialogue if, while doing all this, it seems to be busied only with characterization.

Unassigned dialogue usually makes a reader or hearer promptly recognize his preference for characterized rather than uncharacterized speech. When a group, as in many stage mobs, speaks in chorus, or at best in sections, the result is unreality for many hearers and absurdity for the more critical. Every hearer knows that people do not really, when part of a mob, say absolutely the same thing, and rarely speak in perfect unison. Common sense cries out for individualization among the possible speakers. When we read the following extract from Andreiev's *Life of Man*, we may agree with what is apparently the author's idea, that it makes no difference which one of the speakers delivers a particular line or sentence; but the moment the scene is staged everything changes.

A profound darkness within which nothing moves. Then there can be dimly perceived the outlines of a large, high room and the grey silhouettes of Old Women in strange garments who resemble a troop of grey, hiding mice. In low voices and with laughter to and fro the Old Women converse.

. . . .

When they sent him to the drug store for some medicine he rode up and down past the store for two hours and could not remember what he wanted. So he came back.

> (*Subdued laughter. The crying again becomes louder and then dies away. Silence.*)

What has happened to her? Perhaps she is already dead.

No, in that case we should hear weeping. The doctor would run out and begin to talk nonsense, and they would bring out her husband unconscious, and we should have our hands full. No, she is not dead.

Then why are we sitting here?

Ask Him. How should we know?

He won't tell.

He won't tell. He tells nothing.

He drives us here and there. He rouses us from our beds and makes us watch, and then it turns out that there was no need of our coming.

We came of our own accord. Didn't we come of our own accord? You must be fair to Him. There, she is crying again. Aren't you satisfied?

Are *you*?

I am saying nothing. I am saying nothing and waiting.

How kind-hearted you are!

> (*Laughter. The cries become louder.*)[1]

Of course every rule has its exception, and it may be urged that the final lines of David Pinski's *The Treasure* need no assigning to special speakers. This, if true, results from the fact that Mr. Pinski, as the last touch in his study of the universal perversion of man through lust for money, wishes to represent even all the dead as sharing in this greed. Even here, however, Mr. Pinski is careful, by his headings "Many" and "The Pious Rabbi," to distinguish among speeches to be given by one person, the chorus, and a figure he wishes specially to individualize, the Rabbi.

[1] *Plays*, pp. 71-72. Copyright, 1915, by Chas. Scribner's Sons, New York.

The Dead

(*In shrouds and praying shawls appear singly and in groups amid the graves. They whisper and breathe their words.*) Swiftly into the synagogue! . . . Hasten! . . . The hour of midnight is long past. . . . Hasten. . . .

> (*They hasten to the gate. One sees only their silhouettes in the dim light of the veiled moon.*)

I thought we would not come out today at all.

The dead fear the breath of the living.

We fear them more than they do us. There is no peace betwixt life and death. . . .

No peace . . . no peace. . . .

Indeed life vexed me grievously today.

Vexed is not the word. I lived in their life so really that I shuddered and feared.

Shuddered with fear or with longing? Did you feel a yearning for your money?

> (*Ghostly laughter shakes the rows of the dead.*)

The distinguished and the wealthy must surely have had a bad day.

It fairly smelled of money and they had to lie with the worms.

It almost threw them out of their graves.

Many

Money . . . money . . . money. . . .   (*Ghostly laughter.*)

But you poor devils hadn't a much better time either. It smelled of money and you couldn't even beg.   (*Laughter.*)

It is high time for all of you to be forgetting life. . . . Come quickly into the synagogue. . . .   (*Many of the dead vanish.*)

It gave me really an exalted feeling to see how little fear of us they felt.

Don't flatter yourself. We would have been no better. We were no better either.

Many

(*At the same time.*) Money . . . Money . . . Money. . . .

Others

And that is life . . . that is life . . . that is life. . . .

It exalted me in my grave too. So many women walked about here today. Young ones and pretty ones, I wager. . . . (*Laughter.*)

Who speaks thus? Who opens his mouth to speak such ugly words?

It's the petty field surgeon who lies buried by the wall.

The Pious Rabbi

(*In passing. His praying shawl hangs but loosely over his left shoulder.*) They have dug up my whole grave. . . . They have dug away my right arm. Woe, how shall I now put on my praying shawl? How shall I appear before God? (*To a group.*) Will not some one help me to put on my praying shawl?

   (*They surround and help him. They show signs of deep feeling at the sight of the missing arm. Murmurs of astonishment and compassion.*)

Many

Woe . . . woe . . . woe. . . .

Others

Money . . . money . . . money. . . .

The Rabbi

Now will I go and appear before God. . . . Now I will ask him. . . .

   (*He vanishes through the gate.*)

Many

He will get no answer . . . he will get no answer.

One of the Dead

(*With feeling.*) They who are in life still stand at the same point. Generation dies after generation and all remains as it has been. As it was aforetime, so it was in my time and so it is today.

Many

Money . . . money . . . money. . . .

And yet it must lead to something. Surely there must be a goal.

Only God knows that. . . .

And man must learn what it is.

That will be his greatest victory.

Man's greatest victory.

Several

Man's. . . .

Others

The living one's. . . . And we?
>   (*A ghostly breathing of laughter and sighing.*)

The First

Man's greatest victory . . .

Curtain [1]

Staging this, several facts will confront us. We certainly shall not let different actors of the group speak different lines on successive nights. That is, each supernumerary will be given one speech or more. If certain speeches seem to belong together, they will be given to one actor, and characterization will emerge as he speaks his lines. Unquestionably, too, if speeches which seem in themselves uncharacterizing are given to marked physical types, such as stout, very thin, very tall, or very short people, persons of markedly quick or slow physical movement, some of the speeches may seem unfitting. Rarely, then, is there any value in the unassigned speech. It may pass in the reading, as has been admitted, but the public prefers the assigned speech, and still more the speech so characterized that it must be assigned. Compare this passage from *Julius Cæsar* with its assignments to the First, the Second, the Third, and the Fourth Plebeian with the passage from Andreiev's play. Can there be any question that Shakespeare's assigned speeches are somehow clearer, more dramatic?

SCENE III. *A Street*

Enter Cinna the poet, and after him the Plebeians

Cinna. I dreamt tonight that I did feast with Cæsar,
And things unluckily charge my fantasy.
I have no will to wander forth of doors,
Yet something leads me forth.

[1] B. W. Huebsch, New York.

DIALOGUE

1. Plebeian. What is your name?

2. Plebeian. Whither are you going?

3. Plebeian. Where do you dwell?

4. Plebeian. Are you a married man or a bachelor?

2. Plebeian. Answer every man directly.

1. Plebeian. Ay, and briefly.

4. Plebeian. Ay, and wisely.

3. Plebeian. Ay, and truly, you were best.

Cinna. What is my name? Whither am I going? Where do I dwell? Am I a married man or a bachelor? Then, to answer every man directly and briefly, wisely and truly: wisely I say, I am a bachelor.

2. Plebeian. That's as much as to say, they are fools that marry. You'll bear me a bang for that, I fear. Proceed; directly.

Cinna. Directly, I am going to Cæsar's funeral.

1. Plebeian. As a friend or an enemy?

Cinna. As a friend.

2. Plebeian. That matter is answered directly.

4. Plebeian. For your dwelling, — briefly.

Cinna. Briefly, I dwell by the Capitol.

3. Plebeian. Your name, sir, truly.

Cinna. Truly, my name is Cinna.

1. Plebeian. Tear him to pieces; he's a conspirator.

Cinna. I am Cinna the poet, I am Cinna the poet.

4. Plebeian. Tear him for his bad verses, tear him for his bad verses.

Cinna. I am not Cinna the conspirator.

4. Plebeian. It is no matter, his name's Cinna. Pluck but his name out of his heart and turn him going.

3. Plebeian. Tear him, tear him! Come, ˈbrands, ho! fire-brands! To Brutus', to Cassius'; burn all! Some to Decius' house, and some to Casca's; some to Lingarius'. Away, go! (*Exeunt.*)[1]

It may almost be stated as a general principle that assigning a speech is the first step in focusing the attention of an audience on that speech. The value of such focusing has been discussed earlier under "Characterization." In exceptional cases, as the citation from *The Treasure* shows, there may be some justification for unassigned speeches, but in

[1] *Julius Cæsar*, Act III, Scene 3.

ninety-nine cases out of a hundred, when any lines of the play seem not to need assigning to any particular person, they lack the characterization which belongs to them.

The thesis play or the problem play, which have been so current in the last few years, have brought into special prominence a common fault in so-called dramatic dialogue. The speeches narrate, describe, expound or argue, and well, but not in the character of the supposed speaker. Rather the author himself is speaking. Such dialogue, whether it be as clever as some in Mr. Shaw's plays, as beautiful as certain passages by George Chapman, or as commonplace as in many modern instances, should be rewritten till the author can state the desired idea or facts as the imagined speaker would have stated them. This was the fault with the extract from the John Brown play, and whether it has its source in an intense desire of the author to present his own ideas, or to phrase his sense of beauty, in lack of characterizing power or in mere carelessness, it is reprehensible. In the following instance, the writer is so absorbed in his own ideas that he forgets characterization.

Senator Morse. . . . What great motive —?

Mary. One more imperious than empires or coalitions — (*Mary turns to Mrs. Morse*) — one that mothers know — (*Mary turns to Senator Morse*) — and fathers, too. It is the commonest thing in the world, and the one most completely overlooked. Woman's love and faith and charity are the motives of that great, imperious impulse by which nature is trying to rule this world and perpetuate the human soul. Individual self-control and the governance of the world are themselves in embryo. . . . Creation is from God and *it* is *divine*. It is the thing and the only thing that kills wantonness and makes love pure. The higher modesty is the peculiar inherit-ance of our race. It is our duty to understand it, respect it, make it sacred, and have it raised out of the darkness of ignorance and mystery in its true dignity as patriotic impulse and made the true basis of society, its government, and its provision for the general welfare.

Does this sound like an individual woman or like the author using one of his characters for the sounding phrases of his own thinking?

In the next illustration, from *George Barnwell*, the colorlessness comes from the lack of quickening sympathy with character which marks most of Lillo's work.

Thorowgood. Thou know'st I have no heir, no child but thee; the fruits of many years successful industry must all be thine. Now, it would give me pleasure great as my love, to see on whom you would bestow it. I am daily solicited by men of the greatest rank and merit for leave to address you; but I have hitherto declin'd it, in hopes that by observation I shou'd learn which way your inclination tends; for as I know love to be essential to happiness in the marriage state, I had rather my approbation should confirm your choice than direct it.

Maria. What can I say? How shall I answer, as I ought, this tenderness, so uncommon even in the best of parents? But you are without example; yet had you been less indulgent, I had been most wretched. That I look on the croud of courtiers that visit here with equal esteem, but equal indifference, you have observed, and I must needs confess; yet had you asserted your authority, and insisted on a parent's right to be obey'd, I had submitted and to my duty sacrificed my peace.

Thor. From your perfect obedience in every other instance, I fear'd as much; and therefore wou'd leave you without a byass in an affair wherein your happiness is so immediately concern'd.

Ma. Whether from a want of that just ambition that wou'd become your daughter, or from some other cause, I know not; but I find high birth and titles don't recommend the man who owns them to my affections.

Thor. I wou'd not that they shou'd, unless his merit recommends him more. A noble birth and fortune, tho' they make not a bad man good, yet they are a real advantage to a worthy one, and place his virtues in the fairest light.

Ma. I cannot answer for my inclinations, but they shall ever be submitted to your wisdom and authority; and, as you will not compel me to marry where I cannot love, so love shall never make me act contrary to my duty. Sir, I have your permission to retire?

Thor. I'll see you to your chamber. (*Exeunt.*)[1]

Too often even somewhat skilled dramatists are led astray by the belief that to write in a style approved at the moment, or which they themselves hold beautiful, is better than to let the characters speak their own language. Examining the early plays of John Lyly — *Alexander and Campaspe, Sapho and Phao, Endymion*[2] (1579–1590) — we find in the more serious portions both action and characterization subordinated to standards of expression supposed at the time to be best. Contrasting the lovers' dialogue of *Love's Labor's Lost* with the scenes of Orsino and Viola in *Twelfth Night,* we see perfect illustration of the greater effectiveness of dialogue growing out of the characters as compared with dialogue which puts style first. The Heroic Drama of the second half of the seventeenth century rested upon theory rather than reality. Here is the way in which Almahide and Almanzor state strong feeling.

> *Almahide.* Then, since you needs will all my weakness know,
> I love you; and so well, that you must go.
> I am so much oblig'd, and have withall
> A heart so boundless and so prodigal
> I dare not trust myself, or you, to stay,
> But, like frank gamesters, must foreswear the play.
> *Almanzor.* Fate, thou art kind to strike so hard a blow;
> I am quite stunn'd, and past all feeling now.
> Yet — can you tell me you have pow'r and will
> To save my life, and at that instant, kill![3]

All that these two worthy people are trying to say is

Almahide. I love you; and so well that I dare not trust myself or you to stay.

Almanzor. Can you tell me you have power and will to save my life and at that instant kill!

---

[1] *The London Merchant, or The History of George Barnwell,* Act i, Scene 1. George Lillo. Sir A. W. Ward, ed. Belles-Lettres Series. D. C. Heath & Co., Boston and New York.

[2] *Works,* R. W. Bond, ed. Clarendon Press, Oxford.

[3] *Selected Dramas of John Dryden. Conquest of Granada.* G. R. Noyes, ed.

Dryden makes Almahide describe her own emotional condition and, as is proper at any critical moment in Heroic Drama, drop into simile. Almanzor, too, confidently diagnoses his own condition and apostrophizes fate. All this was quite correct in its own day, not for real life, but for the people of the myth land conjured up by the dramatic theories of the *litterati*. Did people under such circumstances speak in this way? Surely not.

This scene from *George Barnwell*, 1731, illustrates the same substitution of an author's idea of what is effective because "literary" for a phrasing that springs from the real emotion of perfectly individualized figures.

SCENE 7. *Uncle. George Barnwell at a distance*

Uncle. O Death, thou strange mysterious power, — seen every day, yet never understood but by the incommunicative dead — what art thou? The extensive mind of man, that with a thought circles the earth's vast globe, sinks to the centre, or ascends above the stars; that worlds exotick finds, or thinks it finds — thy thick clouds attempts to pass in vain, lost and bewilder'd in the horrid gloom; defeated, she returns more doubtful than before; of nothing certain but of labour lost.

(*During this speech, Barnwell sometimes presents the pistol and draws it back again; at last he drops it, at which his uncle starts and draws his sword.*)

Barnwell. Oh, 'tis impossible!

Uncle. A man so near me, arm'd and masqu'd!

Barn. Nay, then there's no retreat.

(*Plucks a poniard from his bosom, and stabs him.*)

Uncle. Oh! I am slain! All-gracious heaven regard the prayer of thy dying servant! Bless, with thy choicest blessings, my dearest nephew; forgive my murderer, and take my fleeting soul to endless mercy!

(*Barnwell throws off his mask, runs to him, and, kneeling by him, raises and chafes him.*)

Barn. Expiring saint! Oh, murder'd, martyr'd uncle! Lift up your dying eyes, and view your nephew in your murderer! O, do not look so tenderly upon me! Let indignation lighten from your eyes, and blast me e're you die! — By Heaven, he weeps in pity of my woes. Tears, — tears for blood! The murder'd, in the agonies of death, weeps for his murderer. — Oh, speak your pious purpose, pronounce my pardon then — and take me with you! — He wou'd, but cannot. O why with such fond affection do you press my murdering hand! — What! will you kiss me! (*Kisses him. Uncle groans and dies.*) He's gone forever — and oh! I follow. (*Swoons away by his uncle's body.*) Do I still live to press the suffering bosom of the earth? Do I still breathe and taint with my infectious breath the wholesome air! Let Heaven from its high throne, in justice or in mercy, now look down on that dear murder'd saint, and me the murderer. And, if his vengeance spares, let pity strike and end my wretched being! — Murder the worst of crimes, and parricide the worst of murders, and this the worst of parricides! Cain, who stands on record from the birth of time, and must to its last final period, as accurs'd, slew a brother, favour'd above him. Detested Nero by another's hand dispatched a mother that he fear'd and hated. But I, with my own hand, have murder'd a brother, mother, father, and a friend, most loving and belov'd. This execrable act of mine's without a parallel. O may it ever stand alone — the last of murders, as it is the worst!

> The rich man thus, in torment and despair,
> Prefer'd his vain, but charitable prayer.
> The fool, his own soul lost, wou'd fain be wise
> For others good; but Heaven his suit denies.
> By laws and means well known we stand or fall,
> And one eternal rule remains for all.
> *The End of the Third Act.*[1]

Have you noticed that people under stress of strong emotion stop to depict their emotional condition, to analyze it, or neatly to apostrophize fate or Providence? The more real the emotion the more compact and connotative, usually, is its expression. People under high emotional strain who can tell you just what they ought to feel, or who describe elaborately what they are feeling are usually "indeed exceeding calm." Dryden's Lyndaraxa builded better than she knew when she said:

[1] Belles-Lettres Series. Sir A. W. Ward, ed. D. C. Heath & Co., Boston and New York.

> By my own experience I can tell
> Those who love truly do not argue well.

Bulwer-Lytton was thinking of the weakness of self-descriptive woe when he wrote Macready, while composing *Richelieu*, "In Act 4 — in my last alteration, when Richelieu, pitying Julie, says, 'I could weep to see her thus — But' — the effect would I think be better if he felt the tears with indignation at his own weakness — thus:

> 'Are these tears?
> O, shame, shame, Dotage' —"

Emotion, if given free way, finds the right words by which to express itself. When a character stands outside itself, describing what it feels, the speaker is really the author in disguise, describing what he is incompetent, from lack of sympathetic power, to phrase with simple, moving accuracy. M. de Curel has described perfectly the right relation of author to character and dialogue.

During the first days of work I have a very distinct feeling of creation. Later I move on instinctively and that is much better. When the sentiments of my characters are in question I am absolutely in their skins, for my own part indifferent as to their griefs or joys. I can be moved only later in re-reading, and then this emotion seems to arise from the fact that I have to do with characters absolutely strange to me. I experience sometimes, and then personally, a feeling of irony, of flippancy, in regard to my characters who tangle themselves up and get themselves into difficulties. That transpires sometimes in the language of some other character who, at the moment, ceases to speak correctly because he speaks as I should. As a result, corrections later. At the end of a year, my play, when I re-read it, seems something completely apart from me, written by another.[1]

Allowing a character to express itself exactly raises inevitably the question of dialect. On the one hand it must be

---

[1] *L'Année Psychologique*, 1894, p. 120.

admitted that nothing more quickly characterizes a figure, as far as type is concerned, than to let him speak like a Yankee, a Scotchman, a Negro, etc. If the character utters phrases which an audience recognizes instantly as characteristic of his supposed type, there is special satisfaction to the audience in such recognition. On the other hand, very few audiences know any dialect thoroughly enough to permit a writer to use it with absolute accuracy. The moment dialect begins to show the need of a glossary, it is defeating its own ends. As a result a compromise has arisen, dating from the very early days of the drama — stage dialects. A character made up to represent Scotchman, Welshman, Frenchman, Negro, or Indian, speaks in a way that has become time-honored on the stage as representing this or that figure among these types. Till recently most dialect on the stage has been at best a mere popular approximation to real usage. Until within a few years the peasant dialogue of *Gammer Gurton's Needle*, the famous sixteenth-century Interlude, was supposed to represent dialect of its time in the neighborhood of Cambridge, England. Recently philologists have shown that the speech of these peasants is unlike any dialect of the period of the play, and was obviously a stage convention of the time. Study the Welshmen and other dialect parts in Shakespeare, and you will reach approximately the same conclusion. With our developing sense of historical truth and of realism, we have, in recent years, been trying to make our characters speak exactly as they would in real life. The plays of the Abbey Theatre are in large part a revolt from the Irish dialogue which the plays of Dion Boucicault had practically established as true to life. Today we try not only phonetically to represent the ways in which words are spoken by the people of a particular locality, but by the use of words and phrases heard among such people to make the characterization vivid and convincing. Here, in Mr. Sheldon's play, *The Nigger*, is care to reproduce phonetically the speech of negroes:

Jinny. (*Wearily.*) I speck yo' right. Hev yo' got suthin' fo' me t'night? Seems lak I might take it down wif me t' de cabin.

Simms. (*Grumbling.*) Fo' dat young good-fo'-nuffin hawg-grubbah t' swallow w'en he done come home? Laws me, w'y Marse Phil 'lows his fried chicken en' co'n-braid t' feed dat wo'thles rap-scallion, I jes' cain't see! Clar out o' heah, yo' ern'ry yallah gal!

Jinny. (*Crushingly.*) Yallah gal —! Sho'! I was livin' heah fo' yo' was bawn! Don' fo'get dat, yo' imperent, low-down li'tle niggah yo'!

Simms. (*Pacifically.*) Hol' on, Jinny! I ain't said nuffin'. Dat I ain't! Yo' g' long now en' I'll sen' down a gal t' yo' cabin wif a basket.

Jinny. (*Turning away.*) Yo' sho' will — er Marse Phil'd —

Simms. (*As he goes up the steps.*) En' keep yo' gran'chillun out dat saloom, Jinny, ef yo' don' want t' see 'em cross de Jo'dan ahead o' yo'! Dat Joe! Lawd-a-massy! De white in him ain't done no-body no good's fah's dis — 'Scuse me, sah!

> (*He stops suddenly and turns aside, bowing, on seeing Noyes and Georgie, who have opened the door and come out.*)

Here is equal care to represent the speech of Southerners.

Noyes. My fathah? Yes, he gave way t' his Comme'cial ambition by sellin' powda an' bullets t' the Union — way back in '62. That got him into a bunch o' trouble, but it wasn't what *sta'ted* the — slight fam'ly coolness!

Georgie. Wasn't it? Why, I always hea'd —

Noyes. No, it came befo' that. My gran'fathah an' Phil's — they were brothahs-in-law, you know — they began it in the fo'ties.

Georgie. Why?

Noyes. (*Grimly.*) I reckon the Morrows are tryin' now t' keep it da'k. But Lawd! — I don't mind tellin'. It's the old thing — both losin' theah heads ovah the same woman.

Georgie. (*Innocently.*) How romantic! Phil's gran'mothah?

Noyes. (*After a pause.*) No — niggah woman.

Georgie. (*In a low voice, turning away.*) Oh — I didn't — realize —

Noyes. (Clearing his throat.) Phil's gran'fathah — he won out. An' that's the kick that sta'ted the Noyes fam'ly a-rollin' t' pe'-dition.

Georgie. (With difficulty.) But mos' people are willin' to fo'get — at least they ought to be.

Noyes. (Dryly.) Some ain't killed 'emselves tryin'. Howevah, on lookin' ahead I saw Phil an' I might be in a position t' help each othah, so we agreed t' sink it. I — I wish yo' mothah would follow Phil, Miss Byrd. I ce'tainly do wish that!

Georgie. She's old-fashioned — oh, hopelessly so! — in things the world now considers — trivial.

Noyes. (Looking at his hands.) Such as — trade?

Georgie. (Gently.) That's one of them.[1]

Lady Gregory, after writing a rough draft of one of her plays, goes among the people of her community and sets them talking of the subject she is treating. Noting their racy, apt, and highly individualized phrases, she gives them to her characters in the play as she re-writes. Such intimate, loving study of dialect as Lady Gregory, Mr. Yeats, and Synge have shown has given us an accurate representation of the Irish peasant, and may ultimately drive from the English stage the conventional absurdities of the past. Dialect, then, if carefully studied, is highly desirable if two or three facts are borne in mind. First of all, it should be accurate; but secondly it must be clear or must be made clear for any audience. Unquestionably, Mr. Stanley Houghton's memorable play *Hindle Wakes* had a bad title away from its birthplace, — Manchester, England. In the United States, this title is perfectly meaningless. How many in any audience in this country could be expected to know that the title means certain "autumn week-end holidays in the town of Hindle." There could be no harm in using a different title away from the birthplace of the play. Recently, in a manuscript play, appeared a figure

[1] *The Nigger,* Act I. Edward Sheldon. The Macmillan Co., New York.

speaking a strange mixture of Negro and Irish dialects. He
seemed to all readers a clumsy attempt by the author at a
dialect part. Really, the figure was a portrait of a small
political boss who, from boyhood on, had acquired in the
saloons and purlieus of his district words and phrases of
both the Negroes and the Irish. A little preliminary exposition at the right place cleared up this difficulty and turned
what seemed inept characterization into a particularly individual figure of richly characterizing phrase. Obviously,
then, dialect should, first, be written accurately. Then it
should be gone over to see what in it may not be clear to
most auditors. These words or phrases should be made
clear because they are translated by other people on the
stage or by the speaker, who himself sees or is told that some
stage listener does not understand him. Only a little
ingenuity is needed to do away with such vaguenesses. To
substitute for such words and phrases others which, though
incorrect, would be instantly understood by the audience is
to botch the dialect and produce what is, after all, not different from the conventional stage dialect of the past. This
raises a third point in regard to dialect, and one very frequently disregarded. Over and over again in plays using
dialect certain speeches are passed over by the author in his
final revision which neither phonetically nor in the words
and phrases chosen comport with the context. Instantly
the mood and the color of the scene are lost unless the actor
supplies what the author failed to give. That is, dialect, if
used, should be used steadily and consistently. The desid-
erata are, then, accuracy, persistent use, and clearness for
the general public. Thus used, dialect is one of the chief aids
to characterization.

If, in writing dialogue, a dramatist must not speak as
himself but in character, must not be consciously or unconsciously literary if not in character, how may one surely

choose the right words? Perhaps one or two illustrations will help here. The citation in the left-hand column from the first quarto *Hamlet* states the facts clearly enough, but wholly uncolored by the emotion of the speaker. In the right-hand column the passionate sympathy of Shakespeare has given him perfect understanding of Hamlet's feeling.

Hamlet. O fie Horatio, and if thou shouldst die,	*Hamlet.* O good Horatio, what a wounded name
What a scandale wouldst thou leave behinde?	Things standing thus unknowne, shall I leave behind me?
What tongue should tell the story of our deaths,	If thou did'st ever hold me in thy hart,
If not from thee? O my heart sinckes Horatio,	Absent thee from felicity a while,
Mine eyes have lost their sight, my tongue his use:	And in this harsh world drawe thy breath in paine
Farewell Horatio, heaven receive my soule.	To tell my story: What warlike noise is this?
(*Hamlet dies.*)	(*A march a farre off.*)[1]

Speaking, not as the historian, not as the observer, but as Hamlet himself, Shakespeare by his quickened feeling finds a phrasing of which we may say what Swinburne said of some of the lines of John Webster: that the character says, not what he might have said, not what we are satisfied to have him say, but what seems absolutely the only thing he could have said.

When a dramatist works as he should, the emotion of his characters gives him the right words for carrying their feelings to the audience, and every word counts. Writing to Macready of *Money*, Bulwer-Lytton said of his play, "At the end of Act in your closing speech, will you remember to say, you 'would' refuse me ten pounds to spend on benevolence. Not you refuse me. The *would* is important."[2]

In the left-hand column the complete sympathy of Hey-

---

[1] *The Devonshire Hamlets*, p. 99.

[2] *Letters of Bulwer-Lytton to Macready*, p. 130. B. Matthews, ed.

wood with his characters makes them speak simply, out of the fullness of their emotion. In the right-hand column, Heywood's collaborator, Rowley, lacking complete understanding of his characters, is thinking more of phrase for its own sake.

ACT I. SCENE 4. *The street*

Enter Rainsford and Young Forrest, meeting

Young Forrest. Pray let me speak with you.

Rainsford. With me, sir?

Young For. With you.

Rains. Say on.

Young For. Do you not know me?

Rains. Keep off, upon the peril of thy life.

Come not within my sword's length, lest this arm

Prove fatal to thee and bereave thy life,

As it hath done thy brother's.

Young For. Why now thou know'st me truly, by that token,

That thou hast slain my brother. Put up, put up!

So great a quarrel as a brother's life

Must not be made a street-brawl; 'tis not fit

That every prentice should, with his shop club,

Betwixt us play the sticklers. Sheathe thy sword.

Rains. Swear thou wilt act no sudden violence,

Or this sharp sword shall still be interposed

ACT II. SCENE 1. *Hounslow*

Enter Rainsford and Young Forrest

Rainsford. Your resolution holds, then?

Young Forrest. Men that are easily mov'd are soon remov'd

From resolution; but when, with advice

And with foresight we purpose, our intents

Are not without considerate reasons alter'd.

Rains. Thou art resolv'd, and I prepar'd for thee.

Yet thus much know, thy state is desperate,

And thou art now in danger's throat already

Ev'n half devour'd. If I subdue thee, know

Thou art a dead man; for this fatal steel,

That search'd thy brother's entrails is prepar'd

To do as much to thee. If thou survivest,

And I be slain, th'art dead too, my alliance

And greatness in the world will not endure

My slaughter unavenged. Come, I am for thee.

'Twixt me and thy own hatred.

Young For. Sheathe thy sword.

By my religion and that interest

I have in gentry I will not be guilty

Of any base revenge.

Rains. Say on.

Young For. Let's walk.

Trust me. Let not thy guilty soul

Be jealous of my fury. This my hand

Is curbed and govern'd by an honest heart,

Not by just anger. I'll not touch thee foully

For all the world. Let's walk.

Rains. Proceed.

Young For. Sir, you did kill my brother. Had it been

In fair and even encounter, tho' a child,

His death I had not question'd.

Rains. Is this all?

Young For. He's gone. The law is past. Your life is clear'd;

For none of all our kindred laid against

You evidence to hang you. You're a gentleman;

And pity 'twere a man of your descent

Should die a felon's death. See, sir, thus far

We have demeaned fairly, like ourselves.

But, think you, though we wink at base revenge,

Young For. I would my brother liv'd, that this our diff'rence

Might end in an embrace of folded love;

But 'twas Heaven's will that for some guilt of his

He should be scourged by thee; and for the guilt

In scourging him, thou by my vengeance punish'd.

Come; I am both ways arm'd, against thy steel

If I be pierc'd by it, or 'gainst thy greatness

If mine pierce thee.

Rains. Have at thee.

(*They fight and pause.*)

Young For. I will not bid thee hold; but if thy breath

Be as much short as mine, look to thy weakness.

Rains. The breath thou draw'st but weakly,

Thou now shalt draw no more.

(*They fight. Forrest loseth his weapon.*)

Young For. That Heaven knows.

He guard my body that my spirit owes!

(*Guards himself, and puts by with his hat — slips — the other, running, falls over him, and Forrest kills him.*)

Good. My cousin's fall'n — pursue the murderer.

Foster. But not too near, I pray; you see he's armed,

A brother's death can be so soon
forgot?
Our gentry baffled, and our
name disgraced?
No: 'tmust not be; I am a gen-
tleman
Well known; and my demeanor
hitherto
Hath promis'd somewhat.
Should I swallow this,
The scandal would outlive me.
Briefly then,
I'll fight with you.
Rains. I am loath.
Young For. Answer directly,
Whether you dare to meet me
on even terms;
Or mark how I'll proceed.
Rains. Say, I deny it.
Young For. Then I say
thou'rt a villain, and I
challenge thee,
Where'er I meet thee next, in
field or town,
The father's manors, or thy
tenants' grange,
Saving the church, there is no
privilege
In all this land for thy despised
life.
(*Fortune by Land and Sea,*
Act I, Scene 4.)[1]

And in this deep amazement
may commit
Some desperate outrage.
Young For. Had I but known
the terror of this deed,
I would have left it done im-
perfectly,
Rather than in this guilt of con-
science
Labour'd so far. But I forget
my safety.
The gentleman is dead. My
desp'rate life
Will be o'erswayed by his allies
and friends,
And I have now no safety but
my flight.
And see where my pursuers
come. Away!
Certain destruction hovers o'er
my stay.   (*Exit.*)
(*Fortune by Land and Sea,*
Act II, Scene 1.)[1]

Two sets of extracts from the first and final versions of
Ibsen's *A Doll's House* show the way in which perfected
understanding of a character reveals the apt phrase.

[1] *Fortune by Land and Sea.* T. Heywood and W. Rowley. W. B. Clarke Co., Boston.

(*Nora stands motionless. He goes to the door and opens it.*)
The Maid. (*In the Hall.*) Here is a letter for you, ma'am.

Helmer. Give it here. (*He seizes the letter and shuts the door.*) Yes, from him. Look here.

Nora. Read it.
Helmer. I have hardly the courage. I fear the worst. We may both be lost, both you and I. Ah! I must know. (*Hastily tears the letter open; reads a few lines with a cry of joy.*) Nora!
(*Nora looks inquiringly at him.*)
Helmer. Nora! — Oh, I must read it again. Yes, yes, it is so. You are saved, Nora, you are saved.
Nora. How, saved?
Helmer. Look here. He sends you back your promissory note. He writes that he regrets and apologises, that a happy turn in his life — Oh, what matter what he writes. We are saved, Nora! There is nothing to witness against you. Oh, Nora, Nora.[1]

(*Nora stands motionless. Helmer goes to the door and opens it.*)
Ellen. (*Half-dressed in the Hall.*) Here is a letter for you, ma'am.
Helmer. Give it to me. (*Seizes letter and shuts the door.*) Yes, from him. You shall not have it. I shall read it.
Nora. Read it!
Helmer. (*By the lamp.*) I have hardly the courage to. We may both be lost, both you and I! Ah! I must know. (*Hastily tears the letter open; reads a few lines, looks at an enclosure; a cry of joy.*) Nora!
(*Nora looks inquiringly at him.*)
Helmer. Nora! Oh! I must read it again. Yes, yes, it is so. I am saved! Nora, I am saved!

Nora. And I?
Helmer. You too, of course; we are both saved, both of us. Look here, he sends you back your promissory note. He writes that he regrets and apologises; that a happy turn in his life — Oh, what matter what he writes. We are saved, Nora! No one can harm you. Oh, Nora, Nora.[2]

The text of the right-hand column brings out more clearly than the original the complete but unconscious selfishness of Helmer. Ibsen, understanding that character more fully

[1] *From Ibsen's Workshop*, p. 162. Chas. Scribner's Sons, New York.
[2] *Prose Dramas*, vol. I, p. 377. *Idem.*

than in his first draft, makes not only the change from "You are saved, Nora" to the self-revelatory "I am saved!" but also the change to that infinitely more dramatic "And I?" which replaces Nora's "How, saved?"

In a second set of extracts from the same scene, a firmer grasp of the characters has permitted Ibsen to replace the general and conventional in the last two speeches of the left-hand column with the more specific and characterizing lines of Helmer and the lines of Nora that are an inspiration.

Nora. . . . It never for a moment occurred to me that you would think of submitting to that man's conditions, that you would agree to direct your actions by the will of another. I was convinced that you would say to him, "Make it known to the whole world"; and that then —

Helmer. Well? I should give you up to punishment and disgrace.

Nora. No; then I firmly believed that you would come forward, take everything upon yourself, and say, "I am the guilty one" —

Helmer. Nora!

Nora. You mean I would never have accepted such a sacrifice? No, of course not. But what would my word have been in opposition to yours? I so firmly believed that you would sacrifice yourself for me — "don't listen to her," you would say — "she is not responsible; she is out of her senses" — you

Nora. . . . When Krogstad's letter lay in the box, it never occurred to me that you would think of submitting to that man's conditions. I was convinced that you would say to him, "Make it known to all the world"; and that then —

Helmer. Well? When I had given my own wife's name up to disgrace and shame —?

Nora. Then I firmly believed that you would come forward, take everything upon yourself, and say, "I am the guilty one."

Helmer. Nora!

Nora. You mean I would never have accepted such a sacrifice? No, certainly not. But what would my assertions have been worth in opposition to yours? That was the miracle that I hoped for and dreaded. And it was to hinder that that I wanted to die.

would say that it was love of
you — you would move heaven
and earth. I thought you would
get Dr. Rank to witness that I
was mad, unhinged, distracted.
I so firmly believed that you
would ruin yourself to save
me. That is what I dreaded, and
therefore I wanted to die.

Helmer. Oh, Nora, Nora!

Helmer. I would gladly work
for you day and night, Nora —
bear sorrow and want for your
sake — but no man sacrifices
his honour, even for one he loves.

Nora. And how did it turn
out? No thanks, no outburst of
affection, not a shred of a
thought of saving me.[1]

Nora. Millions of women
have done so.[2]

Perfect phrasing rests, then, on character thoroughly
understood and complete emotional accord with the character. Short of that in dialogue, one stops at the commonplace and colorless, the personal, or the literary.

Even, however, when dialogue expounds properly and is
thoroughly in character, it will fail if not fitted for the stage.
John Oliver Hobbes stated a truth, if somewhat exagger-
atedly, in these lines of her preface to *The Ambassador:*

Once I found a speech in prose — prose so subtly balanced,
harmonious, and interesting that it seemed, on paper, a song:
But no actor or actress, though they spoke with the voice of
angels, could make it, on the stage, even tolerable. . . . Yet the
speech is nevertheless fine stuff: it is nevertheless interesting in
substance: it has imagination: it has charm. What, then, was lacking? Emotion in the *tone* and, on the part of the writer, consideration for the speaking voice. Stage dialogue may have or may not
have many qualities, but it must be emotional. It rests primarily
on feeling. Wit, philosophy, moral truths, poetic language —

[1] *From Ibsen's Workshop,* p. 171. Chas. Scribner's Sons, New York.
[2] *Prose Dramas,* vol. 1, p. 386. *Idem.*

all these count as nothing unless there is feeling of an obvious, ordinary kind.[1]

When reading a play aloud, do we give all the stage directions, or, cutting out those which state how certain speeches should be read, try to give these as directed? Even when reading some story aloud, do we not often find troublesome full directions as to just how the speakers delivered their lines? If given by us, they provide an awkward standard by which to judge our reading. If we wish to suppress them, they are not, in rapid reading, always seen in time. As was pointed out very early in this book, gesture, facial expression, movement about the stage, and above all, the voice, aid the dramatist as they cannot aid the novelist. These aids and the time limits of a play have, as we shall see, very great effect on dialogue. Note in the opening of *The Case of Rebellious Susan*, by Henry Arthur Jones, the effects demanded from the aids just named.

ACT I. SCENE. *Drawing-room at Mr. Harabin's; an elegantly furnished room in Mayfair. At back, in centre, fireplace, with fire burning. To right of fireplace a door leading to Lady Susan's sitting-room. A door down stage left.*

Enter footman left showing in Lady Darby

Lady Darby. (*A lady of about fifty.*) Where is Lady Susan now?
Footman. Upstairs in her sitting-room, my lady.
                                        (*Indicating the door right.*)
Lady D. Where is Mr. Harabin?
Footman. Downstairs in the library, my lady.

Enter Second Footman showing in Inez, a widow of about thirty, fascinating, inscrutable

Lady D. (*To First Footman.*) Tell Lady Susan I wish to see her at once.
Inez. And will you say that I am here too?
            (*Exit First Footman at door right. Exit Second Footman at door left.*)

---
[1] *The Ambassador.* T. Fisher Unwin, London.

Lady D. (Going affectionately to Inez, shaking hands very sympathetically.) My dear Mrs. Quesnel, you know?

Inez. Sue wrote me a short note saying that she had discovered that Mr. Harabin had — and that she had made up her mind to leave him.

Lady D. Yes, that's what she wrote me. Now, my dear, you're her oldest friend. You'll help me to persuade her to — to look over it and hush it up.

Inez. Oh, certainly. It's the advice everybody gives in such cases, so I suppose it must be right. What are the particulars?

Lady D. I don't know. But with a man like Harabin — a gentleman in every sense of the word — it can't be a very bad case.

Enter Lady Susan.[1]

If the voice does not deftly stress "now" in Lady Darby's first speech, and the "upstairs" and the "downstairs" of the footman, this opening will fail of its desired effect. Everything in this well-written beginning of an interesting play depends on bringing to the delivery of the lines right use of the dramatist's greatest aids: gesture, facial expression, pantomime, and above all the exquisite intonations of which the human voice is capable. Write this scene as a novelist would handle it, and see to what different proportions it will swell. Note in the final result how much less connotative, how much more commonplace the dialogue probably is. Contrasting two passages — one from a novel, the other in a play drawn from it — will perhaps best illustrate that the dialogue of the novel and of the play treating the same story usually differ greatly.

And when it became clear that somebody, good or bad, was without, Patty, having regard to the lateness of the hour and the probability of supernatural visitations, was much disposed to make as though the knocking were unheard, and to creep quietly off to bed. But Mistress Beatrice prevailed upon her to depart from this prudent course; and the two peered from an upper window to see who stood before the door.

[1] Samuel French, New York.

At first they could see no one; but presently a little figure stepped back from the shadow, looking up to the window above, and Beatrice Cope, although she discerned not the face, felt more than ever certain that this summons was for her.

"'Tis but a child there without, Patty," she said. "Maybe 'tis some poor little creature that has lost its way, and come here for help and shelter. Heaven forbid that we should leave it to wander about, all the dreary night through!"

Patty's fears were not much calmed by the sight of this lonely child. "'Twas the Phantom Child," she murmured, "who comes wailing piteously to honest folks' doors o' nights; and if they take it in and, cherish it, it works them grievous woe."

Mistress Beatrice, however, tried to hear as little as she might of what Patty was saying; and she went downstairs and undid the heavy bar very cautiously. Then she opened the door a little space; and Patty Joyce stood by her staunchly, although disapproving of what she did.

And when the door was opened, this persevering applicant proved to be only the boy Bill Lampeter, who was known at Whiteoaks as at Crowe Hall, and a score of country Granges beside. He did but crave a drink of milk and a bit to eat, he said. He had been a-foot all day, and had had nought to eat; and seeing a light burning in the houseplace, he made bold to knock and ask for what he needed.

The boy's breath was short and hurried, and his grimy face was pale and damp with toil of hard running. He did not seek to enter, but kept glancing over his shoulder into the darkness behind him.

Beatrice sent Patty for food and drink, standing still herself in the doorway; and the maid was no sooner gone than the boy drew nearer and spoke.

"Oh, mistress," he said, hoarsely, "I have been beat to-night — but I told 'em nought. The corporal he raddled my bones terrible — but I set my teeth, and I told 'un nought. I bit him when he took they shining white things o' yourn, wi' the writing; them as I could not give to Mr. Cope, the day I warned the porter at Goodrest that the red-coats was upon 'em. I had the white things safe, mistress, hid in my smock" — (he put his hand to his breast, where the rough garment he wore was heavily quilted and closely drawn). — "And I would ha' giv' them to Mr. Cope, the first chance I got — I would, honest and true. But the scouting party caught me; and they says, 'Thee be allays running from one Grange to another, thee little ne'er-do-weel; thee can tell us what we wants to know about Goodrest in the hills' — And I was telling of 'em just what tales comed into my head, for fear of unpleasantness, mistress, when the corporal, a great rough chap, seizes hold of me, and says, says he, ' 'Tis all a pack o' lies, this here. Search him,' he says, 'and see if he carries messages or tokens.' And then I fought and bit, for I know'd they'd find your bright things in my smock; and I bit his hand nigh upon through, that I did," said Bill, with grim satisfaction, and an oath at which poor Beatrice shuddered.

"Oh, hush!" she said. "There is no help in swearing, boy."

"*He* swore," Bill replied. "But when he got the tablets, he were fine and pleased. And he said, 'This is a stag of ten, my boys; and should he snuff the breeze too soon we have means to keep him where he is till morning. Hold that little viper fast,' says he, 'and for your lives don't let him give us the slip.' — So one of the troopers took me behind him on his horse, with a rope round my body, drawn cruel tight at first. And I panted and groaned, and made as though he were killing of me; and after a bit he slacked the rope a little, so as I could put my head down and gnaw it through in the dark. And at the dip of a valley, where the shadow was deep under the trees, I slipped off quiet-like into the long grass. He knew the rope was loose in a minute, and he snapped his pistol; but the covert was good, and I crope into the heart of a holler tree covered o'er wi' ivy. I bided there, till they was tired o' hunting round. — But oh, mistress, the poor gentleman at Goodrest is undone! — They talked together while the trooper was making me fast upon his horse; and I heard a word now and again, for I listened with all my might. There were but four of 'em; and they said they weren't strong enough to surprise Goodrest, but must ride back to quarters for help. And as we went past Grantford Farm, the corporal called a halt; and one held his horse while he went in and spoke with the farmer. And, mistress, Hugh Stone of Grantford is known for a bitter Whig. . . . And presently Hugh of Grantford comes out, and his little brother with him; and the boy had that as you wrote upon — that as they took from me — in his hand. And the corporal says, looking over his shoulder quick and short, 'Does he understand?' says he. 'Oh, aye,' says Hugh of Grantford, 'he understands fine.' And I could see wee Jock did not like the job he were put upon; and I made a face at him from ahint the trooper's back, and he liked it less nor ever then."

"What job, Bill?"

Bill Lampeter looked in amazement at this beautiful, terrified lady, who did not understand.

"Don't 'ee see?" he said. "Jock o' Grantford were to take your writing to Goodrest, and play upon the gentleman there, to keep him biding till the red-coats come. What were it as you wrote down that day, mistress?"

As in a flash of painful memory Beatrice saw the dainty tablets once more, with words traced upon them in a hand rendered somewhat unsteady by the slow pace of the sorrel horse — a hand unmistakable, however, to the eyes of Charlie Cope.

I pray you, do not stir far from home. There is risk abroad.

B. C.

She understood then; and she turned quickly to Patty Joyce, who had come back bringing bread and milk ere Bill's tale was half done. Bill, even in the eagerness of his disclosure, had clutched the bread and cheese; and now he drained the mug of milk, while the good-natured maid stood open-mouthed, her eyes fixed upon Mistress Beatrice.

"Patty," the young lady whispered, "I think you are faithful and true. . . . I must trust you with a perilous secret. This gentleman whom they seek at Goodrest is my only brother; he has papers of importance in his keeping, and a warrant is out for his arrest. They will lure him to his destruction by means of me, his sister; he knows my handwriting and will trust to my warning. He will lie close at Goodrest, as a hare upon her form; and they will take him — oh! they will take him prisoner! — ere morning dawns. I must to Goodrest now, in the dark night. — Boy! is there time? is there time?"

Bill Lampeter nodded, munching his bread.

"They'll not be back afore the dawning, them troopers," he said. "They've limed the twig, ye see; the bird is made fast. If Mr. Cope do hear the country's up, he'll bide where he be there at Goodrest, reckoning 'tis safest to keep still. Between now and the first streak as shows over the Black Scaur, mistress, you can do as you will."

"Eh, Mistress Beatrice, you can't never go," said Patty, trembling. "You couldn't dare to do it. And this here boy," she whispered, standing close to Mistress Beatrice, "is a very proverb for wicked story-telling. 'Tis a naughty little varlet; who knows that he has not been set on to bring this tale?"

"'Tis true enough, though I be a story-teller," said Bill, whose ears were sharp. "Yon gentleman at Goodrest has need of thee the night, mistress. And now let me lie down on the straw in the big barn, for my bones do ache, and I be dizzy wi' running."

He caught at the doorpost as he spoke; and Patty Joyce's suspicion vanished in pity for the worn-out creature. She kindled a flame to light the lanthorn which hung in the houseplace; and herself crossed the wide courtyard to make Bill a comfortable resting-place in the soft hay and clean straw which filled the great barn.[1]

This is the same scene in the play:

> (*Louder rapping. Trembling with rage and disappointment, Sandiland disappears down the path. Beatrice stands a moment, looking as if waking from a nightmare.*)

Patty. (*Outside, rapping more.*) Miss Beatrice, Miss Beatrice! Quick!

Beatrice. (*Crossing dazedly to door. By it, dully.*) Who?

Patty. Open quick. Me and Bill.

Beat. (*Recovering.*) Bill!

> (*Quickly she unbolts the door. Patty enters, half supporting Bill. She looks about as if surprised at not seeing any one beside Beatrice. Bill's clothes are torn and he is covered with dirt. There is blood on his hands where cords have torn the flesh. He looks white and wretched and breathes hard as if from recent running. He should play the whole scene with nervous excitement that suggests a collapse at the end of it.*)

Bill. (*Apologetically, as he stumbles toward Beatrice.*) I've had a bit of a scrap. (*Aside to Beatrice.*) Get rid o' 'er.

Beat. You can trust her. What has happened?

Bill. Scoutin' party got me. Corporal raddled my bones terrible when I fought and bit, fearin' they'd find your message hid in my smock. They near tore it off, damn 'em.

Beat. You have the tablets?

Bill. No.

Beat. They have them? (*With relief.*) Then they haven't reached James!

---

[1] *Mistress Beatrice Cope.* M. E. Le Clerc. D. Appleton & Co., New York.

Bill. The gentleman? Oh, ay. When we come to Grantford Farm — I were trussed up be'ind a trooper — Corporal called out little Jock o' Grantford — his fayther's a bitter Whig — and bade 'im take your message to Goodrest, to keep the gentleman waitin' till the red coats be come.

Beat. (*To Patty.*) Where's Grizel?

Patty. In the paddock'm. But —

Beat. Saddle her at once. I must to Goodrest.

(Patty hesitates.)

Bill. (*Menacingly as he reaches for a candle-stick.*) She said — To once.

(Unwillingly but quickly, Patty goes out centre.)

Bill. (*Pointing to the door where the full moon shines in clearly.*) Ay, but that ain't 'id yet.

Beat. (*As if struck by a sudden idea.*) How did you get free?

Bill. Gnawed the ropes; slipped off in the long grass. Trooper's pistol missed me. Stayed in a holler oak I knows till they was tired 'untin'.

Beat. Knowing you are loose, they will start at once.

Bill. If they ain't fools. But most folks be. Risk somethin' on that. (*Beatrice is busy with her dress and cloak. He starts to help her but has to support himself by table.*) Don't go through Whitecross Village. There the soldiers be. Take the footpath by Guiting; the bridge be shaky but 'twill hold.

(Enter Patty, centre.)

Patty. Grizel's ready'm.

Beat. (*Nodding her understanding to Bill — to Patty.*) Close up here. Look after Bill. Be ready to let me in when the first cock crows. My stirrup! (*Goes out swiftly, followed protestingly by Patty. Bill drags himself to right of door watching, and says after a minute.*) She's up!

Patty. (*Rushing in as there is the sound of swift hoof beats.*) She's gone! (*She falls sobbing hysterically by the left side of door.*)

Bill. (*As he holds himself up at right.*) The damned brave lady!

Curtain.

First of all, the novelist permits himself an amount of detail which the dramatist must forego because of his more limited space. Interesting details which do not forward the purpose of the scene or act the wise dramatist denies himself — note in Ibsen's revision of certain lines in *A Doll's House* (p. 350) the cutting, between the first and final versions, of what concerns Dr. Rank. It was in part unnecessary detail which made the dialogue of the play on John Brown (pp. 309–313) so ineffective. In what follows immediately, a skilful hand seems in column one to have cut details of column two which, though interesting in themselves, delay the essential movement of the scene and help to swell the whole play to undue proportions.

Horatio. Mary that can I, at least the whisper goes so,
Our late King, who as you know was by Forten-Brasse of Norway,

Thereto prickt on by a most emulous cause, dared to
The combate, in which our valiant Hamlet,
For so this side of our knowne world esteemed him,
Did slay this Fortenbrasse,
Who by a seale compact well ratified, by law
And heraldrie, did forfeit with his life all those
His lands which he stoode seazed of by the conqueror,
Against the which a moity competent,
Was gaged by our King:

Horatio. That can I.
At least the whisper goes so; our last King,
Who[se image even but now appear'd to us,]
Was as you knowe by Fortinbrasse of Norway,

Thereto prickt on by a most emulate pride
Dar'd to the combat; in which our valiant Hamlet,
(For so this side of our knowne world esteemd him)
Did slay this Fortinbrasse, who by a seald compact
Well ratified by lawe and heraldy
Did forfait (with his life) all these his lands
Which he stood seaz'd of, to the conquerour.
Against the which a moitie competent
Was gaged by our King, [which had returne
To the inheritance of Fortinbrasse,
Had he bin vanquisher; as by the same comart,

Now sir, young Fortenbrasse,
Of inapproved mettle hot and
full,
Hath in the skirts of Norway
here and there,
Sharkt up a sight of lawlesse
Resolutes
For food and diet to some enter-
prise,
That hath a stomacke in't: and
this (I take it) is the
Chief head and ground of our
watch.

And carriage of the article des-
seigne,
His fell to Hamlet;] now Sir
young Fortinbrasse
Of unimprooved mettle, hot and
full,
Hath in the skirts of Norway
heere and there
Sharkt up a list of lawelesse
resolutes
For foode and diet to some en-
terprise
That hath a stomacke in't
[which is no other
As it doth well appeare unto
our state
But to recover of us by strong
hand
And tearmes compulsatory,
those foresaid lands
So by his father lost;] and this
I take it
Is [the maine motive of our pre-
parations
The source of this our watch,
and] the chiefe head
Of this post hast and Romadge
in the land.
    [Bar. I thinke it be no other,
    but enso;
Well may it sort that this por-
tentous figure
Comes armed through our
watch so like the King
That was and is the question of
these warres.
    Hora. A moth it is to trouble
    the mindes eye:
In the most high and palmy
state of Rome,
A little ere the mightiest Julius
fell

The graves stood tenantlesse,
and the sheeted dead
Did squeake and gibber in the
Roman streets
As starres, with traines of fier,
and dewes of blood
Disasters in the sunne; and the
moist starre,
Upon whose influence Neptunes
Empier stands,
Was sicke almost to doomes-
day with eclipse.
And even the like precurse of
feare events
As harbindgers preceading still
the fates
And prologue to the Omen com-
ming on
Have heaven and earth together
demonstrated
Unto our Climatures and coun-
trymen.]

Enter the Ghost.	*Enter Ghost.*
But loe, behold, see where it comes againe,	But softe, behold, loe where it comes againe
Ile crosse it, though it blast me: stay illusion,	Ile crosse it though *It spreads* it blast mee: stay *his armes* illusion,
If there be any good thing to be done,	[If thou hast any sound or use of voyce
That may doe ease to thee, and grace to mee,	Speake to me,] if there be any good thing to be done
Speake to mee.	That may to thee doe ease, and grace to mee,
	Speake to me.[1]

Unnecessary detail should, then, be cut from dialogue
both because it is usually the chief offender in making the
play unduly long, and because it weakens the dialogue of

_____
[1] *The Devonshire Hamlets,* pp. 4, 6.

which it is a part. In argument it is a time-honored principle that it is far better not to pile up all the evidence you can on a given point, but by selecting your best argument, or two or three of the better type, to strike hard with the selected material. The same principle underlies writing good dramatic dialogue. Say what you have to say as well as you can, and except for emphasis or when repetition produces some desired effect, don't repeat. In the speech quoted below it became clear in rehearsal that the bracketed part was not necessary because what preceded showed sufficiently the affection Miss Helen had roused in the faithful old servant, Alec. However characterizing or amusing the remainder might be, it clogged the movement of the scene. Consequently it went out.

Dick. Hello — what's this Alec?

Alec. A grand pianner, sir.

Dick. Of course, but where did it come from?

Alec. Miss Helen, she gave it to 'em at Christmas.

Dick. She — gave it to — them —?

Alec. Yes.

Dick. (*Laughing.*) But they don't play it, do they?

Alec. No, she plays it —. An' you oughter hear her play, sir. At evenin's after supper when the wind'd howl around the house she'd make it sound like Heaven in here. If I ever get up there I don't want white angels and gold harps in mine, — I jes' want Miss Helen an' a grand pianner. (*Dick is very sober.* [*He doesn't speak.*]) An' she can sing, too. You oughter hear her, — little soft things, — none o' this screechy stuff. An' all the old dames sit around — an' then when my work was done out in the barn I'd come in an' sit over there in the corner out o' the way like, an' listen like a old lady myself — with my Adam's apple getting tight every once in a while thinkin' o' things. I tell you she's — she's a regular — humdinger.]

Dick. (*Quietly.*) What time do you expect her back?

Time forbids any form of fiction to be encyclopædic. The drama is, as we have seen, the most selective of the forms of fiction. Failure to remember this has hurt the chances of many a promising dramatist. Few have such skilled and loyal advisers as Lord Tennyson found in Sir Henry Irving when his over-long *Becket* must be cut for stage production. How much of the following scene in the original do we think at first sight we can spare? Much which Sir Henry removed we should like to keep, but time-limits forbade and he cut with exceeding skill to the best dramatic phrasing offered of the essentials of the scene.

ACT I. SCENE 1. *Becket's House in London. Chamber barely furnished. Becket unrobing. Herbert of Bosham and Servant.*

ORIGINAL	REVISION
Servant. Shall I not help your lordship to your rest?	*Servant.* Shall I not help your lordship to your rest?
Becket. Friend, am I so much better than thyself	*Becket.* Friend, am I so much better than thyself
That thou shouldst help me? Thou art wearied out	That thou shouldst help me? Thou art wearied out
With this day's work, get thee to thine own bed.	With this day's work, get thee to thine own bed.
Leave me with Herbert, friend.	Leave me with Herbert, friend.
(*Exit Servant.*)	(*Exit Servant.*)
Help me off, Herbert, with this — and this.	Help me off Herbert, with this — and this.
Herbert. Was not the people's blessing as we past	*Herbert.* Was not the people's blessing as we past
Heart-comfort and a balsam to thy blood?	Heart-comfort and a balsam to thy blood?
Becket. The people know their Church a tower of strength,	*Becket.* The people know their Church a tower of strength,
A bulwark against Throne and Baronage.	A bulwark against Throne and Baronage.
Too heavy for me, this; off with it, Herbert!	Too heavy for me, this; off with it, Herbert!
Herbert. Is it so much heavier than thy Chancellor's robe?	*Herbert.* Is it so much heavier than thy Chancellor's robe?

Becket. No; but the Chancellor's and the Archbishop's
Together more than mortal man can bear.
Herbert. Not heavier than thine armour at Thoulouse?
Becket. O Herbert, Herbert, in my chancellorship
I more than once have gone against the Church.
Herbert. To please the King?
Becket. Ay, and the King of kings,
Or justice; for it seem'd to me but just
The Church should pay her scutage like the lords.

But hast thou heard this cry of Gilbert Foliot
That I am not the man to be your Primate,
For Henry could not work a miracle —
Make an Archbishop of a soldier?
Herbert.   Ay,
For Gilbert Foliot held himself the man.
Becket. Am I the man? My mother, ere she bore me,
Dream'd that twelve stars fell glittering out of heaven
Into her bosom.
Herbert. Ay, the fire, the light,
The spirit of the twelve Apostles enter'd
Into thy making.
Becket. And when I was a child,

Becket. No; but the Chancellor's and the Archbishop's
Together more than mortal man can bear.
Herbert. Not heavier than thine armour at Toulouse?

Becket. But hast thou heard this cry of Gilbert Foliot
That I am not the man to be your Primate,
For Henry could not work a miracle —
Make an Archbishop of a soldier?
Herbert.   Ay,
For Gilbert Foliot held himself the man.

The Virgin, in a vision of my
    sleep,
Gave me the golden keys of
    Paradise. Dream,
Or prophecy, that?
    Herbert. Well, dream and
    prophecy both.
    Becket. And when I was
    of Theobald's household,
    once —
The good old man would some-
    times have his jest —
He took his mitre off, and set it
    on me,
And said, "My young Arch-
    bishop—thou wouldst make
A stately Archbishop!" Jest
    or prophecy there?
    Herbert. Both, Thomas, both.
    Becket. Am I the man? That
    rang
Within my head last night, and
    when I slept
Methought I stood in Canter-
    bury Minster,
And spake to the Lord God, and
    said, "O Lord,
I have been a lover of wines
    and delicate meats,
And secular splendours, and a
    favourer
Of players, and a courtier, and
    a feeder
Of dogs and hawks, and apes,
    and lions, and lynxes.
Am *I* the man?" And the Lord
    answer'd me,
"Thou art the man, and all
    the more the man."
And then I asked again, "O
    Lord my God

Becket. Am I the man? That
    rang
Within my head last night, and
    when I slept
Methought I stood in Canter-
    bury Minster,
And spake to the Lord God and
    said,

Henry the King hath been my
 friend, my brother
And mine uplifter in this
 world, and chosen me
For this thy great archbishop-
 rick, believing
That I should go against the
 Church with him,
And I shall go against him with
 the Church,
And I have said no word of this
 to him:
Am *I* the man?" And the Lord
 answer'd me,
"Thou art the man, and all the
 more the man."
And thereupon, methought, He
 drew toward me,
And smote me down upon the
 Minster floor.
I fell.
 Herbert. God make not thee,
 but thy foes, fall.
 Becket. I fell. Why fall?
 Why did he smite me?
 What?
Shall I fall off — to please the
 King once more?
Not fight — tho' somehow
 traitor to the King —
My truest and mine utmost for
 the Church?
 Herbert. Thou canst not fall
 that way. Let traitor
 be;
For how have fought thine ut-
 most for the Church,
Save from the throne of thine
 archbishoprick?
And how been made archbishop
 hadst thou told him,

"Henry the King hath been
 my friend, my brother
And mine uplifter in this world,
 and chosen me
For this thy great archbishop-
 rick, believing
That I should go against the
 Church with him,
And I shall go against him with
 the Church.

Am *I* the man?" And the Lord
 answer'd me,
"Thou art the man and all the
 more the man."
And thereupon, methought, He
 drew toward me,
And smote me down upon the
 Minster floor.
I fell.
 Herbert. God make not thee,
 but thy foes, fall

"I mean to fight mine utmost
for the Church,
Against the King?"
  Becket.   But dost thou
think the King
Forced mine election?
  Herbert.   I do think
the King
Was potent in the election, and
why not?
Why should not Heaven have
so inspired the King?
Be comforted. Thou art the
man — be thou
A mightier Anselm.
  Becket. I do believe thee,
then. I am the man.
And yet I seem appall'd — on
such a sudden
At such an eagle-height I stand
and see
The rift that runs between me
and the King.
I served our Theobald well
when I was with him;
I served King Henry well as
Chancellor;
I am his no more, and I must
serve the Church.
This Canterbury is only less
than Rome,
And all my doubts I fling from
me like dust,
Winnow and scatter all scruples
to the wind,
And all the puissance of the
warrior,
And all the wisdom of the Chan-
cellor,
And all the heap'd experiences
of life,

Becket. And yet I seem appall'd — on such a sudden
At such an eagle-height I stand
and see
The rift that runs between me
and the King.

I cast upon the side of Canter-
bury —
Our holy mother Canterbury,
who sits
With tatter'd robes. Laics and
barons, thro'
The random gifts of careless
kings, have graspt
Her livings, her advowsons,
granges, farms,
And goodly acres — we will
make her whole;
Not one rood lost. And for these
Royal customs,
These ancient Royal customs —
they *are* Royal,
Not of the Church — and let
them be anathema,
And all that speak for them
anathema.

    Herbert. Thomas, thou art
    moved too much.
    Becket. Oh, Herbert here
I gash myself asunder from the
King,
Tho' leaving each, a wound:
mine own, a grief
To show the scar forever —
his, a hate
Not ever to be heal'd.[1]

    Herbert. Thomas, thou art
    moved too much.
    Becket. O Herbert, here
I gash myself asunder from the
King,
Tho' leaving each, a wound;
mine own, a grief
To show the scar forever — his,
a hate
Not ever to be heal'd.[2]

Dialogue, then, should avoid all unnecessary detail, and
should avoid repetition except for desired dramatic ends —
in other words, must select and again select.

Practically every illustration thus far used in treating
dialogue fitted for the stage has shown the enormous importance of facial expression, gesture, and voice. What the
voice may do with just two words is the substance of a little

---

[1] *Becket.* Tennyson. The Macmillan Co.
[2] *Becket.* Arranged by Sir Henry Irving. *Idem.*

one-act piece made famous years ago by Miss Genevieve
Ward and later often read by the late George Riddle. An
actress applying to a manager is tested as to her power to
express in the two words "Come here" all the emotions
described by her examiner. As will be seen, the little play,
when read in the study, lacks effectiveness. Given by an
actress who can put into the two words all that is demanded,
it becomes varied, exciting, and even amazing.

Actress. . . . Your selection may not be in my repertoire.
Manager. Oh! yes, it is. I only require two words: "Come here."
Actress. Come here?
Manager. Yes, and with the words, the meaning, emphasis, and
expressions, that situation, character, and the surroundings would
command.
Actress. (*Takes off her bonnet and shawl.*) Well, then, I am ready.
Manager. Before a mother stand a loving couple, who pray for
her consent; the lover is poor; she battles with her pride, it is a
great struggle for her; at last with open arms she cries —
Actress. Come here!
Manager. A mother calls her little daughter, who has done
something to vex her.
Actress. Come here!
Manager. And now it is her step-child.
Actress. Come here!
Manager. A carriage is dashing by, the child is in the street, the
mother's heart is filled with terror, she calls her darling and
cries out —
Actress. Come here!
Manager. In tears and sorrow a wife has bid adieu to her de-
parting husband, whom the State has called to defend his country
on the battlefield; her only consolation is in her children, these she
calls, and presses to her heart.
Actress. Come here!
Manager. The husband has returned, and full of joy she calls
her children as she observes him coming home.
Actress. Come here!
Manager. While in his arms, she now observes his servant, and
as with every one she would divide her joy she calls to him —

Actress. Come here!

Manager. The feelings of a mother in all her joys and tribulation, you have most perfectly sustained. Now show me, how in despair a widow, who has lost all she possessed through fire, confronts the creditors, who clamor for their dues, and whose cruelty has killed her husband. She stands by his body and points to all that now is left her, the remains of her dead husband, and calls on them to look at their work.

Actress. Come here!

Manager. I must confess you depict pain as if you felt it.[1]

Mark, when running through the scene in which Iago tempts Othello to his final undoing (Act III, Scene 3.), the variety of intonation required in the repetitions of "Honest" and "Think." In a novel containing this scene the absence of the actors' trained intonations would cost the author much labor in describing how the words should be uttered.

Othello. Farewell, my Desdemona; I'll come to thee straight.

Desdemona. Emilia, come. — Be as your fancies teach you; Whate'er you be, I am obedient.

(*Exeunt Desdemona and Emilia.*)

Othello. Excellent wretch! Perdition catch my soul, But I do love thee! and when I love thee not, Chaos is come again.

Iago. My noble lord, —

Othello. What dost thou say, Iago?

Iago. Did Michael Cassio, when you woo'd my lady, Know of your love?

Othello. He did, from first to last. Why dost thou ask?

Iago. But for a satisfaction of my thought; No further harm.

Othello. Why of thy thought, Iago?

Iago. I did not think he had been acquainted with her.

Othello. O, yes; and went between us very oft.

Iago. Indeed!

Othello. Indeed! ay, indeed. Discern'st thou aught in that? Is he not honest?

---

[1] *George Riddle's Readings.* Walter H. Baker & Co., Boston.

Iago.   Honest, my lord?
Othello.   Honest, ay, honest.
Iago. My lord, for aught I know.
Othello. What dost thou think?
Iago.   Think, my lord?
Othello.   Think, my lord!
By heaven, he echoes me,
As if there were some monster in his thought
Too hideous to be shown. — Thou dost mean something.
I heard thee say even now, thou lik'st not that,
When Cassio left my wife. What didst not like?
And when I told thee he was of my counsel,
Of my whole course of wooing, thou criedst, "Indeed!"
And didst contract and purse thy brow together,
As if thou then hadst shut up in thy brain
Some horrible conceit. If thou dost love me,
Show me thy thought.

Even passages in a play which look very unpromising
should not be finally judged till a flexible, well-trained voice
has done its best to bring out any emotion latent in the
words. If they were originally chosen by an author writing
in full sympathetic understanding of his figures, they will,
properly spoken, reveal unexpected emotional values. Here
is a passage from Kyd's *Spanish Tragedy* at which many a
critic has poked fun. At first sight it undoubtedly seems
merely "words, words, words."

Hieronimo. O eyes! no eyes, but fountains fraught with tears:
O life! no life but lively form of death:
O world! no world but mass of public wrongs,
Confus'd and fill'd with murder and misdeeds:
O sacred heav'ns! if this unhallow'd deed,
If this inhuman and barbarous attempt;
If this incomparable murder thus,
Of mine, but now no more my son,
Should unreveal'd and unrevenged pass,
How should we term your dealings to be just
If you unjustly deal with those that in your justice trust? [1]

[1] *The Origin of the English Drama*, vol. II, p. 48. T. Hawkins, ed. Clarendon Press, Oxford, 1773.

If we remember what the play has already told us of Hieronimo: that having found his son hanging murdered in the arbor, he enters in a perfect ecstasy of grief; and if we recall that the Elizabethan loved a style as ornate as this, feeling it no barrier between him and the thought behind it; the look of the passage begins to change. Put the feeling of the father into the voice as one reads, and lo, these lines are not a bad medium for expressing Hieronimo's grief. They may lack the simplicity we demand today, but strong, clear feeling may be brought out from behind them for any audience. For an Elizabethan audience it came forth in a style delightful in itself. The fact is, time cannot wholly spoil the value even of lines phrased according to the standards of some literary vogue of the moment if the author originally wrote them with an imagination kindled to accuracy of feeling by complete sympathy with his characters. Never judge the dialogue of a play only by the eye. Hear it adequately, interpretively spoken. Then, and then only, judge it finally.

It is almost impossible, also, to separate the voice from gesture and facial expression as aids in dramatic dialogue. Unquestionably each of these would help the voice in the illustrations just given from *Come Here*, *Othello*, and the *Spanish Tragedy*. When Antony, absorbed in Cleopatra, and therefore unwilling to listen to the messenger bearing tidings of the utmost importance from Rome, cries, "Grates me: the sum!" [1] it is not merely the intonation but the accompanying gesture in the sense of general bodily movement, and the facial expression, which make the condensed phrasing both natural and immensely effective. When Frankford (*A Woman Killed With Kindness*, Act III, Scene 2) [2] asks his old servant, Nicholas, for proof of Mrs. Frankford's

---

[1] *Antony and Cleopatra*, Act I, Scene 1.
[2] Belles-Lettres Series. K. L. Bates, ed. D. C. Heath & Co., Boston and New York.

unfaithfulness the answer is not, "I saw her," or "I saw her and her lover with my eyes," but simply "Eyes, eyes." The last are what rightly, in dramatic dialogue, may be called "gesture words," words demanding for their full effect not only the right intonation, but facial expression and all that pantomime may mean. The old man lifts his head, and, though unwillingly, looks his master straight in the face as he speaks. Perhaps he even emphasizes by lifting his hand toward his eyes. With the concomitants of action and voice, the words take on finality and equal: "What greater proof could I have? I saw the lovers with these eyes."

So close, indeed, is the relation between action and phrasing that often we cannot tell whether dialogue is good or bad till we have made sure of the "business" implied by it, or to be found in it by an imaginative worker. The following passage from *The Revesby Sword Play* is distinctly misleading because of the word, "looking-glass" unless one studies the context closely for implied business, and above all, understands the sword dances of the period in which the play was written.

> *Fool.* Well, what dost thou call this very pretty thing?
> *Pickle Herring.* Why, I call it a fine large looking-glass.
> *Fool.* Let me see what I can see in this fine large looking-glass. Here's a hole through it, I see. I see, and I see!
> *Pickle Herring.* You see and you see, and what do you see?
> *Fool.* Marry, e'en a fool, — just like thee!
> *Pickle Herring.* It is only your own face in the glass.[1]

A "looking-glass" with "a hole through it" seems nearly a contradiction in terms, but the word "glass" is synonymous with "nut," a name given to the swords of English Folk Dances when so interwoven as to make a kind of frame about a central space. This space is often large enough for a man's head. The Fool has seen the dancers

---

[1] *Pre-Shakesperean Drama*, vol. i, p. 300. J. M. Manly. Ginn & Co., Boston.

make such a nut. Holding it up, he asks Pickle Herring what it is. Pickle Herring, seeing the Fool's face through the opening and seizing his chance for a jest, calls the nut a "looking-glass." The Fool carries on the conceit. Looking through the hole he and Pickle Herring jibe at each other. The whole *Revesby Sword Play* provides illustration after illustration of the inseparability of words and business in good dramatic dialogue.

By "business" is meant ordinarily either illustrative action called for by a stage direction or clearly implied in the text. By "latent business" is meant the illustrative action which a sympathetic and imaginative producer finds in lines either ordinarily left without business or treated with some conventional action. Mr. William Poel's historic revival of *Everyman* was crowded with such imaginative and richly interpretive business. When Death cried,

> Everyman, thou art mad! Thou hast thy wits five,
> And here on earth will not amend thy life!
> For suddenly I do come —

on that last line he stretched out one arm and with the index finger of his hand barely touched the heart of Everyman. In the gesture there was a suggestion of what might be going to happen, even a suggestion that already Death thus claimed Everyman for his own. It pointed finely the immediate cry of Everyman,

> O wretched caitiff, whither shall I flee,
> That I might scape this endless sorrow? [1]

The text did not call for this gesture: it belongs to the best type of interpretive business.

Few untrained persons hear what they write: they merely see it. The skilled dramatist never forgets that he has to help him in his dialogue all that intonation, facial expression,

---

[1] *Early Plays*, p. 72. C. G. Child. Riverside Literature Series, No. 191. Houghton Mifflin Co., Boston.

gesture, and the general action of his characters may do for him. Which, after all, is the more touching, the cry of pleasure with which some child of the streets, at a charity Chrismas tree, gazes at a rag doll some one holds out to her, or the silent mothering gesture with which she draws it close to her, her face alight? It is just because, at times, facial expression, gesture, and movement may so completely express all that is needed that pantomime is coming to play a larger and larger part in our drama. Older readers of this book may recall the late Agnes Booth and her long silent scene in *Jim, The Penman*. By comparison of a letter and a cheque, Kate Ralston becomes aware that her husband is a famous forger, Jim, the Penman. Through all this great scene of an otherwise cheap play, the physical movement was very slight. The actress, three-quarters turned toward the audience, sat near a table. It was her facial expression and, rarely, a slight movement of the arms or body which conveyed her succession of increasingly intense emotions. The significant pantomime began with "She puts cheque with others." The acting of the next seven lines of stage direction held an audience with increasing intensity of feeling for some five minutes.

Nina (Mrs. Ralston) has just told her husband that she discovered Captain Redwood asleep in the conservatory at the end of Act I. Though she does not know it, this shows her husband that all his incriminating interview with Dr. Hartfeld may have been overheard. He falls into disturbed reverie and is so absorbed in thinking out the situation that he is oblivious to what she does.

Nina. Now then, for my pass-book.
      (*Opens pass-book and takes passed cheques out of side pocket of book. Music.*)
Ralston. (*Aside.*) He heard all! If she had told me, she would have saved me.

Nina. (*Looking at a cheque.*) What is this cheque? I don't remember it. A cheque for five guineas in favor of Mrs. Chapstone.
I never gave her a cheque. Oh, I recollect, that same evening
she bothered you to take some tickets and you took them in my
name. I never had the tickets, by-the-bye. I suppose she sold
them over again. Yes, to be sure, you wrote the cheque. You
asked permission to sign my name. How wonderfully like my
writing! Why, it quite deceives me, it's so marvelous!

> (*Ralston, in chair, is lost in thought, and hardly attends to
> what she says. She puts cheque with others and goes
> through accounts. Pauses, puts pass-book down, and
> takes up cheque again, examines it; turns her head and
> looks at Ralston, observes his absorption, and after an-
> other look at him takes from drawer the letter which Per-
> cival gave her and the other. She places them and the
> cheque together, almost in terror; comparing them, a look
> of painful conviction comes over her face, which changes
> into one of terrible determination. She rises from chair.
> Stop music on the word "James."*)[1]

The greatest recent instance of pantomime is undoubtedly the third scene of Act III of Mr. Galsworthy's *Justice.*
Set in Falder's cell, it is meant to illustrate the loneliness,
the excitability, and even the brutishness of a prisoner's life.
Many people, while admitting the effectiveness of this word-
less scene, have declared it emotionally so overwhelming
that they could not endure seeing it a second time.

*Falder's cell, a whitewashed space thirteen feet broad by seven deep,
and nine feet high, with a rounded ceiling. The floor is of shiny black-
ened bricks. The barred window of opaque glass with a ventilator, is
high up in the middle of the end wall. In the middle of the opposite end
wall is a narrow door. In a corner are the mattress and bedding rolled
up (two blankets, two sheets, and a coverlet). Above them is a quarter-
circular wooden shelf, on which is a Bible and several little devotional
books, piled in a symmetrical pyramid; there are also a black hair-
brush, tooth-brush, and a bit of soap. In another corner is the wooden
frame of a bed, standing on end. There is a dark ventilator over the*

[1] Samuel French, New York.

window, and another over the door. Falder's work (a shirt to which he is putting button holes) is hung to a nail on the wall over a small wooden table, on which the novel, "Lorna Doone,"[1] *lies open. Low down in the corner by the door is a thick glass screen, about a foot square, covering the gas-jet let into the wall. There is also a wooden stool, and a pair of shoes beneath it. Three bright round tins are set under the window.*

In the fast failing daylight, Falder, in his stockings, is seen standing motionless, with his head inclined towards the door, listening. He moves a little closer to the door, his stockinged feet making no noise. He stops at the door. He is trying harder and harder to hear something, any little thing that is going on outside. He springs suddenly upright — as if at a sound, and remains perfectly motionless. Then, with a heavy sigh, he moves to his work, and stands looking at it, with his head down; he does a stitch or two, having the air of a man so lost in sadness that each stitch is, as it were, a coming to life. Then turning abruptly, he begins pacing the cell, moving his head, like an animal pacing its cage. He stops again at the door, listens, and, placing the palms of his hands against it with his fingers spread out, leans his forehead against the iron. Turning from it, presently, he moves slowly back towards the window, tracing his way with his finger along the top line of the distemper that runs round the wall. He stops under the window, and, picking up the lid of one of the tins, peers into it. It has grown very nearly dark. Suddenly the lid falls out of his hands with a clatter, the only sound that has broken the silence — and he stands staring intently at the wall where the stuff of the shirt is hanging rather white in the darkness — he seems to be seeing somebody or something there. There is a sharp tap and click; the cell light behind the glass screen has been turned up. The cell is brightly lighted. Falder is seen gasping for breath.

A sound from far away, as of distant, dull beating on thick metal, is suddenly audible. Falder shrinks back, not able to bear this sudden clamour. But the sound grows, as though some great tumbril were rolling towards the cell. And gradually, it seems to hypnotise him. He begins creeping inch by inch nearer to the door. The banging sound, travelling from cell to cell, draws closer and closer; Falder's hands are seen moving as if his spirit had already joined in this beating, and the sound swells till it seems to have entered the very cell.

---

[1] Note that this is a literary detail effective for readers only. At best the first row of spectators alone could identify the title of the book.

He suddenly raises his clenched fists. Panting violently, he flings himself at his door, and beats on it.

The curtain falls.[1]

Perhaps an even more interesting illustration of pantomime, because it gives us, instead of the heightening emotion of one person, the action of two characters upon each other, is found in Hugo von Hofmannsthal's *Die Frau im Fenster.*

She remains leaning over the parapet thus for a long time. Suddenly she thinks she hears something as the curtain behind her, separating her balcony from the room, is thrown open. Turning her head she sees her husband standing in the doorway. She springs up; her features become distorted with the utmost anguish. Messer Braccio stands silent in the doorway. He wears a simple dark green dressing-gown, without weapons; low shoes. He is very tall and strong. His face has the quality that often shows itself in the old pictures of great lords and condottieri. He has an exceedingly large forehead, and little, dark eyes, thick black hair, short and curly, and a small beard round his face. Dianora wishes to speak, but can bring no sound from her throat. Messer. Braccio motions for her to draw in the ladder. Dianora does so automatically, rolls it together, and as though unconscious, lets the bundle fall at her feet. Braccio regards her calmly. Then he grasps his left hip with his right hand, also with his left hand, and looking down, notes that he has no dagger. Making an impatient movement of the lips he glances down into the garden and behind him. He lifts his right hand for an instant and looks at its palm. He goes back into the room with firm, unhurried steps.

Dianora looks after him continually; she cannot take her eyes from him. When the curtain falls behind him, she passes her fingers over her cheeks and through her hair. Then she folds her hands and with wildly twitching lips silently prays. Then she throws her arms backward and grasps the stone coping with her fingers, a movement revealing firm resolution and a hint of triumph.

Braccio steps out through the door again, carrying in his left hand a stool which he places in the doorway, and then sits down opposite his wife. His expression has not changed. From time to time he lifts his right hand mechanically and regards the small wound in its palm.

[1] *Justice.* Copyright, 1910, by John Galsworthy. Chas. Scribner's Sons, New York.

*Braccio. (His tone is cold, slightly disdainful. He indicates the
ladder with his foot and his eyes.)* Who is it?

    (Dianora lifts her shoulders, then lets them fall again slowly.)
Braccio. I know.

    *(Dianora lifts her shoulders, then lets them fall again slowly.
Her teeth are pressed tightly together.)*
*Braccio. (Raising his hand with the movement but touching his
wife only with his glance; then he turns his gaze toward the garden
again.)* Palla degli Albizzi.[1]

Such elaborate pantomime as the cases just cited is naturally rare, but a dramatist is always watching for an opportunity to shorten by pantomime a speech or the dialogue of
a scene, or to intensify by it the effect of his words.[2] Is anything in *Shore Acres*, by James A. Herne, more memorable
than the last scene? In it Uncle Nat, who has established
the happiness of the household, lights his candle deliber-
ately and goes slowly up the long staircase to his bedroom,
humming softly. He is the very picture of spiritual content.
Words would have spoiled that scene as they have spoiled
many and many a scene of an inexperienced dramatist.

Iris, at the end of Act III of Pinero's play of that name, is
on the point of leaving Bellagio. Maldonado has left lying
on her table a checkbook on a bank in which he has placed
a few hundred pounds in her name. Because of the defalca-
tion of her lawyer, she is in financial straits. Maldonado
wishes to help her but also to gain power over her. Unwilling
to take the checkbook, she has urged him to remove it.
Lacking firmness of character, however, she lets him leave
it, saying she will destroy it.

*With a troubled, half-guilty look, Iris attires herself in her hat and
cape ; after which, carrying her gloves, she returns to her dressing-bag.
Glancing round the room to assure herself that she has collected all her
small personal belongings, her eyes rest on the checque-book which lies
open on the writing-table. She contemplates it for a time, a gradually*

---

[1] *Die Frau im Fenster.* Theater in Versen. H. von Hofmannsthal. S. Fischer, Berlin.
[2] The final scene of Act IV of *Nathan Hale* shows effective use of pantomime.

increasing fear showing itself in her face. Ultimately she walks slowly to the table and picks up a book. She is fingering it in an uncertain, frightened way when the servant returns.

Man-servant. (*Standing over the bag.*) Is there anything more, ma'am —?

> (*She hesitates helplessly ; then, becoming conscious that she is being stared at, she advances, drops the book into the bag, and passes out. The man shuts the bag and is following her as the curtain falls.*)[1]

This passage from Act I of *The Great Divide* shows pantomime supplementing speech as the dramatist of experience frequently employs it. A writer of less sure feeling would have permitted his characters some unnecessary or involved speech.

(*Ruth selects a red flower, puts it in the dark mass of her hair, and looks out at the open door.*) What a scandal the moon is making out in that great crazy world! Who but me could think of sleeping on such a night?

> (*She sits down, folds the flowers in her arms, and buries her face in them. After a moment, she starts up, listens, goes hurriedly to the door, draws the curtains before the window, comes swiftly to the table, and blows out the light. The room is left in total darkness. There are muttering voices outside, the latch is tried, then a heavy lunge breaks the bolt. A man pushes in, but is hurled back by a taller man, with a snarling oath. A third figure advances to the table, and strikes a match. As soon as the match is lighted Ruth levels the gun, which she has taken from its rack above the mantel. There is heard the click of the hammer, as the gun misses fire. It is instantly struck from her hand by the first man (Dutch), who attempts to seize her. She evades him and tries to wrest a pistol from a holster on the wall. She is met by the second man (Shorty), who frustrates the attempt, pocketing the weapon. While this has been going on, the third man (Ghent) has been fumbling with the lamp, which he has at last succeeded in*

---

[1] Walter H. Baker & Co., Boston; W. Heinemann, London.

*lighting. All three are dressed in rude frontier fashion,
the one called Shorty is a Mexican half-breed, the others
are Americans. Ghent is younger than Dutch, and taller,
but less powerfully built. All are intoxicated, but not
sufficiently so to incapacitate them from rapid action.
The Mexican has seized Ruth and attempts to drag her
toward the inner room. She breaks loose and flies back
again to the chimney place, where she stands at bay.
Ghent remains motionless and silent by the table, gazing
at her.)*

Dutch. (*Uncorking a whiskey flask.*) Plucky little catamount. I
drink its health.   (*Drinks.*)

Ruth. What do you want here? [1]

Hofmannsthal, in his *Electra*, uses pantomime as only
one detail, but no words could so paint the mad triumph of
the sister of Orestes as does her "incredible dance."

> (*Electra has raised herself. She steps down from the threshold,
> her head thrown back like a Mœnad. She lifts her knees,
> stretches out her arms; it is an incredible dance in which
> she steps forward.*
> *Chrysothemis appearing again at the door, behind her
> torches, a Throng, faces of Men and Women.*)

Chrysothemis.   Electra!

Electra. (*Stands still, gazing at her fixedly.*) Be silent and dance.
Come hither all of you!
Join with me all! I bear the burden of joy,
And I dance before you here. One thing alone
Remains for all who are as happy as we;
To be silent and dance.

> (*She does a few more steps of tense triumph, and falls
> a-heap. Chrysothemis runs to her. Electra lies motionless.
> Chrysothemis runs to the door of the house and knocks.*)

Chrysothemis. Orestes! Orestes!   (*Silence.*)

Curtain. [2]

Without question, then, speech in the drama may often
give way in part or wholly to pantomime. The inexperienced

---

[1] *The Great Divide*, Act I. The Macmillan Co., New York.
[2] Translated by Arthur Symons. Brentano, New York.

dramatist should be constantly alert to see to what extent he can substitute it for dialogue.[1]

In all that has been said of pantomime, of course technical pantomime is not meant. The *Commedia dell' arte*, pantomime artists like the Ravel Brothers or Mme. Pilar-Morin, have a code of gesture to symbolize fixed meanings. What is meant here is the natural human pantomime of people whose faces and bodies portray or betray their feelings.

Another word of warning in regard to pantomime. When a writer of plays once becomes well aware of the great value of pantomime, he is likely to overwork it. Assuming that the actor or actors may convey almost anything by physical movement, he trusts it too much. Let him who is for the moment under the spell of pantomime study the moving picture show. Pantomime may ordinarily convey physical action perfectly. Emotion naturally and easily expressed by action pantomime may convey, but when action for its clearness depends on knowledge of what is going on in the mind of the actor, pantomime begins to fail. Great artists like Mme. Pilar-Morin may carry us far even under these conditions, but most actors cannot. In a motion picture play like *Cabiria*, contrast the scenes in which the Roman and his slave flee before the crowd from part to part of the temple (mere action), or the scene of the terror of the wine merchant (in which the face and body tell the whole story) with the scene in which the nurse meets the Roman and his slave on the wall of the city and begs their aid in saving the child, or the scenes in which Sophonisba struggles with her anxieties and mad desires. The second group of pictures without the explanations thrown on the screen would have little meaning. Pantomime is safe, not when it pleases us to use pantomime rather than to write dialogue, but when

[1] For such skilful substitution of pantomime for words, see pp. 388–89, *Lady Windermere's Fan*.

our characters naturally act rather than speak, or when we can devise for them natural action as clear as speech or clearer than speech. Use pantomime, but use it cautiously. Speech is the greatest emotional weapon of the dramatist. It best reveals emotion, and best of all creates responsive emotion. However, as most inexperienced dramatists use far too many words rather than too few, the value rather than the danger of pantomime should probably be stressed here. What seems natural, what makes for illusion, is the final test.

It is this test of naturalness which has gradually excluded, except in special instances, the soliloquy and the aside. The general movement of drama in the past ten years has been toward better and better characterization in plays of all kinds. The newer melodrama and farce show us, not the mere comic puppets of the past, but people as real as the form represented — be it comedy, farce, tragedy, or melo- drama — will permit. This new tendency has largely driven out the soliloquy and the aside. We should not, however, go to extremes, for occasionally we do swear under our breath or comment in asides, and as long as people do either, such people should be so represented. Moreover, we must admit that the insane, the demented, the invalid left much to himself, the hermit, whether of the woods or the hall bed- room in a city boarding house, do talk to themselves and often at great length. Neither the aside nor the soliloquy is, then, objectionable in itself. It is the use of either by persons who would probably use nothing of the sort, or their use in order to avoid exposition otherwise difficult which is to be decried. It is particularly this latter fault to which Sir Arthur Pinero calls attention when treating the faulty technique of R. L. Stevenson as a playwright:

" I will read you one of the many soliloquies — the faulty method of conducting action and revealing character by soliloquy was one from which Stevenson could never emancipate himself. It is a speech delivered by Deacon Brodie while he is making preparations for a midnight gambling excursion.

> (*Brodie closes, locks, and double-bolts the doors of his bedroom.*)
> *Deacon Brodie.* Now for one of the Deacon's headaches! Rogues all, rogues all! (*He goes to the clothes press and proceeds to change his coat.*) On with the new coat and into the new life! Down with the Deacon and up with the robber! Eh God! How still the house is! There's something in hypocrisy after all. If we were as good as we seem, what would the world be? The city has its vizard on and we — at night we are our naked selves. Trysts are keeping, bottles cracking, knives are stripping; and here is Deacon Brodie flaming forth the man of men he is! How still it is! — My father and Mary — Well! The day for them, the night for me; the grimy cynical night that makes all cats grey, and all honesties of one complexion. Shall a man not have *half* a life of his own? not eight hours out of twenty-four? Eight shall he have should he dare the pit of Tophet. Where's the blunt? I must be cool tonight, or — steady Deacon, you must win; damn you, you must! You must win back the dowry that you've stolen, and marry your sister and pay your debts, and gull the world a little longer! The Deacon's going to bed — the poor sick Deacon! *Allons!* Only the stars to see me! I'm a man once more till morning! [Act 1, Tableau 1, Scene 9.] [1]

Sir Arthur knows whereof he speaks, for past-master as he has shown himself since *The Second Mrs. Tanqueray* in the art of giving necessary exposition and characterization without soliloquy, he was a bad offender in his early days, as the following extract from the opening of *The Money Spinner* shows:

> (*Directly Margot has disappeared, there is a knocking outside the door, right. It is repeated, then the doors slowly open and the head of Monsieur Jules Faubert appears.*)
> *Faubert.* (*Who also speaks with the accent of a foreigner.*) Boycott,

[1] *Robert Louis Stevenson, the Dramatist*, p. 15. Sir A. W. Pinero. Chiswick Press, London. For the play see *Three Plays*, Henley and Stevenson. Chas. Scribner's Sons, New York.

my friend, are you at home? My friend Boycott, do you hear me? (*Receiving no answer, he enters rather cautiously and looks around. He is in black, wearing a long, tightly buttoned frock coat and a tall hat. His hair is red and closely cropped. His voice is soft and his manner stealthy and mechanical.*) Where is Boycott, my friend? Ah, he has not yet taken his breakfast. (*He crosses over to the curtains, left, and looks through.*) No one to be seen. Boycott asks me to call for him at ten o'clock in the morning, and it is now a quarter past ten by the Great Clock, and he is not visible. (*Walking round the room, inspecting the objects with curiosity.*) Yet he could not have left the house for I have been watching at the front door since eight o'clock. (*Takes letters from top of Pianette.*) Besides, here are his letters unopened. (*Examines them narrowly, scrutinizing the writing, and weighing them in his hand.*) One, Mr. Boycott, with the post-mark of London. Two, Monsieur Boycott with the post-mark of Rouen. Three, Madame Boycott with the post-mark of Paris. (*Replacing letters.*) Ah, I have not yet the pleasure of the acquaintance of Madame Boycott. Poor soul, perhaps she will know me some day. (*Going over to the door, right.*) Well, I shall call again after breakfast. My friend Boycott is getting very unpunctual — a bad sign — a very bad sign.[1]

The unnaturalness of the two foregoing illustrations needs no comment. The Elizabethan author, knowing that above all else the dramatist must make clear why his people do what they do, used soliloquy with the utmost frankness as the easiest method of exposition. Here are three specimens, one from Webster and two from Shakespeare.

> *Cardinal.* The reason why I would not suffer these
> About my brother is because at midnight
> I may with better privacy convay
> Julias body, to her owne lodging. O, my conscience!
> I would pray now: but the divell takes away my heart
> For having any confidence in praier.
> About this houre I appointed Bosola
> To fetch the body: when he hath serv'd my turne,
> He dies. (*Exit.*)[2]

[1] Samuel French, New York.
[2] *The Duchesse of Malfi*, Act v, Scene 4. Belles-Lettres Series. M. W. Sampson, ed D. C. Heath & Co., Boston and New York.

Iago. That Cassio loves her I do well believe't;
That she loves him, 'tis apt and of great credit;
The Moor, howbeit that I endure him not,
Is of a constant, loving, noble nature,
And I dare think he'll prove to Desdemona
A most dear husband. Now, I do love her too;
Not out of absolute lust, though peradventure
I stand accountant for as great a sin,
But partly led to diet my revenge,
For that I do suspect the lusty Moor
Hath leap'd into my seat; the thought whereof
Doth, like a poisonous mineral, gnaw my inwards;
And nothing can or shall content my soul
Till I am even'd with him, wife for wife;
Or failing so, yet that I put the Moor
At least into a jealousy so strong
That judgement cannot cure. Which thing to do,
If this poor trash of Venice, whom I trash
For his quick hunting, stand the putting on,
I'll have our Michael Cassio on the hip,
Abuse him to the Moor in the rank garb —
For I fear Cassio with my night-cap too —
Make the Moor thank me, love me, and reward me,
For making him egregiously an ass
And practising upon his peace and quiet
Even to madness. 'Tis here, but yet confus'd;
Knavery's plain face is never seen till us'd.   *(Exit.)*[1]

Emilia. I am glad I have found this napkin;
This was her first remembrance from the Moor.
My wayward husband hath a hundred times
Woo'd me to steal it; but she so loves the token,
For he conjur'd her she should ever keep it,
That she reserves it evermore about her
To kiss and talk to. I'll have the work ta'en out,
And give 't Iago. What he will do with it
Heaven knows, not I;
I nothing but to please his fantasy.[2]

---

[1] *Othello*, Act II, Scene 1.   [2] *Othello*, Act III, Scene 3.

Echegaray's *The Great Galeoto* (1881), though a part of the newer movement in the drama, shows soliloquy.

SCENE. *Madrid of our day.*

PROLOGUE

A study; to the left a balcony; on the right a door; in the middle a table strewn with papers and books, and a lighted lamp upon it. Towards the right a sofa. Night.

SCENE 1.

Ernest. (*Seated at a table and preparing to write.*) Nothing — impossible. It is striving with the impossible. The idea is there; my head is fevered with it; I feel it. At moments an inward light illuminates it, and I see it. I see it in its floating form, vaguely outlined, and suddenly a secret voice seems to animate it, and I hear sounds of sorrow, sonorous sighs, shouts of sardonic laughter — a whole world of passions alive and struggling — They burst forth from me, extend around me and the air is full of them. Then, then I say to myself: "'Tis now the moment." I take up my pen, stare into space, listen attentively, restraining my very heart-beats, and bend over the paper — Ah, but the irony of impotency! The outlines become blurred, the vision fades, the cries and sighs faint away — and nothingness, nothingness encircles me — The monotony of empty space, of inert thought, of dreamy lassitude! and more than all the monotony of an idle pen and lifeless paper that lacks the life of thought! Ah, how varied are the shapes of nothingness, and how, in its dark and silent way, it mocks creatures of my stamp! So many, many forms. Canvas without color, bits of marble without shape, confused noise of chaotic vibrations. But nothing more irritating, more insolent, meaner than this insolent pen of mine (*throws it away*), nothing worse than this white sheet of paper. Oh, if I cannot fill it, at least I may destroy it — vile accomplice of my ambition and my eternal humiliation. Thus, thus — smaller and still smaller. (*Tears up paper. Pauses.*) And then! How lucky that nobody saw me! For in truth, such fury is absurd and unjust. No, I will not yield. I will think and think until

I have conquered or am crushed. No, I will not give up. Let me see, let me see — if in that way — [1]

Such soliloquy, even if conventionally justifiable in its own time, is rarely, if ever, necessary. Scene 2 of Echegaray's play shows Ernest and Don Julian discussing the former's difficulty in working. What could be easier, then, than to cut the scene just cited to Ernest seated at a writing table and showing by his pantomime how impossible he finds composition? Why should he not act out the lines, "I take up my pen, stare into space, listen attentively, — bend over the paper . . . and nothingness, nothingness"? If as a climax he throws away his pen and tears up his paper, it certainly should be clear that he is thoroughly exasperated with his failure to write what he wishes. In Scene 2 a very slight change or amplification in the phrasing will permit him to bring out whatever of importance in Scene 1 the suggested revision has omitted.

Doubtless it would not be so easy to get rid of the soliloquies of the Cardinal, Iago, and Emilia, but ingenuity in handling the scene preceding and the scene following soliloquies will usually dispose of all or most of them. When *Lady Windermere's Fan* of Wilde first appeared, hardly any one seriously objected to its soliloquies. They were an accepted convention of the stage. When Miss Margaret Anglin revived the play very successfully a year or two ago, she rightly felt these soliloquies to be outworn. By use of pantomime, in some cases hardly more than the pantomime called for in the stage directions, she disposed of all except an occasional line or two of the original soliloquies. The instances cited from her prompt book of the play show one soliloquy cut to stage directions and two lines of the original, and the second cut to mere stage direction.

[1] *Drama League Series.* Hannah Lynch, tr. Doubleday, Page & Co.

ACT I.

Lady Windermere. How horrible! I understand now what Lord Darlington meant by the imaginary instance of the couple not two years married. Oh! it can't be true — she spoke of enormous sums of money paid to this woman. I know where Arthur keeps his bank book — in one of the drawers of that desk. I might find out by that. I *will* find out. (*Opens drawer.*) No, it is some hideous mistake. (*Rises and goes C.*) Some silly scandal! He loves *me!* He loves *me!* But why should I not look? I am his wife, I have a right to look! (*Returns to bureau, takes out book and examines it, page by page, smiles and gives a sigh of relief.*) I knew it, there is not a word of truth in this stupid story. (*Puts book back in drawer. As she does so, starts and takes out another book.*) A second book — private — locked! (*Tries to open it but fails. Sees paper knife on bureau, and with it cuts cover from book. Begins to start at the first page.*) Mrs. Erlynne — £600 — Mrs. — Erlynne — £700 — Mrs. Erlynne — £400. Oh! it is true! it is true! How horrible! (*Throws book on floor.*)[1]

(*Lady Windermere sits left of centre, looks toward desk, rises, starts toward desk, hesitates centre, goes to desk, tries drawer, hunts for and finds key, unlocks drawer, takes out check book, looks over stubs, finds nothing and is relieved, then sees first entry.*)

Lady Windermere. Mrs. Erlynne — £600 — Mrs. Erlynne — £700 — Mrs. Erlynne — £400. Oh! it is true! it is true!

---

[1] *Plays,* vol. i. J. W. Luce & Co., Boston.

ACT III.

Lady Windermere. (*Standing by the fireplace.*) Why doesn't he come? This waiting is horrible. He should be here. Why is he not here, to wake by passionate words some fire within me? I am cold — cold as a loveless thing. Arthur must have read my letter by this time. If he cared for me, he would have come after me, and have taken me back by force. But he doesn't care. He's entrammeled by this woman — fascinated by her — dominated by her. If a woman wants to hold a man, she has merely to appeal to what is worst in him. We make gods of men and they leave us. Others make brutes of them and they fawn and are faithful. How hideous life is! . . . Oh! it was mad of me to come here, horribly mad. And yet which is the worst, I wonder, to be at the mercy of a man who loves one, or the wife of a man who in one's own house dishonors one? What woman knows? What woman in the whole world? But will he love me always, this man to whom I am giving my life? What do I bring him? Lips that have lost the note of joy, eyes that are blighted by tears, chill hands and icy heart. I bring him nothing. I must go back — no; I can't go back, my letter

(*Lady Windermere discovered at fireplace, L., crosses to chair, L. of C., takes cloak from chair, puts cloak on crossing to door U.L., stops, decides to stay, crosses to R. of D.C. Enter Mrs. Erlynne.*)

has put me in their power —
Arthur would not take me back!
That fatal letter! No! Lord
Darlington leaves England tomorrow. I will go with him — I
have no choice. (*Sits down for a
few moments. Then starts up and
puts on her cloak.*) No, no! I
will go back, let Arthur do with
me what he pleases. I can't wait
here. It has been madness my
coming. I must go at once. As
for Lord Darlington — Oh! here
he is! What shall I do? What
can I say to him? Will he let me
go away at all? I have heard
that men are brutal, horrible.
. . . Oh! (*Hides her face in her
hands.*)

Enter Mrs. Erlynne, L.[1]

Soliloquy when a character is left alone on the stage is a
perfect illustration of the difference between permanent and
ephemeral technique. As a device for easy exposition, it has
been popular from the beginning of drama till recently.
Now, though one may use it in a rough draft, a technique
which is likely to become permanent in this respect forces
us to go over this draft, cutting soliloquy to mere action and
the few exclamations which the character might utter under
the circumstances. Soliloquy has no such permanent place
in technique as have preliminary exposition, suspense, and
climax. Soliloquy, when other people are on the stage and
known by the speaker to be listening is also absurd. It is
because of this fact that the dramatic or psychologic monologue, the form taken by a very large portion of Browning's
voluminous poetry, breaks down if we attempt to stage it.
"Some speaker is made to reveal his character, and, some-

[1] *Plays,* vol. I. J. W. Luce & Co., Boston.

DIALOGUE 391

times, by reflection, or directly, the character of some one
else — to set forth some subtle and complex soul-mood, some
supreme, all-determining movement or experience of a life,
or, it may be, to ratiocinate subtly on some curious question
of theology, morals, philosophy, or art. Now it is in strictly
preserving the monologue character that obscurity often
results. A monologue often begins with a startling abrupt-
ness, and the reader must read along some distance before
he gathers what the beginning means. Take the monologue
of Fra Lippo Lippi for example. The situation is necessarily
left more or less unexplained. The poet says nothing *in
propria persona*, and no reply is made to the speaker by the
person or persons addressed. Sometimes a look, a gesture or
a remark must be supposed on the part of the one addressed,
which occasions a responsive remark. Sometimes a speaker
imputes a question, and the reader is sometimes obliged to
stop and consider whether a question is imputed by the
speaker to the one he is addressing, or is a direct question
of his own. This is often the case throughout *The Ring and
the Book.*" [1]

> *Giuseppe Caponsacchi.* Answer you, Sirs? Do I
> understand aright?
> Have patience! In this sudden smoke from hell, —
> So things disguise themselves, — I cannot see
> My own hand held thus broad before my face
> And know it again. Answer you? Then that means
> Tell over twice what I, the first time, told
> Six months ago: 'twas here, I do believe,
> Fronting you same three in this very room,
> I stood and told you: yet now no one laughs,
> Who then . . . nay, dear my lords, but laugh you did,
> As good as laugh, what in a judge we style
> Laughter — no levity, nothing indecorous, lords!
> Only, — I think I apprehend the mood:
> There was the blameless shrug, permissible smirk,

[1] *Introduction to Browning*, pp. 85–86. H. Corson. D. C. Heath & Co.

The pen's pretence at play with the pursed mouth,
The titter stifled in the hollow palm
Which rubbed the eyebrow and caressed the nose,
When first I told my tale: they meant, you know,
"The sly one, all this we are bound believe!
"Well, he can say no other than what he says.
"We have been young, too, — come, there's greater guilt!
"Let him but decently disembroil himself,
"Scramble from out the scrape nor move the mud, —
"We solid ones may risk a finger-stretch!"
And now you sit as grave, stare as aghast
As if I were a phantom: now 'tis — "Friend,
"Collect yourself!" — no laughing matter more —
"Counsel the Court in this extremity,
"Tell us again!" — tell that, for telling which,
I got the jocular piece of punishment,
Was sent to lounge a little in the place
Whence now of a sudden here you summon me
To take the intelligence from just — your lips,
You, Judge Tommati, who then tittered most, —
That she I helped eight months since to escape
Her husband, is retaken by the same
Three days ago, if I have seized your sense.[1]

It may be true that when one reads a dramatic monologue, the changes in thought caused by some movement or look of an imagined hearer may seem sufficiently motivated. When, on the other hand, this monologue is staged, it becomes exceedingly unreal because we feel that the second person would not be silent but would interrupt with question or comment. More than this, unless the listening actor changes from pose to pose with rapid plasticity, he will become stiff in attitude, thus making us conscious of him when we should be listening to the speaker. Increasing the number of hearers does not relieve the situation, but merely increases the number of possible interrupters or of people who stand about the stage more and more stiffly. Soliloquy is,

---

[1] *The Ring and the Book.* Robert Browning. Tauchnitz ed., vol. IV. Leipzig.

therefore, to be avoided except when it seems or can be made to seem perfectly natural. Monologue, acceptable perhaps to a reader, becomes well-nigh impossible on the stage.

The aside must be subjected to very nearly the same tests. In *Two Loves and a Life* of Tom Taylor and Charles Reade, Musgrave and his daughter, Anne, are opening letters surreptitiously. They come to the letter of William Hyde, which the girl opens with reluctance, crying, —

Ah, see, father, it is a blank!

Musgrave. A blank! Then it is as I thought!

Anne. How?

Musgrave. Here, girl!
        (*He takes the letter and holds it to the fire in the brazier.*)

Anne. See! Letters become visible!

Musgrave. A stale trick. 'Tis done with lemon juice or milk, when folks would keep what they write from those who are in their secret. Politicians correspond so, Anne, and rebels.

Anne. But William Hyde is neither, father.

Musgrave. Of course not. Now then!

Anne. (*Aside.*) Thank Heaven! 'tis all about his calling!

Musgrave. Read! (*Aside.*) I have learned the key to their cypher, which I have copied from the priest's letter.

Anne. (*Reads.*) "Dear Will, we have thine advices, and shall be at Lancaster Fair. All the smart fellows —"

Musgrave. (*To himself.*) Ah! Bardsea Hole — all the Jacobite gentlemen — good.

Anne. (*Reads.*) "By the time the grilse come ashore —"

Musgrave. (*To himself.*) Grilse? ammunition. Go on.

Anne. (*Reads.*) "Which shall be as you fix, on Tuesday the 16th, at ten of the clock, P.M. There is a bill against you and the old clothier, payable at Ulverstone today, drawn by the butcher. Look out and see that he does not nab either of you —"

Musgrave. (*Aside.*) The proclamation!

Anne. (*Reads.*) "For your friends assembled. John Trusty."

Musgrave. From Townley. It *is* as I suspected.
                                    (*He starts up.*)

Anne. Father!

Musgrave. I'm a made man, Anne. Give me joy — joy! [1]

[1] Act II, Scene 2. Samuel French, New York.

In this once popular drama we have five asides close together, for of course "to himself" is the equivalent of an aside. All are bad, for in each case the other person on the stage must be supposed not to hear, and the aside is merely a device for telling us what the speaker is thinking. They vary in badness, however, for while Musgrave might well explain "grilse" to Anne as "ammunition," he says, "I have learned the key to their cipher, which I have copied from the priest's letter," not as something which he is necessarily thinking at the time, but as something which the audience needs to know at this point. An aside is objectionable when a man speaks what he would be careful only to think, either because of the very nature of his thought or because somebody is near at hand who should not overhear. Asides should be kept for confidential remarks which may be made to some person standing near the speaker, but could not be heard by persons standing at a greater distance; and to what naturally breaks from us in a moment of irritation, terror, or other strong emotion. Asides of the first group, confidential remarks, gain much in naturalness if spoken in half tones. Nothing could be more preposterous than the old stage custom of coming down to the footlights to tell an audience in clear-cut tones confidences which must not be overheard by people close at hand on the stage. Asides which are only brief soliloquies are little better. Asides in which the speaker merely says to the audience what he might perfectly well say to the people on the stage are foolish unless the author wishes to make the point that the character has the habit of talking to himself. The following from Vanbrugh's *The Provoked Wife* shows two entirely natural uses of the aside by Lady Brute, and one debatable use by Sir John.

ACT III. *Scene opens. Sir John, Lady Brute, and Belinda rising from the Table*

Sir John. Will it so, Mrs. Pert? Now I believe it will so increase it, (*sitting and smoaking*) I shall take my own House for a Paper-mill.

Lady Brute. (*To Belinda aside.*) Don't let's mind him; let him say what he will.

Sir John. (*Aside.*) A Woman's Tongue a Cure for the Spleen — Oons — If a Man had got the Head-ach, they'd be for applying the same Remedy.

Lady Brute. You have done a great deal, Belinda, since yes-terday.

Belinda. Yes, I have work'd very hard; how do you like it?

Lady Brute. O, 'tis the prettiest Fringe in the World. Well, Cousin, you have the happiest fancy. Prithee advise me about altering my Crimson Petticoat.

Sir John. A Pox o' your Petticoat; here's such a Prating, a Man can't digest his own Thoughts for you.

Lady Brute. (*Aside.*) Don't answer him. — Well, what do you advise me?

Belinda. Why really I would not alter it at all. Methinks 'tis very pretty as it is.[1]

Sir John's aside, if addressed to the audience, is bad; if meant to illustrate his habit of grumbling to himself, it is permissible.

Mr. Henry Arthur Jones protests against complete disuse of the aside. "In discarding the 'aside' in modern drama we have thrown away a most valuable and, at times, a most necessary convention. Let any one glance at the 'asides' of Sir John Brute in *The Provoked Wife*, and he will see what a splendid instrument of rich comedy the 'aside' may become. How are we as spectators to know what one character on the stage thinks of the situation and of the other characters, unless he tells us; or unless he conveys it by facial play and gestures which are the equivalent of an

[1] *Plays*, vol. ii, pp. 150–51. J. Tonson. London, 1730.

'aside'? The 'aside' is therefore as legitimate a convention of drama as the removal of the fourth wall. More and more the English modern drama seems to be sacrificing everything to the mean ambition of presenting an exact photograph of real life."[1]

Of course Mr. Jones is quite right in wishing to keep the aside for cases in which it is perfectly natural. His illustration of Sir John Brute is, however, not wholly fortunate, for his asides are not conventional but are characterizing touches. Surely we must all admit that a certain type of drunkard likes to mumble to himself insulting speeches which he hasn't quite the courage to speak directly to other people, but rather hopes they may overhear. Study the asides of Sir John Brute — they are not very many after all — and note that practically every one might be said directly to the people on the stage. All of them help to present Sir John as the heavy drinker who talks to himself and selects for his speeches to himself his particularly insulting remarks.

Why, too, are "facial play and gestures" more objectionable than the conventional aside? The fundamental trouble with the aside which should not be overheard by people on the stage is that, if spoken naturally, it would be too low for the audience to hear, and if spoken loud enough to be heard, would so affect the other characters as to change materially the development of the scene. The aside should, therefore, be used with great care.

Congreve, writing of ordinary human speech said, "I believe if a poet should steal a dialogue of any length, from the extempore discourse of the two wittiest men upon earth, he would find the scene but coldly received by the town." [2]

[1] *The Foundations of a National Drama*, p. 23. H. A. Jones. George H. Doran Company, New York.
[2] *Concerning Humour in Comedy. A Letter. European Theories of the Drama*, pp. 213–214. Ed. B. H. Clark. Stewart and Kidd Co., Cincinnati.

In everyday speech, that is, we do not say our say in the most compact, characteristic, and entertaining fashion. To gain all that, we must use more concentration and selection than we give to ordinary human intercourse. Just that concentration of attention, which produces needed selection, a dramatist must give his dialogue. To this concentration and selection he is forced by the time difficulty already explained. Into the period sometimes consumed by a single bit of gossiping, perhaps shot through with occasional flashes of wit, but more probably dull, — into the space of two hours and a quarter, — the dramatist must crowd all the happenings, the growth of his characters, and the close reasoning of his play. Dramatic dialogue is human speech so wisely edited for use under the conditions of the stage that far more quickly than under ordinary circumstances the events are presented, in character, and perhaps in a phrasing delightful of itself.

Picking just the right words to convey with gesture, voice and the other stage aids of dialogue the emotions of the characters is so exacting a task that many a writer tries to dodge it. He thinks that by prefacing nearly every speech with "Tenderly," "Sarcastically," "With much humor," in other words a statement as to how his lines should be read, commonplace phrasings may be made to pass for the right emotional currency. This is a lazy trick of putting off on the actor what would be the delight of the writer if he really cared for his work and knew what he wished to say. Of course, from time to time one needs such stage directions, but the safest way is to insist, in early drafts, on making the text convey the desired emotion without such statements. Otherwise a writer easily falls into writing unemotionalized speeches, the stage directions of which call upon the actor to provide the emotion.

A similar trick is to write incomplete sentences, usually

ending with dashes. Though it is true, as Carlyle long ago pointed out, that a thought or a climax which a reader or hearer completes for himself is likely to give him special satisfaction, the device is easily overdone, and too often the uncompleted line means either that the author does not know exactly what he wishes to say, or that, though he knows, the hearer or reader may not complete the thought as he does. The worst of this last trick is that it may confuse the reader and, as was explained earlier in this chapter, clearness in gaining the desired effect is the chief essential in dialogue.

An allied difficulty comes from writing dialogue in blocks, the author forgetting, in the first place, that the other people on the stage are likely to interrupt and break up such speech, and secondly, that when several ideas are presented to an audience in the same speech, they are likely to confuse hearers. In these parallel passages from the two quartos of *Hamlet*, is not the right-hand column, with its mingling of rapidly exchanged speech and description, much more vivid and moving?

Enter Ofelia;

Corambis. Farewel, how now Ofelia, what's the news with you?

Ofelia. O my deare father, such a change in nature,
So great an alteration in a Prince,
So pitifull to him, fearefull to mee,
A maiden's eye ne're looked on.

Corambis. Why, what's the matter my Ofelia?

Ofelia. O yong Prince Hamlet, the only floure of Denmark,

Enter Ophelia.

Polonius. Farewell. How now Ophelia, what's the matter?

Ophelia. O my Lord, my Lord, I have been so affrighted.

Polonius. With what i'th name of God?

Ophelia. My Lord, as I was sowing in my closset,
Lord Hamlet with his doublet all unbrac'd,
No hat upon his head, his stockins fouled,
Ungartred, and downe gyved to his ancle,

Hee is bereft of all the wealth he
  had,
The Jewell that adorn'd his feature most
Is filcht and stolne away, his
  wit's bereft him.

Pale as his shirt, his knees
  knocking each other,
And with a look so pittious in
  purport
As if he had been loosed out
  of hell
To speake of horrors, he comes
  before me.
    Polonius. Mad for thy love?
    Ophelia. My lord I doe not
  know,
But truly I doe feare it.
    Polonius. What said he?
    Ophelia. He took me by the
  wrist, and held me hard,
Then goes he to the length of
  all his arme,
And with his other hand thus
  ore his brow,
He falls to such perusall of my
  face
As a would draw it.[1]

Is it probable that in the following extract from *A Soul's
Tragedy* of Browning the deeply interested and excited audience would permit the first bystander to complete uninterrupted his third and very long speech? Are the phrasing
and thought really his, or Robert Browning's?

ACT II. *Scene. The market place. Luitolfo in disguise mingling
with the Populace assembled opposite the Provost's Palace.*

1st Bystander. (*To Luitolfo.*) You, a friend of Luitolfo's? Then,
your friend is vanished, — in all probability killed on the night that
his patron the tyrannical Provost was loyally suppressed here,
exactly a month ago, by our illustrious fellow-citizen, thrice-noble
saviour, and new Provost that is like to be, this very morning, —
Chiappino!

. . . .

Luitolfo. (*Aside.*) (If I had not lent that man the money he

[1] *The Devonshire Hamlets*, p. 28.

wanted last spring, I should fear this bitterness was attributable to me.) Luitolfo is dead then, one may conclude?

3rd Bystander. Why, he had a house here, and a woman to whom he was affianced; and as they both pass naturally to the new Provost, his friend and heir . . .

Luitolfo. Ah, I suspected you of imposing upon me with your pleasantry! I know Chiappino better.

1st Bystander. (Our friend has the bile. After all, I do not dislike finding somebody vary a little this general gape of admiration at Chiappino's glorious qualities.) Pray, how much may you know of what has taken place in Faenza since that memorable night?

Luitolfo. It is most to the purpose, that I know Chiappino to have been by profession a hater of that very office of Provost, you now charge him with proposing to accept.

1st Bystander. Sir, I'll tell you. That night was indeed memorable. Up we rose, a mass of us, men, women, children; out fled the guards with the body of the tyrant; we were to defy the world; but, next gray morning, "What will Rome say?" began everybody. You know we are governed by Ravenna, which is governed by Rome. And quietly into the town, by the Ravenna road, comes on muleback a portly personage, Ogniben by name, with the quality of Pontifical Legate; trots briskly through the streets humming a "Cur fremuere gentes," and makes directly for the Provost's Palace — there it faces you. "One Messer Chiappino is your leader? I have known three-and-twenty leaders of revolts!" (laughing gently to himself) — "Give me the help of your arm from my mule to yonder steps under the pillar — So! And now, my revolters and good friend what do you want? The guards burst into Ravenna last night bearing your wounded Provost; and, having had a little talk with him, I take on myself to come and try appease the disorderliness, before Rome, hearing of it, resort to another method: 'tis I come, and not another, from a certain love I confess to, of composing differences. So, do you understand, you are about to experience this unheard-of tyranny from me, that there shall be no heading nor hanging, no confiscation nor exile: I insist on your simply pleasing yourselves. And, now, pray, what does please you? To live without any government at all? Or having decided for one, to see its minister murdered by the first of your body that chooses to find himself wronged, or disposed for reverting to first principles and a justice anterior to all institutions, — and so will you carry matters, that the rest of the world must at length unite and put down such a den of wild beasts? As for vengeance on what had just taken place, — once for all, the wounded man assures me that he cannot conjecture who struck him; and this so earnestly, that one may be sure he knows perfectly well what intimate acquaintance could find admission to speak with him late last evening. I come not for vengeance therefore, but from pure curiosity to hear what you will do next." And thus he ran on, easily and volubly, till he seemed to arrive quite naturally at the praise of law, order, and paternal government by somebody from rather a distance. All our citizens were in the snare and about to be friends with so congenial an adviser; but that Chiappino suddenly stood forth, spoke out indignantly and set things right again.

Luitolfo. Do you see? I recognize him there![1]

People who think ramblingly and not clearly must undoubtedly on the stage speak in similar fashion, but it is wise when possible to avoid stating two or three ideas in the same sentence, or developing two or three ideas in one long speech. An idea to a sentence, with the development of one thought in a speech, is a fairly safe principle, though not unalterable. For instance, the daughter of a widowed mother is facing the fact that if they are to stay in their meagre quarters she may have to ask this as a favor from her employer, Mr. Hollings. The mother, not knowing that he has pressed his attentions objectionably, does not understand the unwillingness of the girl to ask his help. In answer to her pleadings the girl cries, "Oh, I would do anything for you! Poor dear father! Mother, go to Mr. Hollings." Here are three different trains of thought in one speech. The first exclamation is a direct answer to the mother's preceding speech. For the audience there is no clearness of transition to the second exclamation, nor from it to the third. Cut the girl's answer to the first sentence. Then the mother, seizing on the idea that her daughter is willing to do anything, urges her for this and that reason to see her employer, emphasizing the idea that, had the father lived, all

[1] Belles-Lettres Series, pp. 271–273. A. Bates, ed. D. C. Heath & Co., Boston.

their present sorrow would not exist. In this case the second exclamation falls into its proper place, as a natural reply of the girl to her mother. If, too, as the mother urges reason after reason for going to the employer for aid, the girl at last pleads, "Mother, you go to Mr. Hollings," this sentence also falls into its proper place. It becomes the first sign of her yielding, for she is at last willing that some one should intercede with the man. When a writer finds himself skipping from idea to idea within a speech or a sentence, with transitions likely to be unclear for the audience, he should break what he has written into its component parts and let the other people on the stage, by their interruptions, queries, and comments, provide the connectives of speech and thought which will bind these ideas together properly. The following rearrangement by Miss Anglin of the original text of *Lady Windermere's Fan* shows her correct feeling that ideas originally treated together should be separated. Lord Windermere's reply is to the first sentence of Mrs. Erlynne's speech. It is therefore much clearer to shift her two succeeding exclamations to her next speech.

ORIGINAL	REVISION
Mrs. Erlynne. (*C.*) How do you do, again, Lord Windermere? How charming your sweet wife looks! Quite a picture!	*Mrs. Erlynne.* (*C.*) How do you do, again, Lord Windermere?
Lord Windermere. (*In a low voice.*) It was terribly rash of you to come!	*Lord Windermere.* (*In a low voice.*) It was terribly rash of you to come!
Mrs. Erlynne. (*Smiling.*) The wisest thing I ever did in my life. And, by the way, you must pay me a good deal of attention this evening.[1]	*Mrs. Erlynne.* (*Smiling.*) The wisest thing I ever did in my life. How charming your sweet wife looks! Quite a picture! And by the way, you must pay me a good deal of attention this evening.

[1] *Plays of Oscar Wilde*, vol. 1, *Lady Windermere's Fan.* J. W. Luce & Co., Boston.

Often dialogue which is clear sentence by sentence is, as a whole, somewhat confusing to an audience. Frequently a careful re-ordering of the parts of the speech, or of a group of speeches, will dispose of the trouble. Occasionally a playwright allows his ordering of his ideas to obscure the cue, or important idea. Undoubtedly the important word in what follows is "christenings," but Chasuble runs on into various other matters before Jack speaks. Consequently a hearer is a little startled when Jack takes up the idea of christenings instead of anything following it.

Chasuble. In Paris! (*Shakes his head.*) I fear that hardly points to any very serious state of mind at the last. You would no doubt wish me to make some slight allusion to this tragic domestic affliction next Sunday. (*Jack presses his hand convulsively.*) My sermon on the meaning of the manna in the wilderness can be adapted to almost any occasion, joyful, or, as in the present case, distressing. (*All sigh.*) I have preached it at harvest celebrations, christenings, confirmations, on days of humiliation and festal days. The last time I delivered it was in the Cathedral, as a charity sermon on behalf of the Society for the Prevention of Discontent among the Upper Orders. The Bishop, who was present, was much struck by some of the analogies I drew.

Jack. Ah! That reminds me, you mentioned christenings I think, Dr. Chasuble? I suppose you know how to christen all right? (*Dr. Chasuble looks astounded.*) I mean, of course, you are continually christening, aren't you? [1]

It is true that the last part of Chasuble's speech illustrates his volubility, and that the way in which Jack picks up the idea, "christening," shows that he is so absorbed in his purpose as to pay no attention to anything Chasuble says after "christenings." Here, therefore, the method is probably justified, but ordinarily the end of one speech leads into the next, and when something which breaks the sequence stands between, it must prove its right to be there, or be postponed for later treatment, or be cut out altogether.

[1] *Idem,* vol. ii. *The Importance of Being Earnest.*

What re-ordering will do for a dialogue which is uninteresting and somewhat confused was shown in the revising of the extract from the John Brown play (pp. 309–313). There is a brilliant instance, in Miss Anglin's version of *Lady Windermere's Fan*, of re-ordering such that a climax of interest develops from groups of somewhat independent sentences.

ORIGINAL	REVISION
Lady Plymdale. My dear Margaret, what a fascinating woman your husband has been dancing with! I should be quite jealous if I were you! Is she a great friend of yours?	*Dumby.* Awful manners young Hopper has!
Lady Windermere. No.	*Cecil Graham.* Ah! Hopper is one of Nature's gentlemen, the worst type of gentleman I know.
Lady Plymdale. Really? Good night, dear.	*Lady Jedburgh.* What a fascinating woman Mrs. Erlynne is! She is coming to lunch on Thursday, won't you come too? I expect the Bishop and dear Lady Merton.
(*Looks at Mr. Dumby, and exit.*)	
Dumby. Awful manners young Hopper has!	*Lady Windermere.* I am afraid I am engaged, Lady Jedburgh.
Cecil Graham. Ah! Hopper is one of Nature's gentlemen, the worst type of gentleman I know.	*Lady Jedburgh.* So sorry. Good night. Come, dear.
Dumby. Sensible woman, Lady Windermere. Lots of wives would have objected to Mrs. Erlynne coming. But Lady Windermere has that uncommon thing called common sense.	(*Exeunt Lady Jedburgh and Miss Graham.*)
	Dumby. Sensible woman, Lady Windermere. Lots of wives would have objected to Mrs. Erlynne coming. But Lady Windermere has that uncommon thing called common sense.
Cecil Graham. And Windermere knows that nothing looks so like innocence as an indiscretion.	*Cecil Graham.* And Windermere knows that nothing looks so like innocence as an indiscretion.
Dumby. Yes; dear Windermere is becoming almost modern. Never thought he would	*Dumby.* Yes; dear Winder-

(*Bows to Lady Windermere and exit.*)

Lady Jedburgh. Good night, Lady Windermere. What a fascinating woman Mrs. Erlynne is! She is coming to lunch on Thursday. Won't you come too? I expect the Bishop and dear Lady Merton.

Lady Windermere. I am afraid I am engaged, Lady Jedburgh.

Lady Jedburgh. So sorry. Come. dear.

(*Exeunt Lady Jedburgh and Miss Graham.*)

Enter Mrs. Erlynne and Lord Windermere.

Mrs. Erlynne. Charming ball it has been! Quite reminds me of old days. (*Sits on the sofa.*)[1]

mere is becoming almost modern. Never thought he would.

Lady Plymdale. Dumby!

(*Dumby bows to Lady Windermere and exit.*)

Lady Plymdale. My dear Margaret, what a fascinating woman your husband has been dancing with! I should be quite jealous if I were you! Is she a great friend of yours?

Lady Windermere. No!

Lady Plymdale. Really? Good night, dear.

(*Lady Plymdale exits.*)

Enter Mrs. Erlynne and Lord Windermere.

Mrs. Erlynne. Charming ball it has been! Quite reminds me of old days. (*Sits on the sofa.*)

Dialogue may be both clear and characterizing yet fail because it is difficult to speak. Too many writers, as has been said, do not hear their words but see them. Could any one who heard his words have penned the lines, "She says she's sure she'll have a shock if she sees him." That time "apt alliteration" was so artful that, setting her trap, she caught a dramatist. Here is the amusing comment of a critic on an author's protest that her lines have been misquoted and made to sound difficult to deliver:

In the review of the ——— Theatre's opening bill there occurred a line purporting to come from Miss Blank's psychic play, *The Turtle.* Miss Blank writes, "The line, which was either incorrectly spoken or heard, was not, 'How does one know one is one's self?' but 'How is one to know which is one's real self when one feels so different with different people?'" Naturally the reviewer of a play is as open to mistakes in noting down lines as the actor is in speak-

[1] *Plays of Oscar Wilde*, vol. i. J. W. Luce & Co., Boston.

ing them, particularly if the author is much given to the "one-one-one" style of construction. If, however, Miss Blank prefers her own version of the sentence, she is welcome to it.

Of course each writer is perfectly sure that his own ear will keep him from errors of this kind, but even the greatest err. Did Shakespeare write the opening lines of *Measure For Measure*, he the master of exquisitely musical and perfectly chosen dramatic speech? Some scholars believe he did. If so, in that second speech of the Duke which wearies the jaws and tempts to every kind of slurring, Jove certainly nodded.

Enter Duke, Escalus, Lords and Attendants

Duke. Escalus!
Escalus. My lord.
Duke. Of government the properties to unfold,
Would seem in me to affect speech and discourse,
Since I am put to know that your own science
Exceeds, in that, the lists of all advice
My strength can give you: then no more remains,
But that, to your sufficiency . . .
. . . as your worth is able,
And let them work.

Are the following straight translations from the old French farce, *Pierre Patelin*,[1] as easy to speak as the revisions?

TRANSLATION	REVISION
Guillemette. And don't forget your dram, if you can come by it for nothing.	*Guillemette.* And if any one offers to stand treat, don't refuse.
. . . . .	. . . . .
(*Patelin is trying to cheat the Draper out of a piece of cloth.*)	(*Patelin is trying to cheat the Draper out of a piece of cloth.*)
Patelin. I don't care: give me my money's worth. (*Whis-*	*Patelin.* I don't care: give me my money's worth. (*Whisper-*

[1] Walter H. Baker Co., Boston.

pering in the Draper's ear.) I know of another coin or two that nobody ever got a smell of.

Draper. Now you're talking! That would be capital.

Patelin. In a word, I am hot for this piece, and have some I must.

ing in the Draper's ear.) I know of some chink —

Draper. Now you're talking!

Patelin. (*Letting his hand fall on the goods.*) This!

The first revision certainly gives lines easier to speak. The writer of the second revision hears it and knows the gesture, facial expression, and intonation which must go with "This!" Dialogue which is perfectly clear and characterizing should not be allowed to pass in the final revision if at any point it is unnecessarily difficult to deliver.

From the preceding discussion it must be clear that the three essentials of dialogue are clearness, helping the onward movement of the story, and doing all this in character. Dialogue is, naturally, still better if it possesses charm, grace, wit, irony, or beauty of its own. Dialogue which merely states the facts is, as we have seen, likely to be dull or commonplace. Well characterized dialogue still falls short of all dialogue may be if it has none of the attributes just mentioned. Feeling this strongly, the dramatists throughout the ages have striven to give their dialogue attractiveness because of its style, forgetting that above all for the dramatist it is true that "style is the man," and that "style is a thinking out into language." Lyly, Shakespeare, in some of the scenes of his early plays, Kyd in *The Spanish Tragedy*, John Dryden in his Heroic Drama, Cibber and Lillo in their rhythmic prose which often might be perfectly well printed as blank verse, strove to decorate their dialogue from without — something sure to fail, either with the immediate audience or with posterity. If the charm, the grace, the wit, the irony of the dialogue does not come from the characters speaking, that dialogue fails in what has been shown to be one of its chief essentials, right characterization. Congreve emphasized this in that classic of dramatic criticism, his letter *Concerning Humour in Comedy*.[1] "A character of a splenetic and peevish humour should have a satirical wit. A jolly and sanguine humour should have a facetious wit. The former should speak positively; the latter, carelessly: for the former observes and shows things as they are; the latter rather overlooks nature, and speaks things as he would have them; and his wit and humour have both of them a less alloy of judgment than the others." Undoubtedly, however, the dramatist may do much in helping a character to reveal these qualities, particularly beauty of thought or phrasing. It is a conventional use supposed to make for beauty which *The Rehearsal* ridicules in the following scene, for at nearly all crises the Heroic Drama rested on a simile for its strongest effect.

Prettyman. How strange a captive am I grown of late!
Shall I accuse my love or blame my fate?
My love I cannot; that is too divine:
And against fate what mortal dares repine?

Enter Chloris

But here she comes.
Sure 'tis some blazing comet! is it not?   (*Lies down.*)
   Bayes. Blazing comet! Mark that; egad, very fine.
   Prettyman. But I am so surpris'd with sleep, I cannot speak the rest.   (*Sleeps.*)
   Bayes. Does not that, now, surprise you, to fall asleep in the nick? His spirits exhale with the heat of his passion, and all that, and, swop, he falls asleep, as you see. Now, here she must make a simile.
   Smith. Where's the necessity of that, Mr. Bayes?
   Bayes. Because she's surprised. That's a general rule; you must ever make a simile when you're surprised; 'tis the new way of writing.

[1] *Dramatic Works*, vol. II, pp. 222-223. London, 1773.

Chloris. As some tall pine which we on Ætna find
T' have stood the rage of many a boist'rous wind,
Feeling without that flames within do play,
Which would consume his root and sap away;
He spreads his worsted arms unto the skies:
Silently grieves, all pale, repines, and dies:
So, shrouded up, your bright eye disappears.
Break forth, bright scorching sun, and dry my tears.　　(*Exit.*)
　　John. Mr. Bayes, methinks this simile wants a little application,
　　-too.
　　Bayes. No faith; for it alludes to passion, to consuming, to dying,
and all that, which, you know, are the natural effects of an amour.
　　　　　　　　　　　　　　　　　　　　(Act ii, sc. 3.) [1]

Why is it that the citation from Shakespeare in the left-hand column is less satisfactory than that in the right-hand?

York. To do that office of thine own good will
Which tired majesty did make thee offer,
The resignation of thy state and crown
To Henry Bolingbroke.
　　King Richard. Give me the crown. — Here cousin, seize the crown;
Here, cousin,
On this side my hand, and on that side thine.
Now is this golden crown like a deep well
That owes two buckets, filling one another,
The emptier ever dancing in the air,
The other down, unseen, and full of water.
That bucket down and full of tears am I,

Viola. If I did love you in my master's flame,
With such a suffering, such a deadly life,
In your denial I would find no sense,
I would not understand it.
　　Olivia. Why, what would you?
　　Viola. Make me a willow cabin at your gate,
And call upon my soul within the house;
Write loyal cantons of contemned love
And sing them loud even in the dead of night;
Halloo your name to the reverberate hills
And make the babbling gossip of the air
Cry out "Olivia!" O, you should not rest

---

[1] Geo. Villiers, Duke of Buckingham. *Selected Dramas of John Dryden, with The Rehearsal,* p. 399. G. R. Noyes, ed. Scott, Freeman & Co.

Drinking my griefs, whilst you
　　mount up on high.
　　Bolingbroke. I thought you
　　had been willing to resign.
　　King Richard. My crown I
　　am; but still my griefs are
　　mine.
You may my glories and my
　　state depose,
But not my griefs; still I am
　　king of those.[1]

Between the elements of air and
　　earth,
But should pity me!
　　Olivia. You might do much.[2]

The second extract is the more effective because the onward sweep of the emotion of the scene reveals beauty as it
moves, but the first shows King Richard checking the course
of his natural emotion in order suavely and perfectly to
develop his comparison. Of course there is beauty in the
first extract, but it is not genuine dramatic beauty. Why
does one find the following passage from *The Importance of
Being Earnest* (Act I), delightful as it is, less fine than the
passage from *The Way of the World* (Act II, Scene 5)?

THE IMPORTANCE OF BEING EARNEST

Lady Bracknell. (*Sitting down.*) You can take a seat, Mr. Worthing. 　　　　　(*Looks in her pocket for notebook and pencil.*)
Jack. Thank you, Lady Bracknell, I prefer standing.
Lady Bracknell. (*Pencil and notebook in hand.*) I feel bound to
tell you that you are not down on my list of eligible young men,
although I have the same list as the dear Duchess of Bolton has.
We work together, in fact. However, I am quite ready to enter
your name, should your answers be what a really affectionate
mother requires. Do you smoke?
Jack. Well, yes, I must admit I smoke.
Lady Bracknell. I am glad to hear it. A man should always have
an occupation of some kind. There are far too many idle men in
London as it is. How old are you?
Jack. Twenty-nine.

---

[1] *Richard the Second*, Act IV, Scene 1.　　　[2] *Twelfth Night*, Act I, Scene 5.

Lady Bracknell. A very good age to be married at. I have always been of opinion that a man who desires to get married should know either everything or nothing. Which do you know?

Jack. (*After some hesitation.*) I know nothing, Lady Bracknell.

Lady Bracknell. I am pleased to hear it. I do not approve of anything that tempers with natural ignorance. Ignorance is like a delicate exotic fruit; touch it and the bloom is gone. The whole theory of modern education is radically unsound. Fortunately in England, at any rate, education produces no effect whatsoever. If it did, it would prove a serious danger to the upper classes, and probably lead to acts of violence in Grosvenor Square. What is your income?

Jack. Between seven and eight thousand a year.

Lady Bracknell. (*Makes a note in her book.*) In land or investments?

Jack. In investments, chiefly.

Lady Bracknell. That is satisfactory. What between the duties expected of one during one's lifetime, and the duties exacted from one after one's death, land has ceased to be either a profit or a pleasure. It gives one position and prevents one from keeping it up. That's all that can be said about land.

Jack. I have a country house with some land, of course, attached to it, about fifteen hundred acres, I believe; but I don't depend on that for my income. In fact, as far as I can make out, the poachers are the only people who are making anything out of it.

Lady Bracknell. A country house! How many bedrooms? Well, that point can be cleared up afterwards. You have a town house, I hope? A girl with a simple unspoiled nature, like Gwendolen, could hardly be expected to reside in the country.

Jack. Well, I own a house in Belgrave Square, but it is let by the year to Lady Bloxham. Of course, I can get it back whenever I like, at six months' notice.

Lady Bracknell. Lady Bloxham? I don't know her.

Jack. Oh, she goes about very little. She is a lady considerably advanced in years.

Lady Bracknell. Ah, nowadays that is no guarantee of respectability of character. What number in Belgrave Square?

Jack. 149.

Lady Bracknell. (*Shaking her head.*) The unfashionable side. I thought there was something. However, that could easily be altered.

Jack. Do you mean the fashion or the side?

Lady Bracknell. (*Sternly.*) Both, if necessary, I presume. What are your politics?

Jack. Well, I'm afraid I really have none. I am a Liberal Unionist.

Lady Bracknell. Oh, they count as Tories. They dine with us. Or come in the evening, at any rate. Now to minor matters. Are your parents living?

Jack. I have lost both my parents.

Lady Bracknell. Both? — That seems like carelessness. Who was your father? He was evidently a man of some wealth. Was he born in what the Radical papers call the purple of commerce, or did he rise from the ranks of the aristocracy?

Jack. I'm afraid I really don't know. The fact is, Lady Bracknell, I said I had lost my parents. It would be nearer the truth to say that my parents seem to have lost me — I don't actually know who I am by birth. I was — well, I was found.

Lady Bracknell. Found!

Jack. The late Mr. Thomas Cardew, an old gentleman of a very charitable and kindly disposition, found me and gave me the name of Worthing, because he happened to have a first-class ticket for Worthing at the time. Worthing is a place in Sussex. It is a seaside resort.

Lady Bracknell. Where did the gentleman who had a first-class ticket for this seaside resort find you?

Jack. (*Gravely.*) In a hand-bag.

Lady Bracknell. A hand-bag!

Jack. (*Very seriously.*) Yes, Lady Bracknell. I was in a hand-bag — a somewhat large, black leather hand-bag, with handles to it — an ordinary hand-bag in fact.

Lady Bracknell. In what locality did this Mr. James, or Thomas, Cardew come across this ordinary hand-bag?

Jack. In the cloak-room at the Victoria Station. It was given to him in mistake for his own.

Lady Bracknell. The cloak-room at Victoria Station?

Jack. Yes, the Brighton line.

Lady Bracknell. The line is immaterial. Mr. Worthing, I confess I feel somewhat bewildered by what you have just told me. To be born, or at any rate, bred in a hand-bag, whether it had handles or not, seems to me to display a contempt for the ordinary decencies of family life that remind one of the worst excesses of the

French Revolution. And I presume you know what that unfortunate movement led to? As for the particular locality in which the hand-bag was found, a cloak-room at a railway station might serve to conceal a social indiscretion — has probably, indeed, been used for that purpose before now — but it could hardly be regarded as an assured basis for a recognized position in good society.

Jack. May I ask you then what you would advise me to do? I need hardly say I would do anything in the world to ensure Gwendolen's happiness.

Lady Bracknell. I would strongly advise you, Mr. Worthing, to try and acquire some relations as soon as possible, and to make a definite effort to produce at any rate one parent, of either sex, before the season is quite over.

Jack. Well, I don't see how I could possibly manage to do that. I can produce the hand-bag at any moment. It is in my dressing-room at home. I really think that should satisfy you, Lady Bracknell.

Lady Bracknell. Me, sir! What has it to do with me? You can hardly imagine that I and Lord Bracknell would dream of allowing our only daughter — a girl brought up with the utmost care — to marry into a cloak-room, and form an alliance with a parcel? Good morning, Mr. Worthing!

(*Lady Bracknell sweeps out in majestic indignation.*)[1]

THE WAY OF THE WORLD

Enter Mrs. Millamant, Witwoud, Mincing

Mirabell. Here she comes, i'faith, full sail, with her fan spread and streamers out, and a shoal of fools for tenders; ha, no, I cry her mercy.

Mrs. Fainall. I see but one poor empty sculler; and he tows her woman after him.

Mirabell. (*To Mrs. Millamant.*) You seem to be unattended, Madam — you us'd to have the beau monde throng after you; and a flock of gay fine perukes hovering round you.

Witwoud. Like moths about a candle, — I had like to have lost my comparison for want of breath.

Mrs. Millamant. Oh, I have denied myself airs today, I have walk'd as fast through the crowd —

---

[1] *Plays of Oscar Wilde*, vol. II. J. W. Luce & Co., Boston.

Witwoud. As a favourite just disgraced; and with as few followers.

Mrs. Millamant. Dear Mr. Witwoud, truce with your similitudes; for I am as sick of 'em —

Witwoud. As a physician of good air — I cannot help it, Madam, though 'tis against myself.

Mrs. Millamant. Yet again! Mincing, stand between me and his wit.

Witwoud. Do, Mrs. Mincing, like a screen before a great fire. I confess I do blaze today, I am too bright.

Mrs. Fainall. But, dear Millamant, why were you so long?

Mrs. Millamant. Long! Lord, have I not made violent haste? I have ask'd every living thing I met for you; I have enquir'd after you, as after a new fashion.

Witwoud. Madam, truce with your similitudes — no, you met her husband, and did not ask him for her.

Mrs. Millamant. By your leave, Witwoud, that were like enquiring after an old fashion, to ask a husband for his wife.

Witwoud. Hum, a hit, a hit, a palpable hit, I confess it.

Mrs. Fainall. You were dress'd before I came abroad.

Mrs. Millamant. Ay, that's true — O but then I had — Mincing, what had I? why was I so long?

Mincing. O mem, your La'ship staid to peruse a pacquet of letters.

Mrs. Millamant. O, ay, letters — I had letters — I am persecuted with letters — I hate letters — nobody knows how to write letters, and yet one has 'em one does not know why — they serve one to pin up one's hair.

Witwoud. Is that the way? Pray, Madam, do you pin up your hair with all your letters? I find I must keep copies.

Mrs. Millamant. Only with those in verse, Mr. Witwoud, I never pin up my hair with prose. I think I try'd once, Mincing.

Mincing. O mem, I shall never forget it.

Mrs. Millamant. Ay, poor Mincing tift and tift all the morning.

Mincing. 'Till I had the cramp in my fingers, I'll vow, mem. And all to no purpose. But when your Laship pins it up with poetry, it fits so pleasant the next day as anything, and is so pure and so crips.

Witwoud. Indeed, so crips.

Mincing. You're such a critic, Mr. Witwoud.

Mrs. Millamant. Mirabell, did you take exceptions last night?

O ay, and went away — now I think on't, I'm angry — no, now I think on't I'm pleas'd — for I believe I gave you some pain.

Mirabell. Does that please you?

Mrs. Millamant. Infinitely; I love to give pain.

Mirabell. You wou'd affect a cruelty which is not in your nature; your true vanity is in the power of pleasing.

Mrs. Millamant. O I ask your pardon for that — one's cruelty is in one's power; and when one parts with one's cruelty, one parts with one's power; and when one has parted with that, I fancy one's old and ugly.

Mirabell. Ay, ay, suffer your cruelty to ruin the object of your power, to destroy your lover — and then how vain, how lost a thing you'll be! nay, 'tis true: you are no longer handsome when you've lost your lover; your beauty dies upon the instant; for beauty is the lover's gift; 'tis he bestows your charms — your glass is all a cheat. The ugly and the old, whom the looking-glass mortifies, yet after commendation can be flatter'd by it, and discover beauties in it; for that reflects our praises rather than our face.

Mrs. Millamant. O the vanity of these men! Fainall, d'ye hear him? If they did not commend us, we were not handsome! now you must know they cou'd not commend one, if one was not handsome. Beauty the lover's gift — Lord, what is a lover, that it can give? Why, one makes lovers as fast as one pleases, and they live as long as one pleases, and they die as soon as one pleases; and then if one pleases, one makes more.

Witwoud. Very pretty. Why, you make no more of making of lovers, Madam, than of making so many card-matches.

Mrs. Millamant. One no more owes one's beauty to a lover than one's wit to an echo; they can but reflect what we look and say; vain empty things if we are silent or unseen, and want a being.

Mirabell. Yet to those two vain empty things you owe the two greatest pleasures of your life.

Mrs. Millamant. How so?

Mirabell. To your lover you owe the pleasure of hearing yourselves prais'd; and to an echo the pleasure of hearing yourselves talk.

Witwoud. But I know a lady that loves talking so incessantly, she won't give an echo fair play; she has that everlasting rotation of the tongue, that an echo must wait 'till she dies before it can catch her last words.

Mrs. Millamant. O fiction! Fainall, let us leave these men.[1]

[1] *Dramatic Works of William Congreve*, vol. II. pp. 114–117. S. Crowder, London, 1773.

Is not the dialogue of Congreve the finer because one feels in Wilde the ringmaster showing off his figures, and with Congreve is not conscious of the author at all? That is, the wit of the first passage is an assisted wit, edged, underscored, selectively phrased by a skilful author. In the second, everything springs seemingly unassisted from the characters. The range of accomplishment from obvious search for beauty in consciously made similes, through such relatively fine accomplishment as Wilde shows, to such perfect work as that of Congreve, should be carefully studied by the would-be dramatist. John Ford's wonderful lines

> Parthenophil is like to something I remember,
> A great while since, a long, long time ago

hold the memory not merely because of the loveliness of their haunting melody, but because they are in character and help to portray the wistful bewilderment of the moment. Why go far afield searching for the phrase that shall give charm, grace, beauty? Look into the souls of your characters and find them there. Either you haven't seen them or, not being there, they cannot properly appear in your text. Mr. W. B. Yeats tells of rehearsing a young actress who stumbled constantly over the line

And then I looked up and saw you coming toward me, I know not whether from the north, the south, the east or the west.

She gave it with no sense of its contained rhythm, and always came to a full stop after "toward me," adding the last words almost unwillingly. When asked why she did this, she said that all which followed seemed to her unnecessary: the important fact was contained in what preceded. It took much rehearsing to make the young woman see that the music of the line is characteristic of the dales people, and so has characterizing value, and that she had totally forgotten the situation of the woman speaking. A peddler has come to the only hut in a lonely valley. The woman welcomes him heartily, not that she may buy, but because after days in which she has seen no one except her "man," she is greedy for talk. Having bargained as long as she can, very regretfully she sees the man departing, and, other topics being exhausted, she tells him of her pleasure in his coming, spinning out her phrase as long as she possibly can in order to hold him. Out of that set of conditions springs a highly characterizing phrase that also has beauty. If Synge had done no more by his plays than to make us recognize in the speech of the peasant the characterizing power and the beauty for him who has "the eye to see and the ear to hear," his work would deserve permanent fame. He states his ideas in the preface to *The Playboy of the Western World*.

In writing *The Playboy of the Western World*, as in my other plays, I have used one or two words only that I have not heard among the country people of Ireland, or spoken in my own nursery before I could read the newspapers. A certain number of the phrases I employ I have heard also from herds and fishermen along the coast from Kerry to Mayo, or from beggar-women and ballad-singers near Dublin; and I am glad to acknowledge how much I owe to the folk-imagination of these fine people. Any one who has lived in real intimacy with the Irish peasantry will know that the wildest sayings and ideas in this play are tame indeed, compared with the fancies one may hear in any little hillside cabin in Geesala, or Carraroe, or Dingle Bay. All art is a collaboration; and there is little doubt that in the happy ages of literature, striking and beautiful phrases were as ready to the story-teller's or the playwright's hand as the rich cloaks and dresses of his time. It is probable that when the Elizabethan dramatist took his ink-horn and sat down to his work he used many phrases that he had just heard as he sat at dinner, from his mother or his children. In Ireland, those of us who know the people have the same privilege. When I was writing *The Shadow of the Glen*, some years ago, I got more aid than any learning could have given me from a chink in the floor of the old Wicklow house where I was staying, that let me hear what was being said by the servant girls in the kitchen. This matter, I think, is of importance for in countries where the imagination of the people, and the language they use, is rich and living, it is possible for a writer to be rich and copious in his words, and at the same time to give the reality, which is the root of all poetry, in a comprehensive and natural form. In the modern literature of towns, however, richness is found only in sonnets, or prose poems, or in one or two elaborate books that are far away from the profound and common interests of life. One has, on one side, Mallarmé and Huysmans producing this literature; and on the other Ibsen and Zola dealing with the reality of life in joyless and pallid words. On the stage one must have reality, and one must have joy; and that is why the intellectual modern drama has failed, and people have grown sick of the false joy of the musical comedy, that has been given them in place of the rich joy found only in what is superb and wild in reality. In a good play every speech should be as fully flavoured as a nut or apple, and such speeches cannot be written by any one who works among people who have shut their lips on poetry. In Ireland, for a few years more, we have a popular imagination that is fiery and magnificent, and tender; so that those of us who wish to write start with a chance that is not given to writers in places where the springtime of the local life has been forgotten, and the harvest is a memory only, and the straw has been turned into bricks.[1]

As Ibsen says, "Style must conform to the degree of ideality which pervades the representation."

You are of opinion that the drama ought to have been written in verse, and that it would have gained by this. Here I must differ from you. The play is, as you must have observed, conceived in the most realistic style; the illusion I wished to produce was that of reality. I wished to produce the impression on the reader that what he was reading was something that had really happened. If I had employed verse I should have counteracted my own intention and prevented the accomplishment of the task I had set myself. The many ordinary, insignificant characters whom I have intentionally introduced into the play would have become indistinct, and indistinguishable from one another, if I had allowed all of them to speak in one and the same rhythmical measure. We are no longer living in the days of Shakespeare. Speaking generally, the style must

[1] J. W. Luce & Co., Boston.

conform to the degree of ideality which pervades the representation. My new drama is no tragedy in the ancient acceptation; what I desired to depict were human beings, and therefore I would not let them talk "the language of the Gods." [1]

The dramatist who would write dialogue of the highest order should have not only an inborn and highly trained feeling for the emotional significance of the material in hand; a fine feeling for characterization; ability to write dialogue which states facts in character; and the power to bring out whatever charm, grace, irony, wit, or other specially attractive qualities his characters permit; also he should have, or develop, a strong feeling for the nicest use of language. Dumas fils said, "There should be something of the poet, the artist in words, in every dramatist."

[1] *The Letters of Henrik Ibsen*, p. 269. Letter to Edmund Gosse, January 15, 1874. Fox, Duffield & Co., New York.

CHAPTER IX

MAKING A SCENARIO

THERE is frequent and decided divergence of opinion among dramatists as to the value of a scenario, — the outline of a play which the dramatist purposes to write or has already written. Some dramatists very carefully prepare a detailed outline before they settle down to writing a play. Others, equally well-known on the stage assert: "I never think of mapping out in detail what I intend to write. When I begin, I may know only my central situation or little more than my main characters in broadest outline. I simply write and rewrite until the perfected manuscript lies before me." Another declares that although he has no scenario, he does use some notes. Showing these notes, — an accumulation of ideas as they have come to him from time to time, written anywhere on a single sheet without apparent order or form, — he asks triumphantly whether this can be called a scenario. Whatever the opinion of a dramatist as to the usual value to him of a scenario, he can hardly deny that there are times when it is very convenient to have a scenario of a play not yet completed. Plays sometimes have a curious, unexpected way of forcing themselves on the attention of a writer when his mind should be engrossed with another play. Ideas wholly irrelevant to the play in question keep surging into the dramatist's mind and drawing his attention from the subject in which he wishes to be interested. Often he can relieve his mind of this Banquo-like play, not by stopping to write it out in full, but by putting a careful outline of it on paper and storing this away until such time as he has opportunity to work out the play from this scenario.

Or it may be that a dramatist sees that plays he has submitted to some manager or actor are not attractive, but that some subject which as yet lies only half-formed in his mind finds, when mentioned, a ready response. Here is the best opportunity for use of a good scenario. Submit such to the actor or manager in question and even if a contract does not follow, the promise, "I will produce your play if it is as good as your scenario" is very likely to be made. Admitting then, for the moment, that some dramatists believe they can get on equally well without a scenario as a prerequisite for one of their plays, what are the main characteristics of a good scenario — this form of outline which some dramatists have found very useful in their work?

In the first place, the word "scenario" has been very carelessly used. It is often applied to as brief a set of notes as the following, intended by Ibsen merely to suggest to his correspondent in the broadest possible way the play which he thinks might be made from the poem which he has been discussing:

Have you not noticed that you have in the division of your poem entitled, *A Norwegian Sculptor*, the subject for a five-act popular play (Folkeskuespil)? Act 1. In the Mountains. The wood-carver. The art-enthusiast from the capital discovers him and takes him away with him. Act 2. In Christiania. The boy the hero of the day; great hopes; sent to Rome. Act. 3. In Rome. Life there among the artists and the Italian lower class. Act 4. Many years later. Return to Christiania; forgotten; everything changed. Act 5. At home again in the mountain parish; ruin. Write this with songs and dances and popular costumes and irony and devilry.[1] . . .

In the following from *Little Stories of New Plays* we have a far better summary than in the instance just cited, but surely even this is an outline and not a dramatic scenario, for intentionally it does not convey to a reader

---

[1] *Letters of Henrik Ibsen*, p. 325. For a similar outline see that on *Faste*, p. 151.

just that for which he would go to the theatre, the emotional treatment of the scenes — here given only in the merest outline.

GENERAL JOHN REGAN

By George A. Birmingham

Characters

Dr. Lucius O'Grady.	Constable Moriarity, R.I.C.
Timothy Doyle.	Tom Kerrigan, bandmaster.
Major Ken.	Rev. Father McCormack.
Thaddeus Golligher.	Lord Alfred Blakeney.
Horace P. Billing,	Mrs. de Courvy.
C. Gregg, district inspector.	Mrs. Gregg.
Sergeant Colgan, R.I.C.	Mary Ellen.

Into Ballymoy, a sleepy little town in the west of Ireland, comes Horace P. Billing, one gentle summer day, and spins in the market place a tale of a certain General John Regan, who, he said, these many years agone had been born and had sailed from Ballymoy to free the oppressed people of Bolivia, and who was the great national hero of that Republic from that time to the present day.

Comes there to listen to his tale one Doctor Lucius O'Grady, whose nose can no more keep out of other people's business than can his busy brain refrain from all manner of schemings or his tongue from uttering the grandest, gloriousest, whooping lies that the mouth of man e'er uttered.

To the American tourist he unreels anecdote and episode dealing with the romantic life of the great General while he had been yet a boy in Ballymoy. He sends Golligher, the editor of the Connaught Eagle, to show the American gentleman the birthplace of the General, a broken down cow-shed, in a nearby field.

The American leaves Ballymoy wildly excited and fermenting under the constant nagging of the doctor's busy self and never resting tongue, and promises that he will be back in a few days, and that in the meantime, should the citizens of Ballymoy have enough patriotism in them to erect a statue of their great townie in the market place, he would contribute a hundred pounds towards it.

This sets the Doctor at work with even more (if possible) vim. He gets Doyle to promise to contribute ten pounds, the parish priest (though it nearly breaks the good father's heart) ten also, Major Kent, the local landlord, another ten, and keeps the list himself — explaining that it is not necessary for him to put himself down for anything for that reason.

It develops that Doyle has a nephew in Dublin who is a mortuary sculptor, and has a statue of some deceased citizen on hand which was never paid for. This statue Doyle's nephew agrees to sell to Ballymoy for some eighty-odd pounds. The Doctor arranges to buy it, thus figuring that there will be a balance of twenty pounds out of the American's contribution to divide among themselves. This pleases Doyle, Father McCormack, and Golligher (who form the statue committee) very much; but unfortunately, it develops also that Doyle has neglected to get the money from the American for the statue before he left.

This does not stump the Doctor in the least, however. Among his plans for the unveiling of the statue is the appearance of Mary Ellen, the servant in Doyle's hotel, as a green fairy, and the appearance of the Lord Lieutenant of Ireland to make a speech. He suggests that when the Lord Lieutenant appears, they ask him for five hundred pounds for a pier — as the town already has but five or six piers — and that the money for the statue be taken out of that. The Major objects to this, but the Doctor's ability to explain does not desert him, and the Major is satisfied.

The great day of the unveiling finally arrives. The statue from the mortuary sculptor in Dublin is standing in the market place, with a veil over it. A letter comes from the Lord Lieutenant to the effect that he has never heard of General John Regan, can find no record of him in any history of any country on the globe, and, in the person of his aide de camp, Lord Al Blakeney, protests and accuses Ballymoy of having put a hoax over on him and all that sort of bally rot, by Jove.

The Doctor rises to the occasion beautifully. The aide de camp is made to make a speech as a representative of the Lord Lieutenant, and Mary Ellen unveils the statue, disclosing a hideous caricature of a grinning dead man in an ill-fitting business suit.

At that moment the American appears, explains grandly that there is no such man as General John Regan, and says that if the Doctor can prove to him that the General is not a fiction he himself will give the five hundred pounds for the pier — as, he says, "the show is worth it!"

The Doctor merely asks the American to prove to the satisfaction of the assembled townsfolk that the General does not exist.

Billing gives it up and writes out a check to the Doctor's order for five hundred pounds, while the Doctor poses grandly before the cheers of the assembled and admiring populace of Ballymoy.[1]

Here, too, is an outline which led to a very dramatic sermon. Obviously it is a satisfactory summary of the story underlying the sermon, but just what it would give a reader, if it were a perfect scenario, is lacking — namely, suggestion of the emotional treatment of the scenes which is to make them worth the manager's or actor's producing:

AT THE TOP OF THE TENEMENT

The arrangement of the platform will suggest the bare condition of the home in the first part of the sermon, and in the second part will show the improved condition a year later.

PART I

Dan Howard comes home discouraged. He cannot get work. Christmas is approaching. His wife keeps his courage up and that of the family. The Minister calls and is not received kindly by Dan Howard, who does not believe in the church. He promises to get Dan work and thus proves himself a true friend in need. Misfortune has come to the home. The oldest boy is drinking and the next son has been arrested for theft. Things looks very black. It is Christmas eve and the father compels the children to go to bed. He tells them Santa Claus will not come to-night. But they hang up their stockings by the fireplace.

PART II

A year later. Things have changed. The home is better. All are happy tonight. The father has had steady work and so they are to have a good Christmas this year. The boys are doing well. The family all go to church now and it has made a difference in them all. The children have gone to bed with joy tonight. Dan Howard tells his wife what a help she has been to him through thick and thin. While they stand talking they hear the carol singers from the church, singing outside their home. The Minister comes in and is made very welcome. While they exchange greetings the Christmas Carol is sung and the beautiful illuminated star shines out in the night.

[1] *The Green Book Magazine*, February, 1914.

The following may be full of dramatic suggestion for its writer, but if we mean by scenario a document which, when handed to a manager or actor, is to arouse his enthusiasm because it tells him interestingly just what a proposed play will do, this is not a scenario at all.

THE ETERNAL TRIANGLE: A NIGHTMARE

[Diagram of stage]

Dramatis Personæ

Sylvia Macshane, the actress.
Norman Pritchard, the manager.
Laddie Benton, the poet.
The Imp, sentinel at Ventilator X-10, Hell.

SCENE: *Room in a well-furnished apartment, New York City. Large round-topped window back right, matched by large semicircular mirror over fireplace back left. Mirror space later serves as Ventilator X-10.*

SCENARIO

I. Curtain rises on crimson sunset in room of apartment.
    Actress and Manager in jealous love scene.
    Enter the bone of contention — the Poet.
    Quarrel scene — Poet crushed.
    By accident Actress drinks Poet's suicide potion.
    Poet strangles Manager, Actress smashes chair on Poet.
    The lamp is knocked over.
    Black darkness accompanied by shrieks.
II. In red glow of semi-circular opening appear Imp and two mutes.
    Humorous talk of their job, guarding this ventilator of Hell.
    The Poet's face appears, followed by Manager's and Actress'.
    Both Heaven and Hell have refused them admission.
    Explanations by Imp — they are not truly dead.
    Renewed quarrels — Actress shows she loves neither one.
    She returns to earth.
    They pursue her.
    Imp is ordered to close ventilator.
    Black darkness again.

III. Moonlight in the apartment.

> *Actress, Poet, and Manager where they fell on the floor.*
> *They arouse — each believes the others ghosts.*
> *Explanations — light; — the men's quarrel renewed and dropped forever.*
> *Poet and Manager plan to make a play of the nightmare.*
> *Actress is wildly jealous of their new-found friendship.*
> *She cajoles each — then quarrels ferociously with each.*
> *They are proof against her and prepare to go.*
> *She demands a part in the play, gets it, and stamps off to her room.*
> *Poet and Manager depart cheerily planning.*

Obviously *General John Regan* is offered not as a scenario, but a summary. All the other so-called "scenarios" are planned only to suggest to the writer or somebody fully acquainted with the content of his mind on the subject what, in broadest terms, may be done with the material. They are all too broadly referential, too vague, to be of real use to a manager or actor looking for a play to produce.

What, then, is the work a real scenario should do? It must show clearly just what is the story, slight or complicated, which the play is to present. It must make the reader understand who the people of the play are, their relations to one another, and anything in their past or present history which he must know if the play at the outset or in its course is to produce upon him the effect desired by the writer. It must tell him where the play takes place — that is, what the settings are, and in such a way as to create atmosphere if anything more than a mere suggestion of background is desirable. It must let the reader see into how many acts the play will break up, and into what scenes if there be more than one setting to an act. Above all, it must make perfectly clear what is the nature of the play — comedy, tragedy, tragi-comedy, farce, or melodrama, and whether it merely tells a story, is a character study, a play of ideas, a problem play, or a fantasy. Proportioning and emphasis as already explained in chapters V and VI will, if rightly understood, bring out correctly in a scenario all these matters of form and purpose.

A good scenario begins with a list of the *dramatis personæ*, that is, a statement of the names and, broadly, the relations of the characters to one another. If the ages are important, they may be given. Without a list of *dramatis personæ* a reader must go far into the scenario before he can decide who the people are and what are their relations to one another. As the following scenario shows, he may easily guess wrong and is sure to be uncertain:

SCENARIO. *As the curtain rises Nat is seated at the right of centre table, planning an attack upon a fort of blocks with an army of wooden soldiers. A drum lies on the floor beside him. Enter Benny, a bag over his shoulder. They salute each other and throughout use frequent military terms in their talk. Benny has just returned from the village and he gives an account of his trip and his purchases. Mention is made of the probable war with Spain. Benny then surprises Nat with a letter from Harold, which proves to contain an announcement that war has been declared and that Harold has enlisted. The two are proud and delighted at the thought of their hero. They recall his former discontent on the farm, the day of his departure to seek his fortune in the city, his statement that he was "no soldier" — now so gloriously disproved. Harold enters in the midst of their preparations for dinner. He is gaunt and shabby and has a nervous hunted air. He receives their plaudits sullenly. He explains that he is away on a week's furlough and answers their questions concerning the regiment and his plans with nervous impatience. . . .*

In this next so-called scenario who is Professor Ward? What is his relation to Phronie? What is her age? What is the age of Keith Sanford and what are the relations of each of these to Professor Ward himself? A good list of *dramatis personæ* would clear all this at once.

THE EYES OF THE BLIND

ACT I

Professor Ward, roused at daybreak after a night at his desk, shows intense disappointment and nervous fatigue.

In brief scene with Phronie, he shows the essential part she plays in his life as one on whom he can absolutely depend; but when he expresses his disapproval of her admirer, Keith Sanford, she shows clear signs of rebellious spirit.

In rapid scene with Phronie and Keith, their spirit of youthful romance is made clear; and Keith indicates his college ambition, his predicament regarding his "cribbed" thesis, and his new attitude therein, ending with his evident resolve to make a clean breast of the matter. . . .

There follows a scenario which is somewhat clearer than the others because it identifies the figures, but it certainly leaves their relations rather confused.

An old white-haired man, the Sire de Maletroit, is seated in the chair to right of fireplace, in a listening attitude. The sound of a heavy door banging is heard and a minute later a young man, sword in hand, parts the curtains on left and stands blinking in the opening. He enters and explains that he has accidentally gained entrance to the house and is unable to re-open the door. His name is Denis de Beaulieu. He seems amazed to have the old man say that he has been waiting for him. Denis suggests that he must be going, at which the old man bursts into a fit of laughter. Denis is insulted and offers to hew the Maletroit's door to pieces. He is convinced that this is folly; the place is full of armed men. The old man rises, goes to door on right and calls upon his niece to leave her prayers and receive her lover. She comes in attended by a priest and protests that this is not the man. The uncle is incredulous and withdraws with a leer.

Again a good list of *dramatis personæ* would be helpful. Prefix to this the following:

THE SIRE DE MALETROIT'S DOOR

> Place: *Château Landon.*
> Time: *Fourteenth century.*

Dramatis Personæ

Blanche, *orphan niece of Sire de Maletroit.*
A Priest, *chaplain to Sire de Maletroit.*
The Sire de Maletroit.
Denis de Beaulieu, *a stranger.*

With this prefixed we can read the scenario just quoted far more comprehendingly.

Note how clearly the following two lists of *dramatis personæ* take us to the scenario proper:

THE LEGACY

The Persons

David Brice, *a young attorney.*
Reene Brice, *his uncle.*
Benjamin Doyle, *his fiancée's father.*
Dr. Wangren, *family physician.*
Mrs. Brice, *the mother.*
"Ditto" Brice, *the sister.*
Katherine Doyle, *fiancée.*

THE CAPTAIN: A MELODRAMA

Dramatis Personæ

Captain La Rue, *a little sea captain.*
Bromley Barnes, *former special investigator for the U.S. customs service.*
Patrick Clancy, *his friend.*
A burly Butler.
John Felspar, *junior partner of the firm of Felspar & Felspar, wine merchants.*
Two Dinner Guests, *members of the firm.*
Carl Cozzens, *the firm's Canadian representative.*

It is easy, however, to let this list of characters go too far descriptively. For instance, this next list tells much which might better appear first in the body of the scenario. The danger here is one already mentioned in this book, namely, that such careful characterizing in the *dramatis personæ* or program is likely to make the characterization of the scenario or play inadequate.[1]

AN ENCORE

Adapted from the story by Margaret Deland

In Two Acts

Time: About 1830 in June.
Place: Little town of Old Chester.
Between the first and second acts three weeks elapse.

Dramatis Personæ

Captain Price: Retired sea-captain, big, bluff, and hearty, with white hair and big white mustachios, rather untidy as to dress. Age, about 68.

Cyrus Price: His son, weak and neat-looking, very thin and of sandy complexion. Age, about 35.

Mrs. North: Sprightly, pretty, white-haired little lady of about 65. Always in black silk.

Miss North: Her daughter, nervous and shy, but truthful with a mania for taking care of her mother and no knowledge of how to wear her clothes; about 40.

Mrs. Gussie Price: A stout, colorless blond, a weeping, vividly gowned lady, who rules her husband, Cyrus, through her tears. Age, about 30.

Flora: A colored maid.

The danger is shown to the utmost in the following. The characterization in the scenario to which this was prefixed was practically *nil*.

Forsythe Savile: A young lawyer of about thirty, clever, and rather versatile. While of great promise in his profession, he is not at all

See pp. 276–278.

pedantic, but has many interests. He is well-read, widely travelled, fond of outdoor sports, and is very popular. Perhaps his most prominent characteristic is his ready wit. He is rarely non-plussed, and while quick and pointed in his remarks, is yet not ill-natured with them. He has been Dennings' most intimate friend ever since they were in college together, although their lives lie along very divergent lines.

Richard Dennings: A globe trotter, as a hunter, explorer, and war-correspondent. He is clever and able, with a tendency to act on impulse rather than after deliberation. He is the closest kind of friend to Forsythe. He has been engaged to Frances Langdon, but the engagement has been broken off. This last fact is not known to any save the two themselves.

Judge Savile: A widower, and Forsythe's father. He has been a very successful man, and holds a high place in his profession. He is devoted to books, and cannot understand his son's taste for out-of-door life, and athletics in general. He philosophically accepts the inevitable, however, and is very proud of Forsythe. The Judge does not approve of the engagement of Frances Langdon to Dennings; he cannot understand Dennings' uncertain methods of life. The Judge while saying very little of his opinion foresees that matters are very far from being finally settled, and is quietly awaiting developments.

Margaret Savile: Forsythe's younger sister, and a feminine edition of him. She is very pretty, bright, and attractive. She and Forsythe are most intimate, more so than brother and sister usually are.

Frances Langdon: An intimate friend of Margaret, and familiarly known as "Frank." She is essentially feminine, attractive, witty and talented. She is very nervous and high-strung — a strong character, but susceptible to her feelings. She has known the Saviles since she was a child and is considered exactly as a relative. She has broken her engagement to Richard Dennings.

A butler: The usual English type.

That list tells so much about the characters that the scenario proper could do little but repeat. The writer, troubled by his sense of repetition, rested for his characterization on the slight chance that a reader would remember every detail of the *dramatis personæ*. All that a reader needs to know at the outset of a scenario is who the characters are, and, in the broadest way, their relations to one another.

A list of *dramatis personæ* should be followed with a statement of the time and place if they are important, and of the settings for all the acts. A detailed description of each new setting should precede its scene or act.[1] In the scenarios already quoted notice how difficult it is to place the characters as far as setting is concerned and how much would be gained if a good description of the setting were added. Keep the description of a setting to essentials, that is, furniture and decorations necessary to give requisite atmosphere or required in the action of the piece. As always in scenarios and acting editions use "left" and "right" as "left" and "right" of the actor, not of the audience.

THE SIRE DE MALETROIT'S DOOR (*See p.* 428)

SCENE: *A large room in the house of the Sire de Maletroit; large fireplace at centre back; curtained door on left leads to stairway; curtained door right leads to chapel. The room is well illuminated by candles, reflecting the polish of stone walls. It is scantily furnished.*

THE LEGACY (*See p.* 464)

THE SCENE: *The Brice living-room comfortably furnished in walnut. A piano centre L., a round table, rear R. Four entrances: upper L., rear centre, upper right, right centre. Curtained windows rear R. & L.*

As has already been pointed out earlier in this book, it is wholly unwise to call, in a description of a setting, for details not really necessary. Here is the setting for the *dramatis personæ* quoted on p. 431. It is over-elaborate because the action of the proposed play involves use of hardly any of the properties called for.

SCENE: *Forsythe Savile's "den." It is an odd room, a curious mixture of library, smoking-room, and museum. On the right is a large fireplace, over which are hung an elk's head, a couple of rifles,*

1 See Kismet Scenario, pp. 474–507.

*queer-looking Eastern weapons, and other sporting trophies and evi-
dences of travel. The room is panelled in dark oak; low bookcases
line the walls, and on top of the cases are small bronzes, photographs,
strange bits of bric-à-brac, and a medley of things, — such truck as a
man with cultivated tastes would insist on accumulating. There are
numerous pictures, a rather heterogeneous lot; valuable engravings, —
portraits of famous lights of the bench and the bar, to judge by their
wigs, — a few oils of the Meissonier type; and others which are obviously relics of college, with medals slung across them by brightly coloured ribbons. The furniture of the room is of heavy oak, upholstered
in dull crimson leather. Capacious club armchairs are in convenient
places, near lamps and books. Around the hearth is a high English
fender, and before it is a great Davenport sofa. On the left, is a broad-
topped table-desk, covered with papers and books, and bearing a squat
bronze lamp with a crimson shade. At one end of the Davenport is a
low cabinet, on which are glasses and decanters. There is a wide doorway at the back of the stage which gives the only entrance and is hung
with heavy crimson portières. The centre of the floor is filled by a huge
polar bear-skin rug, with massive head and the odd spaces are covered
by smaller fur rugs. The stage is dark, save for the uncertain, wavering
light cast by the wood fire.*

Time: The present, and about half-past eight on a winter evening.

A sketch of the desired arrangement of the stage should
be prefixed to the description of the setting. This may be
as simple as comports with clear picturing of the exact conditions required. Such drawings not only help to clearness,
they sometimes bring out difficulties in a proposed setting
not at once evident in a description. Perhaps the staging
called for in what immediately follows may not seem over-
elaborate in the reading. A diagram at once shows its awk-
wardness, expensiveness, and undesirability.

THE SIRE DE MALETROIT'S DOOR

*The scene represents a mediæval outer hall of a powerful nobleman
of Paris with the approach thereto, the streets adjacent and several
other buildings thereon, at 11.30 P.M., the streets in semi-darkness.
This hall runs clear down the stage to within the width of a narrow*

street of the footlights. This street is supposed to run clear across the stage. The approach to the hall from without is through two doors left which open into a gloomy passageway large enough to contain a dozen soldiers. The door to the left of these two entrances opens inward from the street running up left at right angles to the street by the footlights, leaving room enough at the extreme left for several doorways which should be set into the houses so as to form a place sufficient to hide a man who was being searched for on the sidewalk. At the extreme rear of the street going up the stage is stone pavement. The walls of the palace are of thick stones and the furnishings of the hall are plain and gloomy consisting of chairs and a table, a tall clock with a loud tick, curtains at the doors; and over the fireplace, which is huge, hang a shield and helmet, the former emblazoned with the device of the family, the latter beplumed, while under them are two long swords, crossed, with their points hidden behind the shield, these blades both in their scabbards. The floors are all of stone.

At the right of the fireplace are two wide doors which when opened give a full view of the chapel beyond, with the altar to the rear in the centre. The chapel need show no more than a private altar, the accompanying candles, drapery, and steps, lighted with a single hanging lamp of the period that swings before the first step of the altar.

The chairs and table in the hall are of mission style. The doors opening on the street from all of the establishments are very wide, embossed in iron bands and supplied with knockers, heavy bolts and bars on the inside wherever the inside is exposed. There is a large fire in the fireplace. A lamp of the period is swung with heavy chains over the table.

The diagram on the next page shows how this would look.

It is in many ways a bad setting. Waiving all question whether any attempt to suggest the fourth wall of a room, as in *The Passing of the Third Floor Back* by the fireplace at centre front of stage is wise, surely there can be no doubt that to ask an audience to imagine a street between them and the room into which they are looking, particularly when no necessary action takes place in that street, is undesirable. Therefore the suggested "street" across the front of the stage may go. Where is the value of the street

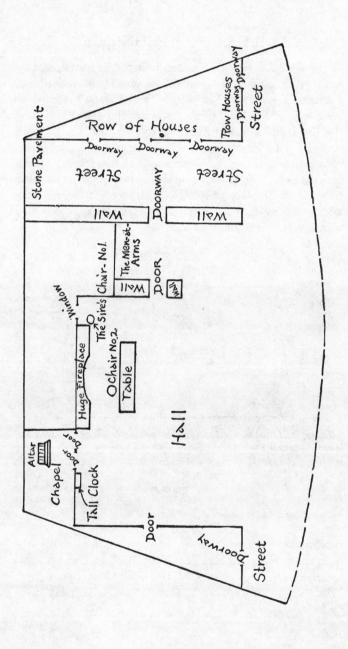

at the side? Little, if any, action in it will be seen except by
the very small part of the audience directly in line with it.
For these the settings below the doors at stage left must be
decidedly pushed back or they will lose important action by
the fireplace. It is questionable, too, whether the fireplace
should not be moved down stage to one side or the other,
so important is the facial expression of the Sire de Maletroit as he sits by it. For effective action, it is better, also,
to separate fireplace and chapel entrance. It is both easy
and for acting purposes better, to stage this proposed play
with a setting as simple as this:

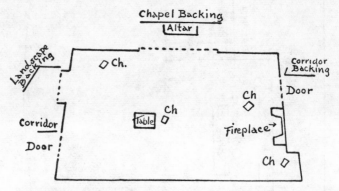

*Gothic stone interior: Doors, centre leading to Chapel or Oratory;
lower right and up left. All doors with old tapestry curtains. Deep
mullioned window up right with landscape backing. Large Gothic
fireplace, with hooded chimney, left. Corridor backings for all doors.
Large armchair left centre in front of fireplace; large oak table right
centre, with chairs on either side; other furniture of period to dress
stage. Altar and furnishings for Chapel.*

Nowadays descriptions of settings are noticeably free
from the mystic R.U.E., L. 2 E., D.L.C., etc., which characterized stage directions of the early Victorian period.
When wings and flats, as in some wood-scenes today, were

used for indoor as well as outdoor scenes — that is, before the coming of the box-set — the stage was divided in this way:

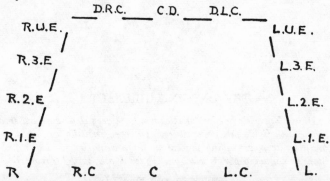

Now that the box-set has replaced the older fashion and new devices are steadily improving on the old wood-wings, it is enough to indicate clearly in the diagram and in the description what doors, windows, fireplaces, and properties are necessary, and exactly where, if their positions are essential in the action. If not, they may be placed to suit the sense of proportion of the designer of the scenery and the sense of fitness of the producer. In any case, rarely today does an author need to use all or many of these stage divisions of an older day. The first of the following diagrams shows how simply an interior set which makes no special demands may be indicated.

THE DANCING GIRL. ACT I [1]

Diana Valrose's boudoir at Richmond. A very elegantly furnished room, with light, pretty furniture. Discover Drusilla in handsome morning dress arranging flowers in large china bowl. Enter footman, announcing Mr. Christison. Enter John. Exit Footman.

[1] Samuel French, publisher, New York.

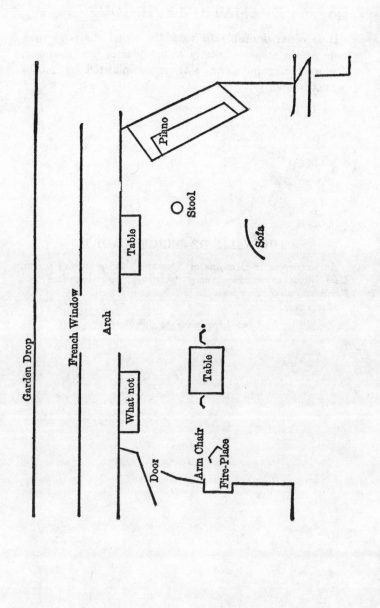

It is often desirable to vary the usual shape given a room on the stage — exactly rectangular or nearly square. The next diagram shows a more complicated setting, of unusual shape.

THE WALLS OF JERICHO. ACT I [1]

An ante-room in Marquis of Steventon's house during a ball. Miss Wyatt, a vivacious young American, has cake-walked with Twelvetrees all the way from the ball-room.
Music under stage.

[1] Samuel French, publisher, New York.

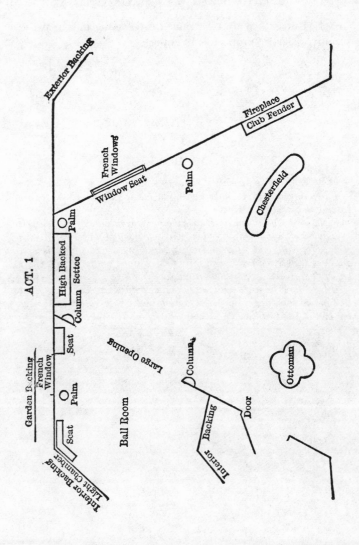

ACT. 1

Act II of *Young America* calls for a setting in which the placing of heavy properties is important.

YOUNG AMERICA. ACT II[1]

SCENE. *The Juvenile Court, 10* A.M. — *Two days later.*

Two entrances, R. U. door leading to Judge's chamber. L. 2 door leading to corridor.

Right — Judge's bench. It extends up and down stage. Below it Clerk's bench upon which are two card catalogue filing cases for court records for children. At L. of Judge's bench small docket for prisoner. At L. of docket, witness stand. It is an 18-inch platform with chair on it. The docket and witness stand face front.

Left — three benches for spectators and witnesses. They face front and are enclosed within a picket railing. Gate with spring lock, near left end of front railing.

---

[1] Samuel French, publisher, New York.

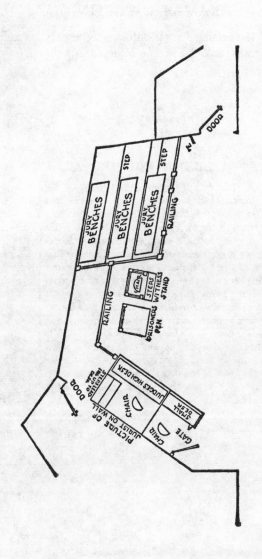

How the setting for an outdoor scene may be indicated the diagram for Act I of *The Dancing Girl* shows.

THE DANCING GIRL. ACT I [1]

SCENE. *The Island of Saint Endellion, off the Cornish Coast. At the back is a line of low rocks, and beyond, the sea. A pathway leads through the rocks down to the sea. On the right side of the stage is the Quakers' meeting-house, a plain square granite building, showing a door and two windows. The meeting-house is built on a low insular rock that rises some three or four feet above the stage; it is approached by pathways, leading up from the stage. On the left side of the stage, down towards the audience, is David Ives's house; another plain granite building, with a door down stage, and above the door, a window. The house is built into a cliff that rises above it. Beyond the house is a pathway that leads up the cliff and disappears amongst the rocks on the left side towards the centre of the stage; a little to the right is a piece of rock rising about two feet from the stage.*

I. Call.
John Christison.
Faith Ives.
David Ives.
Drusilla Ives.

Time, An Autumn evening.

[1] Samuel French, publisher, New York.

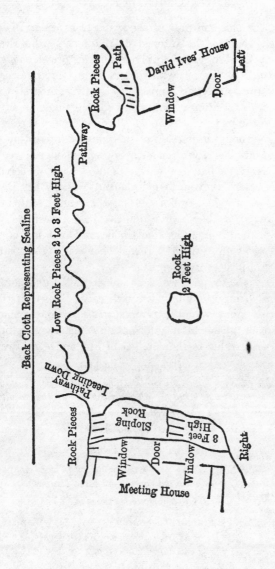

Back Cloth Representing Sealine

Low Rock Pieces 2 to 3 Feet High

Pathway

Rock Pieces

Path

David Ives' House

Window

Door

Left

Rock
2 Feet High

Pathway Leading Down

Rock Pieces

Sloping
Rock

Window

Door

Window

3 Feet High

Right

Meeting House

As the chief purpose of the writer of a scenario is immediately to grip the interest of the reader, this dramatic outline must obviously provide any historical background necessary to sympathetic understanding of the story. In other words, a scenario must very briefly summarize the preliminary exposition about which so much has already been said in the body of this book.[1] The opening of the scenario, already quoted in part on p. 428, may be interesting, but it is also puzzling, for a reader is not told enough in regard to the past of the figures involved to know how to receive what information is given. Much depends on whether Denis de Beaulieu is lying or not. Make the reader somehow understand that Denis and Blanche have never met before and that although the uncle believes Denis is her lover, he is completely in the wrong. Then comedy immediately emerges, interest increases.

Here is a scenario which remained vague and confusing, till just before the final curtain, because the writer thought surprise more valuable than suspense. Consequently he held back the one bit of information which gives significance and comic value to the conduct of Mr. and Mrs. Brede.

[Diagram of setting]

SCENE. *The piazza of a mountain boarding-house. R, practicable door. L, practicable window. C, practicable step. On the piazza are a number of chairs. The bit of lawn in front is not too well kept.*

Characters

Mr. Jones }
Mrs. Jones } *ordinary, well-educated people.*
Major Halkit, retired business man, interested in stock companies.
Mrs. Halkit, his wife, an old gossip, prim and censorious.
Mr. Brede }
Mrs. Brede } *young, handsome, "nice."*
Jacobus, Yankee boarding-house keeper.

Brede and Jones come from the house and discuss the view from the piazza. Brede is enthusiastic and compares it with that from the

---

[1] See pp. 154–182.

Matterhorn. Mrs. Brede and Mrs. Jones come from the house in time to hear "Matterhorn" and Mrs. Brede expresses surprise that her husband has climbed it. Mr. Brede, confused, says it was five years ago, and Mrs. Brede gently chides him for doing such a thing during the first year of their marriage. Mr. Jones and Mrs. Brede talk aside while Mr. Brede explains to Mrs. Jones that he had left his wife in New York some months after their marriage for a hasty trip to Europe and had climbed the Matterhorn then.

Mr. and Mrs. Brede go down the side steps and off at R.C. for a stroll. Mr. and Mrs. Jones discuss them, and decide that they are very "nice" people. During their talk it develops that while Mr. Brede had been telling Mr. Jones that Mrs. Brede had been in this country when he climbed the Matterhorn, Mrs. Brede had informed Mrs. Jones that her husband had left her at Geneva and afterwards taken her to Basle, where their first child was born.

At this point Mrs. Halkit comes from the house. She censures Mrs. Brede for not knowing how to care for her husband and children and it comes out that Mrs. Brede has told Mrs. Halkit that they have two children who have been left with her aunt, whereas Mr. Brede has told Mr. Jones that they have three children at present under the care of his mother-in-law.

Enter Major Halkit from the house. He criticizes Mr. Brede, who purports to be looking for a business opening, for his failure to take a fine chance the Major has pointed out to him.

The party come to the conclusion that there is something queer about the couple and are about to call Jacobus when he appears, coming from the left. Before any of the boarders have a chance to speak, Jacobus asks some question about the numbering of streets in New York and the fact is brought out that Mr. Brede told Mrs. Jacobus, when he was engaging the room, that he lived at number thirty-four of his street, and that the day before Mrs. Brede had informed Mrs. Jacobus that their number was thirty-five. . . .

A reader struggling through the paragraphs of this scenario finds very little that is dramatic because the dramatic values the writer feels in his sentences cannot be the reader's till he learns that Mr. and Mrs. Brede are a newly married couple who wish to conceal the fact. Re-read the quotation with that in mind and all confusion disappears.

On the other hand, it is not always easy to convey needed

preliminary exposition interestingly. When much is needed, there is always danger that the opening of the scenario will be talky and referential rather than definite and full of dramatic action. The following is by no means as bad an example as might be found of a slow opening caused by need for much historical exposition, but it certainly lacks gripping action:

SCENARIO OF CONISTON

When the curtain is raised, Millicent Skinner is working about; a second later Chester Perkins comes slinking in, looking back as though pursued by the Evil One, and close on his heels, another local politician, Mr. Dodd, of the Brampton prudential school committee, enters with the same stealthy and harassed air. Millicent twits them with having run away from Bijah Bixby who is at Jonah Winch's store. They deny that they are afraid of Bije or any one. It is brought out in a sentence or two that Jethro Bass, Cynthia and Ephraim Prescott are away on their Washington trip, and that Bijah, knowing of Jethro's absence, is not likely to come here, which is why the two men have chosen the yard for a refuge; as they have been planning petty treason against the political control of the town by Jethro Bass. Millicent laughs at them and goes in the house. Mr. Dodd and Chester recover their swagger and begin to discuss Bijah and his sneaking ways. Bob Worthington enters, goes to the porch and calls Millicent. She responds from a nearby window. He enquires when she expects Cynthia to return. She tells him they will be here today. Bob announces that he will return, a little later, and goes out. Chester and Dodd discuss Bob's attention to Cynthia and how furious the elder Worthington will be if his son marries the ward of Jethro Bass. Then they drift back to their first topic and are soon absorbed in their wordy revolt against Jethro Bass and Bijah.

Chester. This town's tired of puttin' up with a king!
> (*Behind them Bijah enters silently and stands at their elbows unperceived.*)

Bijah. Leetle early for campaignin', Chester, leetle early.
> (*The other two stand aghast.*)

The scene which follows between the three men gives their characters, the Coniston political atmosphere, Jethro's position as boss of the State

*and his character, the cumulating antagonism between Jethro Bass and
Isaac Worthington, the relation between Jethro and Cynthia, his ward.
Bijah confides to the two that a new era is dawning; that "the railroads,
represented by Worthington, Sr., are tired of paying tribute" to
Jethro and are about to turn and exterminate him. Bixby says that
Jethro's power is gone, that a greater than he has risen, that Isaac
Worthington's campaign, brought forth under cover of a great reform
movement, will sweep the State in the next few months and leave Jethro
politically dead. Bijah brings out a copy of the last issue of the New-
castle Guardian (leading newspaper of the State), and reads them
"The scathing arraignment of Jethro Bass . . . showing how he had
debauched his own town of Coniston; how, enlarging on the same
methods, he had gradually extended his grip over the county and finally
over the State; how he had bought and sold men for his own power
and profit, deceived those who had trusted him, corrupted governors and
legislators . . . how he had trafficked ruthlessly in the enterprises of
the people." Bijah tells them that the whole State is in a stir over this
article, that it is the open declaration of war against Jethro.*

*Here Alva Hopkins and his daughter Cassandra enter. Hopkins has
read the article and come post-haste to see Jethro. He and Bijah discuss the situation and Bijah tells them that the postmastership which
Jethro has promised to Ephraim Prescott (and which it is surmised
they have gone to Washington to secure) is to go to Dave Wheelock;
that that will be the first tangible sign to the public of the fall of Jethro
Bass. . . .*

The cardinal principle in scenario writing, as in the play
itself, is that not talk but action is basal. In a scenario,
however, action is described rather than represented. As
we have just seen, the lengthy historical account of what lies
behind the opening scene is hard to convey without talki-
ness. Many would-be dramatists dodge this difficulty, indeed the whole task of making clear the emotional significance of the action which the play involves, by writing
scenarios which are little more than schedules of the entrances and exits of their characters. There was something
of this in the "Coniston" scenario. The difficulty is still
more marked in the following:

THE SIRE DE MALETROIT'S DOOR

SCENE: *The Maletroit Entrance-Hall*

[Diagram of Setting]

Characters

A Priest.
The Sire de Maletroit.
Blanche de Maletroit, his niece.
Denis de Beaulieu.
Retainer.

Discovered, Retainer finishing work on the door, C. Enter Priest, L.U.E. Slight exposition suggesting that a trap is being set for a girl's gallant. Exit Priest. Enter R.U.E. the Sire. Commends the workman's results, increasing the suspense regarding purpose. Rope outside window R, examined without explanation. Retainer, questioned as to news in the town, remarks the presence of a dare-devil young French soldier under safe-conduct who is likely to get into trouble with the troops quartered in town, unless he keeps a civil tongue in his head. Retainer dismissed R, with suggestion that he understands what is expected of him.

The Sire calls Priest, questions him regarding Blanche, furthering the exposition.

Blanche enters, dressed as bride, and bursts forth in troubled questions as to the meaning of her uncle's orders regarding her appearance at this hour in such costume. The cause is hinted at as an intrigue, and Blanche is ordered to retire and wait in the chapel.

The Sire indicates that the hour is approaching for the "arrival" and the lights are extinguished.

As has been pointed out already,[1] entrances and exits are of the slightest possible consequence except when they count in characterization or dramatic action. It is what takes place for the characters between an entrance and exit which a scenario must bring out as briefly yet clearly as possible.

This fault of over-emphasizing entrances and exits is closely related to the "referential" treatment of possible

[1] See p. 287.

dramatic material. The method for this is: "Mr. and Mrs. Brown enter and talk passionately about their future." "Anne and Sarah now have a tempestuous scene in which Anne discloses to the full her agony." Such scenario writing is all too easy, for the value of the scenario, like the value of the play, will depend upon the ability of the author to make the first scene passionate and the second tempestuous and agonizing. A scenario which constantly states that at a given point something of interest will be done or a very powerful scene dealing with the emotions of one or more of the characters will be written is both useless and exasperating. Nobody wants to buy such a dramatic "pig in a poke." Compare a referential scenario, the first of the three which follow, with the other two. They may, as parts of scenarios, have faults, but at least they move, not by references to "sarcasm, a horror that transfixes, violent threats," etc., but by definitely roused emotional interest.

THE SIRE DE MALETROIT'S DOOR

[Diagram of Setting]

SCENE. *A baronial apartment in heavy polished stone. At the back a large doorway hung with rich tapestry leads to a small chapel. At the right are two doors also with tapestry. In the left back corner is a huge fireplace carved with the arms of the Maletroits. At the left is a large open window looking over the parapets of the castle. A heavy table and a chair or two are all the furnishings.*

Place: Château Landon.
Time: Fourteenth Century.

Dramatis Personæ

Blanche, orphan niece of Sire de Maletroit.
A Priest, chaplain to Sire de Maletroit.
Sire de Maletroit.
Denis de Beaulieu, a stranger.

As the curtain rises Blanche is seen in the chapel kneeling as the priest is finishing the chanting of the vesper service. At the close she rises and walks toward the window, glancing hastily about to see that no one is in the room. As soon as the priest has left she draws from her breast a letter which she starts to read. She is soon interrupted by the entrance of her uncle the Sire de Maletroit, whose keen glance detects her hasty crumpling of the note which she has not had time to conceal. He greets her jovially and starts to walk hand in hand with her. Forcing open her hand, he finds the note, which he reads in a bitterly sarcastic tone, while Blanche stands transfixed with horror. It is a note asking her to leave the house door open at midnight so that the writer may enter and exchange words with her on the stairs. With cold sarcasm, ill concealing his rage, the Sire forces from her the story that a young captain has met her in church and given her the note. She denies that she knows his name, and the most violent threats will not induce her to tell it. She is then sent to her room to dress in sackcloth of repentance and told to prepare to spend the night in the chapel.

THE SIRE DE MALETROIT'S DOOR

Persons represented

The Sire de Maletroit.
Blanche de Maletroit, his niece.
Denis de Beaulieu, a young soldier.
A Priest.

SCENE. *Large apartment of stone. On each of the three sides of the room, three doors curtained with tapestry. On left, beside the door a window. Stone chimney-piece, carved with arms of the Maletroits. Furniture, mainly consisting of table, and heavy chair beside chimney.*

Place: Château Landon, France.
Time: September, 1429.

Curtain rises showing an old gentleman in a fur tipped coat seated in the heavy chair. The old man is mumbling to himself a sort of strange murmur, smiling and nodding, as he sips a cup of wine. The room is silent save for the muttering of the old man.

Suddenly, from the direction of the arras covering the door to left, a muffled sound begins to obtrude itself. This sound, at first vague, then waxing more and more distinct, resolves itself into steps cautiously mounting a flight of stairs. The steps, gradually less vague, finally firm and assertive, reach the tapestried doorway. The click of metal, probably that of a sword, accompanying the steps, echoes in the hush of the room.

The arras parts, and a young man blinking from dark into sudden light, stumbles into the room. (As the tapestry closes behind the youth, a dark passageway and shadowy flight of stairs beyond are visible.)

Another pause ensues, during which the young man and the old man continue to gaze at one another.

"Pray step in," begins the old man; "I have been expecting you all the evening."

The youth shivers slightly, hesitating for speech. Finally he manages to answer. . . .

MISTRESS BEATRICE COPE
ACT III. SCENE 1

Next day, White Oaks. Late twilight. Night falls during early part of scene. Later, moonlight. The great dining hall. It opens at the back on a terrace with a large door at centre. Dame Pettigrew, Joyce and Eliza discovered in a flutter over the news of the war. Scotch raids are threatened from over the border. There are terrible tales of the lootings by the King's soldiers of places suspected of Jacobitry. Dame Pettigrew, as she hears now this story, now that, is first Whig and then Jacobite, until she bewilders herself and the maids. They play on one another's nerves until they are in sore fright. Pettigrew begins to collect her goods against leaving on the morrow, regretting that she has sent for Beatrice to stay with her, who is momentarily expected. At height of nervous strain, when all windows have been closed, all lights but the fire are out, and the women sit cowering and silent, the mournful shrilling of bagpipes and the heavy tread of feet coming nearer and nearer are heard. Joyce gasps about ghosts. Chilled with terror, no one dares go to the window. The procession reaches the end of the lane and passes. Sudden sharp rapping at door. Frightened parley with spirits, as maids think. Beatrice forces them to open, and appears. The pipes are the funeral train of a Jacobite killed on the neighboring border and now on the way to Goodrest for a final mass. Beatrice is excited and anxious but brings order out of chaos in the room. Turns up lights, gets rid of Dame Pettigrew, and one maid, and sends other maid for supper. Bids Joyce, should Bill Lampeter appear, send him to her at once. She has a message for Crowe Hall. When Joyce has departed wonderingly, it appears that all day Beatrice has been trying to warn Cope at Goodrest that they were watched the day before, but has been unable till as she rode over with Jessie she met Bill Lampe-

ter on the road. Dropping behind, she wrote hastily on her tablets a warning, and dropping them into Bill's hands made him fly to Goodrest, he to report his success at once. A knock at the big door softly. Raymond's voice. When she opens to him, a passionate scene follows. She is at first full of affection, mingled with dread of what he may know. He is fighting suspicion, passion for her, and inability to believe her guilty. Seeking her at Crowe Hall, he has followed her thither. At first she is too sincere to play with him. He is too anxious to be able to diplomatize. He shows his fears — that she is intriguing with another, with the Pretender. She is maddeningly incomprehensible — swears she knows no Pretender, but will not say yes or no as to meeting any one in the wood. In his anger and his desire to force the truth from her, by making her feel the uselessness of protecting the Pretender, he lets drop more than he realizes of plans to catch him and for the campaign. Seeing that, had her message not gone, her brother would have been trapped, Beatrice works to delay Raymond. She is first coldly repellent, then alluring, then silent, then apparently almost on the point of revelation. At last in despair he breaks away into the night, vowing vengeance on the destroyer of his happiness and cursing her for a fickle, ambitious thing, unworthy a good man's love. She stands motionless by the table, then hurries to the wide open door through which the moonlight streams in from the garden, calls again and again softly, staggers back, and falls sobbing on the great settle. Van Brugh appears at the open doors, closes them softly and speaks. He is leaving the Hunters for good, for the final Jacobite blows are to be struck. Seeing Raymond ahead of him, he hid in the garden till Raymond went. He calls on "The Daughter of Charles Cope" to tell him for the good of the cause what she knows of Raymond's plans. She denies that she knows them fully, but cannot deny that she knows something of them. He shows that everything depends for the Jacobites on knowing the movements of the local forces for the next few days. He uses every appeal he can, her brother among others. To this she only answers that she has warned and saved him. All his appeals are in vain. "Raymond is my husband in the sight of God. His secrets should be my secrets, but my brother I cannot help to kill. To save him I must deceive the man I love best in all the world; so be it. So much I must do, more I will not." Sandiland, the fanatic breaking out in him, curses her as a renegade and unworthy her name and race. He goes. As she stands murmuring: "Unworthy love, unworthy my father's name!" suddenly her face softens. She drops to the settle and prays for a moment. Quietly she rises, saying, "Why count the cost if Charles' life be saved." The door opens and Joyce enters in great excitement to say, "Bill has come, but in bad plight." She fetches the boy, his clothes torn, his hands bleeding where ropes have cut the wrists. He has been taken shortly after leaving Beatrice and searched. He snatched the tablets from a captor's hand and licked off the message before it was read. He was then trussed up behind a soldier on horseback, and started for the "Maid in the Valley" Tavern, the rendezvous from which the journey to Goodrest was to begin. By daring and ingenuity he slipped away at the inn. "Then my brother knows nothing." "No, and they'll be starting by now from the Maid in the Valley. They were waiting for the moon to be covered." "Where's Philly, my mare?" "In the paddock, miss." "What do you mean?" cries Joyce. "I am going to Goodrest." "Alone? To-night, with these rake-hell soldiers abroad?" Beatrice's only answer is to find her whip and pass quickly out into the night. Joyce sinks down sobbing in window seat. Bill is in the doorway, wild with excitement. "Now, ride, ride, Miss Beatrice. Ride, like Hell!"

Quick Curtain

If it is clear that illustrative action is as essential in a scenario as in a play, it is as true for one form as the other that right proportioning and emphasis must make clear the purpose of the author in writing the scenario and must take a reader clearly to its conclusion. Read any one of the following three scenarios and decide whether you are clear as to the purpose of the author. What did he think was attractively dramatic in his material? What is the central interest of his proposed play? Just what is the suspense created near the beginning of the play and developed throughout from sub-climaxes to a final climax? As has been carefully explained, plays must do all this. Therefore their scenarios must also.

THE FISHING OF SUZANNE

SCENARIO. *Curtain rises discovering Madame knitting in chair, upper right, Hélène embroidering in window-seat, Suzanne on sofa, trying to sew. Suzanne gets into trouble and Hélène helps her. Then grandmother offers to tell her a story. Suzanne says that her stories are so sad, always about her dead parents. Hélène represses her. Enter grandfather, the Colonel, rear. Suzanne starts to show him her sewing and is repulsed. Colonel denounces the Dreyfus situation; Madame trying to interfere when he begins on the American attitude, finally gets Hélène and Suzanne from room. Then Colonel learns that George Williams, an American, loves Hélène. He is overcome. Enter George rear. Embarrassing situation; finally George gets up courage and asks for Hélène's hand, is refused, but goes away undaunted. Enter Hélène, side. Colonel says, "I will have no friend of traitors place his foot in my house." Scene. Exit Hélène sobbing angrily. Colonel disturbed, but when wife starts after her, forbids her going. Exit the Colonel. Madame again starts toward door. Suzanne and Marie enter. Madame has Suzanne play with fishing rod; dismisses Marie from room. Suzanne hears Hélène's sobs. Asks if she is sick. Says she will comfort her. Madame feels guilty and leaves. Suzanne persuades Hélène to come out and watch her fish. Catches some imaginary ones. Discovers George. He sends up notes like fish. Later Hélène furnishes bait. Then she fishes him up. Suzanne is dismissed with candy, and he persuades Hélène to elope. Suzanne comes and says the cab is there. Steps heard. George goes down rope. Marie tells of the cab. Hélène rushes into packing. Leaves note for mother with Suzanne, who wins a promise for a speedy return from her. Exit Hélène rear. Marie and Suzanne wave from window. Talk. Soon Colonel and Madame enter. See disorderly room. Suzanne gives them the note. Madame reads it and breaks news to her husband. Defends Hélène; reminds Colonel of their parents' political differences. Suzanne tells how Hélène thought they did not care for her in her sorrow. Both in tears. Colonel in desperation starts to send for them by Marie. Enter George and Hélène; Hélène unable to leave without seeing them. Colonel says he may have been too hasty. Then Suzanne discovers George's Legion of Honor badge. He and Colonel shake on the old friendship of the Republics.*

Curtain

AN ENCORE

Adapted from a Story by Margaret Deland

Time: *About 1830, in June.*
Place: *Little town of Old Chester.*
Between the first and second act three weeks elapse.

Dramatis Personæ

Captain Price: Retired sea-captain, big, bluff, and hearty, with white hair and big white mustachios, rather untidy as to dress. Age, about 68.

Cyrus Price: His son, weak and neat-looking, very thin and of sandy complexion. Age, about 35.

Mrs. North: Sprightly, pretty, white-haired little lady of about 65. Always in black silk.

Miss North: Her daughter, nervous and shy, but truthful with a mania for taking care of her mother and no knowledge of how to wear her clothes; about 40.

Mrs. Gussie Price: A stout, colorless blond, a weeping, vividly gowned lady, who rules her husband, Cyrus, through her tears. Age, about 30.

Flora: A colored maid.

Stage setting: A drawing-room with a door on either side of the back, leading into the long front hall. A window at the right, looking into the street. Between the window and the door, a stuffed armchair, a hair-cloth sofa. Between the doors, under a mantel-shelf, a Franklin stove, on either side of which, but a little down stage, are two rockers just alike. To the left and back, grand piano. To the left, front, another big chair. Hassocks; and a knit shawl on almost every chair. The only ornament on the shelf is a stuffed bird in a glass case.

ACT I

Miss North is discovered in a very much starched gown, big apron, dusting-cap, and gloves; arranging the chairs more evenly and dusting. Expression of heavy responsibility in her face and manner.

Flora announces Mrs. Price, who enters — right door — at once. Though Mary explains she is busy, Mrs. Price stays. Sits on the sofa. Mary in rocking-chair to left of stove. Dialogue in which Mary explains she is determined to let her mother end life happily in her native town and she expects her to arrive any moment. Mrs. Price offers assist-

ance in fixing up the house and begins to gossip about the fact that her father-in-law, the Captain, who lives in the Price house just across the street, tried to elope with Mrs. North when she was eighteen. Mary becomes very indignant, but sees her mother through the window and dismisses Mrs. Price politely but not sweetly. Exit Mrs. Price by the right door, Mary by the left. Enter Mrs. North by the right and Mary is seen hurrying by the right door with a small wooden chair in her hand.

Mrs. North begins to look about the room while she takes off her calash and leaves it on the piano, her shawl and puts it on the shelf, her gloves and leaves them on a chair. Mary enters, right, with the chair, during this business and remonstrates with her mother for getting out of the chaise without the aid of the chair. As Mrs. North drops her things Mary picks them up. Mrs. North sees the Price house through the window and mentions, cheerily, that the Captain used to be her beau. Mary is shocked. Tries to have her mother put on one of the little shawls and goes to make her some beef-tea. Hangs her things on the hat-tree in hall beyond left door as she goes out.

Mrs. North discovers the Captain going down street and calls him in. Enters right door with his pipe. Both sit in the rockers before the stove and are deep in reminiscences when Mary enters left door. The Captain is requested to put up his pipe, not to talk quite so loud, and not to stay long because of Mrs. North's delicacy. When Mary offers to make him some beef-tea, too, so her mother can take hers, he leaves precipitately, very much cowed.

While Mary is trying to soothe Mrs. North after the undue excitement, Flora announces Cyrus Price who has come in search of his father — at Gussie's tearful instigation. Mary and Cyrus hold an anxious aside, while Mrs. North expresses her pleasure at seeing the Captain again. Curtain falls on Mrs. North trying to pick out some of the old tunes on the piano, and Cyrus and Mary bidding each other a stiff "Good-morning."

ACT II

The Captain and Mrs. North discovered, the Captain with his harmonica trying to teach Mrs. North the old airs. Enter Mary at right door, from outdoors. Consternation ensues and in a few moments the Captain leaves guiltily. Then Mary explains that she has been over to the Prices and requested Cyrus to tell the Captain he must keep away, for they are both too old to be married. Mrs. North exits left, in *despair. Flora announces Mr. and Mrs. Price: a conference of war is held during which it is decided that Cyrus must consult the minister, Dr. Lavender, and Gussie must speak to the Captain himself. Exeunt Mr. and Mrs. Price.*

Enter Mrs. North for her knitting. Mary wraps her up in a shawl, puts a hassock at her feet, suggests lighting a fire in the stove, and tries to comfort her mother by telling her she will take her away from Old Chester if the Captain keeps on bothering her. Mrs. North remonstrates feebly, and Mary decides she needs some beef-tea after the excitement. Exit Mary to make the tea.

Enter the Captain without ringing or knocking, in great wrath. Gussie has spoken to him. At first they laugh at the children's stupidity and by degrees decide to carry out and confirm the children's suspicions by eloping. Enter Mary. Confusion, but the Captain pretends he has come to say good-bye to her because he is going away for a few weeks and under that cover, makes the appointment for the eloping.

Curtain with his exit

THE CAPTAIN, A MELODRAMA

[Diagram]

Dramatis Personœ

Captain La Rue, a little sea captain.
Bromley Barnes, former special investigator for the U.S. Customs Service.
Patrick Clancy, his friend.
A burly Butler.
John Felspar, junior partner of the firm of Felspar & Felspar, wine merchants.
Two Dinner Guests, members of the firm.
Carl Cozzens, the firm's Canadian representative.

SCENE. *The dining-room of Felspar's Summer Cottage*

Time: Early evening

The Captain is discovered sitting on the end of the table next the window with his legs dangling dejectedly. Suddenly he sees something and, rushing to the window, goes through a violent pantomime imploring help and caution from some one without and indicating the

*way to enter the house. He then wrings his hands and paces the floor
excitedly ending at D. R. C. where he listens. The key turns in the lock
and Barnes and Clancy enter cautiously. The Captain throws himself
at their feet and tells them of being kidnapped and confined and his
Ship's papers taken from him and asks frantically for the time.
Barnes tells him, and the Captain becomes at once dejected and silent.
The other two, however, draw from him the story of how he has been
racing over the Atlantic to get a cargo of champagne to an American
port in time to get the benefit of the old tariff rate, just increased by the
governments concerned. He got in in time but was drugged and confined in this house till too late and his papers taken from him. They
advise him to stay where he is and, promising to help him at once, slip
out as they came. The Butler comes in D. R. C. and begins setting
table, joking the Captain about the supper to be held in his honor, but
growling about the suddenness of his master's decision to have it. The
Captain is excited and helps him in mock politeness. As they are
working, Felspar comes in. Butler tells him that he has hired a waiter
for the evening, subject to his approval — a man who happened to be
walking by, with a friend. Felspar congratulates him and the new
waiter is called. It is Clancy. La Rue controls himself as he recognizes him. Felspar orders the Butler to lock La Rue in the up-stairs
bedroom, which has been prepared, till he shall be wanted, telling him
at the same time that all the guests have arrived but Mr. Cozzens, who
is to be brought directly to the dining-room when he arrives. The others
will not wait for him. The Butler hurries La Rue off. Felspar gives a
few parting instructions to the new waiter and goes to bring the guests.
Clancy finishes the preparations and signals out the window to Barnes
to come. Felspar comes back with the guests D. L. C. The Butler
reappears, is called to the door-bell and ushers in Barnes as "Mr.
Cozzens." Felspar introduces him as the Canadian representative of
the firm whom he has never seen before. Barnes takes the cue and excuses his costume, saying that he arrived late and has not had time to
change. All sit again and Felspar, telling the Butler to bring La Rue,
tells the company that the ship's papers of the rival business house
have come into his hands. These he produces and passes along the
table. Barnes, at the opposite end, pockets them as they come to him
and refuses to give them up. All are astonished and half-angry. The
Butler, having brought in the Captain at Felspar's order (who stands
unnoticed at the back) again answers the bell and ushers in Mr. Cozzens, announcing him in a doubtful voice. Felspar stutters, "You —
you Mr. Cozzens?" "So me mother and father says" the new-comer*

replies. "And you?" says the wine-merchant wheeling on Barnes. Barnes presents his card which is read aloud by Felspar, who goes into a white heat and demands the papers back. Barnes blandly refuses. Felspar threatens, saying he has four to one. At this point Clancy and La Rue step forward and signify their readiness to side with Barnes. Felspar laughs and tells them to take the papers then as the new law went into effect at four-thirty that afternoon. But Barnes informs him that the provisions of the French-American commercial treaty demand that the customs houses remain open till midnight when such a law goes through, and that they still have several hours. Felspar is again furious and orders them out and the three go together leaving the company in an angry stupor.

Curtain

Let it be clearly understood that there is no definitely established length for a scenario. It may run from one to two pages for a play of one act to twenty or more pages for a longer play. Obviously, a scenario should be as brief as clear presentation of what it must give permits, for it primarily exists as a short cut for the person who reads it to necessary information about a proposed play. Clearness is the first essential; brevity the second. The exact length must in each case be decided by the particular needs of the subject treated and the best judgment of the writer.

Above all, it should be remembered that a scenario unless it is simply an abbreviated presentation of a play already in manuscript should be considered something flexible. What is meant by this is that many a writer working with a scenario which has been approved by a manager or actor feels hampered because as he writes he has almost irresistible impulses to break away from the scenario as planned into situations or details of characterization and even of general treatment which, though they occur to him at the moment, seem to him undoubted improvements. Yet he hesitates to change his plan because it has been approved. This is folly. A scenario is at its best when it concerns not a completed but a proposed play and is held to be not fixed but thoroughly flexible. If changes suggesting themselves are felt by the writer to be improvements, he should by all means incorporate them. A good scenario bears much the same relation to a completed play that an architect's plans bear to a completed house. Where would the carpenter be without such plans, yet where is the set of plans which has not been modified or even greatly changed while the building is in construction? "Ibsen had no respect for any dramatist who proceeded otherwise [than from a carefully prepared scenario]. Once besought by a young dramatist to read the manuscript of his new play, Ibsen curtly asked for the scenario. When the young man proudly replied that he needed no scenario, having followed his inspiration whithersoever it led him from scene to scene, Ibsen grew furious and showed the pseudo-dramatist the door, declaring that any one who dispensed with a scenario didn't know what a drama was and couldn't possibly write one. And yet, after all, the scenario as first outlined by Ibsen may best be regarded as an experimental foreshadowing subject to radical modification as the writing of the play itself proceeds. It serves as the skeleton framework for Ibsen's later ideation. . . . While it is true, then, that the material took shape in his mind long before he wrote a word of actual dialogue, yet Ibsen expressly acknowledged that it never took such unalterable shape in his mind as to permit him to write the last act first or the first act last. During the course of the work the details emerged by degrees."[1]

The fact is, a scenario is almost always a photograph of the mind of the person who writes it. If he is not ready to write his play, the scenario will show it, making clear whether this unreadiness comes from insufficiently under-

---

[1] *European Dramatists. Henrik Ibsen.* A. Henderson. Pp. 175–176. Stewart & Kidd Co., Cincinnati.

stood characterization; thin or incomplete story; a lack of right proportioning of the material so that what is unimportant seems important; or a general vagueness as to what the author wants to do with his material. Just here lies the strong reason why every would-be dramatist will do well to become expert in scenario writing. He may for a long time fool himself into thinking that he can work better without a scenario; he may be able to write without putting on paper all that in this chapter has been required from the writer of a scenario, but sooner or later he goes through all the processes in his mind and either on paper or in his brain fulfils these requirements. The very people who shrink from forcing themselves to work out all the details required by a good scenario are merely dodging the inevitable. They avoid something irksome as a preliminary merely to do all this work before the completed play is ready. He who wants to write his play rapidly will find that he makes time in his final composition by taking all the time he needs in the preliminary task of drawing a good scenario. Undeniably, a scenario is the most effective way of forcing oneself to know the characters and the story of a play before one begins to write the play in detail. Work out a scenario carefully and all the difficult problems the play involves will have been solved except those of dialogue and perhaps some subtleties of characterization. Regard the resulting scenario as something entirely flexible and the composition of the play should be safe and even sure. He who steers by the compass knows how with safety to change his course. He who steers by dead reckoning is liable to error and delay.

Often questions as to scenarios are asked which imply that there must be some set form fulfilling all the requirements stated which can be adhered to strictly. Not at all. These various requirements may be met in almost as many ways as there are writers. One man may use more descrip-

tion. Another writer may use more narration. Some
will use dialogue very freely. Some will characterize more
than others. Yet all these different workers may produce
scenarios equally good in that they are clear, brief, move
by suggested dramatic action, are definite in *genre*, and
make thoroughly evident their elements of suspense and
climax.

Here are some scenarios which use dialogue rather freely.
They are given not because such use is especially commendable but merely to illustrate it.

THE LEGACY

The persons

David Brice, a young attorney.
Reene Brice, his uncle.
Benjamin Doyle, his fiancée's father.
Dr. Wangren, family physician.
Mrs. Brice, the mother.
"Ditto" Brice, the sister.
Katherine Doyle, fiancée.

The Time: The present.
The Place: Any city.

SCENE. *The Brice living-room comfortably furnished in walnut.
A piano centre L., a round table rear R. Four entrances: upper L.,
rear centre, upper right, right centre. Curtained windows rear R. & L.
Joy seems to radiate through the household. Ditto and Katherine
are discovered; Katherine, a pretty enthusiast of 22 playing diminuendo a joy-melody at piano; Ditto, pretty, 20 and nervous, crossing R.
with an armload of tagged packages of various sizes and prettily tied —
birthday presents for her brother David. Arrived at table, rear R., she
deposits them.*

Ditto. (*Stacking packages.*) Don't you wish you were getting
these birthday presents, Katherine?
Katherine. (*Playing.*) I am, Ditto, dear. David is mine; therefore, what is David's belongs to me.

Ditto. (Petulantly.) And what is yours . . .

Katherine. (In fun.) . . . Belongs to father.

> *(Begins to sing merrily.)*
> *(Exit Ditto, R.)*

Enter Mrs. Brice, L., a thoughtful woman of 50, quite grey and though careworn, attractive. She carries a linen spread and goes to the table. Katherine sings softly, playing diminuendo.

Mrs. Brice. (Covering presents.) You are very happy tonight, aren't you?

Katherine. (Cheerily.) Why shouldn't I be, Mrs. Brice? It is David's birthday. *(Going to her.)* But you aren't.

Mrs. Brice. (Bravely.) Yes, I am. But you see this is probably David's last birthday at home and . . .

Katherine. (Lovingly.) By no means! I shall bring him home every birthday. *(Kissing her.)* . . . And once in a while between.

Mrs. Brice. (As they go down, arm in arm.) I know you will, Katherine, but we mothers . . .

David. (Entering centre rear, overcoat, hat and traveling grip.) Hello everybody! . . . *(Tosses grip on table and makes for them.)* . . . Merry Christmas, Happy New Year *(kisses mother)* and a quiet Fourth of July. *(Kisses Katherine.)*

> *(David is a well-built handsome man of 28 neatly dressed in business suit, light-weight overcoat and hat.)*

David. (Removing coat, Katherine assisting.) Well, how are all the little details?

> *(Coat off, he begins kissing Katherine again. Enter Ditto, R.)*

Ditto. (Petulantly.) Do you realize this is your birthday?

David. (Kissing mother.) I am doing my best to show it! *(Tossing Ditto his coat.)* Hang that up and I will show you.

> *(Exit Ditto, R., with his coat and hat.)*

David. (Coming down from table with blue-print in hand.) Now, mother and child, look ye!

> *(He shows them the architectural plans of the new cottage he is going to build as a wedding present to Katherine. They like them very much. More joy. Ditto, reëntering, is also enthusiastic over plans.*
>
> *David next announces that he has been invited to become a member of his employer's law firm, one of the most successful in the State. More joy, manifested by another round of kisses.*
>
> *But he has not only been asked to join the firm; the firm*

*has promised him a straight loan, without interest, with
which to build his house. Otherwise he would have had to
borrow from a building and loan association. Therefore,
bids are now being advertised for and work will begin very
soon. Great joy. Ditto seizes mother's hand and Katherine's and dances a ring around David.*

*As the jollification subsides, David inquires for his uncle,
Reene. He must approve the plans, for he was a great architect in his day. His mother informs him that the uncle
went for a ride with Doctor Wangren.)*

David. How is he feeling today?

Mrs. Brice. Not quite so well. In fact, I never saw him so
despondent.

David. He must not look at it that way. We all have our little
troubles. (*To Katherine.*) Don't we?

(*They go toward piano. Exit Mrs. Brice, L., taking Ditto
with her.*

*In a short scene at the piano, during which Katherine plays
diminuendo, the fact is revealed that her father opposes
the match between her and David; not because he does not
like David but for reasons which he has not divulged to his
daughter. This cloud passes by quickly, however.)*

THE CONSULTATION

The persons of the play

Marian,
Katherine.
Dr. Thomas Wells.
Dr. Benjamin Crawford.

*The scene represents a sitting room in Marian's home. It is very
cheaply furnished. There is a door at back centre, and also one at
R. At upper left is a curtained window, not practicable. In the centre
is a table, on which is a lighted lamp. Near the window is a couch.
There are chairs about the room, and a few cheap pictures on the walls.
It is evening, and the room is dimly lighted.*

[Diagram]

*When the curtain rises, there is no one in the room, but in a moment
the door at rear opens, and Katherine enters noiselessly. She is a*

pleasant looking woman of 30. She is followed by Dr. Wells, who closes the door behind him very softly. He is a young man, with a Van Dyke beard. The two go to right of table, and Katherine looks at the doctor inquiringly. He speaks with some hesitation.

Dr. Wells. You want the truth?

Katherine. Of course.

Dr. Wells. I think he's dying. This is the crisis, and the chances are a thousand to one against him.

Katherine. I'm afraid my sister can't bear the shock. She loves her husband more than I can tell you, Doctor.

(They are discussing the case when Marian enters from the rear. She lingers a moment and looks back into the other room. Then she slowly closes the door, and advances towards the others. She is a pretty woman, about 25, but she looks pale and anxious.

Dr. Wells and Katherine stop talking when she comes near and watch her. She turns to the Doctor and asks for his verdict. He doesn't reply, but looks inquiringly at Katherine. After a moment, she says he'd better tell her. Very gently he breaks the news, and informs her that her husband will probably die. The disease is vicious and can't be checked.)

Marian. (*Anxiously.*) You mean my husband will die?

Dr. Wells. I fear so.

Marian. Don't say that, Doctor. It will kill me. You don't know what John means to me.

(The Doctor assures her that he has done his best, and the patient is now in the hands of God. He's sorry but in all honesty he believes the man will die.

Marian refuses to believe, and maintains that her husband will not die. No doubt he's a very sick man, but he will live. She declares she has sent for a man who can save him.)

Marian. You've been good, Doctor, and God will bless you. But you won't blame me for saying that perhaps some one else might look at the case differently. You don't feel hurt? Don't blame me, but I've sent for Dr. Crawford, so you can have — what do you call it? — a consultation. I know he can save my husband's life.

Dr. Wells. (*Surprised.*) You mean Dr. William Crawford, the famous specialist?

Marian. Yes. Oh, Doctor, he's so wonderful!
Dr. Wells. (*Enthusiastically.*) Wonderful? I should say so. He's
one of the most remarkable men in the profession. If there's any
one in the world who can save your husband's life, he is the man.
(*Doubtfully.*) But can you pay his fee?

SCENARIO

THE WINNING OF GENERAL JANE

(*A farce of three persons, a dog, and a gun "that wasn't loaded"*)

Cast

Jane, *about twenty.*
Aunt Sophy, *her maiden aunt, about 45.*
Bobby Holloway, *a lodger, about 23.*

Place, Jane's bedroom. Time about 11 at night

SETTING. *Lower left a closet, door opening inward. Upper left
a door leading to Aunt Sophy's room, opening inward. Rear centre,
double-windows set in a shallow alcove. The curtains are draped to
right and left. Right, up stage, a fireplace without a fire. Left, down
stage, a dressing-table with mirror. A low stool stands before it. Against
rear wall to left a washstand half-hidden by a Japanese screen,
shoulder height. Against right wall and about halfway down stage a
bed. It is low and preferably wooden.*

[Diagram of Setting]

*At rise Jane is discovered at dressing-table occupied in braiding
her hair. Enter Aunt Sophy. She asks Jane if Mr. Holloway, their
single lodger, is in for the night. Jane replies with some petulance that
she does not know. A dissection of that gentleman's character ensues
in which Jane anathematizes him, while Aunt Sophy, despite her
avowed dislike for all things masculine, champions his cause. At last
Jane intimates that in all probability Mr. Holloway will propose to
Aunt Sophy at a very early date. The latter cannot conceal her delight.
She is not content with Jane's assurance on this point but must know
how she discovered the state of Bobby's affections. Jane finally admits
that she bases her deduction upon the fact that he "proposes to everybody, in season and out!" — that he has proposed to her, Jane, no
less than 237 times.*

Aunt Sophy is hurt and shocked at this revelation of perfidy and immediately sides with Jane, declaring that she will oust Mr. Hollo-way on the following morning. Jane however does not want to be sided with. With true feminine variability she shifts her attitude as completely as Aunt Sophy has hers, and pleads with the outraged old maid to reverse her decision. She shows that she really cares for Bobby more than at first appeared. Aunt Sophy however is obdurate, and departs, leaving Jane almost dissolved in tears.

At this juncture a racket arises outside Jane's window. It is a mix-ture of blasphemous English, growls and hurried footsteps. Jane starts to investigate, but seeing an arm and a leg thrust hastily over the sill, retreats to the door in alarm. Immediately Bobby climbs in, and a smothered exclamation from Jane identifies him. He glances about hurriedly, and not perceiving her, turns his attention to the dog who still growls below. He epitomizes him with surprising fluency, until Jane, unable to stand more, interrupts. This precipitates a profuse apology for the intrusion and other things, an explanation, and later a proposal.

Jane is angered beyond measure not only at this invasion of her privacy but also at Bobby's attitude towards the whole affair. She orders him to leave. He attempts to do so by way of the door.

Jane. (*Frightened.*) W-w-where are you going?

Bobby. (*Shrugging.*) Hump! — to heaven — eventually!

Jane. (*Barring way.*) N-n-not through Aunt Sophy's room!

> (*She informs him that he must depart the way he came. He consents but only in a very half-hearted manner. Between Aunt Sophy and Towser he is in a quandary. After sev-eral unsuccessful starts he flatly refuses to descend, and upbraids Jane for her cruelty. He dwells at length on the horrors of dog-bites, hydrophobia, madness, and death.*)

Bobby. (*Injured.*) As if I had not already been chewed up so that I can scarcely sit — (*hastily*) — I mean walk.

Jane. (*Relenting.*) Gracious! Bobby, did he bite you?

Bobby. Did he?

Jane. (*Seizing bottle from table.*) Heavens! You must put some-thing on it! Some antiseptic! Bobby come here!

Bobby. Oh, no, no! No, it's not serious!

Jane. Come here this instant!

Bobby. (*Flatly.*) I won't do it!

> (*He succeeds so well in working upon her sympathies that even a knock at Aunt Sophy's door is not enough to make her change her attitude. She now as obstinately refuses to*

let him descend to certain death as previously he had re-
fused to do it. The knocks are continued. Jane is rapidly
losing her head when it suddenly occurs to her that if she
stores Bobby away under the bed until Towser has de-
parted or Aunt Sophy has gone to sleep, all may yet be
well. While Bobby is ensconcing himself in this new posi-
tion a three cornered conversation takes place, in which
Jane becomes more and more involved.)

Aunt Sophy. (*Outside.*) Jane, Jane, are you ill?
Jane. Ill? Oh, oh! I don't know!
Aunt Sophy. Open the door this minute or I'll break it down!
Jane. Break it down?
Aunt Sophy. Yes, this instant!
Jane. Oh, oh! Don't do that! It's not locked! . . .

It may be interesting to compare the scenario of *A Doll's House* from which Ibsen wrote his first draft with his original notes. Here is perfect illustration of the difference between sketchy notes which mean much to the writer and a scenario which at least broadly will convey to a reader the artistic and ethical purposes in the play the dramatist means to write.

NOTES FOR THE MODERN TRAGEDY

Rome, 19. 10, 78.

There are two kinds of spiritual law, two kinds of conscience, one in man and another, altogether different, in woman. They do not understand each other; but in practical life the woman is judged by man's law, as though she were not a woman but a man.

The wife in the play ends by having no idea of what is right or wrong; natural feeling on the one hand and belief in authority on the other have altogether bewildered her.

A woman cannot be herself in the society of the present day, which is an exclusively masculine society, with laws framed by men and with a judicial system that judges feminine conduct from a masculine point of view.

She has committed forgery, and she is proud of it; for she did it out of love for her husband, to save his life. But this husband, with his commonplace principles of honour is on the side of the law and regards the question with masculine eyes.

SCENARIOS 471

Spiritual conflicts. Oppressed and bewildered by the belief in
authority, she loses faith in her moral right and ability to bring
up her children. Bitterness. A mother in modern society, like
certain insects who go away and die when she has done her duty
in the propagation of the race.[1] Love of life, of home, of husband
and children and family. Here and there a womanly shaking-off
of her thoughts. Sudden return of anxiety and terror. She must
bear it all alone. The catastrophe approaches, inexorably, inevitably. Despair, conflict, and destruction.

(Krogstad has acted dishonourably and thereby become well-
to-do; now his prosperity does not help him, he cannot recover his
honour.)[2]

_____

Persons

Stenborg, a Government clerk.
Nora, his wife.
Miss (Mrs.) Linde (a widow).
Attorney Krogstad.
Karen, nurse at the Stenborgs'.
A Parlour-Maid at the Stenborgs'.
A Porter.
The Stenborgs' three little children.
Doctor Hank.

SCENARIO. FIRST ACT

*A room comfortably, but not showily, furnished. In the back, on the
right, a door leads to the hall; on the left another door leads to the
room or office of the master of the house, which can be seen when the
door is opened. A fire in the stove. Winter day.*

*She enters from the back, humming gaily; she is in outdoor dress and
carries several parcels, has been shopping. As she opens the door,
a Porter is seen in the hall, carrying a Christmas-tree. She: Put it
down there for the present. (Taking out her purse.) How much?
Porter: Fifty öre. She: Here is a crown. No, keep the change. The
Porter thanks her and goes. She continues humming and smiling
with quiet glee as she opens several of the parcels she has brought.
Calls off, is he at home? Yes! At first, conversation through the closed
door; then he opens it and goes on talking to her while continuing to
work most of the time, standing at his desk. There is a ring at the hall-*

---

[1] The sentence is elliptical in the original.
[2] *Ibsen's Workshop*, pp. 91-92. Copyright, 1911, by Chas. Scribner's Sons, New York.

door; he does not want to be disturbed; shuts himself in. The maid opens the door to her mistress's friend, just arrived in town. Happy surprise. Mutual explanation of the position of affairs. He has received the post of manager in the new joint-stock bank and is to enter on his duties at the New Year; all financial worries are at an end. The friend has come to town to look for some small employment in an office or whatever may present itself. Mrs. Stenborg gives her good hopes, is certain that all will turn out well. The maid opens the front door to the debt-collector. Mrs. Stenborg, terrified; they exchange a few words; he is shown into the office. Mrs. Stenborg and her friend; the circumstances of the debt-collector are touched upon. Stenborg enters in his overcoat; has sent the collector out the other way. Conversation about the friend's affairs; hesitation on his part. He and the friend go out; his wife follows them into the hall; the Nurse enters with the children. Mother and children play. The collector enters. Mrs. Stenborg sends the children out to the left. Great scene between her and him. He goes. Stenborg enters; has met him on the stairs; displeased; wants to know what he came back for ? Her support ? No intrigues. His wife cautiously tries to pump him. Strict legal answers. Exit to his room. She (repeating her words when the collector went out) : But that's impossible. Why, I did it from love !

SCENARIO. SECOND ACT

The last day of the year. Midday. Nora and the old Nurse. Nora, impelled by uneasiness, is putting on her things to go out. Anxious random questions of one kind and another give a hint that thoughts of death are in her mind. Tries to banish these thoughts, to turn it off, hopes that something or other may intervene. But what ? The Nurse goes off to the left. — Stenborg enters from his room. Short dialogue between him and Nora. — The Nurse re-enters, looking for Nora; the youngest child is crying. Annoyance and questioning on Stenborg's part; exit the Nurse; Stenborg is going in to the children. — Doctor Hank enters. Scene between him and Stenborg. — Nora soon re-enters; she has turned back; anxiety has driven her home again. Scene between her, the Doctor and Stenborg. Stenborg goes into his room. — Scene between Nora and the Doctor. The Doctor goes out. — Nora alone. — Mrs. Linde enters. Short scene between her and Nora. — Krogstad enters. Short scene between him and Mrs. Linde and Nora. Mrs. Linde goes in to the children. — Scene between Krogstad and Nora. — She entreats and implores him for the sake of her little children;

in vain. Krogstad goes out. The letter is seen to fall from outside into the letter-box. — Mrs. Linde re-enters after a short pause. Scene between her and Nora. Half confession. Mrs. Linde goes out. — Nora alone. — Stenborg enters. Scene between him and Nora. He wants to empty the letter-box. Entreaties, jests, half playful persuasion. He promises to let business wait till after New Year's Day; but at 12 o'clock midnight —! Exit. Nora alone. Nora (looking at the clock): It is five o'clock. Five; — seven hours till midnight. Twenty-four hours till the next midnight. Twenty-four and seven — thirty-one. Thirty-one hours to live. —

THIRD ACT

A muffled sound of dance music is heard from the floor above. A lighted lamp on the table. Mrs. Linde sits in an armchair and absently turns the pages of a book, tries to read, but seems unable to fix her attention; once or twice she looks at her watch. Nora comes down from the dance; uneasiness has driven her; surprise at finding Mrs. Linde, who pretends that she wanted to see Nora in her costume. Helmer, displeased at her going away, comes to fetch her back. The Doctor also enters, but to say good-bye. Meanwhile Mrs. Linde has gone into the side room on the right. Scene between the Doctor, Helmer, and Nora. He is going to bed, he says, never to get up again; they are not to come and see him; there is ugliness about a death-bed. He goes out. Helmer goes upstairs again with Nora, after the latter has exchanged a few words of farewell with Mrs. Linde. Mrs. Linde alone. Then Krogstad. Scene and explanation between them. Both go out. Nora and the children. Then she alone. Then Helmer. He takes the letters out of the letter-box. Short scene; goodnight; he goes into his room. Nora in despair prepares for the final step; is already at the door when Helmer enters with the open letter in his hand. Great scene. A ring. Letter to Nora from Krogstad. Final scene. Divorce. Nora leaves the house.[1]

Finally, here is the full scenario of a play which made a great success both in England and the United States and was seen by practically all the Continental countries, namely, *Kismet*. Notice how well it fulfils the requirements for a good scenario stated in this chapter, not because Mr. Knobloch had these rules in mind as he composed it, but

---

[1] *Ibsen's Workshop*, pp. 92–95.

because, as a trained dramatist, he instinctively gave these qualities to his scenario. Carefully studied in relation to the essentials of scenario writing just stated, it should remove all doubt in the mind of a student as to what a good scenario is and why it is an essential preliminary to a good play.

KISMET
or
HAJJI'S DAY

Scenario for a play in three acts, by
EDWARD KNOBLOCH [1]

CHARACTERS

(in order of their appearance)

Original Names	Later Names
Hajji.	*Hajj (as Hajji is Persian, Hajj Arabian).*
A Priest.	*Imam Mahmud.*
Guide.	*Nasir.*
Sheikh of the Desert.	*Jawan.*
Young Beggar.	*Kasim.*
Sultan.	*The Caliph Abdallah.*
His Vizier.	*Abu Bakr.*
Shopkeeper I.	*Amru.*
Shopkeeper II.	*Fayd.*
Zira.	*Marsinah.*
Old Woman I.	*Narjis.*
Officer of Guard.	*Captain of the Watch.*
Executioner.	*Mansur, Chief of Police.*
His Scribe.	*{ Turned into two characters: Kafur, the Sworder. Afife, the Hunchback.*
Old Woman II.	
Executioner's Wife.	*Kut-Al-Kulub.*
Gaoler.	*Kutayt.*
Peasant. } Trial scene at Two Wives. } Sultan's.	*{ Cut out in final draft.*
Dancers, Soldiers, Courtiers, Women, the People.	

[1] Printed by permission of Mr. Knobloch from his own manuscript.

ACT I

[Scene later introduced before the curtain.]
Scene 1. A Street before a Mosque.
Scene 2. The Bazaar.
Scene 3. Courtyard of a Poor House.
Scene 4. Courtyard of Executioner's House.

ACT II

Scene 1. Interior Room of Executioner's House.
Scene 2. Courtyard of a Poor House. (Act I, Scene 3.)
Scene 3. The Sultan's Audience Hall.
Scene 4. A Dungeon.

ACT III

Scene 1. Courtyard of a Poor House (Act I, Scene 3) [cut in final version].
Scene 2. The Bath of the Executioner's House.
Scene 3. A street before a Mosque. (Act I, Scene 1.)

The Scene is laid in Bagdad.
The action takes place from morning to night.

ACT I

SCENE 1

A narrow street with stone steps leading up to a Mosque left. (Small set.)

The sun is just beginning to rise.

Asleep on a large stone which juts out from the angle of the wall C. sits Hajji wrapped in his beggar's cloak. On the minaret of the Mosque appears the priest, a venerable white bearded man. He calls to prayer. [See alterations in actual play.]

The crowd begins to pass into the Mosque as the sun rises. Hajji wakes up, rubs his eyes, and has a drink of water from a gourd which he draws out from behind his seat. He begins to beg from the passers-by.

An Old Man (Jawan) preceded by a guide (Nasir) is carried across the scene in a litter. He fixes his gaze on Hajji and is carried off into the Mosque. The guide remains in the portico. Hajji follows the Old Man on his knees to the steps of the Mosque, begging.

As he does so a lean Beggar of a younger cast of countenance takes Hajji's place.

Hajji returns to his seat.

Hajji.	Hajji curses young Beggar.
	Explains young Beggar must be stranger.
	Who is he that he does not know of Hajji?
	He has sat on this seat for thirty years.
	His father has sat there before him.
	His grandfather before *him*.
	Great pride in his ancestry of beggardom.
Young Beggar. (Kasim.)	The young Beggar tries to retaliate.
	Hajji tells him to go and sit on a seat round the corner — "where other swine have sat before you."
	He kicks the young Beggar.

The Guide (Nasir) of the Old Man comes down to interfere.

The Young Beggar (Kasim) sulks into a corner nursing his kick.

Hajji.	Hajji and Guide get into conversation.
The Guide. (Kasim.)	Guide explains Rich Man here on a pilgrimage.
	Is really a famous old Robber Chief, a Cûrd,
	One of the Sheikhs of the desert: all of whom were notorious and banished by late Sultan (*Caliph*).
	Sheikh old and dying.
	Come to pray to Allah to restore his son to him before he dies (if son still alive).
[*Sultan* is used throughout this scenario — for which, in play, *Caliph* is substituted. *Caliph* is correct, as being Arabian. The title *Sultan* is of later origin and of Turkish influence.]	Sheikh was attacked by Sultan's troops twenty-five years ago, and his son, then four years old, carried off.
	Hajji says he knows what that means. Had his wife carried off many years ago. The only woman he ever loved — really loved.
	The Guide: "I know, Hajji, and I pity you.
	I have a proposition to make:

I know the Sheikh will give money to
charity to save his soul just before dying.
Now if you could predict something to
him, —
Say that he will find his son again, —
The Sheikh will give you money."
And for this advice Guide and Hajji are
to divide money.
Hajji agrees to this.

Prayers are over.

*The crowd disperses coming from the Mosque.
Sheikh is carried out of the Mosque in his litter.*

Hajji.

Hajji throws himself in front of litter.
Crying out: "Listen to me.
I can see why you have come.
You are looking for some one, — your
son.
You shall find him. Give me money."
Sheikh amazed at Hajji's knowledge.
Hajji says his wits have been sharpened
through grief and suffering.
"I had a wife and a son.
They were stolen by my enemy.
My son was murdered,
My wife carried off.
The swine of a beggar who sat round the
corner did it.
He is my enemy. The curse of my life."
Sheikh holds out purse, chinking it.
Hajji blesses Sheikh.
Sheikh bursts out laughing.
Reveals himself to Hajji.
He (Sheikh) is his enemy.
He ran away with Hajji's wife.
And became a robber under her inspir-
ing influence. One of a band of robbers
that attacked the caravans.
It is their son (by Hajji's wife) that the
Sultan captured when he attacked the
robbers.

[Some of this is incor-
porated in the scene with
Nasir.]

Laughs at Hajji for blessing him.
Thanks him ironically.
Throws the purse and is carried off by
his men.
Hajji shouts curses after him.
And kicks away the money.

Hajji. (*Alone.*)   He is torn in two by the hatred for his
enemy.

Young Beggar, in corner. And the love of the money.
What he could do with the money.
He could do so much for Zira (the
daughter),
The pride of his heart, the consolation
of his old age,
The one balm to his fatherly heart.
But his enemy's money?
Never.
But Zira? Trinkets for her. Her laugh-
ter.

[This was cut at re-
hearsals, as halting the
action,]   Her smile.
But the Sheikh's money — The beast
who robbed him of his wife.
Who was Zira's mother? No one. A
dancing girl, a passing whim. The fancy
of a late spring.
But his wife — the one that the Sheikh
took — she was everything. His joy, his
pride, the first finding of his manhood.
To the purse: "I'll not touch thee." (*He
spits at it.*)

> *He sees some one coming.*
> *He quickly pockets the purse.*

The Guide reënters

Hajji.
Guide.
Young Beggar.   Guide comes to claim half of his money.
Hajji does not know anything of the
bargain;
"I saw no purse."
Guide furious.
Hajji laughs at him.
He appeals to young Beggar.

Was there a purse there?
The young Beggar sides with Hajji.
Guide off, furious, vowing vengeance.
Hajji says, "Go thy way in peace."

Hajji.
Young Beggar.

Young Beggar: "What do I get for sid-
ing with you?"
"What?"
"I saw you pick up the purse.
I heard the agreement: you promised
him half."
Hajji says the money was given him,
not by the Sheikh, but by fate.
We all have a day in life.
This is Hajji's day.
There is a future before him.
The Sheikh rose from the mud to power
and riches.
Why not Hajji?
Fortune is smiling on him at last.
He will forsake the seat he has sat on
these thirty years.
Go forth into the world.
What shall he give the Young Beggar?
His throne and his beggar's cloak.
(He instates him in his seat and goes off.)

[Here the Priest is in-
troduced in the play to
heighten the effect at the
end. Also to make him a
friend of Hajji's, as Hajji
sends his daughter to him
at the end of the Hareem
scene. Act III, Scene 1.]

Curtain

SCENE 2

The Bazaar. (Large set)

Shopkeeper I and Shopkeeper II lying outside of adjoining shops. They are very friendly.
Crowd.
Young Sultan (Caliph) rides through the bazaar on a white donkey. His Vizier (Abu Bakr) follows him. Also guards.

Hajji appears. Political discussion.
Shopkeeper I. Young Sultan just come through bazaar.
Shopkeeper II. Hajji regrets he missed seeing him.
  Sultan only been Sultan ten days.
[Read *Caliph* for *Sultan*.] Nephew of old Sultan now dead.
  Young Sultan brought up in a monastery,
[In the play, the shopkeepers have a scene of explanation before Hajj enters, — altered when writing play.] Said to be a dreamer and a poet.
  The real ruler said to be the Executioner,
  A favourite of late Sultan,
  Young man, too, but very strong,
  Very cruel and selfish.
  Young Sultan does not see much of Executioner (*Mansur*).
  Supposed to disappear on nightly expeditions,
  To get to know his people,
  To have some love adventures.
  Has been brought up strictly in monastery.
  Has never yet, they say, tested the "charm of his beard."
[This altered. See note above. In the play Hajj enters here.] Hajji listens to all this humbly,
  Sitting almost under the counter.
  Then begins to finger stuffs.
  The shopkeeper is going to drive him off.
  But Hajji is in earnest.
  Shows his purse. He means to buy.
  Clothes are forthcoming.
  He selects some.

Once he has gone to the bath and the barber he will be resplendent — as noble as the noblest.

Hajji asks the price.

It is very high.

He begins to bargain.

Shopkeeper No. II chimes in.

Hajji pits Shopkeeper No. I against No. II.

They quarrel.

Hajji fans the quarrel into flame.

They almost come to blows.

Hajji escapes with his clothes.

Shopkeeper No. I.   The shopkeepers notice his escape.
and   They combine at once against the com-
Shopkeeper No. II   mon enemy.

Shopkeeper I will go for the guard, And have Hajji followed and caught.

Shopkeeper II to meet him at the Executioner's to witness against Hajji.

[Here Nasir the Guide is introduced to give away Hajj. This was done when the play was revised for production.]

Curtain

SCENE 3

(For "Zira" read "Marsinah.")

Zira's home. Small courtyard of a poor house. On right side a large gate backing to street. Fountain in courtyard.

Old Woman.   Old woman is spinning.

Zira, the daughter of   Zira is lazily hanging her hand into
Hajji.   fountain. (She works instead.)

[*Marsinah works.* This   Old Woman reprimands her for not
was altered when writing   working.
play, because of Arabian   She has changed in last three days.
embroidery frame seen   Zira, who hides her wools, says her
in the Museum of Tunis.]   thread has given out.

Old Woman will go to bazaar for thread.
Locks door carefully, going out.

Zira springs up and goes to the casement in Courtyard and then, plucking a rose, throws it out. She then unlocks casement and goes back to the fountain.

Young Sultan appears in simple clothes, climbing in.

Zira.
Young Sultan.

Love scene.

His madness to come at daytime.
Since he saw her first three nights ago from neighboring roof-tops cannot rest.
She asks who he is.
He is so different from her father.
His hands so beautiful.
He has love scene,
In which they exchange rhymed couplets
In Arabian Nights fashion.
He puts a question (line one and two rhyming)
She caps it (line three not rhyming, but line four rhyming with one and two).
The girl is witty but natural.
This charms the Sultan beyond measure.
All the women he has had presented to him are so stupid.
She says: "'All the women'!" Who is he?
He says a simple scribe — brought up in a monastery. His uncle wishes him to marry.
He has never loved before,
Till meeting Zira.
They embrace.

Noise of key in gate.

They hear noise.
They separate — He will come back after sundown to see her. She gives him a rose. Then he will tell her something which will surprise her.
He escapes through the window.

Zira back to fountain, (to her work).

Old Woman reënters breathless.

Old Woman.	Old Woman says Zira's father is coming.
Zira.	Thing he has never done during daytime.
	Luckily she saw him as she returned from bazaar.
	He was coming out of Public Bath,
	Beautifully dressed.
	They pretend to be busy working.

Noise of key.

Hajji arrives, dressed in good clothes, curls trimmed and beard combed.

Hajji.	Greetings.
Zira.	Zira admires her father.
Old Woman.	Old Woman sent off to get meal ready.
Hajji.	Hajji has great plans for his daughter.
Zira.	His affection for her profound.
	He plans for her future.
	She is very charming to him,
	As she naturally wishes to hide her love affair, and get into his good graces.
	She takes out her guitar.
	Begins to sing to him.
	He sways before her admiringly on his knees.
	Says she is beautiful.
[This altered in the writing of play.]	Her mother was not beautiful.
	Not like his wife that he loved
	Not like his son now dead.
	But she is more beautiful than all,
	The light of his eyes.
	She laughs and sings.
	He claps his hands in ecstasy
	He has great ambitions for her.

A knock on the door.

Zira is sent by her father into the inner house.

The Old Woman comes out of house and says it will be some pedlar at door.

She opens.

The Officer of the Guard and Guard enter with the Shopkeeper I

Hajji.	Shopkeeper accuses **Hajji** of stealing
Shopkeeper.	garments he has on.
Officer.	Hajji denies it.
	Shopkeeper will have him taken before
	the Executioner (*Mansur*).
	Hajji protests.
	He is taken off in spite of his assurances
	that the Shopkeeper is a madman.
[Re-introduction of Na- sir, saying, "I saw no purse!" Change made during rehearsals]	*Curtain*

SCENE 4

Hall in Executioner's House (large set). A colonnade at back,
showing courtyard.

Executioner (Mansur).	Executioner very discontented.
His Scribe (Afife), an	Young Sultan means to curtail Execu-
old man.	tioner's prerogatives.
[*Kafur his Sworder,* —	Executioner was old Sultan's favorite.
added when play was	Scribe and Executioner plan to assas-
written. This first scene	sinate Sultan.
is enlarged in play by a	They need a clever man.
letter from the Caliph.	Whom shall they get?
See play.]	

Hajji is brought by the Guard, followed by Shopkeeper and
a Crowd, in which is the Guide of Scene 1.

Hajji.	Hajji accused by Shopkeeper I.
Executioner.	Shopkeeper II bearing No. I witness.
Scribe.	Hajji protests.
Guide.	Meant to pay — Excitement of new
Shopkeeper I.	clothes made him forget.
Shopkeeper II.	Produces money.
Crowd.	Where did he get his money?
	Sheikh of desert.
	They all laugh.
	Sheikh of desert does not give money.
	Sheikhs are outlaws, robbers.

Not allowed in town.

Hajji says he is in town.

Notices Guide (*Nasir*) in crowd.

Appeals to Guide —

Guide says it is true that Sheikh is in town.

Then, says Executioner, Sheikh must be taken before Sultan.

All Cûrds banished by old Sultan.

Sultan has an audience this afternoon.

Sheikh an exile (by old Sultan).

Executioner cannot allow the word of the deceased monarch to be disregarded.

Sends Guide off to show the Guard the caravansary at which Sheikh is stopping.

Hajji interrupts.

One word.

He asks Guide did he, the Sheikh, not throw Hajji a purse.

Guide repeating Hajji's words (Scene 1) "I saw no purse."

All laugh.

Guide off with the Guard.

[Afterwards, "his hand cut off," as this is the law of the Koran. Change made when writing play.] Executioner orders Hajji to have his ears cut off.

Hajji discourses on Fate, Kismet.

Is very witty.

Executioner becomes interested in Hajji's brilliancy.

Hajji is pardoned suddenly by Executioner.

Executioner does more.

He takes Hajji into his household

Into his personal guard.

A sword is sent for.

Hajji kneels in gratitude at the Executioner's feet.

"His servant always."

The sword is brought in.

Executioner takes it and hands it to Hajji.

"Rise, Hajji, and learn to use this sword in my service."

Hajji rises.

He begs he may begin his career by an act of clemency.

Executioner grants permission.

Hajji makes the Shopkeepers kneel, forgives them for daring to accuse a servant of the Executioner's of stealing — tickles their beards with his sword and orders them to pay a fine to the Executioner.

They leave more dead than alive.

Hajji turns to Executioner.

H. "Have I begun well?"

E. "The beginning is nothing. Go now and the Captain will instruct you in your duties."

H. (*with enormous swagger*) "Captain?"

He goes out, the rest following him.

The Scribe.
Executioner.

Is amazed at Executioner's clemency.

E. "Don't you see why I have pardoned him?"

S. "No, Master."

E. "This man shall do the deed."

S. "The deed?"

E. "Murder the Sultan for me."

S. "I see."

(*They both turn and look after Hajji who is seen traversing the courtyard at the back and twirling his moustaches, the servants all bowing low to him.*)

Curtain

ACT II

An inner chamber in Executioner's House. Door leading to Hareem.
[This is the same hall as at the end of Act I, only that curtains are drawn to hide the courtyard.]

Hajji.
Executioner.
Scribe.
[Coffee and smoking suppressed, as both were found to be anachronisms.]

[This altered. Eastern men do not speak of their wives to strangers.]

Executioner and Scribe seated on a platform drinking coffee and smoking. Hajji seated below them entertaining them with amorous stories. They are all laughing. Hajji finishes a story.

Executioner says it reminds him of his principal wife.

A slight pause.

The Executioner gives Scribe a look as if to say "To business."

He says to Hajji —

How would Hajji like to become a great power in the state?

He broaches plan of assassinating the Sultan.

Hajji hesitates.

Executioner unfolds scheme.

There is an audience in half an hour.

Hajji can come as a Fakir.

[See play. All of this scene was split in half, and Mansur does not now suggest the assassination till at the end of the second half. The reason is clear: Hajj could not have a love scene (as he does now) if he were brooding about the assassination. This was altered in rehearsal at the suggestion of Mr. Grimwood, who played Mansur in England.]

Has told Executioner he could juggle — used to play tricks at his corner when begging. Hajji could get close to Sultan and kill him. No danger to Hajji, As the Guards are under command of Executioner Executioner will be there. But, of course, Hajji must under no condition recognize the Executioner. Hajji feels doubts. Executioner fills him full of promises. Executioner will be made Sultan. Hajji shall become Executioner.

Executioner off to put on his armour for audience.

Scribe goes with him.

Executioner: "Think it over. If you don't like it — there is always room for a strangled body in the river."

Hajji (Alone).

"So this is why I was pardoned this morning?

Oh, Hajji! What a fool you are!

And you thought your personal charm did it all."

Hajji.
Old Woman No II.
[Changed to young slave Miskah. The note becomes a message, with dialogue between Hajj and Miskah]

Door of Hareem opens. Old Woman No. II appears with a note, gives it to Hajji.

Hajji reads it, smiles and nods.

Old Woman disappears.

Hajji (Alone).

"After all I cannot be so utterly without charm, if *this* can happen to me."

He twirls his moustaches up and looks at himself in the blade of his sword.

Old Woman No. II reënters with veiled woman (Executioner's Wife). Old Woman stands guard.

Hajji.
Wife. ⌡

The Wife has seen him from her window.

As he crossed the courtyard at noon, she lost her heart to him.

Her husband neglects her.

She comes to Hajji for sympathy.

Hajji makes love to her.

She refuses to unveil, — at least, at once.

She makes appointment with him.

To meet him in the Executioner's Bath at moonrise.

All the women bathe then.

She will leave a little screen unlatched that leads to the furnaces under the baths.

These furnaces reached also from men's
quarters through the door in the Court.
(She points it out to him.)
He can come and see her there in Bath,
when the other women are back in the
Hareem.
The Executioner never returns from the
Sultan till after supper.
They hear a noise.
She withdraws.
                ´Hajji struts about in great glee.
He hears Executioner coming
He throws himself on his knees and
prays.

Executioner.   Executioner returns armed.
Hajji.   What has Hajji decided?
Scribe.   Hajji says he has been wrestling in
prayer.
He cannot make up his mind to kill Sul-
tan, a descendant of the Prophet.
Executioner says he also is a descendant
of Prophet.
Hajji is accused of cowardice.
He denies it.
He says he has ties that bind him.
The risk is too great because of his
daughter, his daughter, Zira.
He tells about her.
Finally he consents to kill Sultan on one
condition.
No matter what happens to him the
Executioner must marry the daughter.
The Executioner consents.
Hajji is overjoyed.
He quite forgets his own danger when he
thinks his daughter will be the Sultana.
He will hurry off to his daughter's house,
And have her conveyed to Executioner's
house after sun-down.
Too beautiful to pass through the streets
at day time.

Begs for a guard to convey her.
Once he has arranged with her he will
come on to young Sultan's palace, —
"The Sultan who will be dead. Who
is dead!"
He hurries off in great exultation.

[When the play was
written, the mid-after-
noon call to prayer was
introduced here as a
Curtain.]

Curtain

SCENE 2

*Zira's home. Same scene as Scene 3, Act **I**. Small courtyard.*
Zira sits with her guitar singing a love song.

Zira.
Old Woman.
[Cut when play was
written.]

⎧ Zira tries to get the Old Woman to go
⎪ out that night.
⎨ Old Woman suspicious.
⎪ Zira calms her fears.
⎩ Coaxes her, pets her.

Hajji arrives.

Hajji.
Zira.
Old Woman.

Hajji has come to break news to Zira.
Great news!
He is going to give her to Executioner
as wife.
Zira dumb with horror.
Violent scene of cursing and cajoling.
Finally she rebels.
The Old Woman agrees with Hajji
whenever he appeals to her.
He finally calls in the Guard, and makes
them guard door.

[Altered during rehear-
sal. The guard, — eu-
nuchs of Mansur — take
the daughter away at
once. Hajj remains on
the scene, smiling in a
self-satisfied fashion.]

At sundown they are to take the girl to
Executioner's house.
Ungrateful child!
Zira in tears. Hajji off.

Curtain

SCENE 3

The Sultan's Audience Hall (The Caliph's Diwan). (Large set.)
Sultan seated on a Divan.
His Vizier by his side.
Dances of Women.
Sultan melancholy. He says to Vizier that all these dances are
nothing to the faded rose in his hand.
Hour for audience strikes.
The women dismissed.
The gates are opened to the crowd.
The various dignitaries enter.
The Executioner and the Guard come and kneel to the Sultan.
Different cases for trial called.
First of all the old Sheikh is called.
His whereabouts have been ascertained through the Guide.
The Sheikh is carried in on his litter and with greatest difficulty
descends to do obeisance to the Sultan.

Sultan.	Sultan asks him how he, an exile, dare
Sheikh.	enter the city, defying the decree of his
Executioner.	late uncle.
Crowd, etc.	Sheikh says he came on peaceful mission, not to rob.

He is old; one of many robbers. No
longer of consequence.
Came to pray at shrine and give alms,
the shrine where he had prayed in his
youth.
Invokes protection of High Priest.
Sultan says Sheikh must be imprisoned.
If High Priest proves that Sheikh came
to give alms and to repent, he shall be
released forthwith.
Meanwhile, for his many sins, a short
repentance in prison will not be harmful to his soul.

The Goaler comes forward and with two guards drags the
lame man off. The Sheikh goes, blessing the Sultan for his
wisdom and justice. The Sultan says : " Send to the High
Priest at once to see if this old man spoke true."

Sultan.
A Peasant with Two Wives.
[This scene was cut at rehearsal, as having nothing to do with the story. Instead of which, Hajj was introduced by a speech of Mansur's. See play.]

This should be some comic trial with a difficult question to solve. Such as: "Should a man honour his first wife more — who is old and ugly, but devoted — or his second wife whom he mistrusts but adores for her beauty?" Or something of the kind drawn from Arabian Nights.

The Sultan is puzzled.
He has no answer.
Who can solve the riddle ?

Hajji, pushing through the crowd, — "Let me, oh Sire !" — throws himself before Sultan.

Hajji.
Sultan.
Others

[Cut:]

Hajji decides in a witty, whimsical way.
The Sultan amused by him. Who is he?
Hajji says he is a Fakir.
He plays some tricks.
{ While doing one, addresses the Executioner as a slave, asking him to bring a table.
Pretends not to know who Executioner is, and begs his pardon when he is told of his rank.
He then gets near the Sultan.
Does a trick with a sword.
Tries suddenly to stab the Sultan.
The Sultan wears a coat of mail.
The assassination has failed.
Hajji is surrounded at once.
He is to be cut to pieces.
The Sultan says "Stay!"
This man shall be made an example of.
I have heard there are rumours of sedition, and conspiracies against my person.
Therefore I wear this coat of mail.
I shall have this man burnt in my pleasure gardens tomorrow and the public shall be admitted to the spectacle.

This shall show conspirators I am in earnest; mean to uphold my uncle's policy.

Take this man away."

Hajji appeals, he turns to the Executioner.

The Executioner says he does not know him.

Hajji says he does.

He can prove it. He was in the house of the Executioner. In his pay.

Executioner: "The man is mad."

The Sultan fixes Executioner with his eye.

Sultan says he will sift matter to bottom.

Hajji shall be tortured.

The truth shall be wrung from him.

[Hajj is gagged here:] "At once?" asks the Gaoler.

Sultan: "No — let him starve the night first."

Tonight (*smelling the rose*) Sultan has other affairs of import to tend to.

Tomorrow (*with a meaning look*) he expects the Executioner to carry out the tortures himself.

The Executioner bows.

(*To Goaler*) "Take the man away!"

Hajji is dragged off, screaming.

The Sultan to his Vizier: "Oh Mesrur! Mesrur! (Abu Bakr) When does the sun set?"

"Another half an hour, sire"

"Half an hour! Oh, would it were that now!

Why can I not make the sun set — I — the Sultan?

Bring forward the next case."

Curtain.

SCENE 4

A Dungeon. A massive door at the back leads to an endless flight of shallow steps. It is dark : Hardly any light except from one barred window high up: through this come the rays of the setting sun.

The Sheikh is alone in one corner saying his prayers. He then lies down and goes to sleep.

The Gaoler opens the door.

Hajji is thrown in and chained.

Hajji alone.	Repentance.
	Curses every one.
	Raves.
	If only he hadn't received money that morning, he would not have been tempted to steal.
	If he had not stolen, he would not have been taken to the Executioner.
	If he hadn't been taken to the Executioner, he would not have been driven to kill the Sultan.
	The Sheikh is the cause of all his misfortunes.
	He stole his wife.
	He killed his son.
	Now he is killing him.
	Cursed be the Sheikh!
The Sheikh from the corner :	"Who uses my name in vain?"
Hajji.	Hajji recognizes him.
Sheikh.	What is he doing there?
	Sheikh says he is condemned to prison by Sultan.
	Hajji delighted.
	Says this is his only consolation in his trouble.
	Never a sorrow without a grain of joy.
	Joy to see his enemy suffer.
	He could almost feel friendly towards Sheikh, when he thinks how they will be executed together.

[Sheikh's story of the broken coin and his lost son introduced here. See play.

Allusions to wife were cut as unnecessary to the story.]

How strangely their lives have been interwoven.

They talk of the dead woman they have shared.

She is dead now.

Better so. She would have been old and ugly now.

Sheikh says: "She developed a bad temper."

Hajji furiously: "That was your fault. She was the sweetest tempered creature when she was mine. You ruined her, body and soul.

You fiend you — but no matter. You will be tortured tomorrow."

He shrieks with delight.

Gaoler reënters with a decree and a soldier carrying some instruments of torture.

Gaoler.
Sheikh.
Hajji.

Soldier.

Gaoler says that it has been found that Sheikh did come on a pilgrimage.

The High Priest has testified in his favor.

Therefore the Sultan forgives him.

He is free, but must leave the city at once and never return.

Sheikh asks Gaoler to thank Sultan.

Would go — but his limbs are too weak. Could Gaoler send for his litter?

Gaoler says he fears Sheikh's litter gone, but could procure him a chair out of Sultan's palace used to convey the lesser women of the Hareem when Sultan travels.

[Changed to a stretcher used to "carry away the dead." Alteration made when play was written.]

Sheikh gives Gaoler money.

Gaoler now turns to Hajji.

Says he is to come to him.

Makes him kneel down.

Hajji: "I am free too, am I?"

Gaoler: "Free? Here! (*turns to Soldier and takes a casket from him and is about*

[The torture was cut *to put it on Hajji's head*). Sometimes

as too long and too ugly. Altered during rehearsal.]

these head screws and thumb screws don't fit. There must be no hitch in the performance tomorrow."

"Head screw?" says Hajji, trembling. Gaoler tears off Hajji's turban and tries on the torture helmet.

Gaoler: "Does it feel comfortable?"

[All this cut. Instead of which, the Gaoler strikes Hajj with his key which makes Hajj faint.]

Hajji: "Comfortable!"

Gaoler: "It ought to. It's just as if it had been made for your Highness." (Takes it off, laughing loudly; the soldier joins politely.)

Gaoler (to Sheikh): "I'll see to your Excellency's chair."

Gaoler and Soldier off with instruments. *Hajji is on the floor, more dead than alive.*

Hajji.
Sheikh.

Hajji bemoans his fate.

Why should he have to suffer, and Sheikh be pardoned, when Sheikh is the cause of all of Hajji's woe?

Here is Sheikh, an old robber chief, forgiven.

Here is Hajji, a simple, honest beggar, to be tortured and burnt.

Who is dependent on the Sheikh?

He has lost his son — has never found him again — he may be dead.

No one dependent on Sheikh.

But Hajji has a daughter dependent on him.

A daughter! And the sun is setting.

And at this hour she is being taken to the Executioner!

The Executioner who has so cruelly forsaken Hajji.

His daughter going to him, with Hajji powerless — and the Sheikh to live.

It is unjust, cruel, not to be borne.

"It shan't be borne — it —"

[When the play was

He gives the Sheikh an awful look.

written, the breaking of the chains was introduced here.]

The Sheikh realizes his thoughts and draws his knife.

Hajji springs at him, overpowers him, and cuts his throat.

The Sheikh's last words: "My son! My son!"

A moment's thought — then Hajji wipes the knife on his own turban (torn off by Gaoler).

Quickly he exchanges clothes with the dead man.

Puts on his turban

Then rifles pockets.

Finds round the dead man's throat a chain with the broken half of a coin.

Slips it over his own neck.

He puts the dead body into the corner where he (Hajji) lay when the Gaoler left the dungeon.

He hears the tread on the steps.

He assumes the old man's attitude.

The sunlight has died out: the scene grows quite dark.

The Gaoler reënters with the Soldier and a chair borne by two porters. They lift Hajji into the chair. Then take up the chair and carry it up the broad stone stairs.

Gaoler. (*Turning to the dead body.*) "Why not laugh tonight, Hajji? Tomorrow morning will be time enough to weep, when you are tortured in the Pleasure Gardens of the Prophet's descendant." (*He kicks the body, then goes out laughing, and locks the door.*)

Curtain.

ACT III

SCENE 1

[This scene (suggested by a friend) was entirely cut before rehearsals began.]

Zira's house. Same scene as Act I, Scene 3. Small courtyard.
The sun has just set. It is dusk.
The gate is opened from the street.

Old Woman I (Narjis) enters, locks the gate, and lights a lamp.
Knocking at the gate.
Old Woman I opens the gate.
The two porters bring in the chair.
Hajji gets out, bent double, and trembling.
He pays the porters: they withdraw.
The Old Woman says: "Who are you?"

Hajji.   Hajji throws back the shawl.
            He reveals himself, asks for food and
            his daughter.

Old Woman I.   "Hajji!"
            Hajji explains that he must escape:
            Leave the city at once.
            Too long to explain.
            He can never come to Bagdad again.
            Old Woman to bring his daughter at once,
            Old Woman says she has just taken
            daughter to Executioner's house.
            Hajji: "I said not before sundown"
            "It is sundown."
            Hajji curses Old Woman.
            Says that it is her fault that he took
            his daughter to Executioner.
            "My fault?" says she.
            "Yes! You urged me on.
            You agreed with me.
            If I have lost her, you are to blame.
            But I can't lose her.
            I must risk everything.
            I must get her out of his clutches."
            Where did Old Woman leave her?
            With principal wife.
            An idea!
            He had appointment with wife in bath
            at moon rise —
            He will go.
            If it costs him his life, he must try to
            get his daughter.
            He goes to door; as he does so, there is
            knocking at door from without.

They have found him.

What shall he do?

Old Woman opens lattice in Courtyard.

"Escape that way!

When I was young many a time my lover came through that window."

Haj i off through window.

> *More knocking at door.*
> *Old Woman opens.*

Sultan.
Vizier
and a Guard.
Old Woman.

Sultan enters, splendidly attired.

Has come to claim his bride.

Old Woman amazed.

Is he not the Sultan?

She has seen him the day of his entry into the town.

Sultan: "You have guessed.   Bring forth Zira!"

Alas! Zira not here.

At Executioner's house.

Her father has destined her for Executioner.

Sultan furious.

When was she taken there?

Not an hour ago.

Sultan will go to Executioner's house.

The Old Woman I is to lead the way and show the entrance she took the girl to.

> *Curtain.*

SCENE 2

[In the play Act III begins here.]

The Bath in the Executioner's house. (Large set.)

Up five marble steps (almost fifteen feet up stage) a colonnade. Beyond it a courtyard, with a large swimming bath. The front part of the stage, couches and pierced screens. Door right to women's apartments, door left to men's apartments.

Early moonlight in the courtyard beyond the columns. Hanging lamps in the front part of the bath.

Women are robing and disrobing. Some are swimming in the tank. Laughter and chatter.

Principal Wife.   Wife at her toilet.

Old Woman II (Miskah.) Old Woman helping.

               Has Hajji not come back yet?

               "No sign," says Old Woman.

               Has been to outer gate twice.

               Only person there a young woman

               Guarded by two soldiers (eunuchs),

               Weeping this last half hour.

               They say she has been brought by Executioner's orders.

               "Another woman?

               Have her brought here!"

               Old Woman takes order to doorkeeper at door L.

Principal Wife goes to top of steps and orders the other women to dress and retire.

The women swim to the right end of the bath. The talk is silenced.

Zira is brought in by the slave doorkeeper, followed by the Old Woman II.

Wife.   Wife: "What have we here?"

Zira.   She abuses girl.

Old Woman II.   Ill treats her.

[This scene enlarged during rehearsal. Marsinah (Zira) does not leave the stage, but veils. See play.]   Leads off into inner chamber of slaves. Zira in tears goes off by colonnade right with the Old Woman.

Wife.   "I'll soon break your spirit!"

                              The door left opens.

The Executioner enters in a bad humour

Executioner.   *Wife:* "This is an unexpected delight!

Wife.   So early? Did the Sultan not keep you to supper?"

               Executioner: "What are you doing in the bath at this time of night?"

               W. "I was but waiting for you to ask what you wish done with the new slave."

               E. "What new slave?"

               W. "The woman who has just arrived, guarded by two of your men."

The Doorkeeper. "The men you dispatched with Hajji, sir, this afternoon."

E. "Oh, that woman!"

I shall have her strangled."

Wife agrees.

Says girl a slut.

Executioner finds his wife agrees with him to such an extent that he thinks the girl must be beautiful.

Rings a bell.

Old Woman II comes from Colonnade.

[This altered. Marsinah has not left the stage. See note above.] He orders her to bring Zira.

The wife tries to interfere.

Executioner angry.

Wife wonders why he is in such an angry mood.

Because he may lose his head any moment.

"Lose his head?" she asks.

"Yes. This new Sultan —"

Zira is brought in from R. on steps by Old Woman. Zira is veiled.

Executioner.	Executioner orders her to unveil.
Zira.	She hesitates.
Wife.	He tears the veil from her face.
Old Woman.	He sees she is beautiful.

Says to his wife that she has lied.

"Go, get the girl ready.

I will come to her as soon as I have had my bath.

Until tomorrow, at least, I shall enjoy life.

After that — who knows? "

He goes off up the Colonnade to left.

Wife orders Old Woman to take the girl away with her again.

Zira goes off by small door right with Old Woman.

There is a tapping sound on a screen on the right side.

Wife.	"Hajji!"

Wife goes and opens screen in the wall right. Hajji enters.

Wife.	Wife tells him to be quiet.
Hajji.	Executioner near at hand.

Expects an amorous embrace.

Hajji says there is no time for love making.

He has come about his daughter.

W. "Your daughter?"

H. "Yes. Zira — She came here for the Executioner. Has he seen her? Has he gone in to her?"

W. "So she's your daughter?
I have you to thank for this creature, Another rival."

Hajji wants to know where the girl is.

Can't Wife bring her out here and let the girl escape with him.

W. "Escape?"

H. "In that way you can get rid of a rival."

W. "And be strangled myself?"

He urges her.

If she won't let the girl escape, at least won't she take the girl to a sanctuary?

Sanctuary? What for?

To get her out of the way — away from Executioner.

Why not take her to the Mosque?

The Mosque of the Carpenters, where the venerable priest is?

He entreats Wife by the love she has for him.

Points out the dangerous charm of his daughter.

She will prove a great rival.

Wife is torn between jealousy and fear for her own life.

H. "You can say you took her to the Sanctuary for purification — Take her there!"

They are interrupted.

The Executioner appears in a thin robe in the colonnade with two slaves. Wife escapes rapidly into inner room to right. Hajji's escape is cut off. He grovels on the floor.

Hajji.
Executioner.

[All this much more direct and brutal in play. Change made when play was written.]

Executioner sees Hajji and dismisses the slaves.

Amazed at Hajji's presence.

Hajji says he has done everything to get back to Executioner. Bribed the Sultan's Gaoler, faced untold dangers. Grovels and at the same time tries to find out the Executioner's position in regard to the Sultan.

Has he lost his power?

What has Sultan done to Executioner?

Executioner in a boundless rage.

How dare Hajji come and ask him questions?

How dare he break into the women's quarters and then ask for mercy?

How dare he appeal to the Executioner, after betraying him to the Sultan?

Who was Hajji before the Executioner looked with favor on him?

A swine, an abomination picked out of the gutter.

A cur, a dog, — a —

He approaches Hajji.

Hajji hurries up the steps.

The Executioner is too quick, gets up after him and takes Hajji by the throat. Doing so, he catches hold of the chain with the coin that Hajji stole from Sheikh (Act II, Scene 4.)

Where did Hajji get this?

Hajji lies, saying it is his.

It has always been his.

Executioner produces the other half on a massive gold chain.

Miraculous!

Hajji must be Executioner's father.

H. "You — my son?"

E. "Don't you remember?"

[This was altered so Executioner tells how he can just re-that Hajji tells the Executioner all this. See Act II, Scene 4, where the Sheikh gives Hajji the facts.]

member his father breaking a coin when they were being attacked in the desert, before he, the boy, was carried away by the Sultan's troops.

H. "You mean when I was—Sheikh?"

E. "Were you Sheikh or just a robber, then?"

H. "Just a robber at the time — just a robber — And your mother — do you remember her?"

E. "I have tried to often — Her name escapes me."

H. Mentions name of first wife: "Zcenab — whom I loved above all things."

"Zcenab! That was her name!"

H. "She had eyes like stars; and tall, she was tall like a poplar.

How wonderful is fate!

So you are her son!"

E. "Your son."

Hajji, slowly eyeing him and taking the Executioner's chain.

H. "And the halves fit! What a splendid chain! What a heavy chain! Heavier than mine. You have prospered in life, my son —"

E. "My father —"

H. "Your father, yes. I am your father — Come to my arms."

With that he takes the gold chain round the Executioner's neck and twists it till the Executioner chokes. Forces him down on his knees.

Then he pushes him backward into the bath. Holds him under the water and drowns him. "I killed the old rat! I'll kill his spawn! Blessed be Allah for this day of days." He laughs wildly and exultantly.

There is one more splash, then silence in the bath.
Knocking on the door left.

More knocking.
Then the door is broken open.
The Sultan enters with his Guard and Torchbearers, the
  old Woman No. I. following.

The Sultan.	"Where is the woman? Where is Zira? Search the Hareem!"
	Some of the Soldiers cross into door right.
Sultan.	Sultan turns and see Hajji on the steps
Hajji.	by the bath.
	"You?"
	H. "Yes." Allah allowed him to escape in order to serve the Sultan.
	S. "Cut him down!"
	H. "Stop! Look first whether I am not a good servant.
	Look in the bath!"
	The Sultan looks.
	S. "The Executioner!"
	H. "It was all his fault.
	He drove me to attempt your life."

Soldiers reënter, bringing in Wife. Other women of the
  Hareem follow.

Wife.	Soldier says Zira not there.
Sultan.	Wife confesses she has sent her to
Hajji.	Sanctuary.
Old Woman No. I.	Hajji begged her to do so.
	S. "Hajji! Ever Hajji! Why should he have any say in regard to Zira?"
	H. "She is my daughter."
	S. "Yours!"
	H. "Now say I am not a good servant when I serve you with such a daughter. Will you still kill me?"
	Old Woman No. I testifies he is speaking the truth, is Zira's father.
	S. "You have attempted my life. What would my piety be if I pardoned the dagger that tried to kill the descendant of the Prophet?

Taking the law into your own hands
(*points to bath*) does not wipe out your
crime.
But you are the father of Zira,
The woman whom I mean to make my
Sultana.
Her father's blood must not be shed by
me.
Go, then, be banished, forgotten!
Your life is spared — but only under one
condition.
Henceforth you shall be as dead to me
— to your daughter."
H. "To my daughter? Never to speak
to her again, to feel her cheek against
mine? Never?
S. "I have spoken."
Hajji tears his clothes, strews ashes on
his head from the brazier by his side and
goes out, staggering, by door left.
The Sultan will go the Mosque to beg
the High Priest to release Zira from the
Sanctuary.

Curtain

LAST SCENE

The same as the first scene, Act I. Before the Mosque, moonlight.
Young Beggar of Act I is seated on the
seat on which Hajji installed him.
Hajji enters staggering down the street.
He stands at the Mosque a moment.
[Here was introduced a *Wants to enter, then turns away in*
scene with the Priest. *despair.*
Meccah is to be Hajj's *Comes to his accustomed seat.*
goal. Altered when play *Young Beggar is there.*
was written.] [The scene *As Hajji approaches, the Young Beggar*
with the Young Beggar *begins to beg of him.*
is postponed until after *Hajji kicks him off the seat and resumes*
the Caliph and Marsinah *his old place.*

leave. Altered when the *Young Beggar slinks away.*
play was written.]

*Scarcely is Hajji seated when the Sultan
enters on his white donkey with a torch-
light procession.*

*The Sultan dismounts and knocks at the
Mosque.*

The Mosque is opened by the Priest.

*The Priest, when he learns it is the Sultan,
brings out Zira to him.*

*The Sultan reveals himself in a verse to
Zira.*

Zira replies in a rhyme.

The Sultan conducts Zira to a litter.

He re-mounts his donkey.

The procession moves past Hajji.

*Hajji stretches out his hand for alms,
veiling his face.*

*The procession disappears. The street
grows dark again.*

The Mosque is shut.

Hajji is left alone in the moonlight.

*He draws out the old gourd from behind
the stone seat.*

*A line of philosophy summing up his day.
Something, perhaps, on "life and water."*

*He drinks his fill, puts the gourd away,
leans back, and goes to sleep, breathing
regularly.*

Curtain [1]

Does not this careful scenario make very clear what are
the steps in good scenario writing? First comes structure, —
ordering for clearness and correct emphasis in the story-telling. Then, with the scenario kept flexible and subject to
change till the last possible moment, come many changes
big and little, for better characterization and more atmosphere — see pp. 461–463.

[1] For the play see *Kismet*, Methuen & Co., Ltd., London.

Finally, more than anything else, as the author puts last touches to his scenario, or revises the play he has written from it, he scans its details in relation to the probable attitude toward them of his public. In the relation of that public to his subject and his treatment of it lie the most difficult problems of the dramatist. Solving them means the difference between the will to conquer and victory.

CHAPTER X

THE DRAMATIST AND HIS PUBLIC

PROBABLY most dramatists have found that any play, either as a scenario or a completed manuscript, is not a matter of writing but of frequent re-writing. Study *From Ibsen's Workshop* or most of the cases cited by Binet and Passy,[1] and it becomes evident that the first draft of a scenario or play is usually made mainly for clearness. That will be gained by good construction and correct emphasis. There follows a re-writing in which characterization improves greatly and dialogue becomes characterizing and attractive in itself. Either in this or possible later re-writings, the dramatist shapes his material more and more in relation to the public he wishes to address, for a dramatist is, after all, a sort of public speaker. Unlike the platform orator, however, he speaks indirectly to his audience — through people and under conditions he cannot wholly control. None the less, much if not all that concerns the persuasion of public argumentation concerns the dramatist. This does not in any sense mean that an author must truckle to his audience. Far from it. Yet no dramatist can work care free in regard to his audience. He must consider their natural likes and dislikes, interests and indifferences, their probable knowledge of his subject as well as their probable approach to it. As Mr. Archer has pointed out. "The moment a playwright confines his work within the two or three hours' limit prescribed by Western custom for a theatrical performance, he is currying favour with an audience. That limit is imposed simply by the physical endurance and power of sustained attention

[1] *L'Année Psychologique*, 1894.

that can be demanded of Western human beings assembled
in a theatre. Doubtless an author could express himself more
fully and more subtly if he ignored these limitations; the
moment he submits to them, he renounces the pretence that
mere self-expression is his aim." [1]

Once for all, what is "truckling to an audience"? When
an author, believing that the end of his play should be tragic,
so plans his work that until the last act or even the middle
of that act, a tragic ending is the logical conclusion, and
then because he is told or believes that an audience will
quit the theatre much more contented if the ending be happy,
he forces a pleasant ending on his play, he is untrue to himself, dishonest with his art, and truckles to his public. A
very large part of American audiences and many producers
believe that any play is only mere entertainment and consequently may and should be so manipulated as to please
the public even in its most unthinking mood. No man who
does that is a dramatist. He is merely a hack playwright,
bribed by the hope of immediate gain into slavish obedience
to the most unthinking part of the public.

On the other hand, an author is very foolish if he does not
remember certain fundamental principles about audiences
in a theatre. First, no matter what in his material attracts him, people rather than ideas arouse the interest of
the general public. Secondly, even yet action far more than
characterization wins and holds the attention of the great
majority. These facts do not mean, however, that a dramatist must busy himself only with plays of action or characterization, foregoing all problems or thesis material. They
do mean that if he is to write a play of ideas he must recognize that his task is the more difficult because of his public
and that he must so handle it through the characterization
and the action as to make his ideas widely interesting. In

---

[1] *Play-Making*, p. 14. William Archer. Small, Maynard & Co.

brief, insisting on saying what he wishes to say, he must
learn to speak in terms his audience will readily understand.

More than once a play good in itself has gone astray
because written too much unto the author's self, in the
sense that certain figures have interested him more than
others and he has forgotten that they are not likely to be interesting to the public at large and must be made so. For instance, a would-be adapter believed that the hero of the
tale he was dramatizing would remain on the stage the
hero still, but in action another character, with his songs
and rough humor, and his constant action, in sharp contrast with the quiet speech and restrained movement of
the central figure of the story, ran off with the interest.
Consequently this adaptation, though unusually well done
in all other respects, went awry.

Another aspect of the same difficulty is that an author forgets to consider carefully whether something he finds comic
or tragic will naturally be the same for his audiences. In a
prize play produced some years ago in Germany, *Belinda*,
the author found much comedy in the following situation.
A rather addle-pated man has for some years been paying
large sums to a correspondent, a woman as he believes, who
has been painting his portrait again and again from photographs he has sent her. Little by little he has fallen in love
with this correspondent. The day comes when he is awaiting
a visit from her with the utmost delight. A servant, who
knows that the woman is expected, enters looking utterly
bewildered, and announces her arrival. There walks into
the room a wizened Jewish picture dealer, who has all these
years been playing on the vanity of the younger man for his
own gain. Unfortunately the author forgot that an off-stage
figure must be made very attractive if sympathy is to go
with it rather than with a figure seen and known, or that
the on-stage figure must be very unattractive if sympathy

is not to go with it in contrast to a figure unseen. Consequently, when the Jew walked on he was greeted, not as the author expected with shouts of laughter, but with an aghast silence and obvious sympathy for the deceived man. Just at that point the play began to go to pieces because the author had misjudged, or not at all considered, the relation of the public to his material.

Where, perhaps, authors fail with their public more than anywhere else is in motivation of the conduct of their characters.[1] Too frequently a play slips because conduct as explained in it, though wholly convincing to the dramatist, does not similarly affect his public. It is useless for him to say stoutly that he knows the incident happened just in this way, or that the audience ought to know better than to think it could happen differently. As it is hopeless in life merely to protest that you are telling the truth when everybody is convinced that you are lying, it is wasted time for a dramatist to stand his ground in a matter of motivation if he has not succeeded in making that motivation convincing. For instance, there suddenly appears in the office of the hero of a play a former acquaintance of his, an actress. She has come to see him, if you please, even as her act in the theatre is playing. That is, simply because she so wished she has left the theatre during the performance. Now the dramatist may have known of such a case and people unacquainted with life behind the curtain may accept the situation, but people of the slightest experience in the theatre will know that no actor or actress playing an important rôle is allowed to leave during the performance. Instantly the scene becomes improbable for those people — and they are many. It must be so motivated as to be a probable exception in conduct, or the whole situation must be changed.

If it be clear that, though a dramatist should never truckle

[1] See pp. 248–276.

to his audience, he cannot hope to write successfully unless at some time in his composition he revises his material with a view to the general intelligence, natural interests, and prejudices of his audience so far as his special subject is concerned, it is equally true that publics change greatly in their tastes. A young dramatist may learn much as to such shiftings in public taste by watching the revivals of plays once very successful. In Shakespeare's day, for instance, the public would accept a mingling of the real and unreal with equanimity. Today it takes all the genius of Shakespeare to make the scenes of the ghost of Hamlet's father convincing. In reading Chapman's *Bussy d'Ambois*, with its strange commingling of real figures and ghosts, we today draw back disappointed because we feel that what has seemed real becomes with the entrance of the ghost only melodrama sublimated by some excellent characterization and fine poetry. As has already been pointed out, in Elizabethan days the public found cause for mirth in much which today is painful. Watch in performance the scene of *Twelfth Night* in which Toby, the Fool, and Maria deride Malvolio until they almost make him believe himself mad, and you have an admirable instance of changed taste. When first produced, it probably went with shouts of laughter. Because of sympathy for Malvolio it never goes well today. The public no longer finds madness unquestionably comic; it has its hesitations on practical jokes; it has lost a very little its sure enjoyment of drunkenness, especially in women. The day may conceivably come of which no one could say, as of the stage of our time: "The single expletive 'Damn' has saved many a would-be comic situation."

The attitude of a playwright should not be, "If my public ordinarily does not feel about this as I do, I will cut it out or make it conform to their usual tastes," but "Knowing perfectly what the attitude of the public is toward my material, I will not cut it out until I have proved that it is not in my power to make the audience feel it as I do." Just here lies the worst temptation of the playwright. He who keeps his eye more on the money box than artistic self-respect will little by little limit his choice of subjects and conventionalize his treatment of them because he is told or believes that the public will not stand for this or that. Is it not, however, a little strange that almost everything which leading playplacers, managers, and actors have in the past twenty-five years declared the public would unwillingly accept or would not accept at all has since become not only acceptable but often popular. Some years ago it was a truism among readers of manuscript plays that college life was too limited in interest to appeal to the general theatre public. Then Mr. Ade's *The College Widow* proved these prophets wrong. After this play trailed *Brown of Harvard* and a half-dozen other college plays which, whether good, bad, or indifferent artistically, were all warmly received by the public. Another statement once accepted in the theatrical world of New York was that American audiences no longer cared for farce, but *Seven Days*, followed by a crowding group of successes, changed all that. All this was not the result of any sudden revulsion on the part of the public, but came because some intelligent and clever workman, determining to make his interests and his sense of values the public's, labored until he accomplished the task. Forthwith a delighted public begged for more and what was declared impossible became the vogue. Just at present there is a troublesome convention that the American public will not accept anything but farce or comedy. This means only that at the moment our writers of serious plays are not adept enough to win away large audiences from farce and comedy or to build up special audiences for their plays. Nevertheless, sooner or later, they or their sucessors will conquer such a public.

In curious contradiction to the existing attitude that audiences will like only what they at present like, much advice
is given as to novelty. "Find something new in substance or
form and your fortune is made" is the implication. Wherein
lies novelty of plot has already been explained.[1] Certainly
the large amount of experimentation which has been going
on in recent years in one-act plays, two-act plays, or groups
of one-act pieces bound together by a prologue and an epilogue, has all been well worth while, making as it does for
greater flexibility of dramatic form. Yet it is unfortunately
true at the present moment that most audiences prefer a
three- or four-act play to something in two acts because the
uninterrupted attention demanded by the last form asks too
much from them. They prefer the three-act or four-act division to a group of one-act plays tied together by a prologue
and an epilogue, because mere difference of form has no particular attraction for them and they do not willingly shift
their interest as frequently as a group of one-act plays requires. Nevertheless there is nothing completely deterrent
for a dramatist in any of these circumstances; merely cause
why, in every case, after thinking of the subject in relation
to himself, he should ultimately consider it with equal care
in relation to the audience for which he intends it. When,
too, he is selecting his form he should observe whether
though attractive to him, it may not be so difficult or repellent for the general public that another more conventional form is desirable. If he becomes sure that he cannot
get his desired effects except in the form first chosen he
must work until he makes it acceptable to the public or
put aside his subject. The final test is not: "What ordinarily do the public like in a subject like mine and in what
form are they accustomed to see my subject treated," but:
"Can I so present the form I prefer as to make the public

[1] See pp. 62–67.

like equally with me what I find interesting in my subject?"
That is, though presentation of a chosen subject should be
flexible, the central purposes, human and artistic, of the
play, should be maintained inflexibly.

Bearing the audience in mind as one writes may affect
the whole play, but more often it affects details — particularly order. The scenario of *Kismet*[1] has been printed in
full chiefly that the many changes it underwent in shaping
it for final presentation might be clear. Among the many
instances note, in Act II, that in the original form the love
passage of Hajji followed plotting for the murder. When the
play was in rehearsal, both actor and author felt at once that
the sympathy it was necessary to maintain in the audience
for Hajji would be lost if he turned immediately from
such bloody plotting to the love scene. For this reason the
order was changed. Surely there is no harm in such a shifting, for the story develops just as well and the characterization is as humanly true. This is a perfect illustration of persuasive arrangement. Take now the case of the torturing
of Hajji, of which much was made in the original scenario.
It is changed to the blow with the key because the horror
of the scene when acted was too great and everything necessary is accomplished with the key. Here is a change made
not to please the author but to make the material as treated
produce in the audience the desired results, yet the change in
no way interferes with any of the purposes of the dramatist.
An illustration of the way in which a dramatist standing his
ground because he is sure of the rightness of his psychology
may win over his public is found in *La Princesse Georges* of
Dumas fils. So great was the sympathy of the audience with
Severine in her mortified wifehood that at the original performance, when she forgave her husband at the end, there
were many dissenting cries. Dumas fils had foreseen this,

[1] See pp. 474–507.

but believing the ending truer to life than any other could be, he insisted on it. Ultimately the ending was accepted by the public as made necessary by the rest of the play.

In all this discussion of the difference between truckling to an audience and necessary regard for its interests and prejudices, of changing public taste, the important point is that until a dramatist has considered his material in relation to the public, his play is by no means ready for production. Just because the persuasive side of dramatic art is so often neglected, play after play goes on the boards in such condition that it must be greatly changed before it can succeed. Often before these ample changes can be made, the public has lost interest in the piece. If a general principle might be laid down here it would be something like this. "If you wish, first write your play so that to you it is something clear and convincing as well as something that moves to laughter or to tears. Before, however, it is tried on the stage, make sure that you have considered it in all details in so detached a way that you have a right to believe that, as a result of your careful revising, it will produce with the public the same interest, and the same emotions to the same degree as the original version did with you."

Just here arises the ever present query, "Why struggle to write what the public does not readily and quickly accept? Why not study their unthinking likes and dislikes and give them what they want?" Certainly write in that way if it brings contentment, as it surely will bring monetary success if the play thus written really hits popular approval. However, aiming to hit popular taste is like shooting at a shifting target and a play so made may be staged just as the public makes one of its swift changes in theatrical mood. Of course, too, he who writes in this way is in no sense a leader but merely the slave of his public. In any case, his play is but an imitation, not an expression of the author's individuality.

Even would-be dramatists who do not hold the opportunist ideas just considered may draw back after reading what has been stated in this book, saying: "How difficult and painstaking is this art of the drama which I have thought so fascinating and spontaneous." Of course, it is a difficult art. A good many years ago Sir Arthur Pinero said of it:

"When you sit in your stall at the theatre and see a play moving across the stage, it all seems so easy and so natural, you feel as though the author had improvised it. The characters, being, let us hope, ordinary human beings, say nothing very remarkable, nothing, you think (thereby paying the author the highest possible compliment) that might not quite well have occurred to you. When you take up a play-book (if you ever do take one up) it strikes you as being a very trifling thing — a mere insubstantial pamphlet beside the imposing bulk of the latest six-shilling novel. Little do you guess that every page of the play has cost more care, severer mental tension, if not more actual manual labor, than any chapter of a novel, though it be fifty pages long. It is the height of the author's art, according to the old maxim, that the ordinary spectator should never be clearly conscious of the skill and travail that have gone to the making of the finished product. But the artist who would achieve a like feat must realize that no ingots are to be got out of this mine, save after sleepless nights, days of gloom and discouragement, and other days, again, of feverish toil the result of which proves in the end to be misapplied and has to be thrown to the winds."

Nevertheless, this difficult art remains fascinating; and in practice, if rightly understood, it rapidly grows easier. In the understanding of any art there must be two stages. First comes the spontaneous doing of work very encouraging to the author and sufficiently good to warrant a person more experienced in encouraging him to proceed. Then begins the second stage, when he learns what can be taught him of technique in his chosen field. It is bound to be a time when consciousness of rules first learned and limitations first perceived make writing far less attractive and often so irksome that the worker is tempted to throw his task aside for good. He who does not really love his art will cast away his work. He who really cares cannot do this. He may from the hampering of these newly recognized rules become irritable, have his moments of self-doubt and despair, but he cannot stop practicing his art. With each new effort, the rules which have been so troublesome will become more and more a matter of habit. Little by little the writer will gain a curious subconscious power of using almost unthinkingly the principles he needs, giving no thought to those not needed. Then, and then only, will he write with the art that conceals art; and it is only when he has attained to delight in the difficulties of the art he practices that he is in any true sense an artist.

What ultimately happens is probably this. The critical attitude is strong in the scenario period, perhaps predominant as the dramatist works out construction, emphasis, proportion, etc., but when, with the scenario before him, he takes his pen in hand, he lets the creative impulse swamp completely the critical sense and loses himself in his task. Or he reverses the process. He writes in pure creative abandon, until at least an act of a play lies completed before him. Then, with his critical training brought to the front, he goes over and over the manuscript until what was a pure creative effort has been chastened and sublimated by his trained critical sense. The main point is: Don't stultify your creative instincts by trying to use critical training at the same time. As far as possible, let one precede the other. Write creatively. Then correct. Or write with the critical instinct strongly to the front until all plans are made. Then forget everything except the spirit of creation. Where dramatists in training waste their nervous energy and often stultify their best desires is in keeping critical tab upon themselves as they create. Writing something with pure delight, they are suddenly blocked by the critical spirit saying: "This or that is bad. You cannot keep this or that as you have written it," and presto! no more creative work that day. Unless the critical and creative faculties interwork sympathetically and coöperatively, keep them separate.

Whoever aims to write plays chiefly or wholly because he would like fame or money or because he wishes to show that he is as strong in one fictional art as another, — the story, the essay, the poem, whatever it may be, — in fact he who writes plays for any other reason than that he cannot be happy except in writing plays, better give over such writing. Play-making is an exceedingly difficult art, and in so far as it is in any sense a transcript from life or a beautified presentation of life past, present, or imagined, it grows more difficult as the years pass because of the accumulating mass of dramatic masterpieces. Yet for him who cares for dramatic writing more than any form of self-expression, no time has been more promising than the present. There has been more good drama in the past twenty-five years the world over than at any time in the history of the stage. It has been more varied in subject and form, more individual in treatment. The drama is today more flexible, more daring and experimental, than ever before. It is in closer relation to all the subtlest and most advanced of man's thinking. It has been breaking new ways for itself, and it has new ways yet to break. All that has been said in this book concerns merely the historic foundations of this very great art. Accept these principles as stated or quarrel with most of them; but realize that any principles, whether accepted from others or self-taught, should be but the beginning of a life-long training by which the individual will pass from what he shares of general dramatic experience to what is peculiarly his own expression.

INDEX OF AUTHORS

INDEX OF QUOTATIONS

INDEX OF SUBJECTS